NAOKI URASAWA'S
20th CENTURY BOYS

Naoki Urasawa's 20th Century Boys
Volume 04

VIZ Signature Edition

STORY AND ART BY NAOKI URASAWA

English Adaptation/Akemi Wegmüller
Touch-up Art & Lettering/Freeman Wong
Cover & Interior Design/Sam Elzway
Editor/Kit Fox

VP, Production/Alvin Lu
VP, Publishing Licensing/Rika Inouye
VP, Sales & Product Marketing/Gonzalo Ferreyra
VP, Creative/Linda Espinosa
Publisher/Hyoe Narita

20 SEIKI SHONEN 4 by Naoki URASAWA/Studio Nuts
© 2001 Naoki URASAWA/Studio Nuts
With the cooperation of Takashi NAGASAKI
All rights reserved. Original Japanese
edition published in 2001 by Shogakukan Inc., Tokyo.

Printed in the U.S.A.

Published by VIZ Media, LLC
P.O. Box 77010
San Francisco, CA 94107

10 9 8 7 6 5 4 3 2 1
First printing, August 2009

www.viz.com
store.viz.com

NAOKI URASAWA'S
20th CENTURY BOYS

VOL 04
LOVE AND PEACE

Story & Art by

NAOKI URASAWA

With the cooperation of

Takashi NAGASAKI

NAOKI URASAWA'S 20th CENTURY BOYS

PROFILES

The Friend's plan to destroy the world is being carried out exactly in line with "The Book of Prophecy" written by Kenji in his childhood. And now the terror and mystery have spread to Bangkok, Thailand... The men who hold the fate of the world in their hands finally take action!

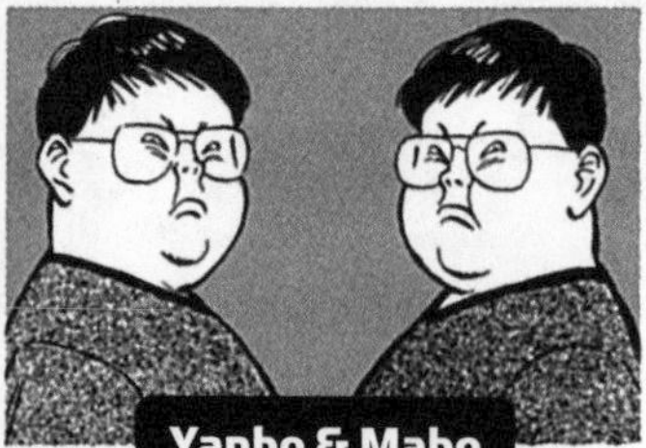

Yanbo & Mabo

The "evilest twins in history." Cruel and brutal and always a double whammy.

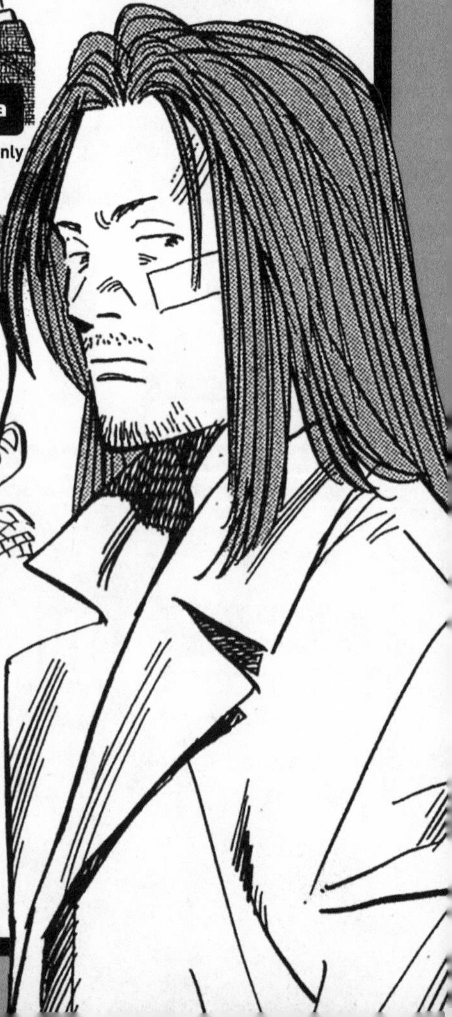

Shogun

A man living in the Bangkok underworld who seems to be Japanese. What is his true identity?

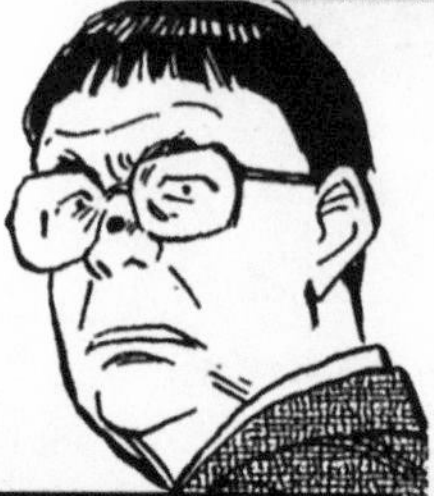

Professor Shikishima

Renowned roboticist who suddenly went missing three years ago.

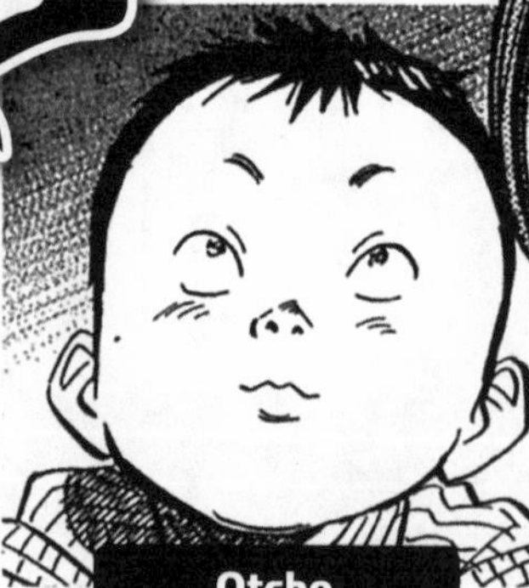

Otcho

A leader of Kenji's group of friends. Went missing overseas where he was posted by a large trading corporation.

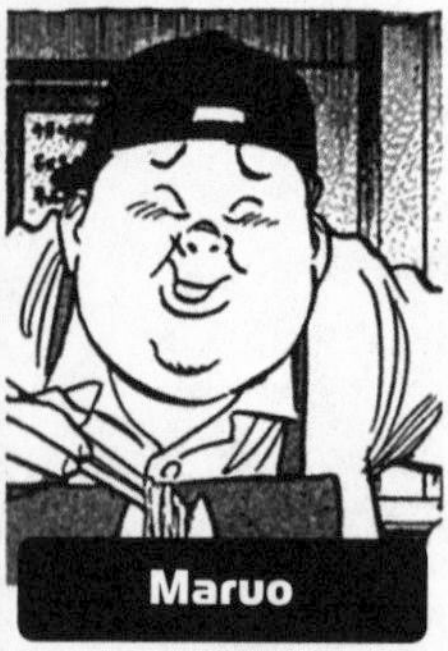

Maruo

Close friend of Kenji's who runs a fancy goods shop in the neighborhood.

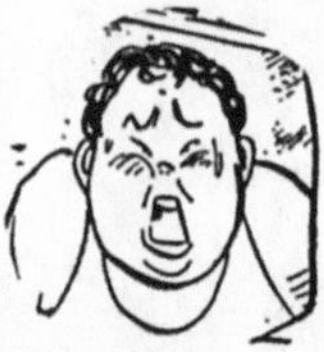

← Maruo as a kid

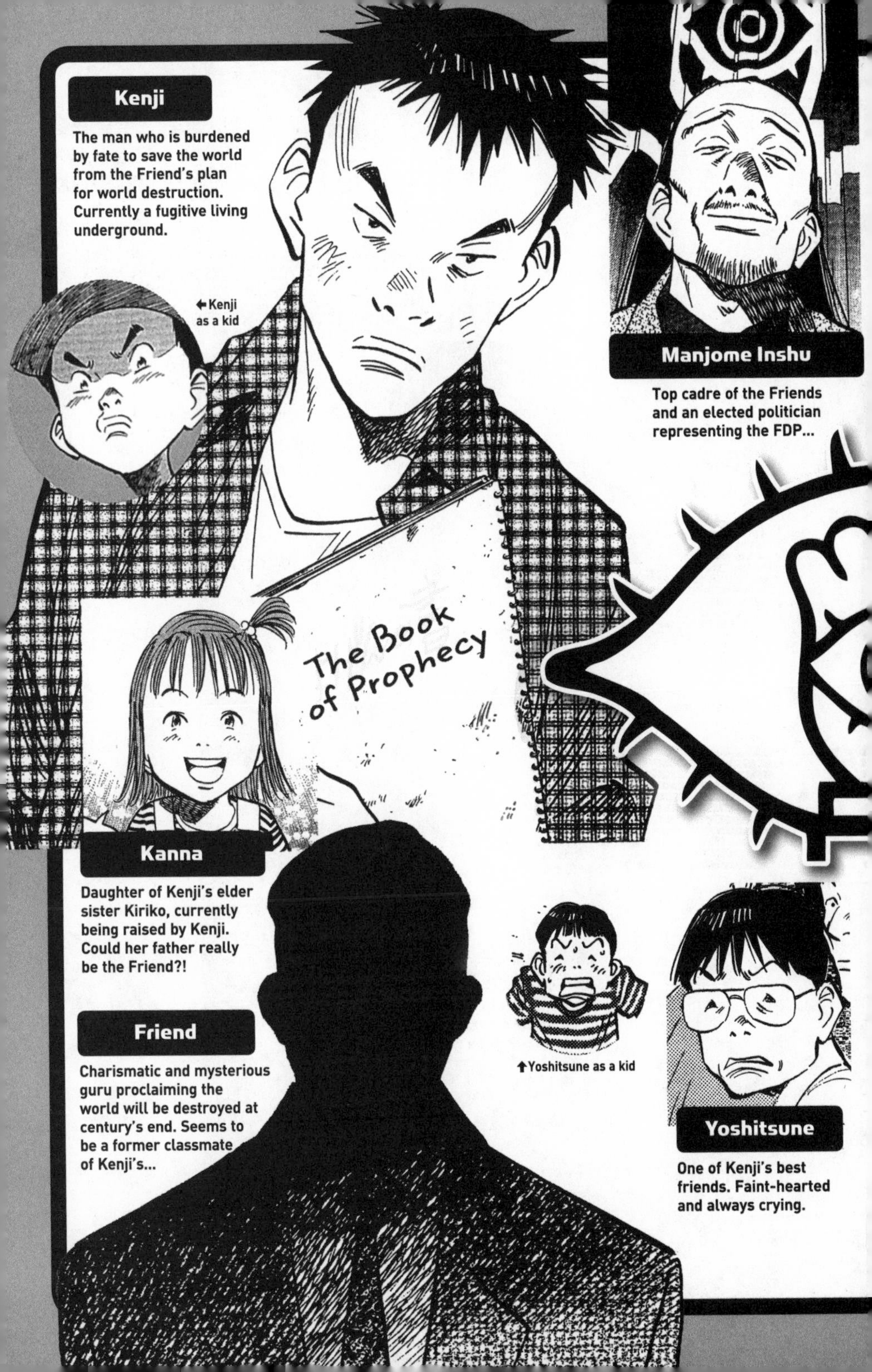
Kenji
The man who is burdened by fate to save the world from the Friend's plan for world destruction. Currently a fugitive living underground.
Manjome Inshu
Top cadre of the Friends and an elected politician representing the FDP...
Kenji as a kid
The Book of Prophecy
Kanna
Daughter of Kenji's elder sister Kiriko, currently being raised by Kenji. Could her father really be the Friend?!
Yoshitsune
One of Kenji's best friends. Faint-hearted and always crying.
Yoshitsune as a kid
Friend
Charismatic and mysterious guru proclaiming the world will be destroyed at century's end. Seems to be a former classmate of Kenji's...

CONTENTS
VOL 04
LOVE AND PEACE

NAOKI URASAWA'S 20th CENTURY BOYS

Chapter 1 FDP

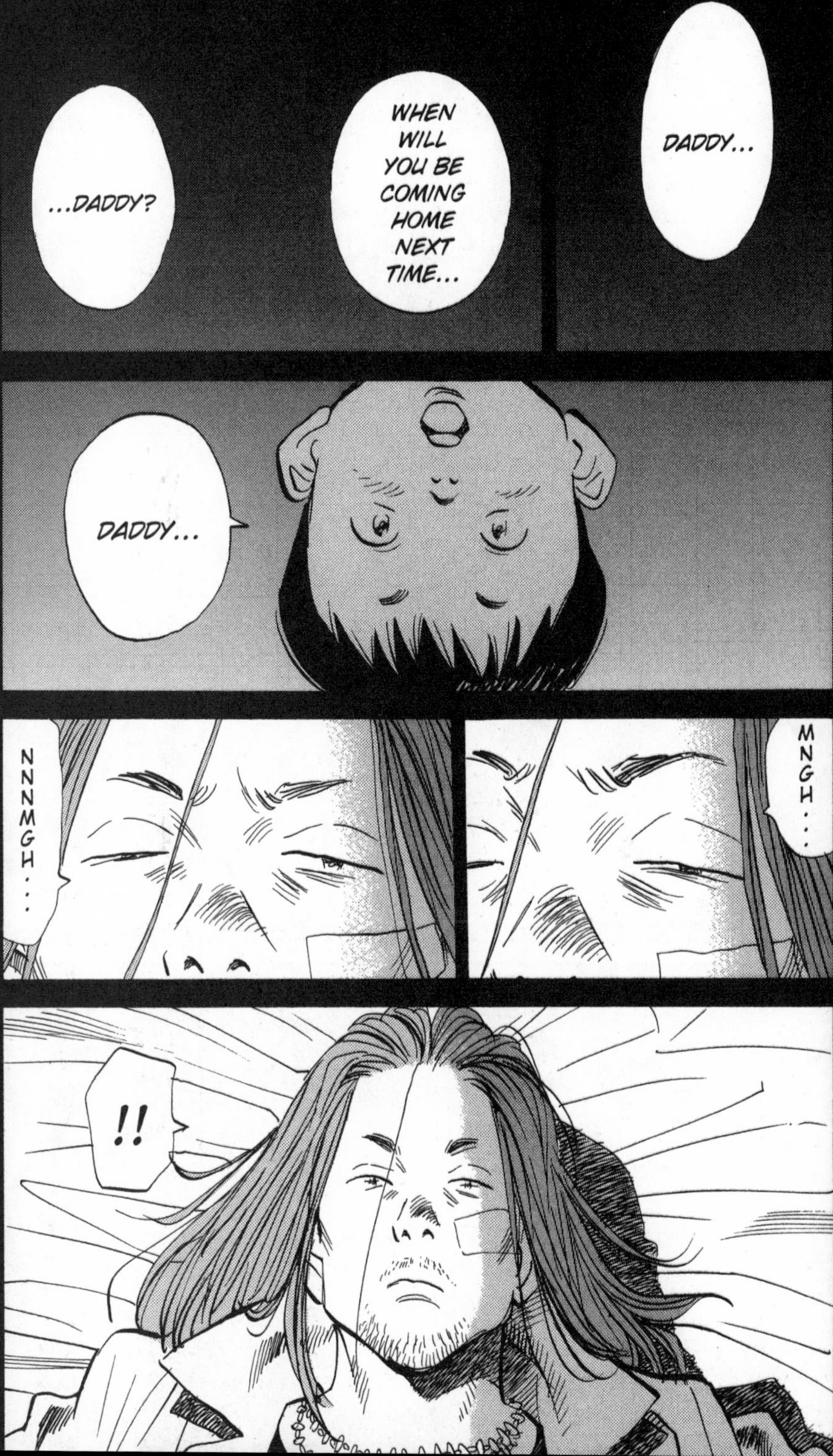
DADDY...
WHEN WILL YOU BE COMING HOME NEXT TIME...
...DADDY?
DADDY...
MNGH...
NNNMGH...
!!

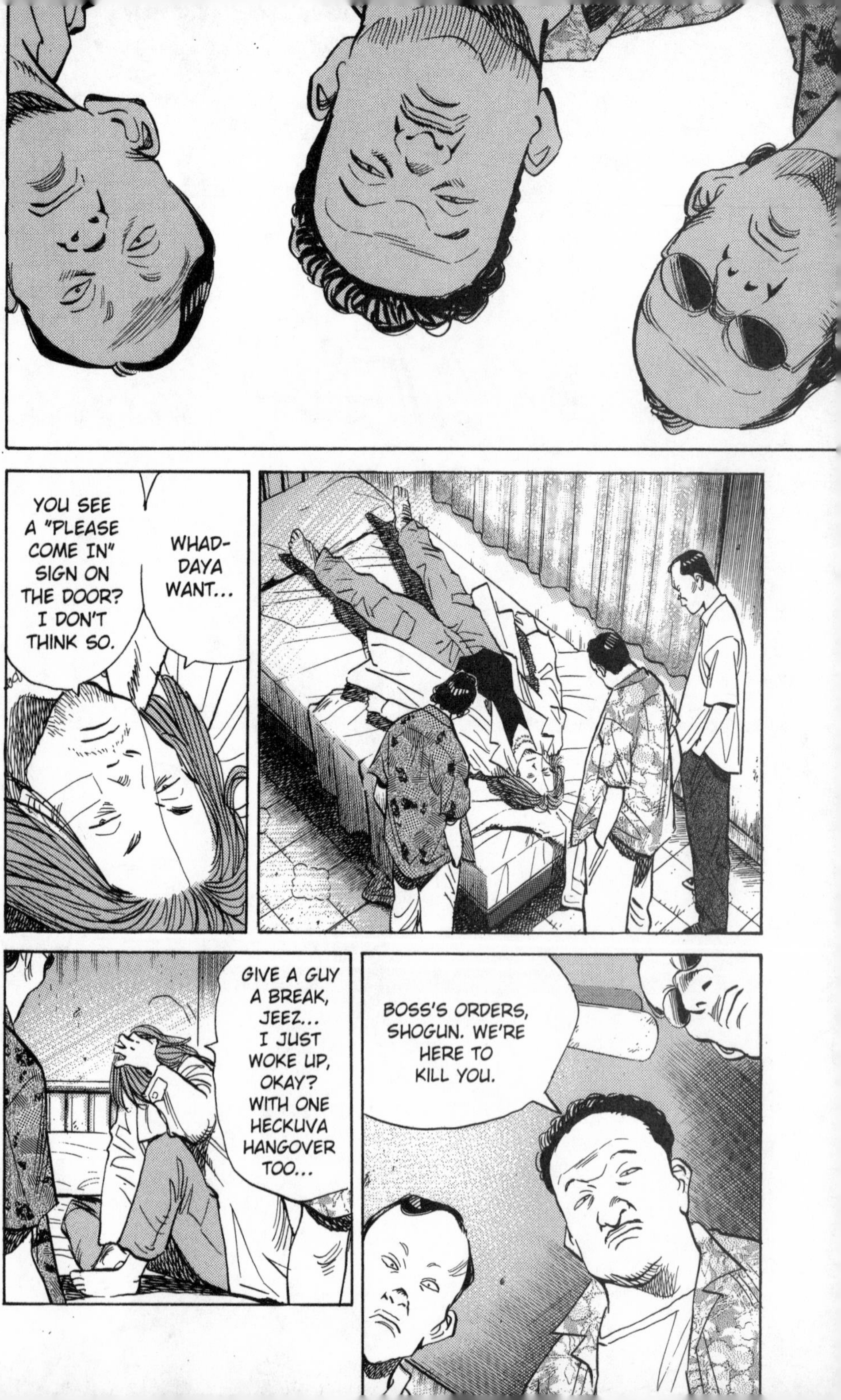
WHAD-DAYA WANT...
YOU SEE A "PLEASE COME IN" SIGN ON THE DOOR? I DON'T THINK SO.
BOSS'S ORDERS, SHOGUN. WE'RE HERE TO KILL YOU.
GIVE A GUY A BREAK, JEEZ... I JUST WOKE UP, OKAY? WITH ONE HECKUVA HANGOVER TOO...

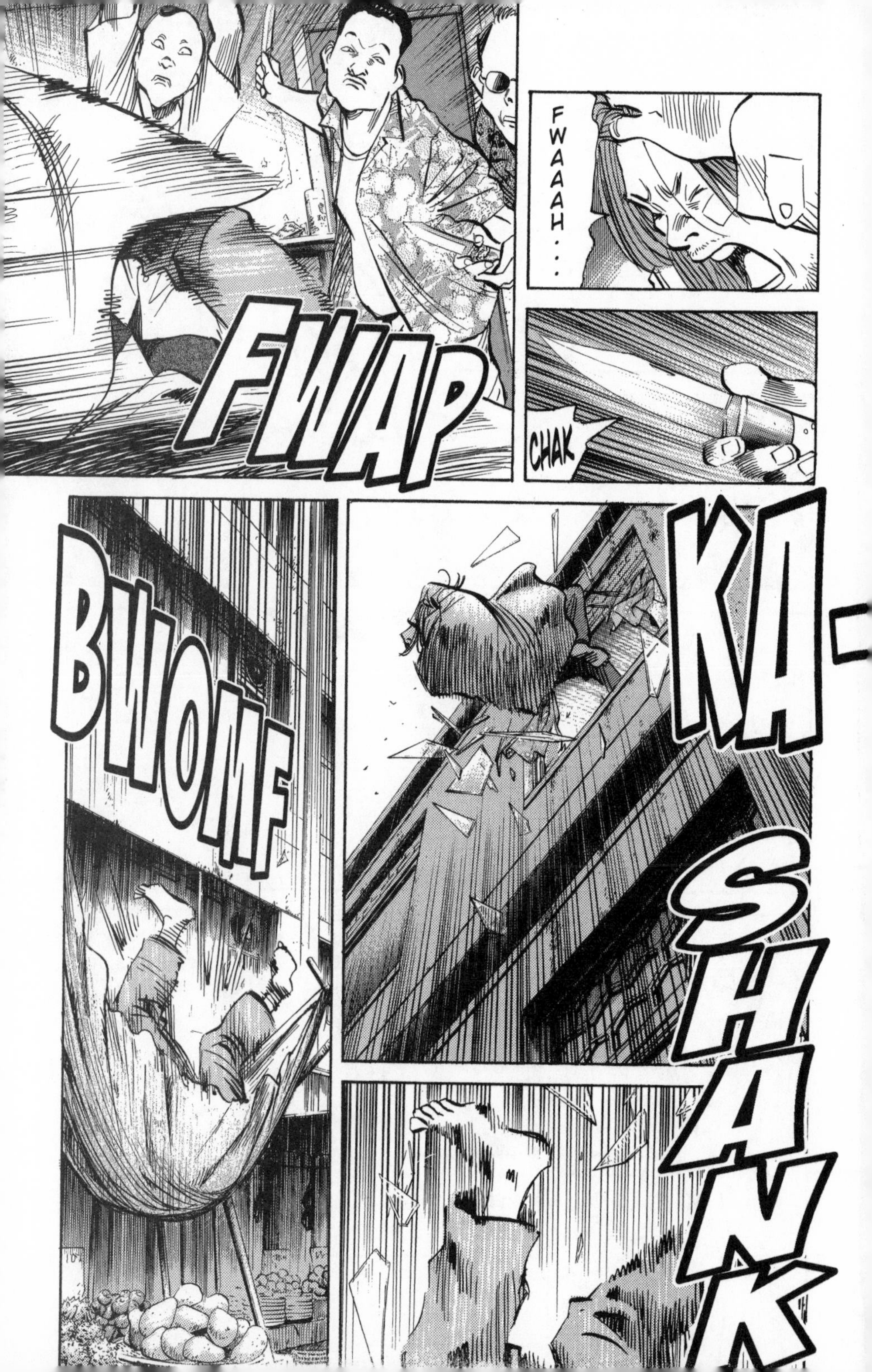
FWAAAH...
CHAK
FWAP
KA-SHANK
BWOMF

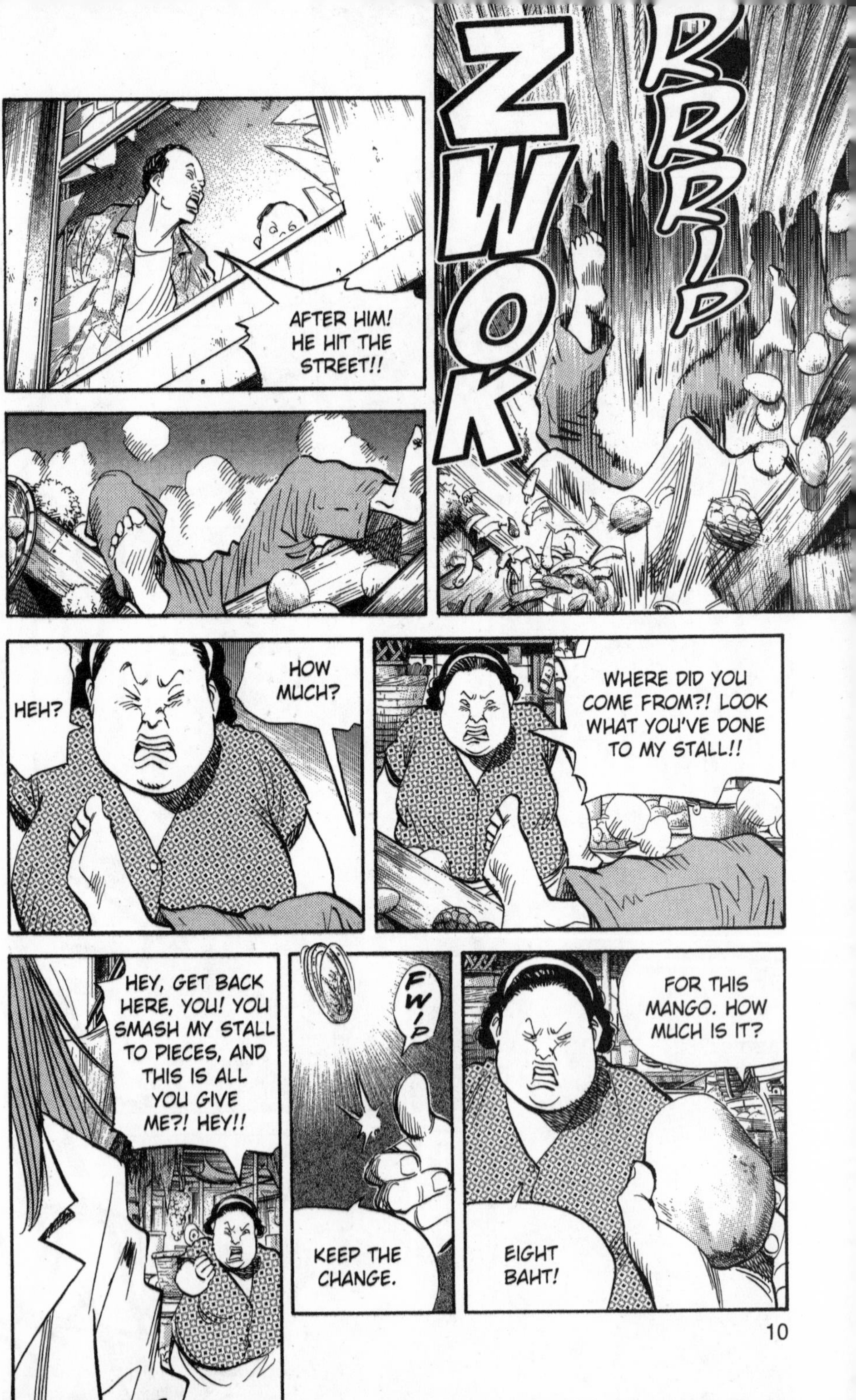
BRRRIP
ZWOK
AFTER HIM! HE HIT THE STREET!!
WHERE DID YOU COME FROM?! LOOK WHAT YOU'VE DONE TO MY STALL!!
HOW MUCH?
HEH?
FOR THIS MANGO. HOW MUCH IS IT?
EIGHT BAHT!
FWIP
KEEP THE CHANGE.
HEY, GET BACK HERE, YOU! YOU SMASH MY STALL TO PIECES, AND THIS IS ALL YOU GIVE ME?! HEY!!

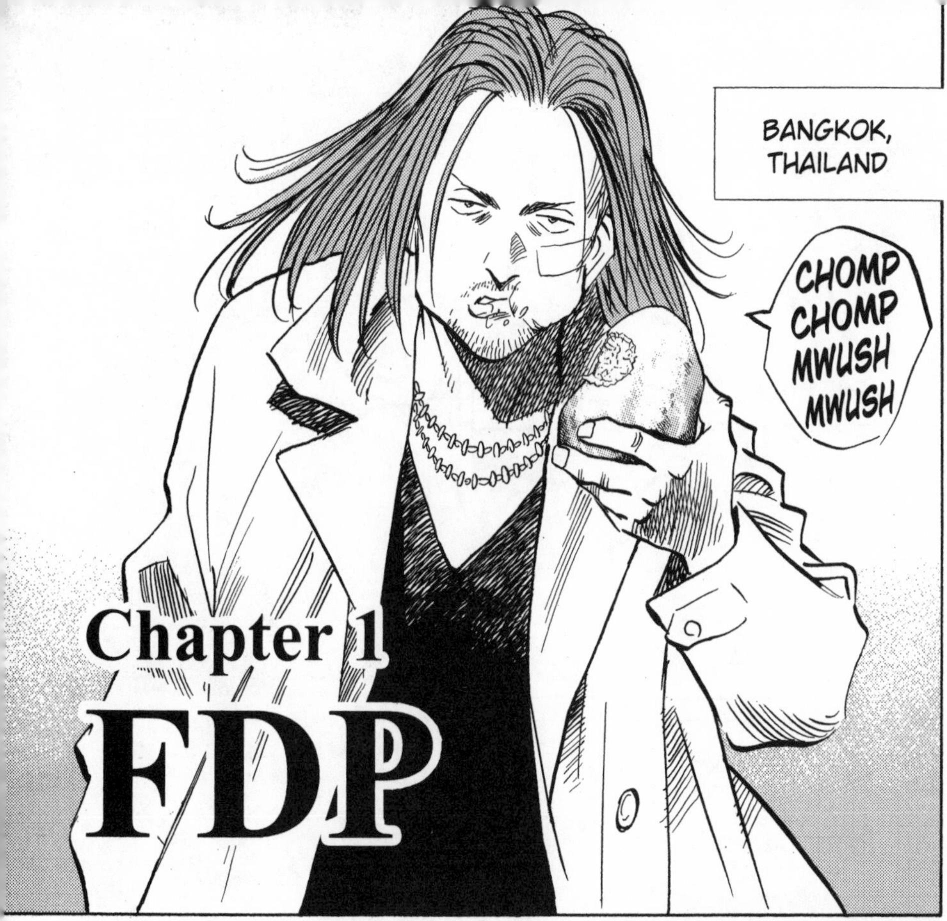
BANGKOK, THAILAND
CHOMP CHOMP MWUSH MWUSH
Chapter 1
FDP

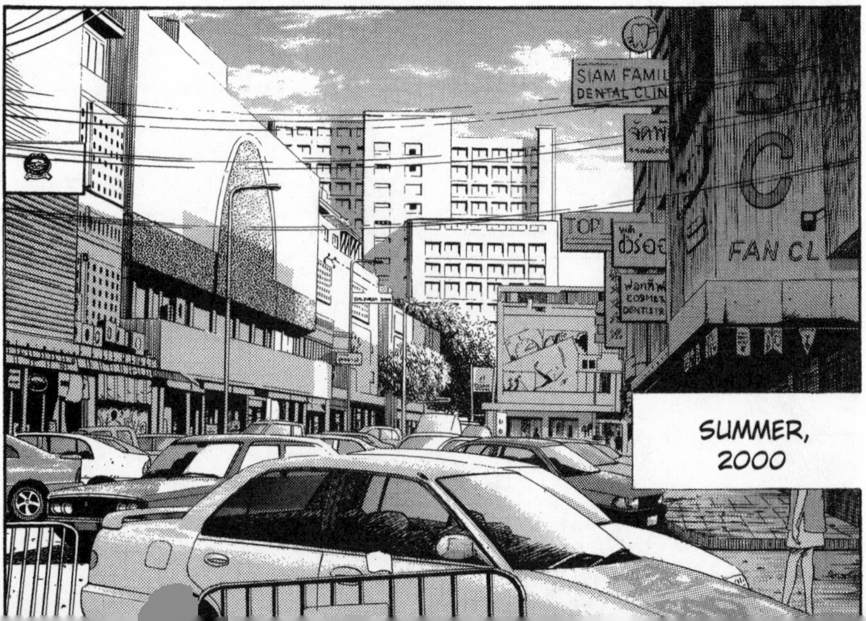
FAN CL
SIAM FAMIL
DENTAL CLIN
TOP
SUMMER, 2000

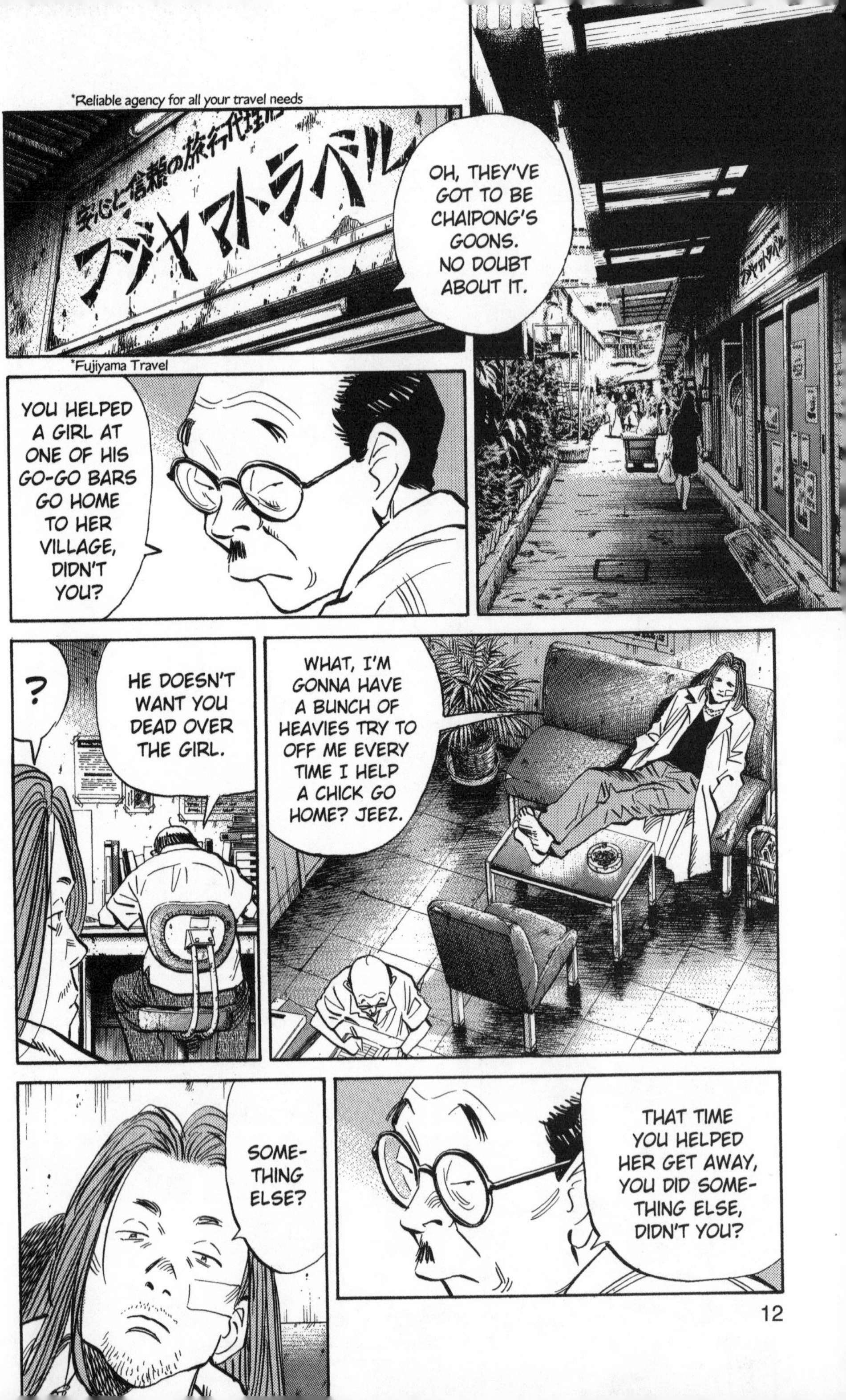
OH, THEY'VE GOT TO BE CHAIPONG'S GOONS. NO DOUBT ABOUT IT.
*Reliable agency for all your travel needs
*Fujiyama Travel
YOU HELPED A GIRL AT ONE OF HIS GO-GO BARS GO HOME TO HER VILLAGE, DIDN'T YOU?
WHAT, I'M GONNA HAVE A BUNCH OF HEAVIES TRY TO OFF ME EVERY TIME I HELP A CHICK GO HOME? JEEZ.
HE DOESN'T WANT YOU DEAD OVER THE GIRL.
?
THAT TIME YOU HELPED HER GET AWAY, YOU DID SOME-THING ELSE, DIDN'T YOU?
SOME-THING ELSE?

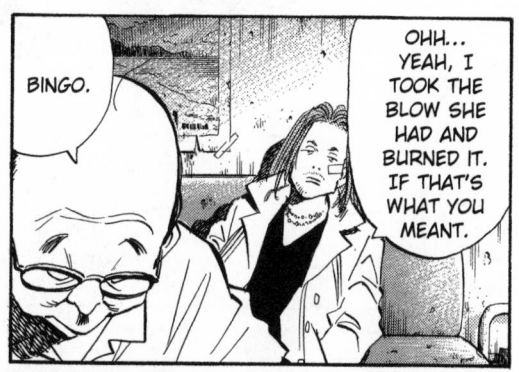

OHH... YEAH, I TOOK THE BLOW SHE HAD AND BURNED IT. IF THAT'S WHAT YOU MEANT.
BINGO.
CHAIPONG'S LATEST BUSINESS VENTURE IS TRAFFICKING SOME NEW TYPE OF DRUG.
THE STUFF YOU BURNED WAS CHAIPONG'S PRODUCT, AND VERY VALUABLE PRODUCT AT THAT.
IT'S CALLED "RAINBOW KID," THIS STUFF, AND IT'S DOING A VERY, VERY BRISK TRADE IN JAPAN, FROM WHAT I HEARD.
YOU WOULDN'T BELIEVE WHAT IT SELLS FOR ON THE STREET OVER THERE.
NOT JAPAN AGAIN...
WHAT'S GOING ON WITH THAT PLACE?
JAPAN? SEEMS LIKE IT'S FINALLY COME OUT OF THAT LONG, DARK RECESSION. THINGS'RE LOOKING GOOD OVER THERE.

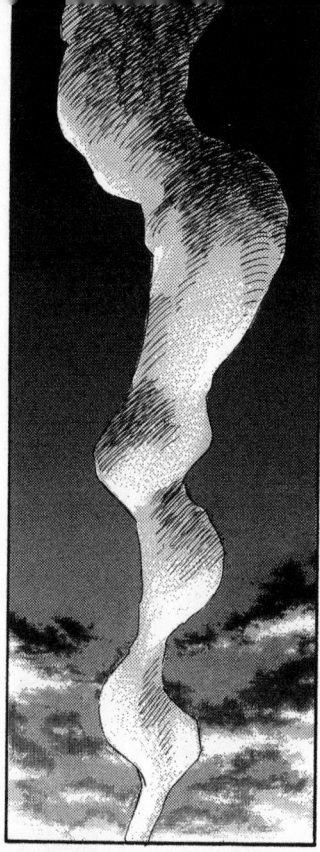

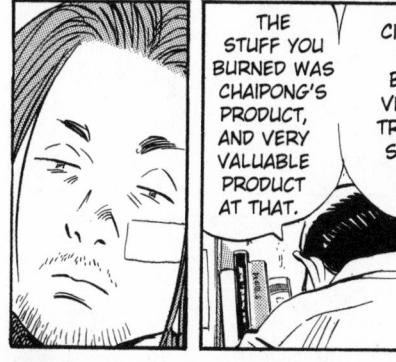

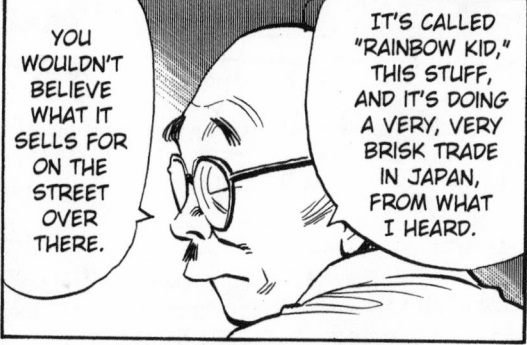

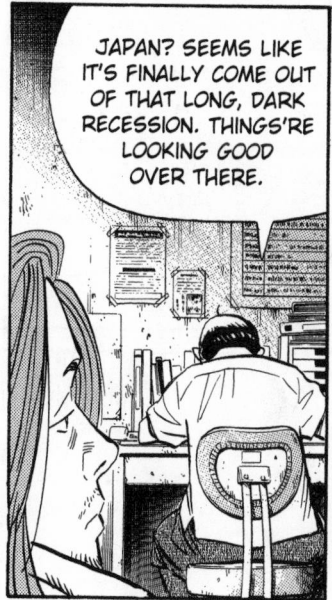

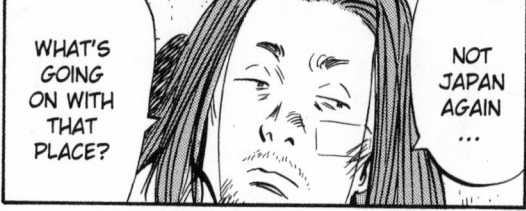

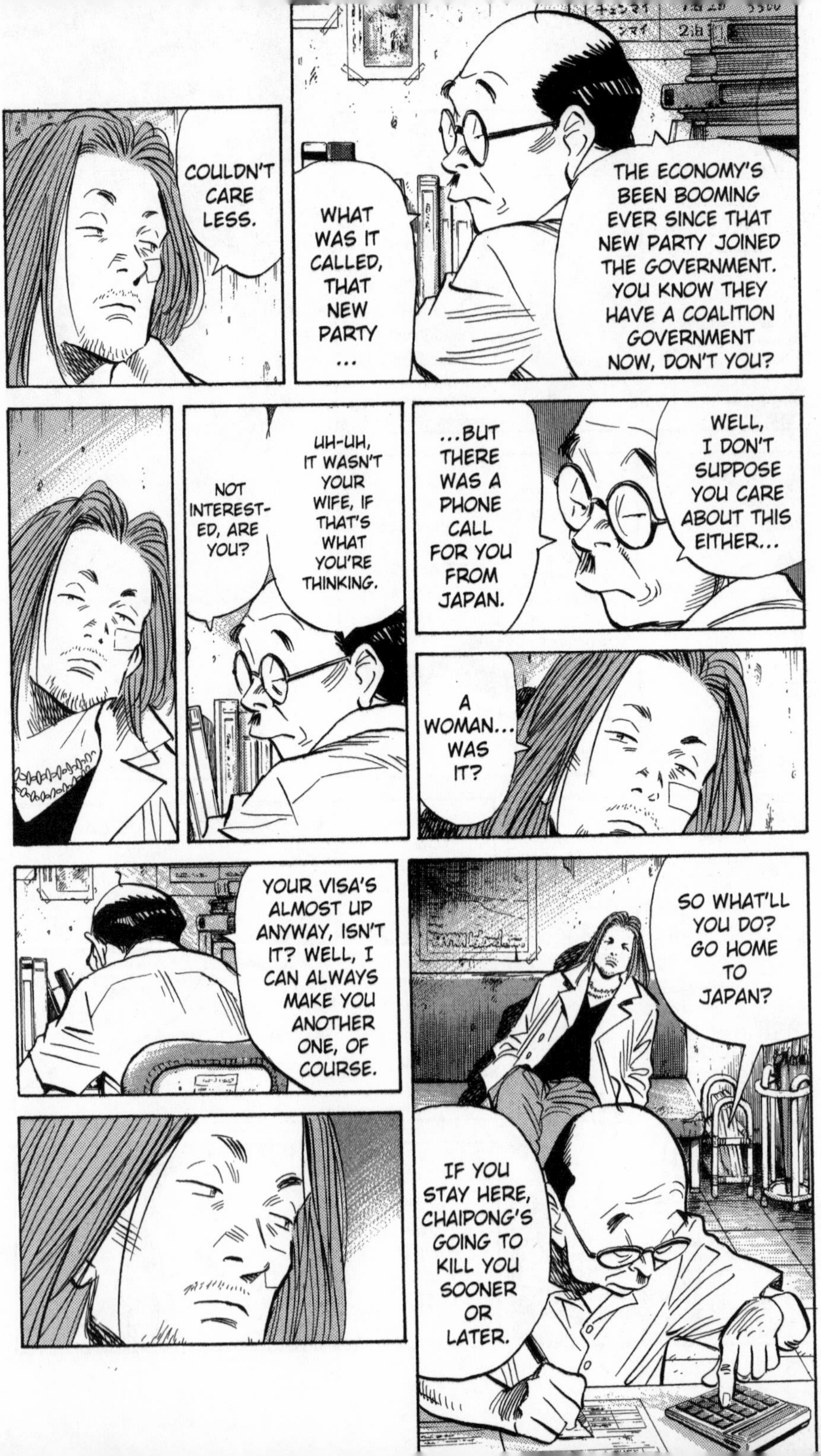
THE ECONOMY'S BEEN BOOMING EVER SINCE THAT NEW PARTY JOINED THE GOVERNMENT. YOU KNOW THEY HAVE A COALITION GOVERNMENT NOW, DON'T YOU?
WHAT WAS IT CALLED, THAT NEW PARTY ...
COULDN'T CARE LESS.
WELL, I DON'T SUPPOSE YOU CARE ABOUT THIS EITHER...
...BUT THERE WAS A PHONE CALL FOR YOU FROM JAPAN.
A WOMAN... WAS IT?
UH-UH, IT WASN'T YOUR WIFE, IF THAT'S WHAT YOU'RE THINKING.
NOT INTEREST-ED, ARE YOU?
SO WHAT'LL YOU DO? GO HOME TO JAPAN?
IF YOU STAY HERE, CHAIPONG'S GOING TO KILL YOU SOONER OR LATER.
YOUR VISA'S ALMOST UP ANYWAY, ISN'T IT? WELL, I CAN ALWAYS MAKE YOU ANOTHER ONE, OF COURSE.

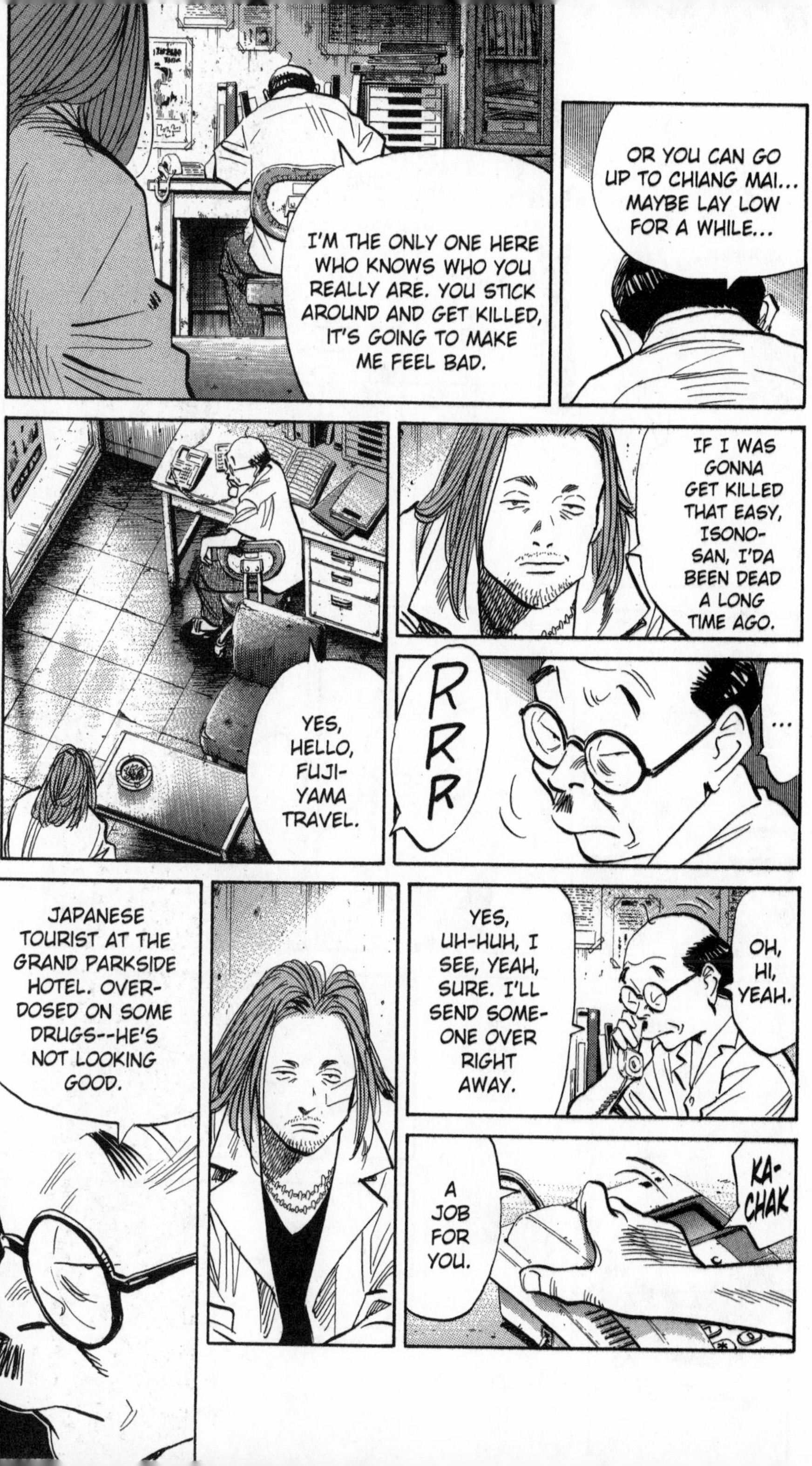
OR YOU CAN GO UP TO CHIANG MAI... MAYBE LAY LOW FOR A WHILE...
I'M THE ONLY ONE HERE WHO KNOWS WHO YOU REALLY ARE. YOU STICK AROUND AND GET KILLED, IT'S GOING TO MAKE ME FEEL BAD.
IF I WAS GONNA GET KILLED THAT EASY, ISONO-SAN, I'DA BEEN DEAD A LONG TIME AGO.
...
RRR
YES, HELLO, FUJI-YAMA TRAVEL.
OH, HI, YEAH.
YES, UH-HUH, I SEE, YEAH, SURE. I'LL SEND SOME-ONE OVER RIGHT AWAY.
KA-CHAK
A JOB FOR YOU.
JAPANESE TOURIST AT THE GRAND PARKSIDE HOTEL. OVER-DOSED ON SOME DRUGS--HE'S NOT LOOKING GOOD.

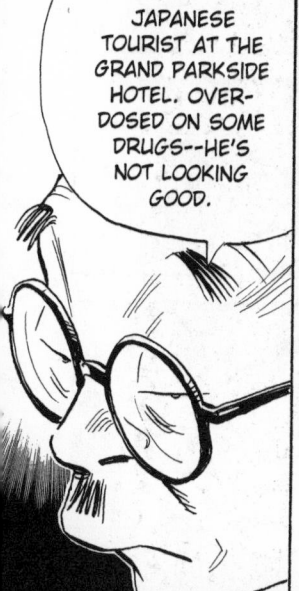

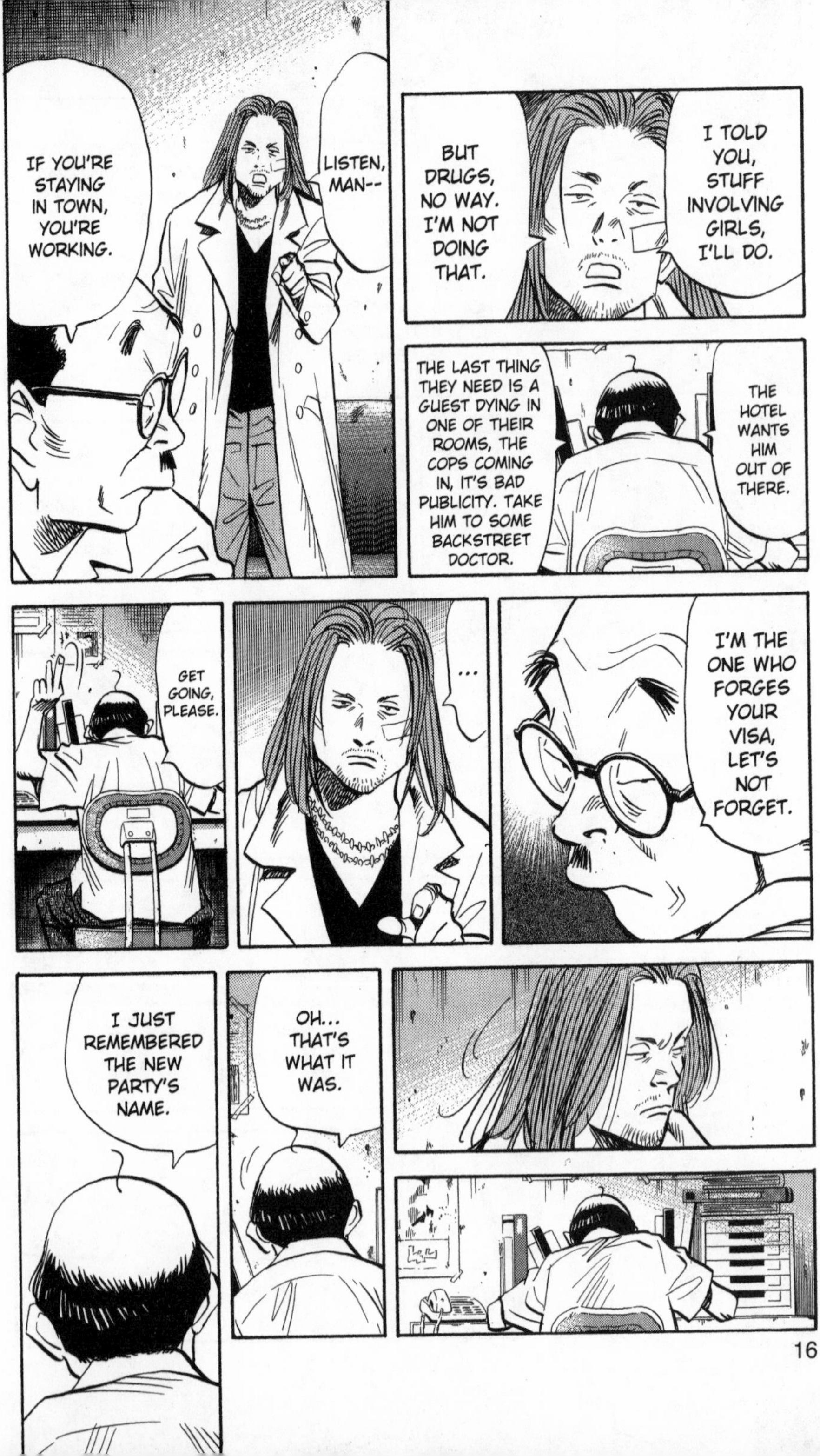
I TOLD YOU, STUFF INVOLVING GIRLS, I'LL DO.
BUT DRUGS, NO WAY. I'M NOT DOING THAT.
THE HOTEL WANTS HIM OUT OF THERE.
THE LAST THING THEY NEED IS A GUEST DYING IN ONE OF THEIR ROOMS, THE COPS COMING IN, IT'S BAD PUBLICITY. TAKE HIM TO SOME BACKSTREET DOCTOR.
LISTEN, MAN--
IF YOU'RE STAYING IN TOWN, YOU'RE WORKING.
I'M THE ONE WHO FORGES YOUR VISA, LET'S NOT FORGET.
...
GET GOING, PLEASE.
OH... THAT'S WHAT IT WAS.
I JUST REMEMBERED THE NEW PARTY'S NAME.

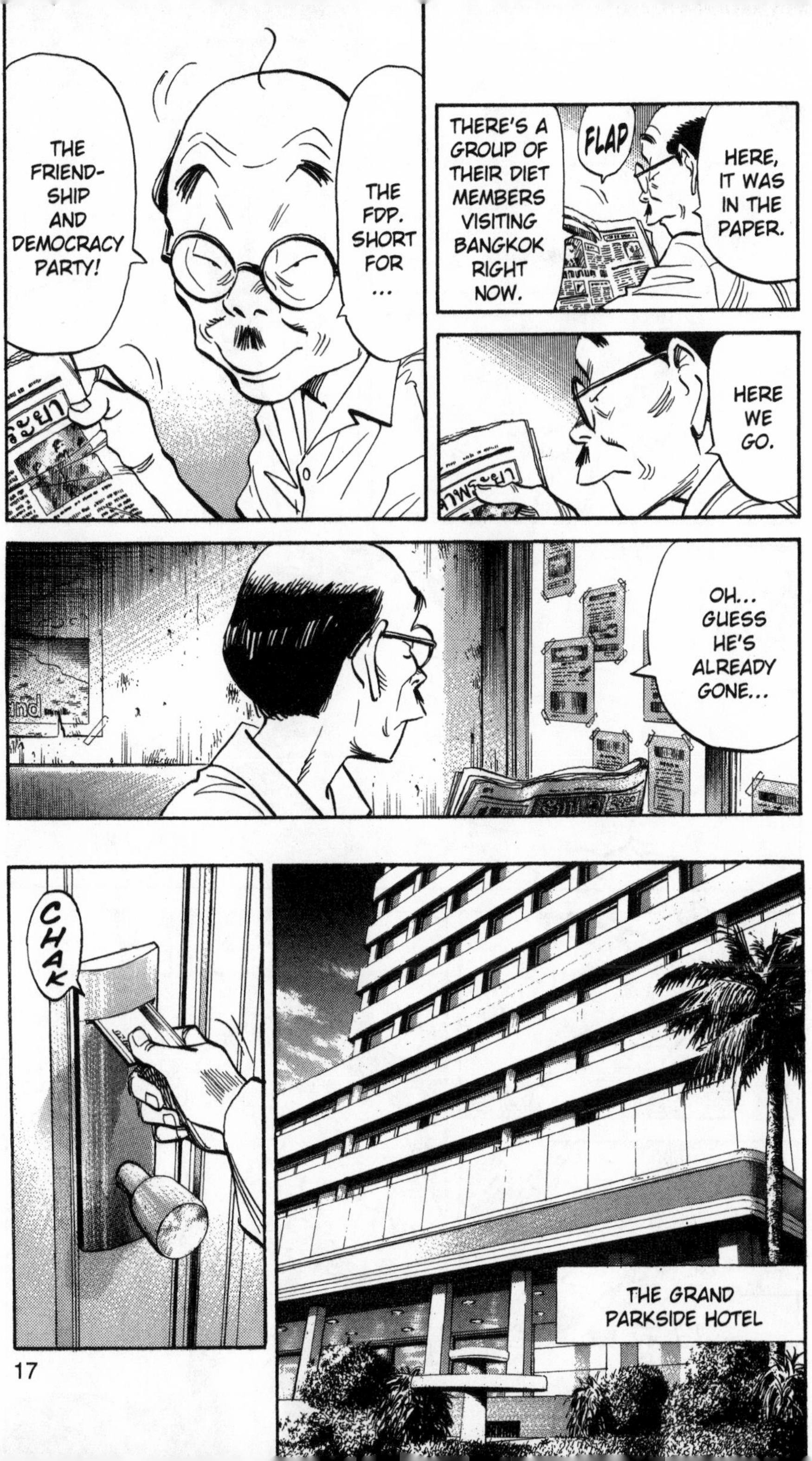

HERE, IT WAS IN THE PAPER.
FLAP
THERE'S A GROUP OF THEIR DIET MEMBERS VISITING BANGKOK RIGHT NOW.
HERE WE GO.
THE FDP. SHORT FOR ...
THE FRIEND-SHIP AND DEMOCRACY PARTY!
OH... GUESS HE'S ALREADY GONE...
THE GRAND PARKSIDE HOTEL
CHAK

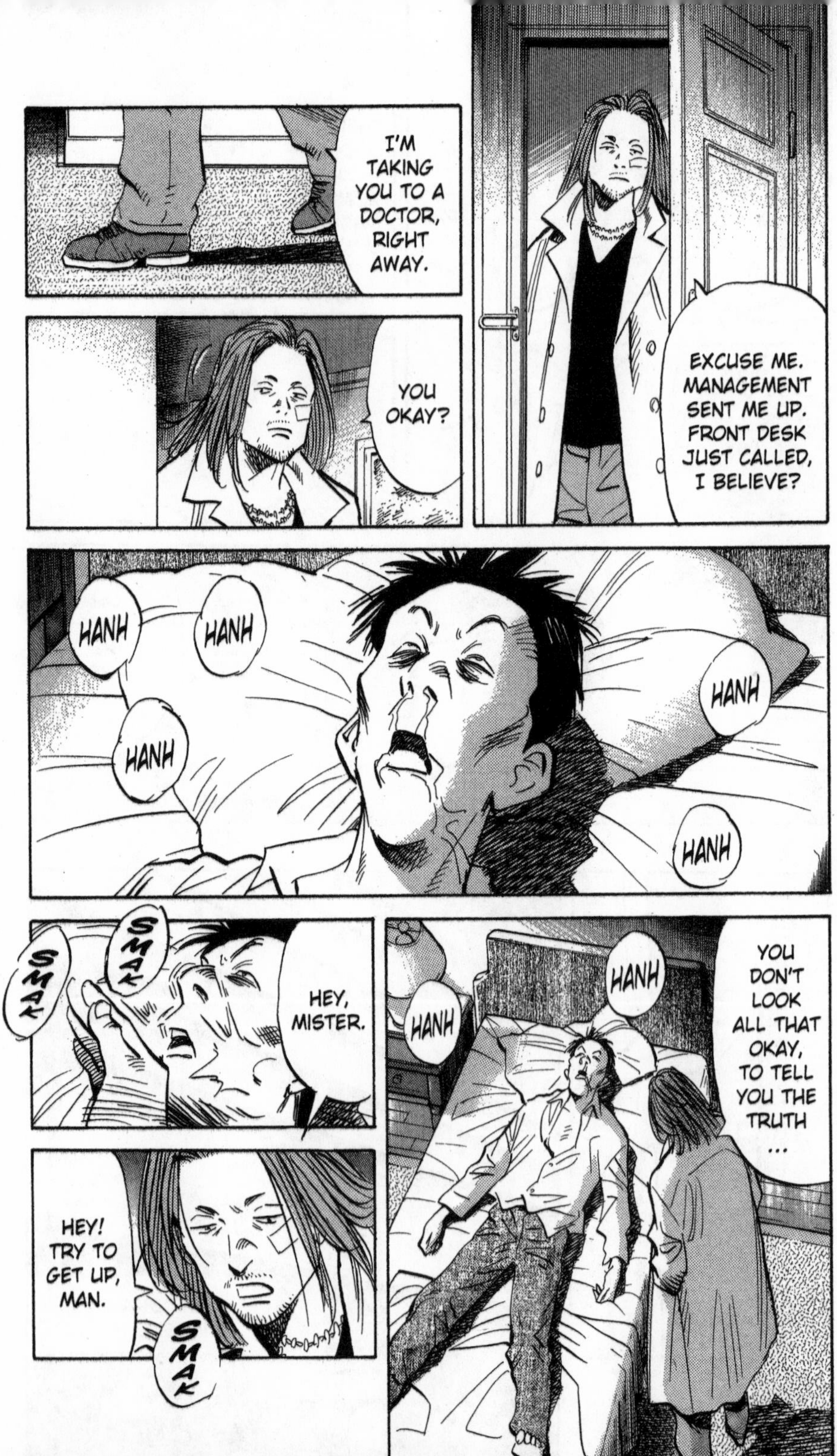
EXCUSE ME. MANAGEMENT SENT ME UP. FRONT DESK JUST CALLED, I BELIEVE?
I'M TAKING YOU TO A DOCTOR, RIGHT AWAY.
YOU OKAY?
HANH
HANH
HANH
HANH
HANH
HANH
HANH
YOU DON'T LOOK ALL THAT OKAY, TO TELL YOU THE TRUTH...
SMAK
SMAK
HEY, MISTER.
HEY! TRY TO GET UP, MAN.
SMAK

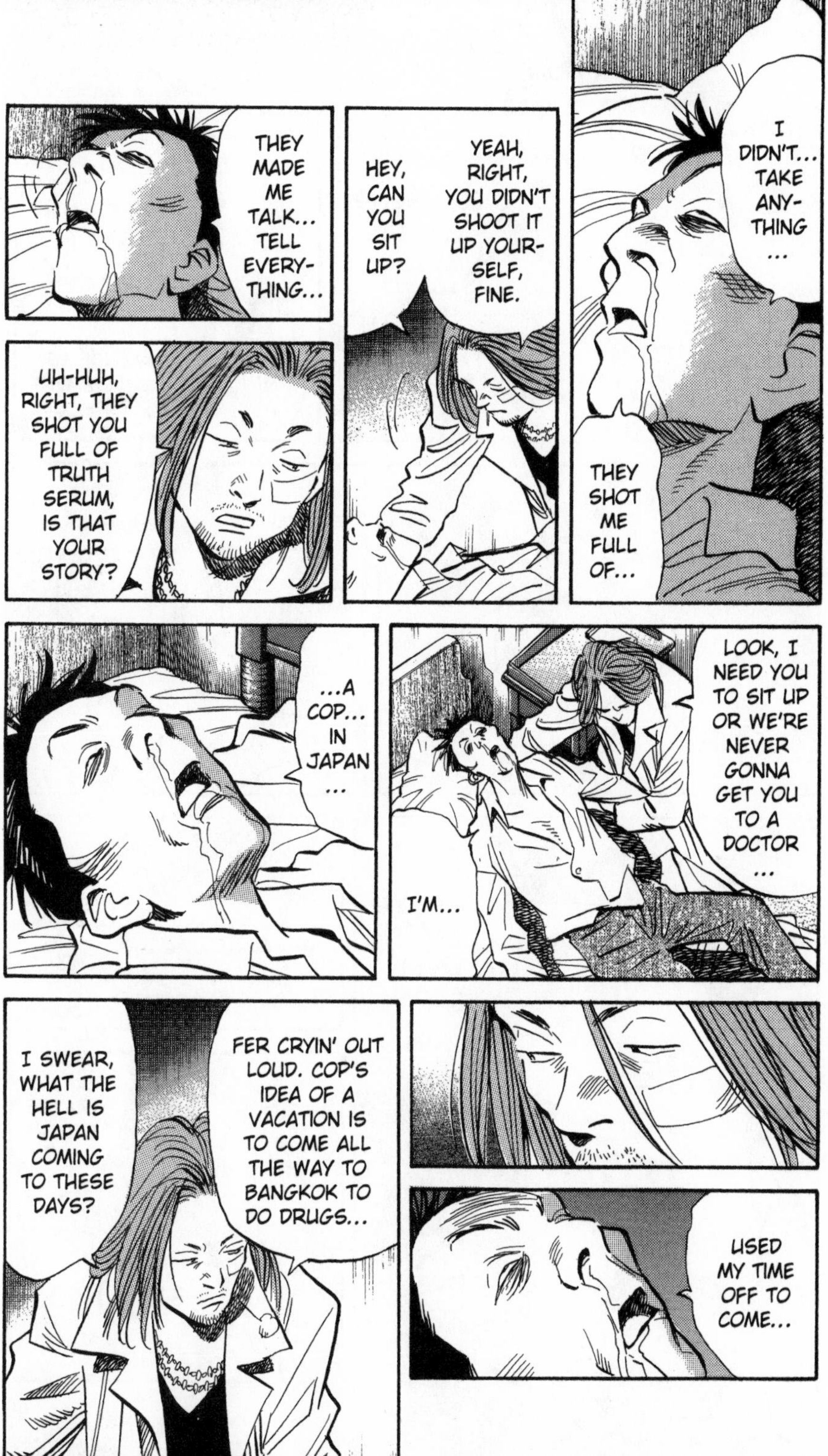
I DIDN'T... TAKE ANYTHING...
THEY SHOT ME FULL OF...
YEAH, RIGHT, YOU DIDN'T SHOOT IT UP YOURSELF, FINE.
HEY, CAN YOU SIT UP?
THEY MADE ME TALK... TELL EVERYTHING...
UH-HUH, RIGHT, THEY SHOT YOU FULL OF TRUTH SERUM, IS THAT YOUR STORY?
LOOK, I NEED YOU TO SIT UP OR WE'RE NEVER GONNA GET YOU TO A DOCTOR...
I'M...
...A COP... IN JAPAN...
USED MY TIME OFF TO COME...
FER CRYIN' OUT LOUD. COP'S IDEA OF A VACATION IS TO COME ALL THE WAY TO BANGKOK TO DO DRUGS...
I SWEAR, WHAT THE HELL IS JAPAN COMING TO THESE DAYS?

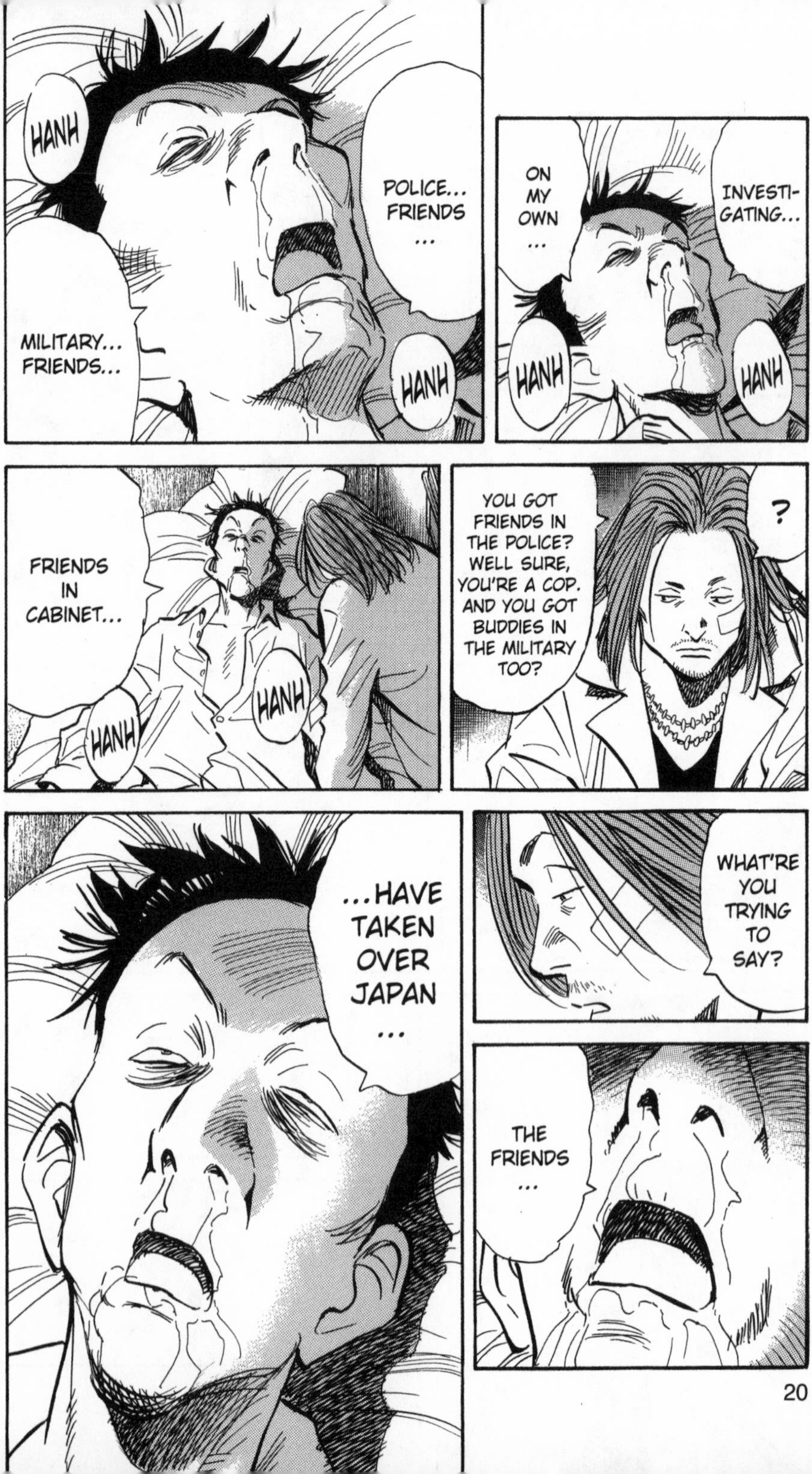
INVESTI-GATING...
ON MY OWN ...
HANH
HANH
POLICE... FRIENDS ...
HANH
MILITARY... FRIENDS...
HANH
?
YOU GOT FRIENDS IN THE POLICE? WELL SURE, YOU'RE A COP. AND YOU GOT BUDDIES IN THE MILITARY TOO?
FRIENDS IN CABINET...
HANH
HANH
WHAT'RE YOU TRYING TO SAY?
THE FRIENDS ...
...HAVE TAKEN OVER JAPAN ...

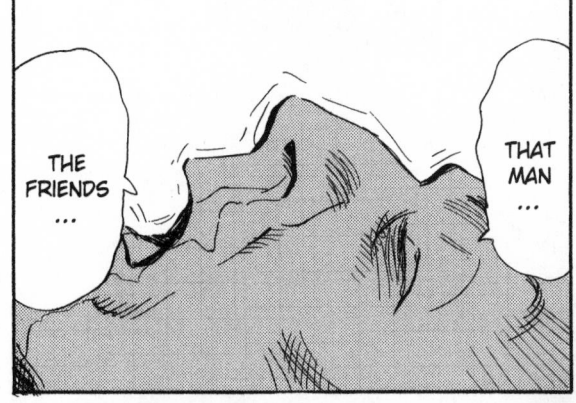

THE FRIENDS...

THAT MAN...

PROOF...

STOLE HIS BADGE...

THEY'VE GOT ANOTHER PLAN...

PLAN...

DESTRUC- TION... OF THE WORLD...

HANH

HANH

HANH

HEY, MISTER.

HEY.

21

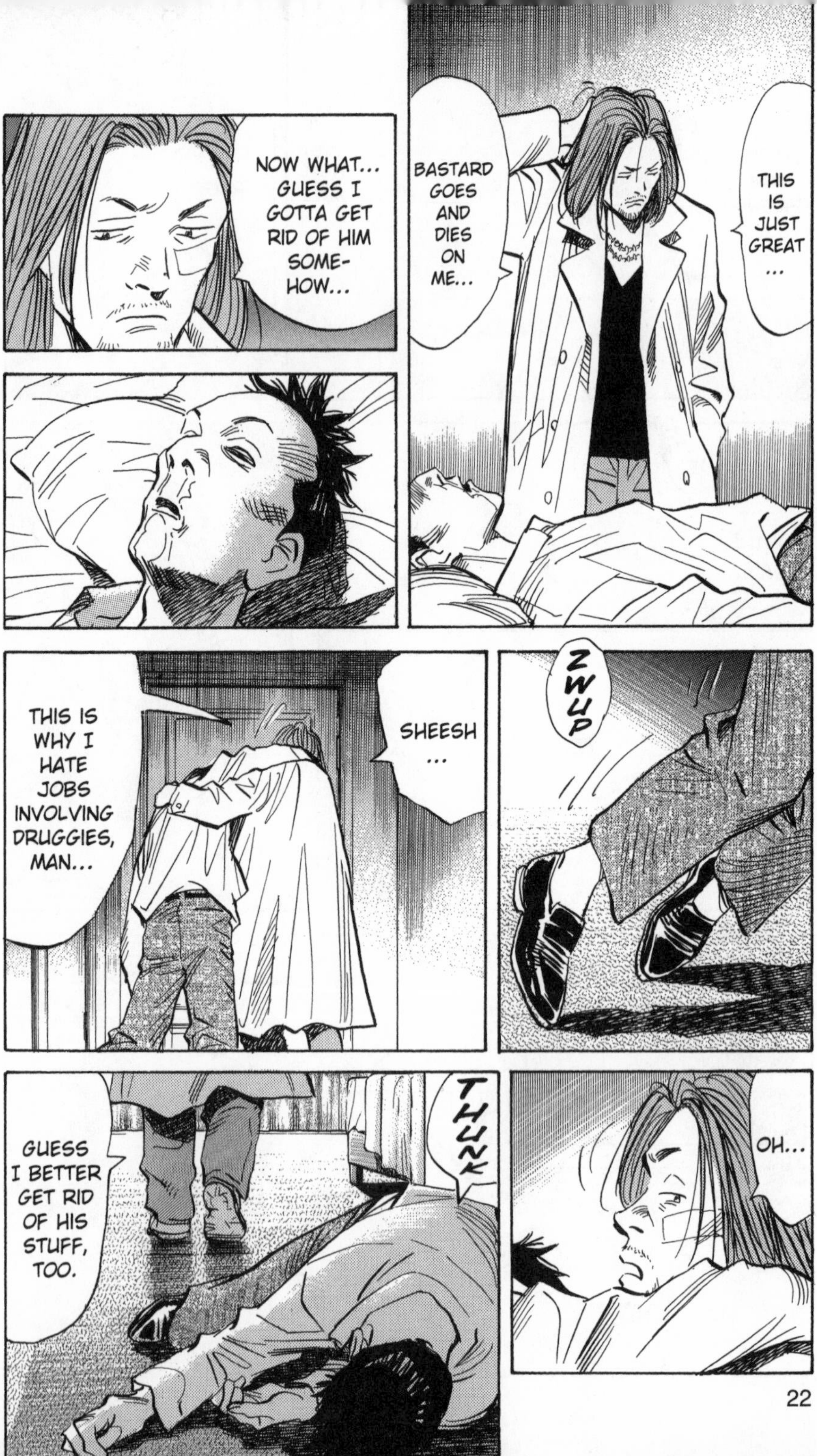
THIS IS JUST GREAT ...
BASTARD GOES AND DIES ON ME...
NOW WHAT... GUESS I GOTTA GET RID OF HIM SOME-HOW...
ZWUP
SHEESH ...
THIS IS WHY I HATE JOBS INVOLVING DRUGGIES, MAN...
OH...
THUNK
GUESS I BETTER GET RID OF HIS STUFF, TOO.

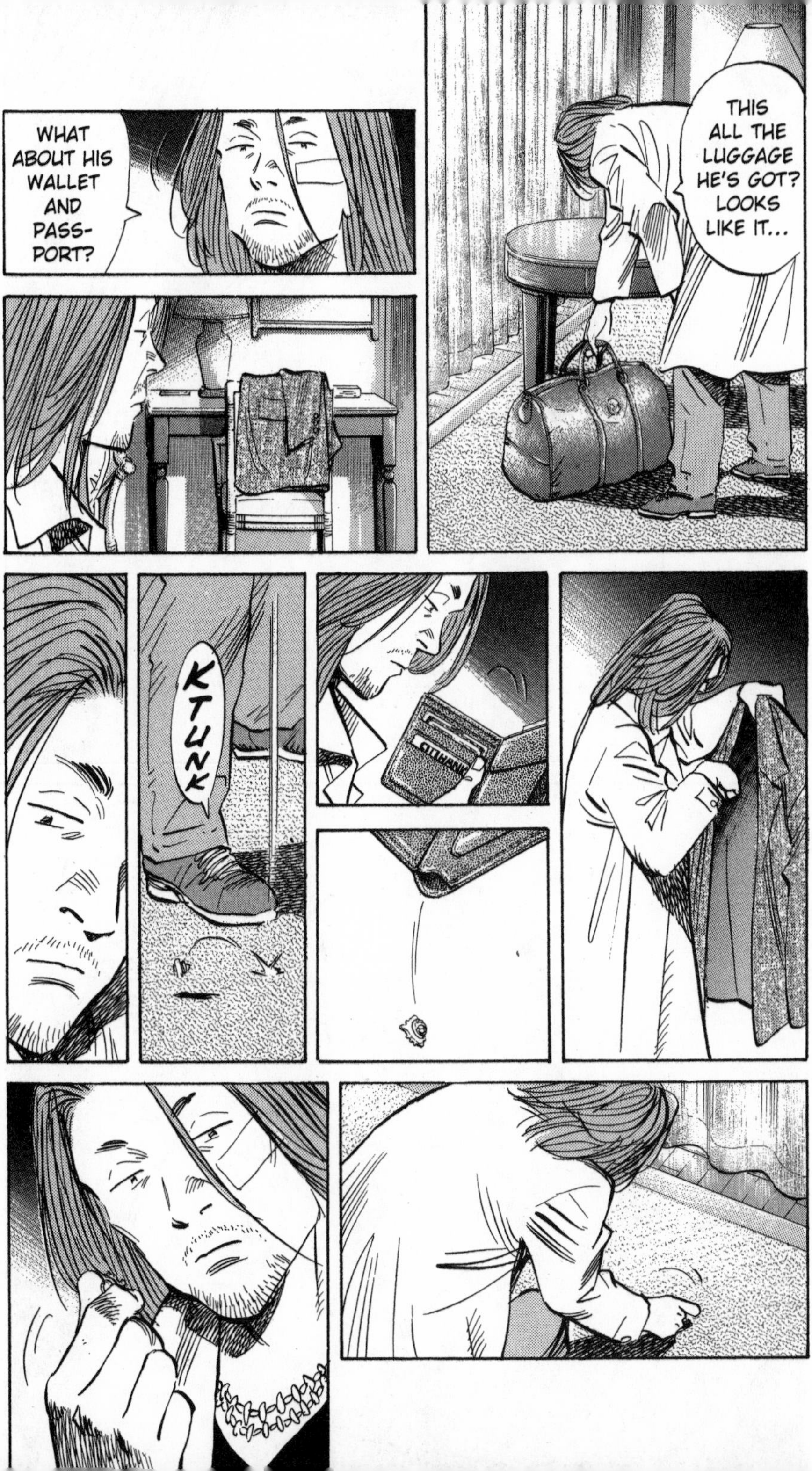
THIS ALL THE LUGGAGE HE'S GOT? LOOKS LIKE IT...
WHAT ABOUT HIS WALLET AND PASS-PORT?
KTUNK

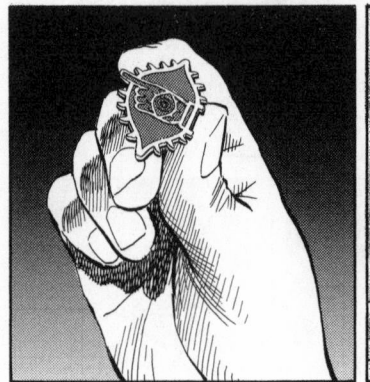

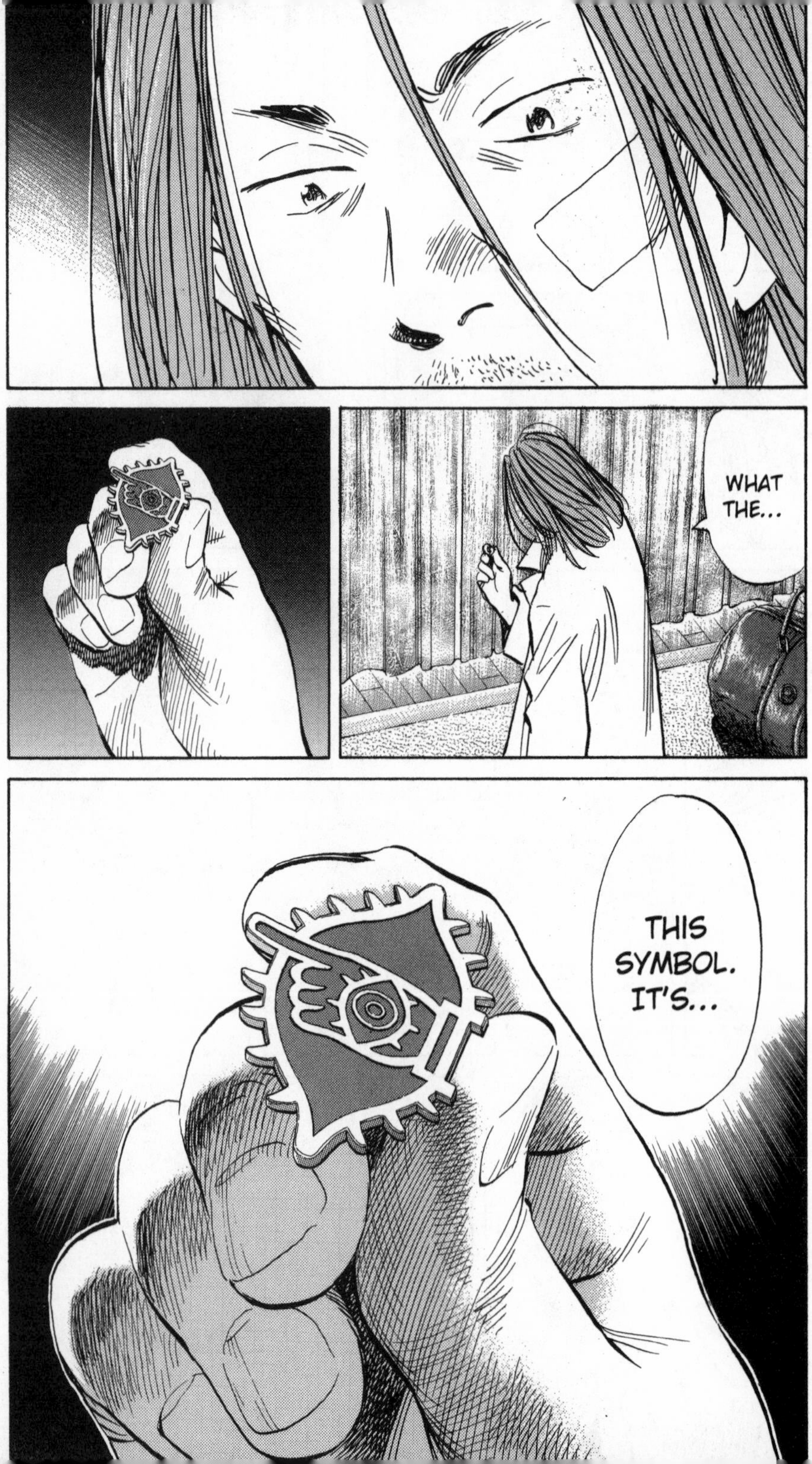

WHAT THE...

THIS
SYMBOL.
IT'S...

Chapter 2 Flight

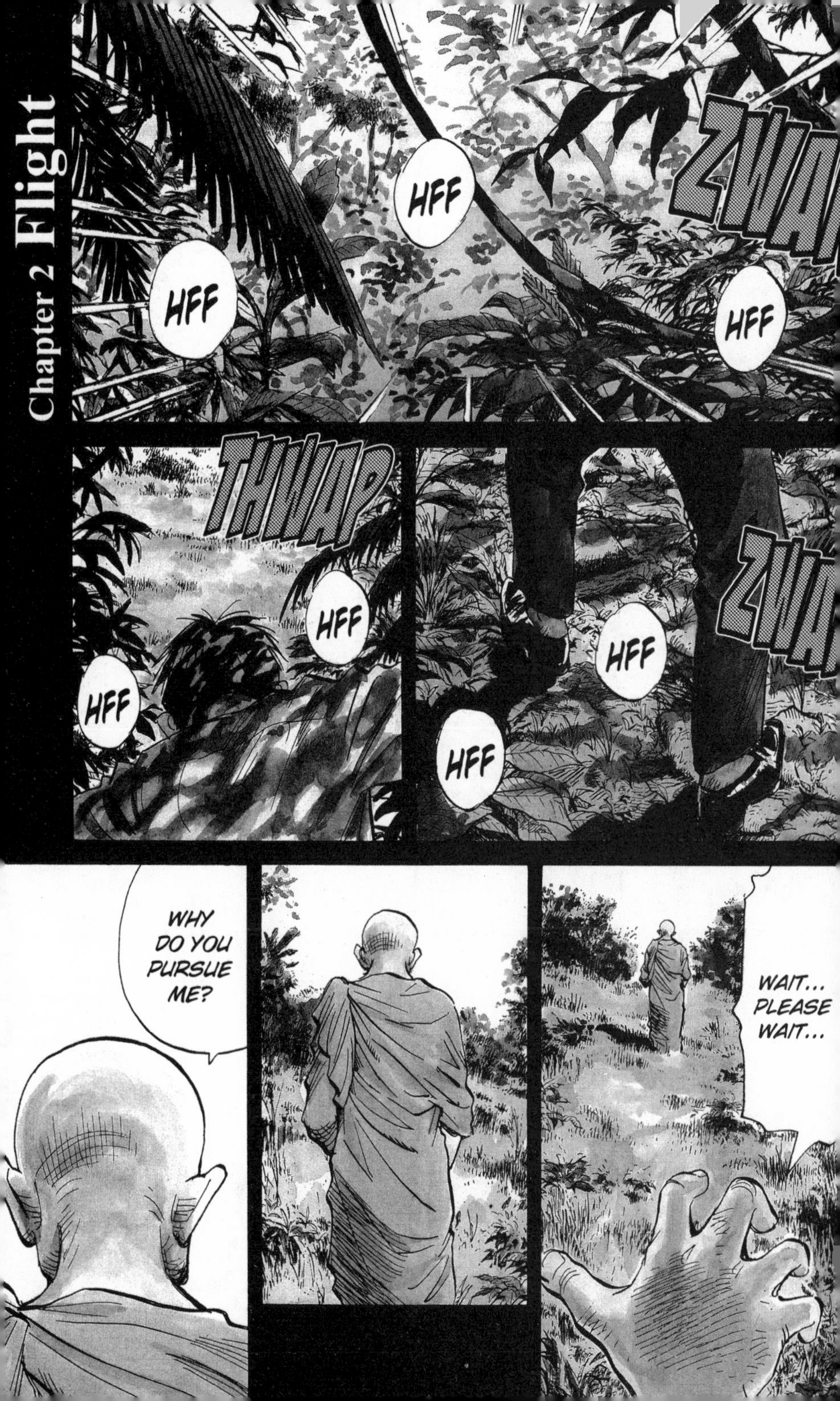
ZWA
HFF
HFF
HFF
ZWA
HFF
HFF
THWAP
HFF
HFF
WAIT... PLEASE WAIT...
WHY DO YOU PURSUE ME?

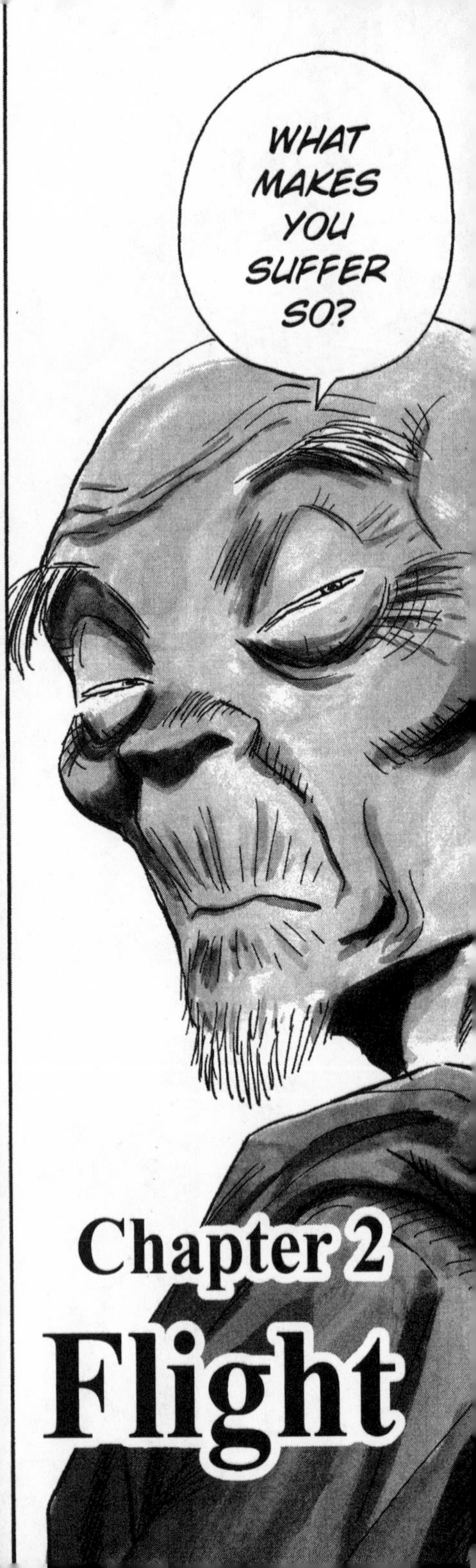
WHAT MAKES YOU SUFFER SO?

Chapter 2 Flight

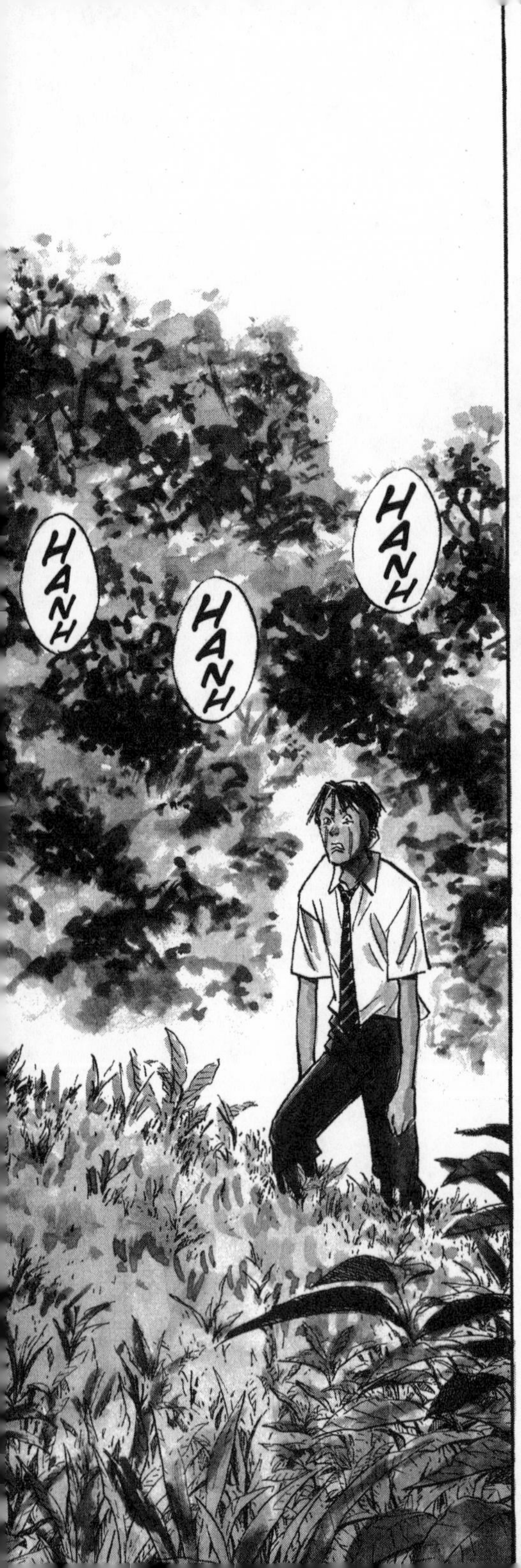
HANH
HANH
HANH

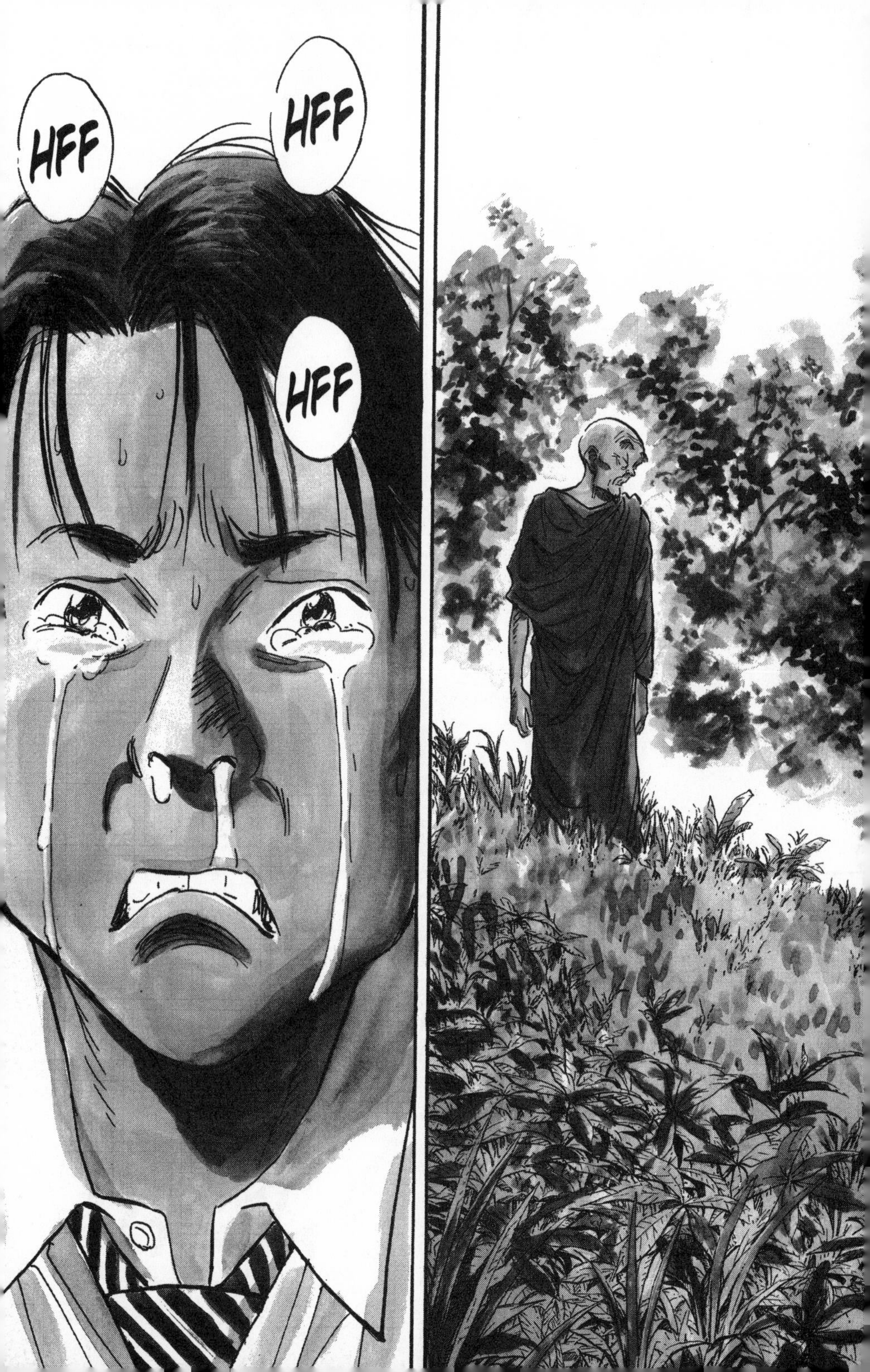
HFF
HFF
HFF

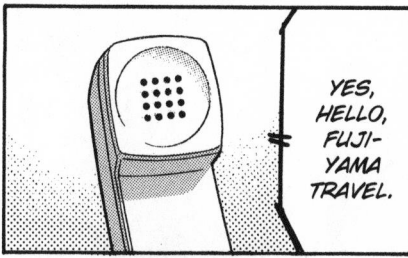

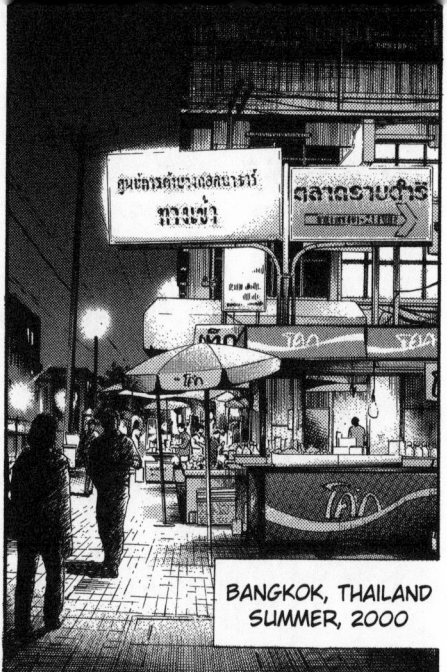

BANGKOK, THAILAND
SUMMER, 2000
YES, HELLO, FUJI-YAMA TRAVEL.
THAT YOU, ISONO-SAN? WHERE THE HECK HAVE YOU BEEN?! I'VE BEEN CALLING THE OFFICE FOR I DON'T KNOW HOW LONG!!
AH, SHOGUN. I WENT OUT FOR A BITE TO EAT. SO, DID YOU GET THE JOB DONE?
DID I GET THE JOB DONE, HE ASKS ME. LIKE I WAS PAINTING A WALL. LISTEN UP. I AM NEVER, UNDER ANY CIRCUMSTANCES, DOING THAT KIND OF JOB AGAIN. YOU HEAR ME?
OH, COME ON, SHOGUN. HOW MUCH TROUBLE COULD IT BE TO DRAG AN OD'D JAPANESE TO A DOCTOR?
A LOT. SINCE HE *DIED*.

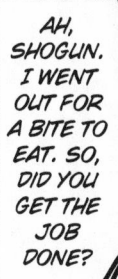

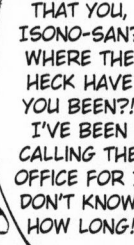

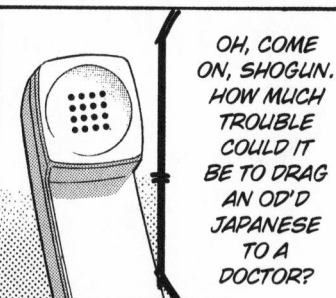

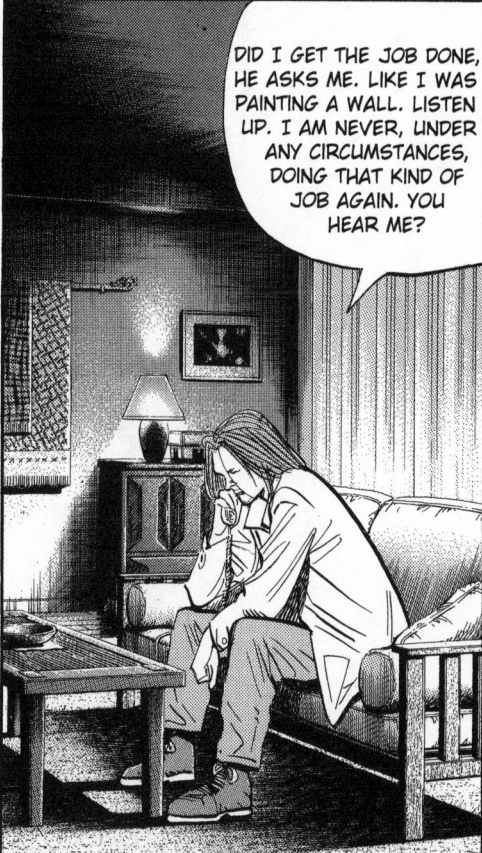

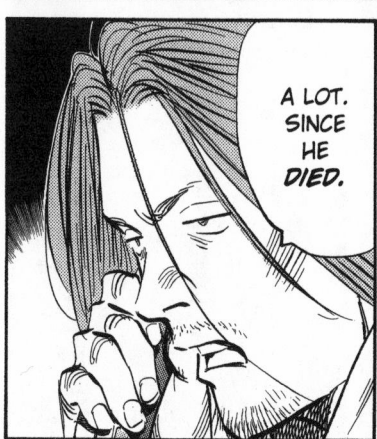

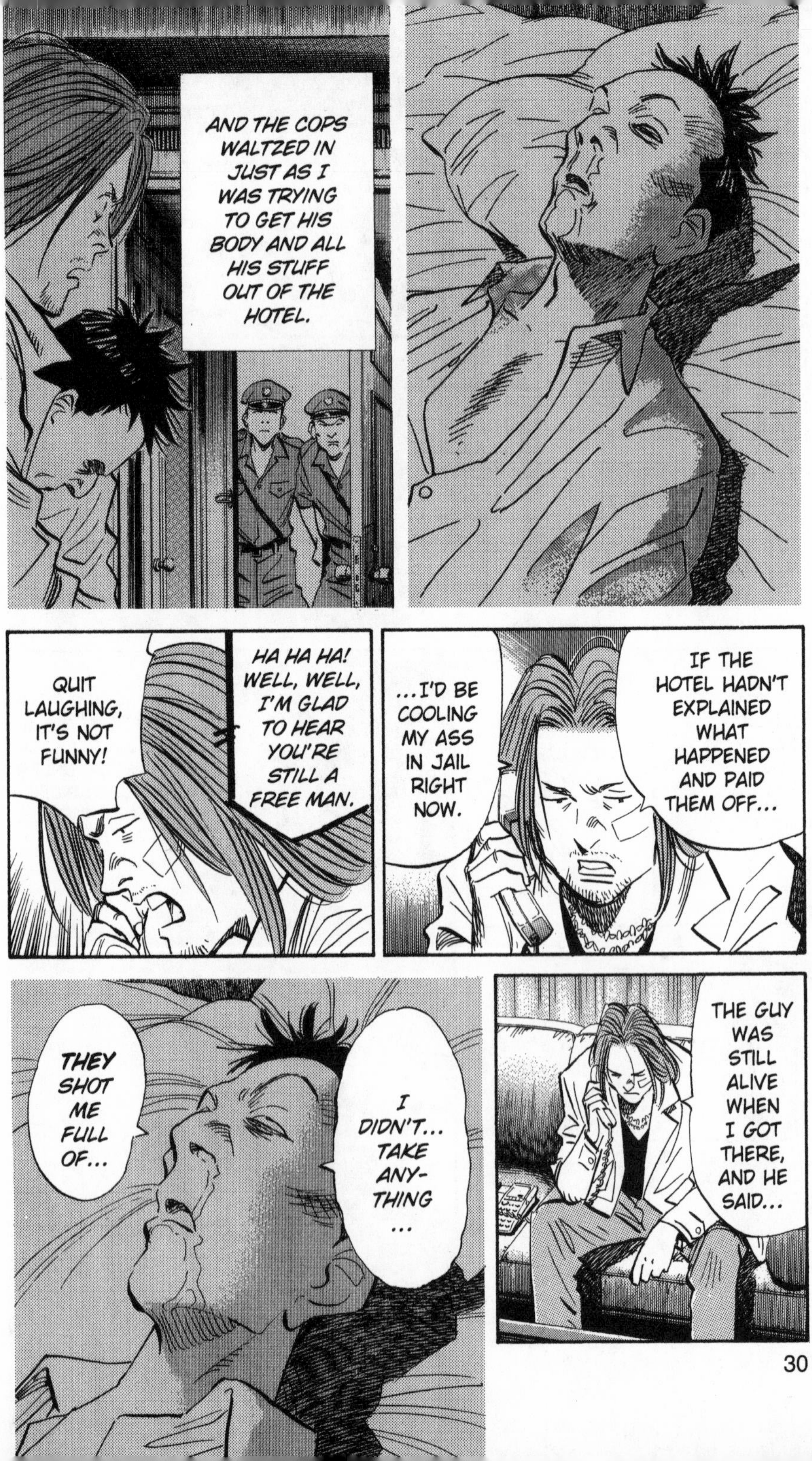
AND THE COPS WALTZED IN JUST AS I WAS TRYING TO GET HIS BODY AND ALL HIS STUFF OUT OF THE HOTEL.
IF THE HOTEL HADN'T EXPLAINED WHAT HAPPENED AND PAID THEM OFF...
...I'D BE COOLING MY ASS IN JAIL RIGHT NOW.
HA HA HA! WELL, WELL, I'M GLAD TO HEAR YOU'RE STILL A FREE MAN.
QUIT LAUGHING, IT'S NOT FUNNY!
THE GUY WAS STILL ALIVE WHEN I GOT THERE, AND HE SAID...
I DIDN'T... TAKE ANY-THING...
THEY SHOT ME FULL OF...

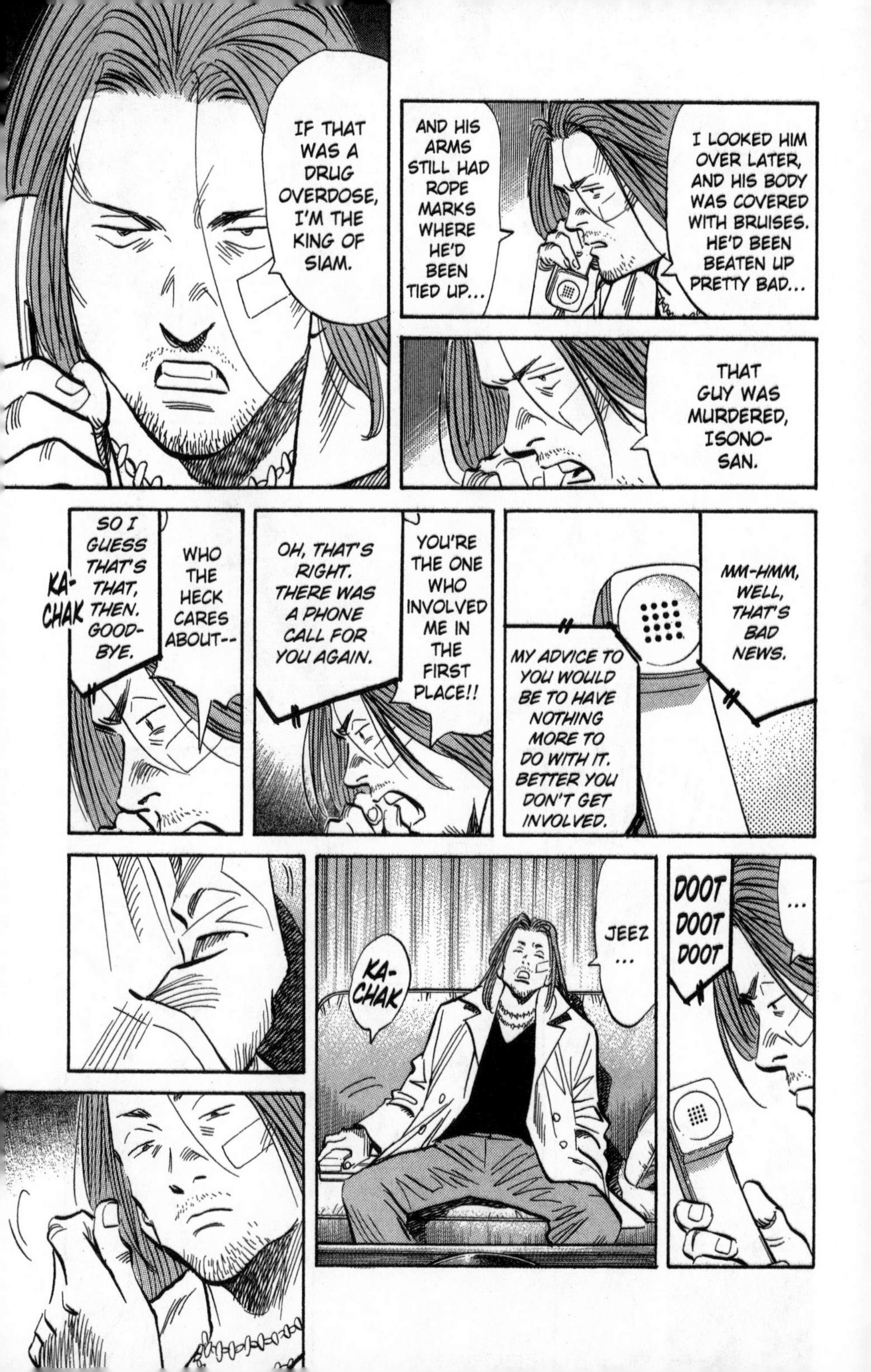
I LOOKED HIM OVER LATER, AND HIS BODY WAS COVERED WITH BRUISES. HE'D BEEN BEATEN UP PRETTY BAD...
AND HIS ARMS STILL HAD ROPE MARKS WHERE HE'D BEEN TIED UP...
THAT GUY WAS MURDERED, ISONO-SAN.
IF THAT WAS A DRUG OVERDOSE, I'M THE KING OF SIAM.
MM-HMM, WELL, THAT'S BAD NEWS.
MY ADVICE TO YOU WOULD BE TO HAVE NOTHING MORE TO DO WITH IT. BETTER YOU DON'T GET INVOLVED.
YOU'RE THE ONE WHO INVOLVED ME IN THE FIRST PLACE!!
OH, THAT'S RIGHT. THERE WAS A PHONE CALL FOR YOU AGAIN.
WHO THE HECK CARES ABOUT--
SO I GUESS THAT'S THAT, THEN. GOOD-BYE.
KA-CHAK
DOOT DOOT DOOT
...
JEEZ...
KA-CHAK

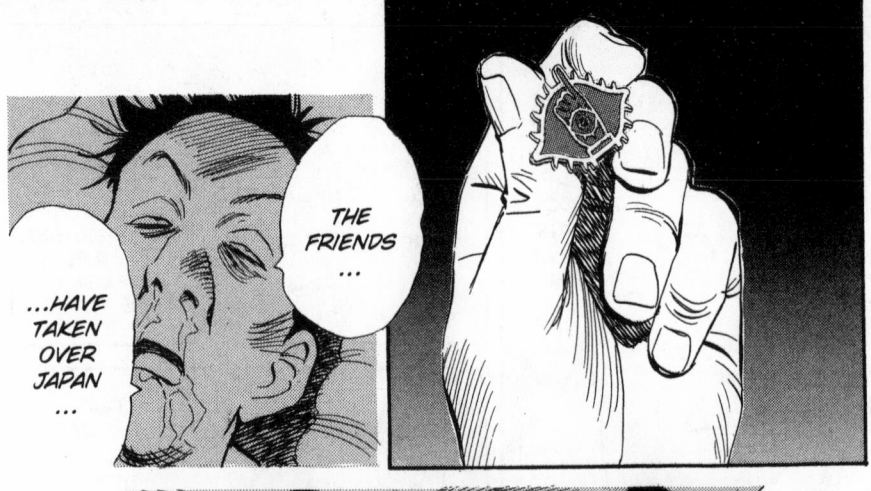

...HAVE TAKEN OVER JAPAN...

THE FRIENDS...

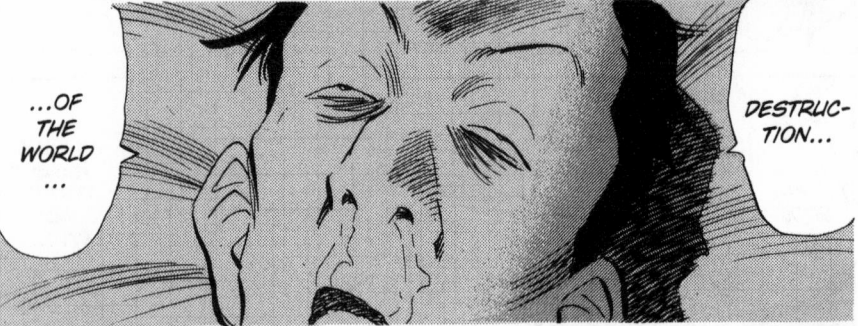

...OF THE WORLD...

DESTRUC- TION...

KLAMP

...

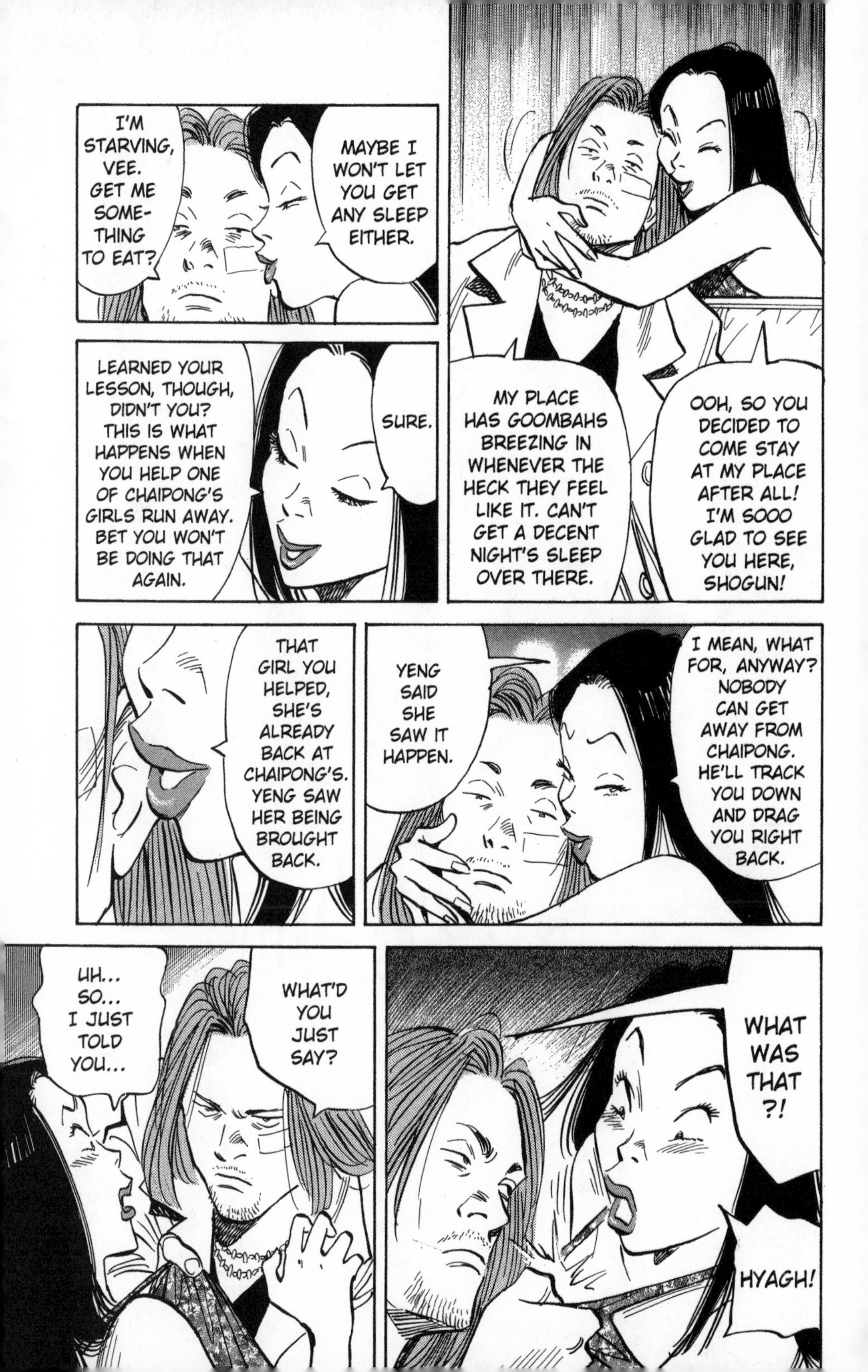
OOH, SO YOU DECIDED TO COME STAY AT MY PLACE AFTER ALL! I'M SOOO GLAD TO SEE YOU HERE, SHOGUN!
MY PLACE HAS GOOMBAHS BREEZING IN WHENEVER THE HECK THEY FEEL LIKE IT. CAN'T GET A DECENT NIGHT'S SLEEP OVER THERE.
MAYBE I WON'T LET YOU GET ANY SLEEP EITHER.
I'M STARVING, VEE. GET ME SOME-THING TO EAT?
SURE.
LEARNED YOUR LESSON, THOUGH, DIDN'T YOU? THIS IS WHAT HAPPENS WHEN YOU HELP ONE OF CHAIPONG'S GIRLS RUN AWAY. BET YOU WON'T BE DOING THAT AGAIN.
I MEAN, WHAT FOR, ANYWAY? NOBODY CAN GET AWAY FROM CHAIPONG. HE'LL TRACK YOU DOWN AND DRAG YOU RIGHT BACK.
YENG SAID SHE SAW IT HAPPEN.
THAT GIRL YOU HELPED, SHE'S ALREADY BACK AT CHAIPONG'S. YENG SAW HER BEING BROUGHT BACK.
WHAT WAS THAT ?!
HYAGH!
WHAT'D YOU JUST SAY?
UH... SO... I JUST TOLD YOU...

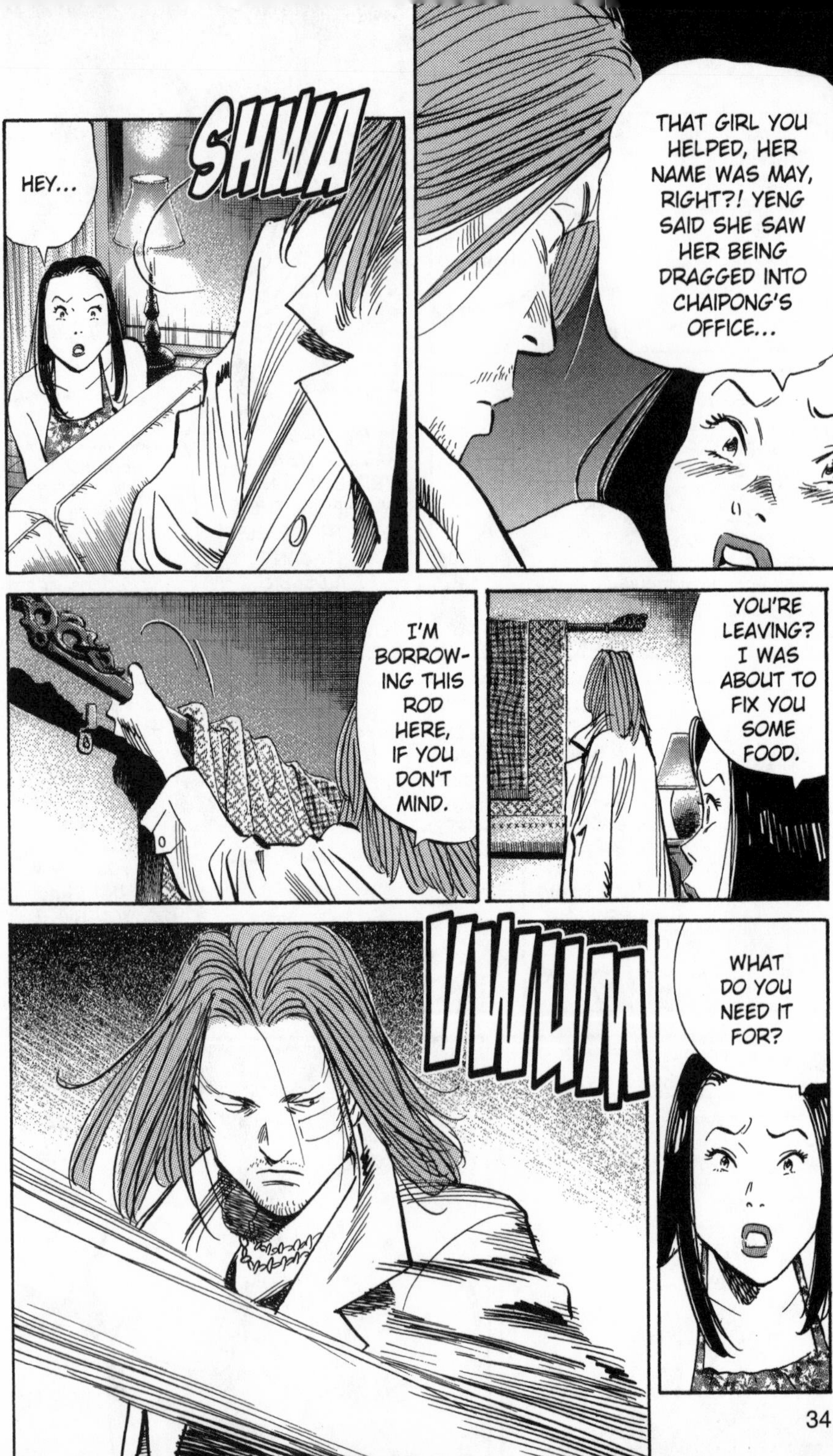
THAT GIRL YOU HELPED, HER NAME WAS MAY, RIGHT?! YENG SAID SHE SAW HER BEING DRAGGED INTO CHAIPONG'S OFFICE...
SHWA
HEY...
YOU'RE LEAVING? I WAS ABOUT TO FIX YOU SOME FOOD.
I'M BORROW-ING THIS ROD HERE, IF YOU DON'T MIND.
WHAT DO YOU NEED IT FOR?
VWUM

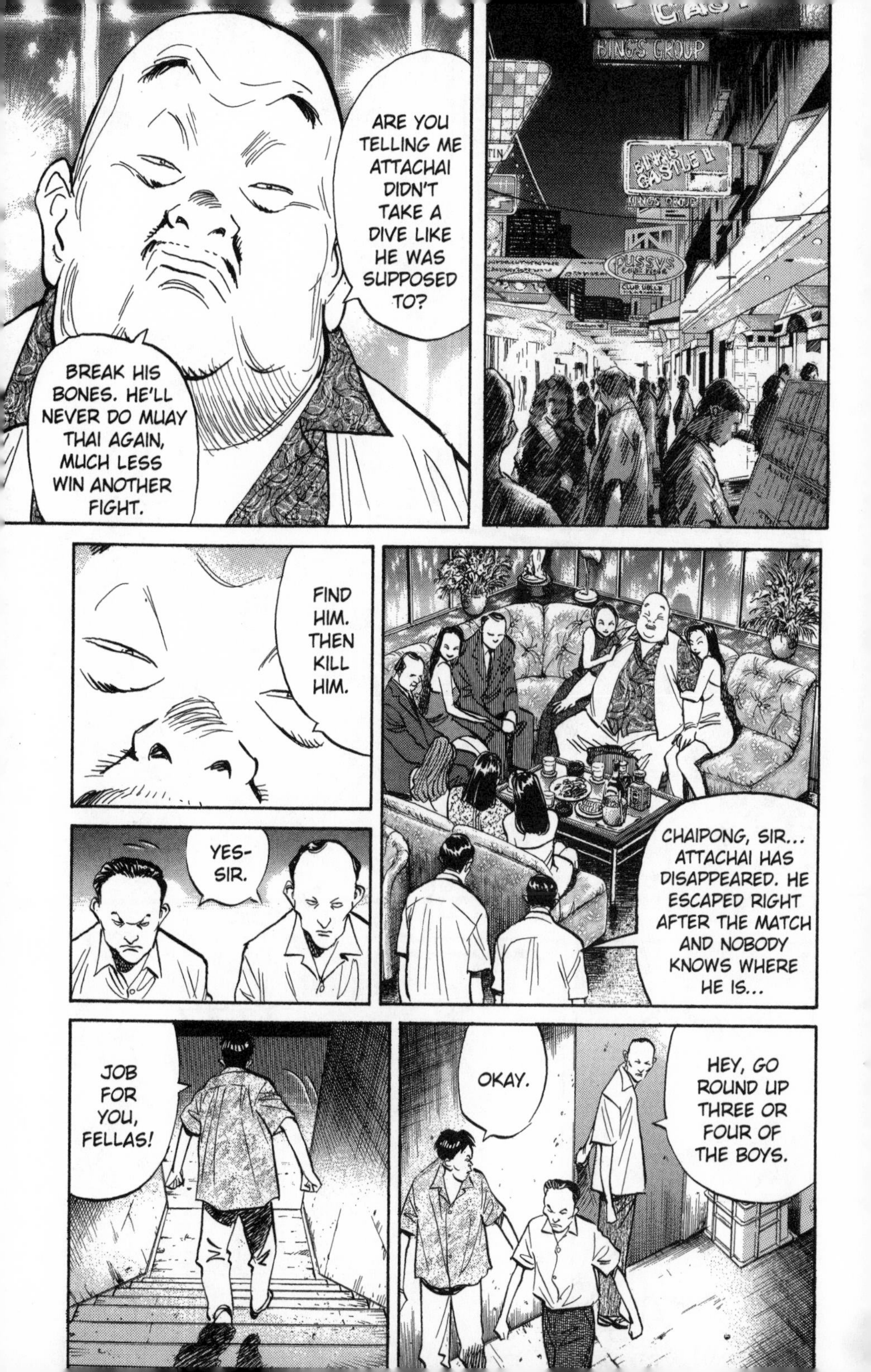
ARE YOU TELLING ME ATTACHAI DIDN'T TAKE A DIVE LIKE HE WAS SUPPOSED TO?
BREAK HIS BONES. HE'LL NEVER DO MUAY THAI AGAIN, MUCH LESS WIN ANOTHER FIGHT.
CHAIPONG, SIR... ATTACHAI HAS DISAPPEARED. HE ESCAPED RIGHT AFTER THE MATCH AND NOBODY KNOWS WHERE HE IS...
FIND HIM. THEN KILL HIM.
YES-SIR.
HEY, GO ROUND UP THREE OR FOUR OF THE BOYS.
OKAY.
JOB FOR YOU, FELLAS!

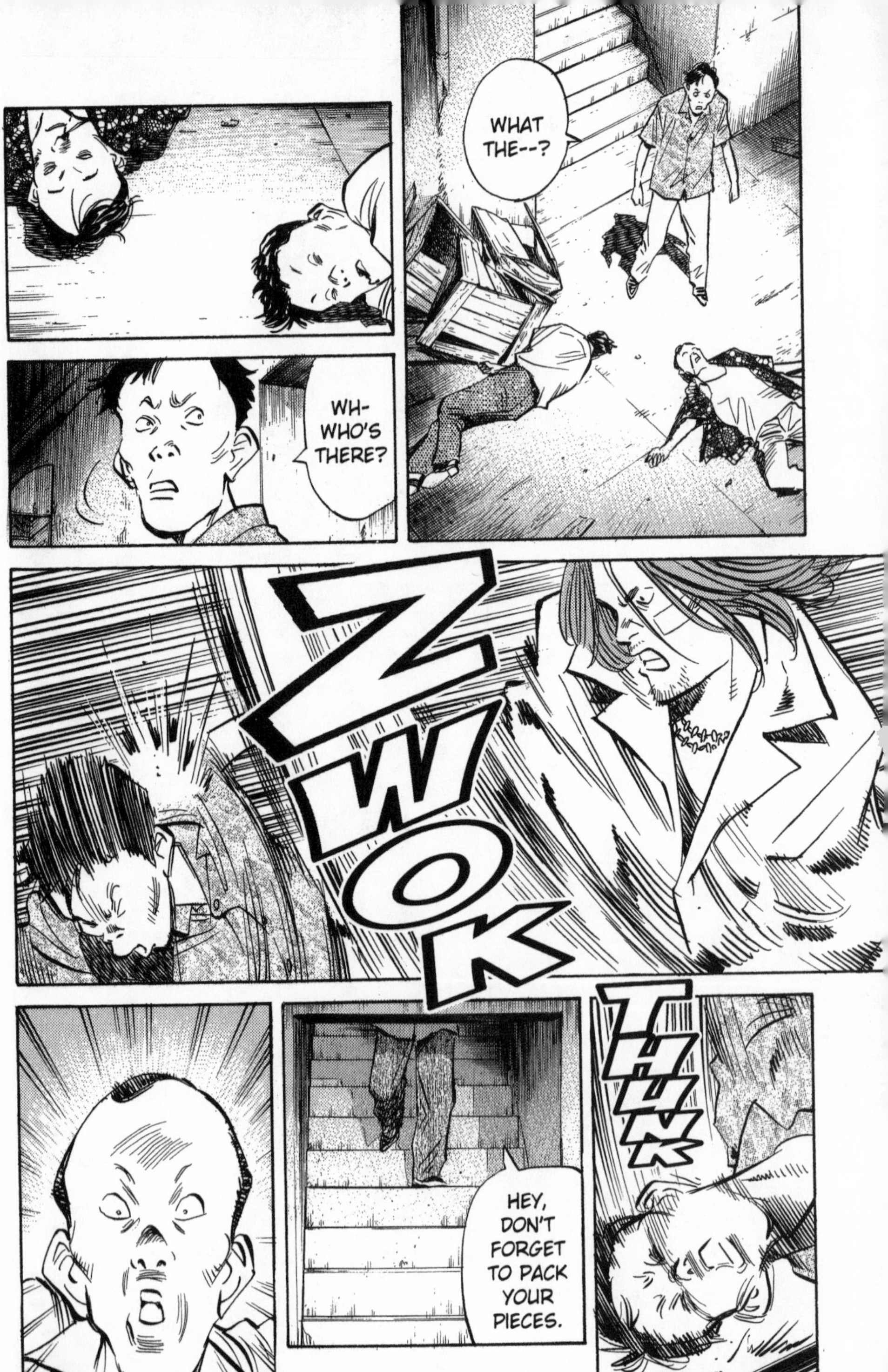
WHAT THE--?
WH-WHO'S THERE?
ZWOK
THUNK
HEY, DON'T FORGET TO PACK YOUR PIECES.

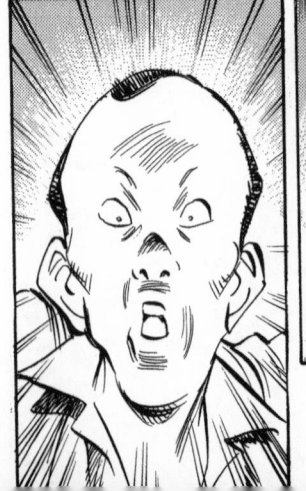

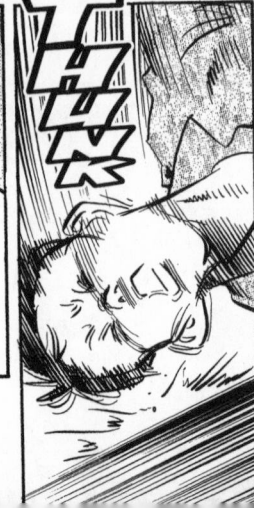

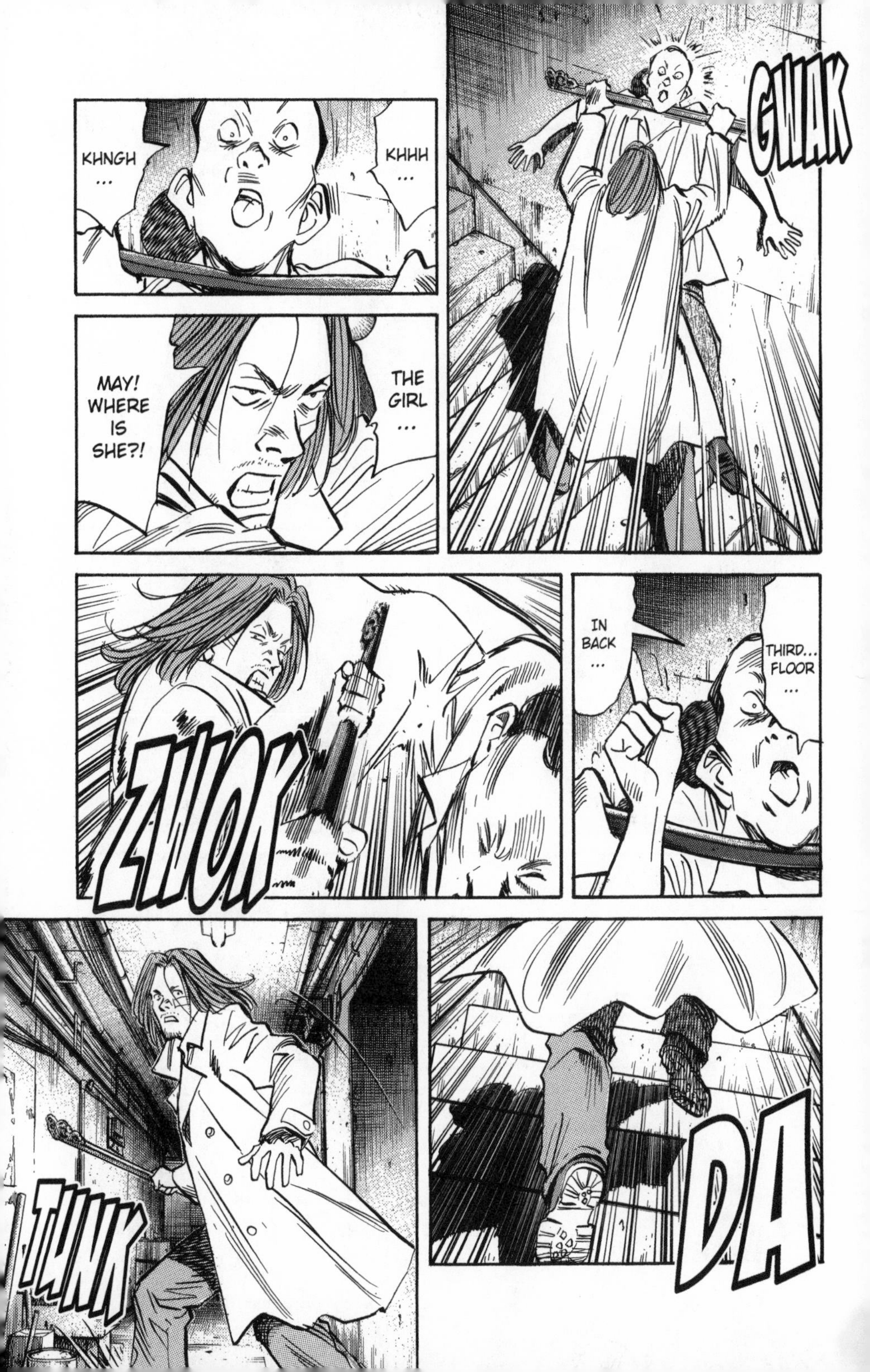
GWAK
KHHH...
KHNGH...
THE GIRL...
MAY! WHERE IS SHE?!
THIRD... FLOOR...
IN BACK...
ZWOK
DA
TUNK

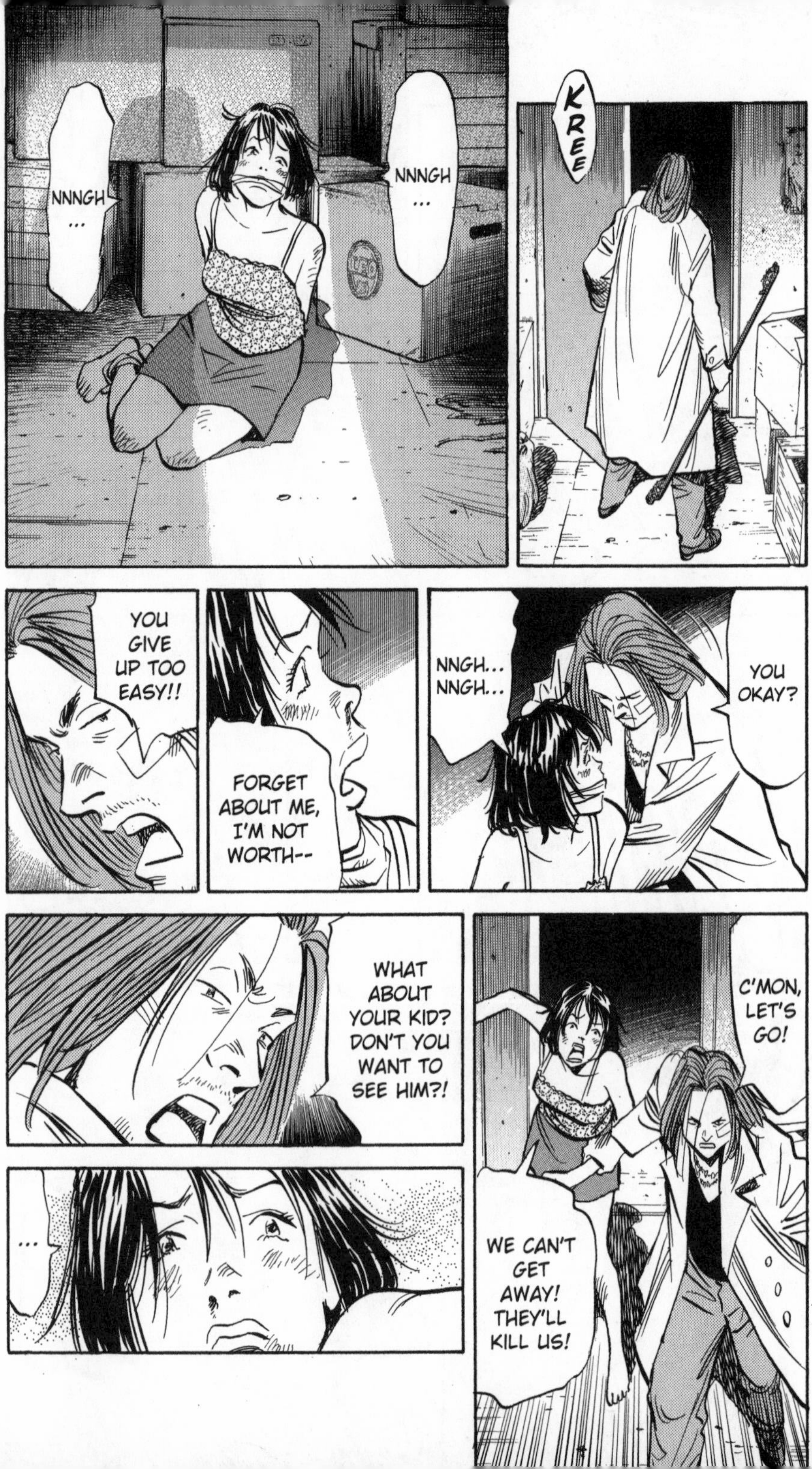
KREE
NNNGH ...
NNNGH ...
YOU OKAY?
NNGH... NNGH...
FORGET ABOUT ME, I'M NOT WORTH--
YOU GIVE UP TOO EASY!!
C'MON, LET'S GO!
WE CAN'T GET AWAY! THEY'LL KILL US!
WHAT ABOUT YOUR KID? DON'T YOU WANT TO SEE HIM?!
...

MAY! RUN!!

SON-OF-A--!!

HEY, WHAT THE HELL ARE YOU DOIN'?!

KRAK

THWUNK

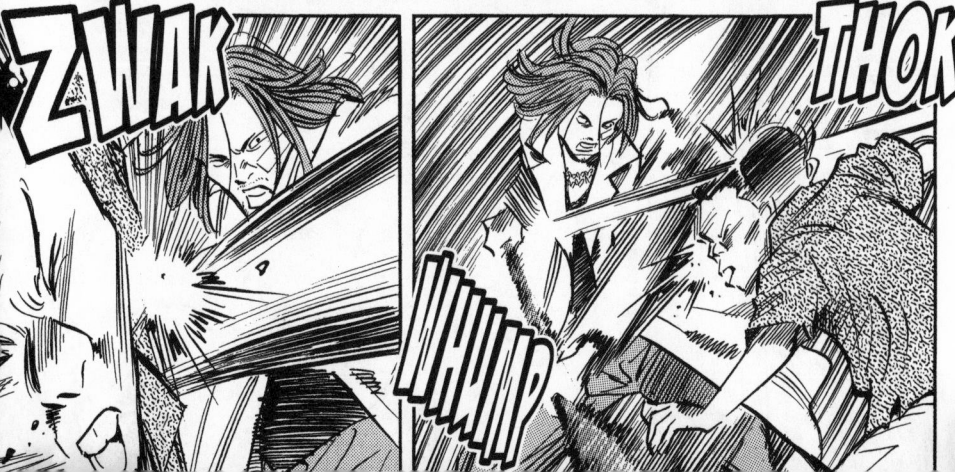

ZWAK

THOK

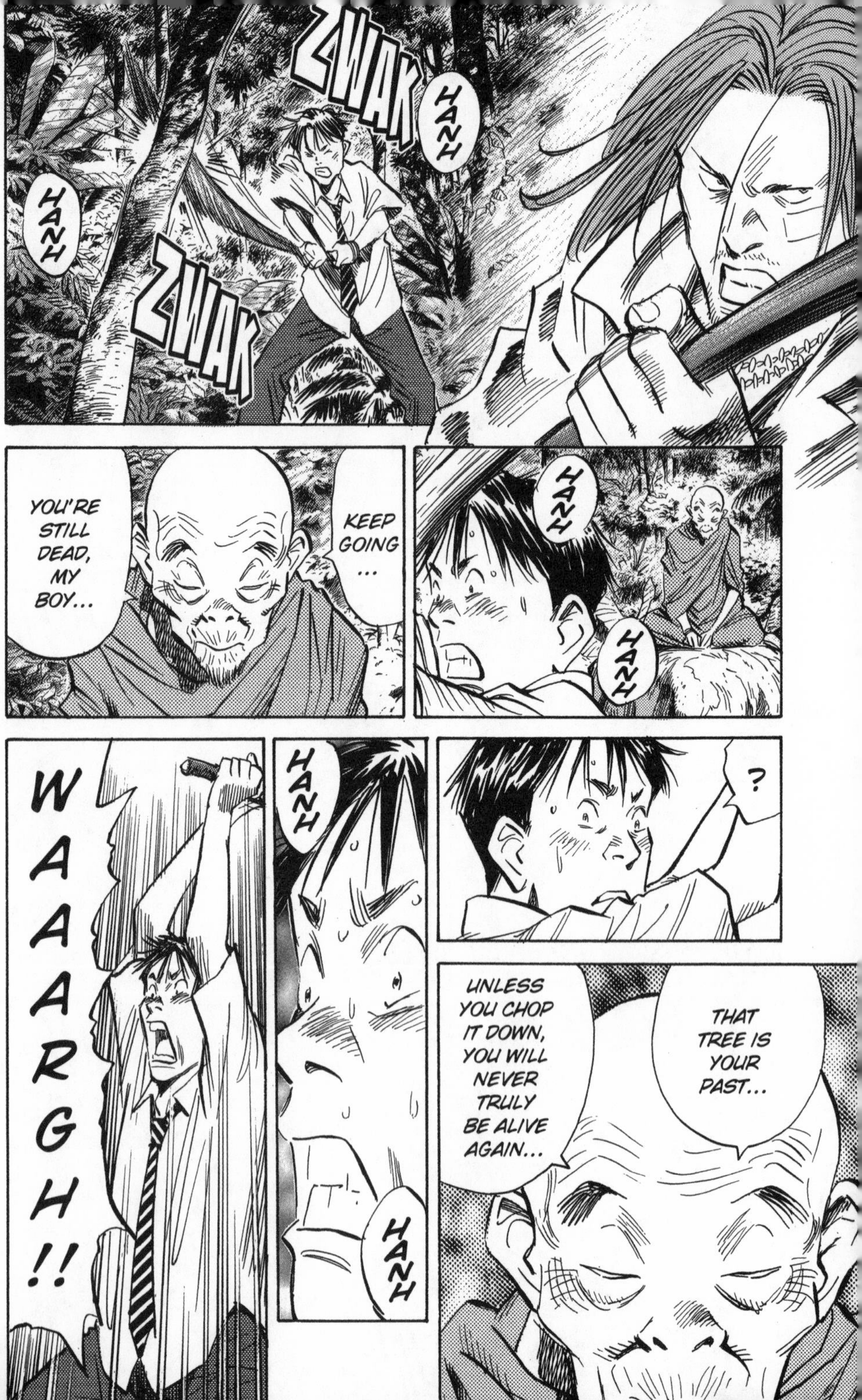
ZWAK
HANH
HANH
ZWAK
HANH
HANH
KEEP GOING...
YOU'RE STILL DEAD, MY BOY...
?
THAT TREE IS YOUR PAST...
UNLESS YOU CHOP IT DOWN, YOU WILL NEVER TRULY BE ALIVE AGAIN...
HANH
HANH
WAAAARGH!!

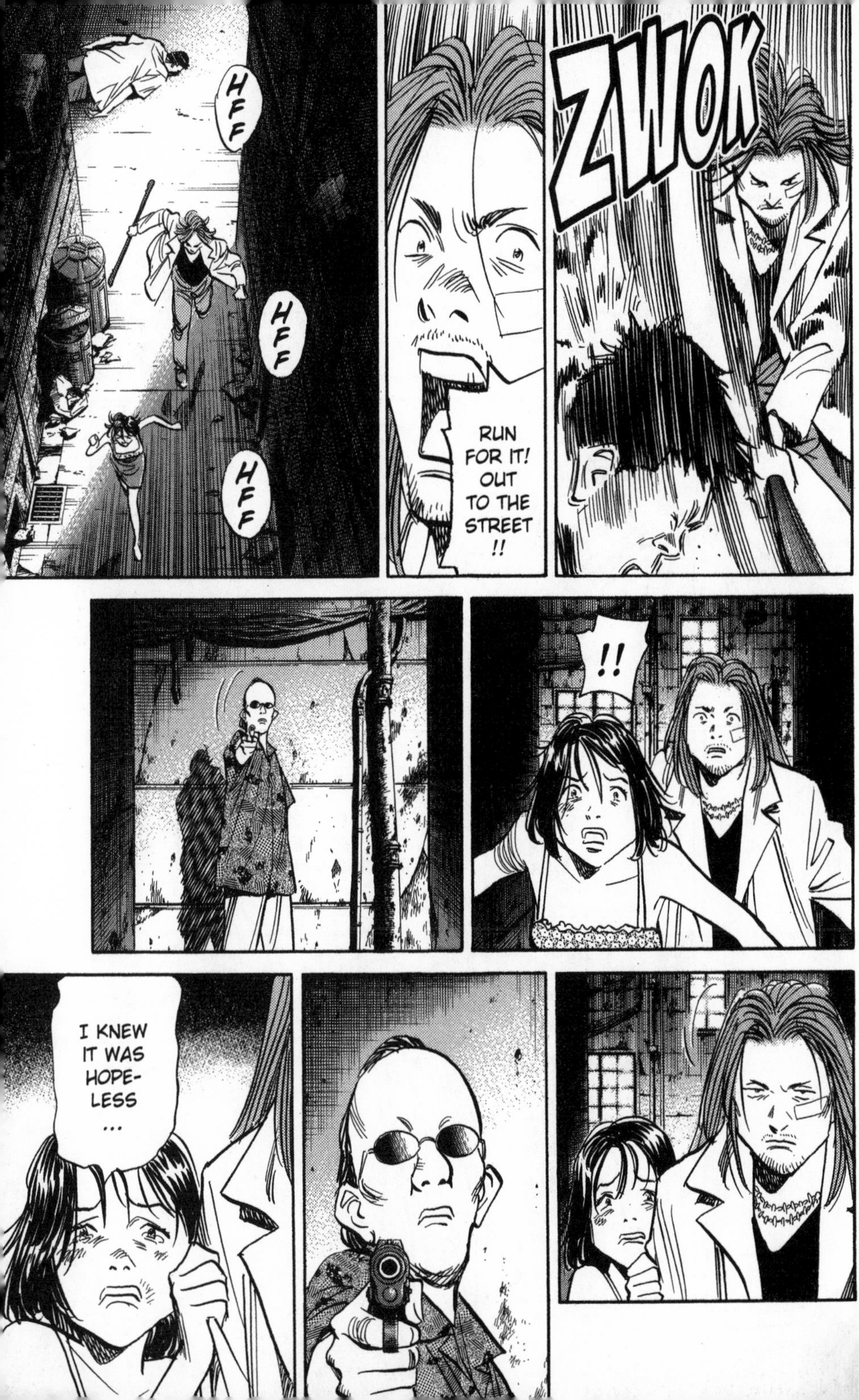
ZWOK
RUN FOR IT! OUT TO THE STREET !!
HFF
HFF
HFF
!!
I KNEW IT WAS HOPE-LESS ...

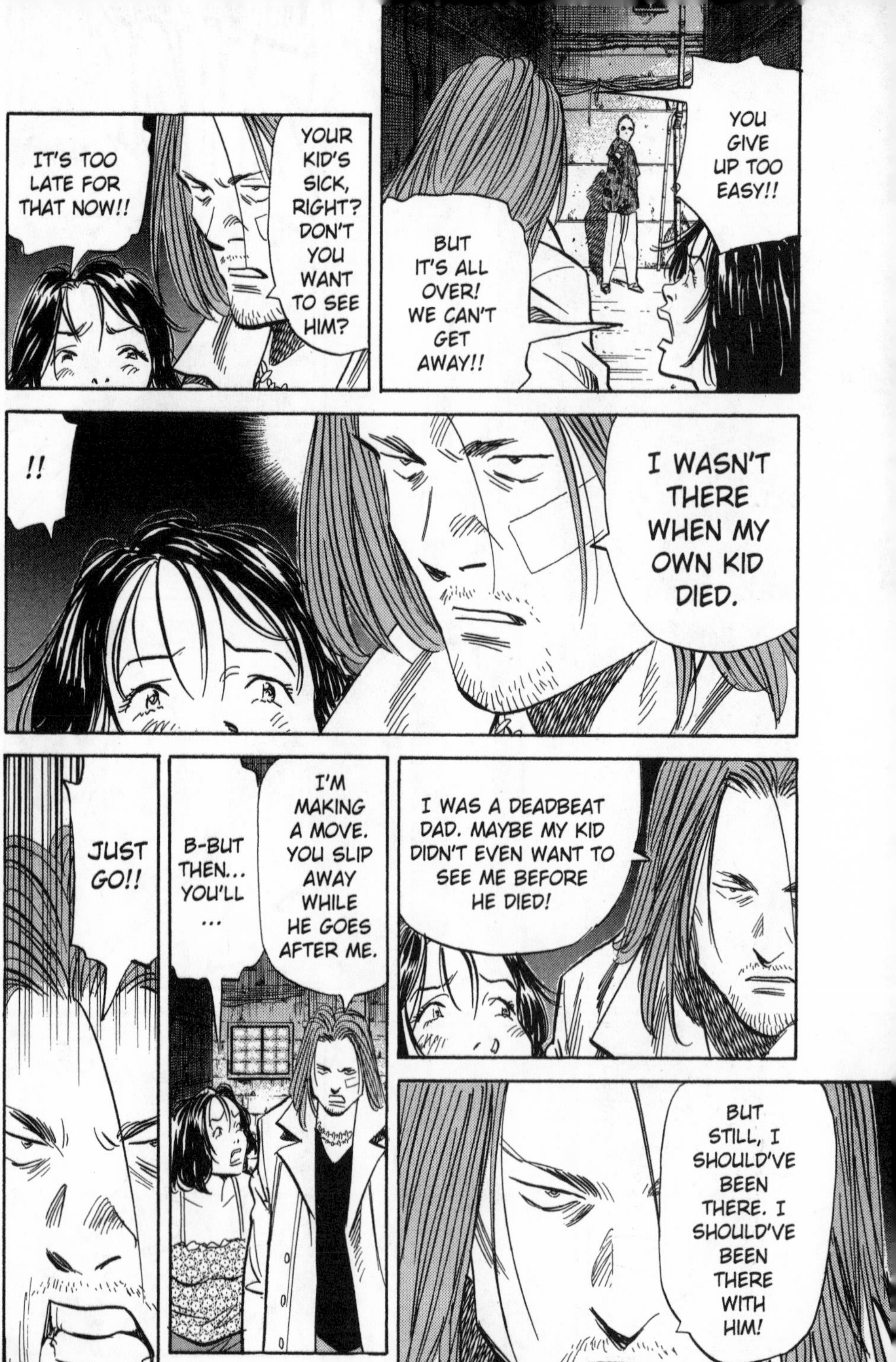
YOU GIVE UP TOO EASY!!
BUT IT'S ALL OVER! WE CAN'T GET AWAY!!
YOUR KID'S SICK, RIGHT? DON'T YOU WANT TO SEE HIM?
IT'S TOO LATE FOR THAT NOW!!
I WASN'T THERE WHEN MY OWN KID DIED.
!!
I WAS A DEADBEAT DAD. MAYBE MY KID DIDN'T EVEN WANT TO SEE ME BEFORE HE DIED!
BUT STILL, I SHOULD'VE BEEN THERE. I SHOULD'VE BEEN THERE WITH HIM!
I'M MAKING A MOVE. YOU SLIP AWAY WHILE HE GOES AFTER ME.
B-BUT THEN... YOU'LL ...
JUST GO!!

PARDON ME, BUT WE'VE LOST OUR WAY...

...

?!

ER... EXCUSE ME.

?!

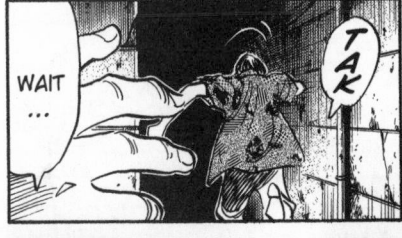

WAIT...

TAK

...

COULD YOU PLEASE TELL ME HOW TO GET TO PATPONG ROAD FROM HERE?

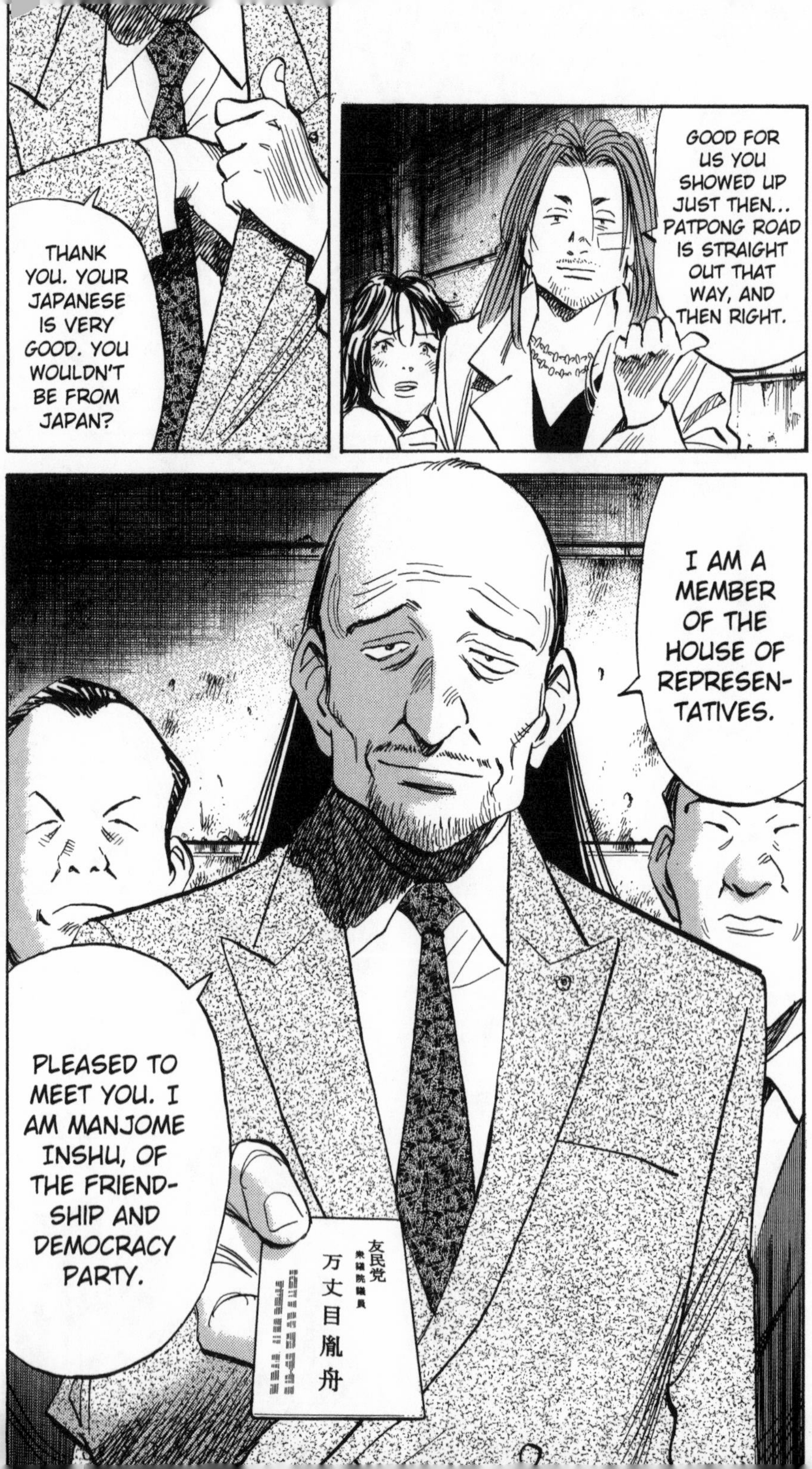
GOOD FOR US YOU SHOWED UP JUST THEN... PATPONG ROAD IS STRAIGHT OUT THAT WAY, AND THEN RIGHT.
THANK YOU. YOUR JAPANESE IS VERY GOOD. YOU WOULDN'T BE FROM JAPAN?
I AM A MEMBER OF THE HOUSE OF REPRESEN-TATIVES.
PLEASED TO MEET YOU. I AM MANJOME INSHU, OF THE FRIEND-SHIP AND DEMOCRACY PARTY.
友民党
衆議院議員
万丈目胤舟

20世紀少年

Twentieth Century Boys

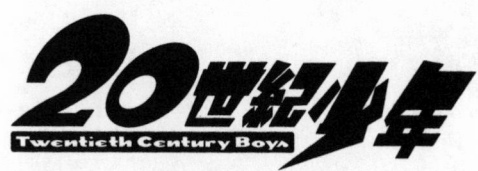

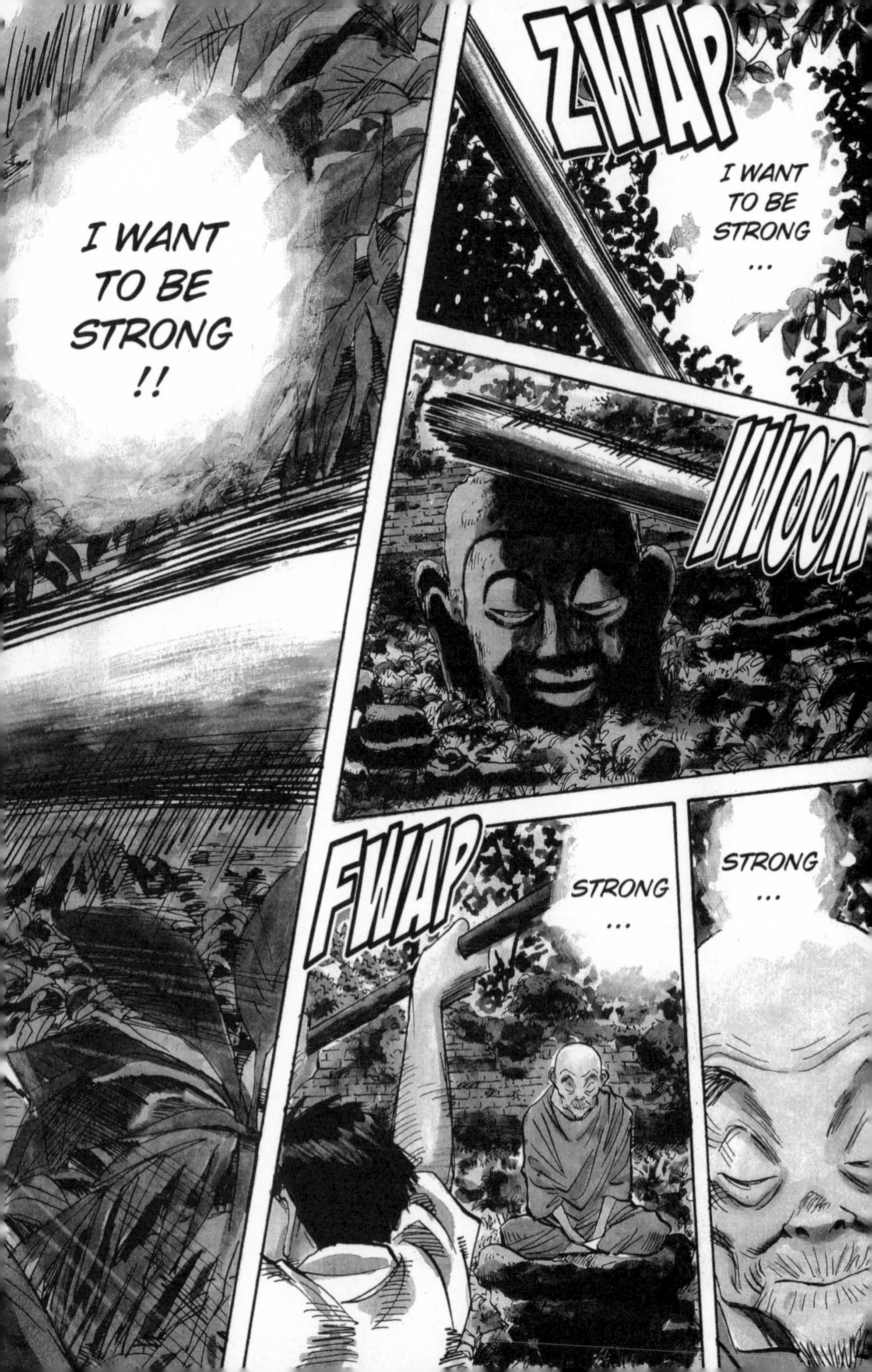
ZWAP
I WANT TO BE STRONG ...
WOOM
STRONG ...
FWAP
STRONG ...
I WANT TO BE STRONG !!

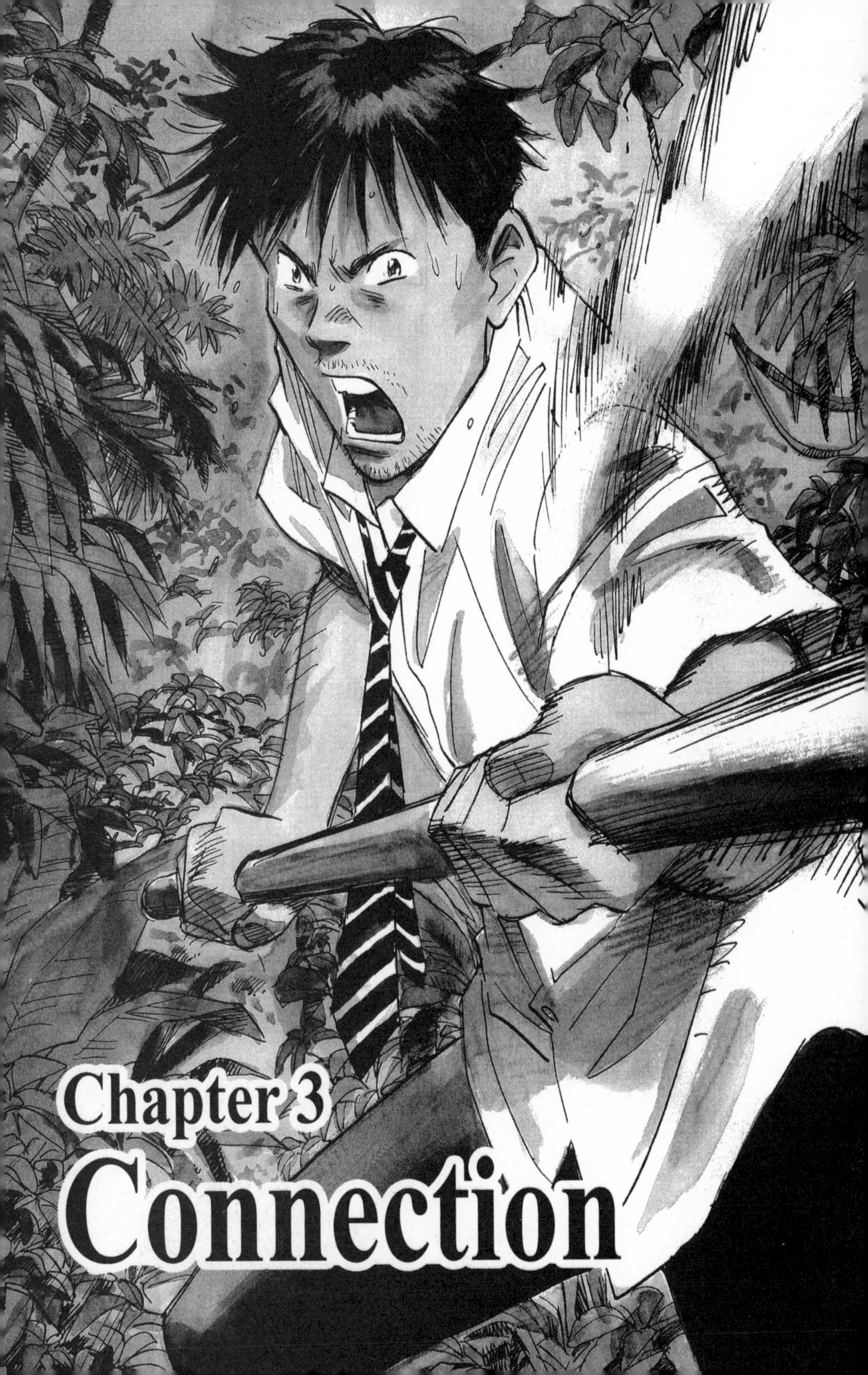
Chapter 3
Connection

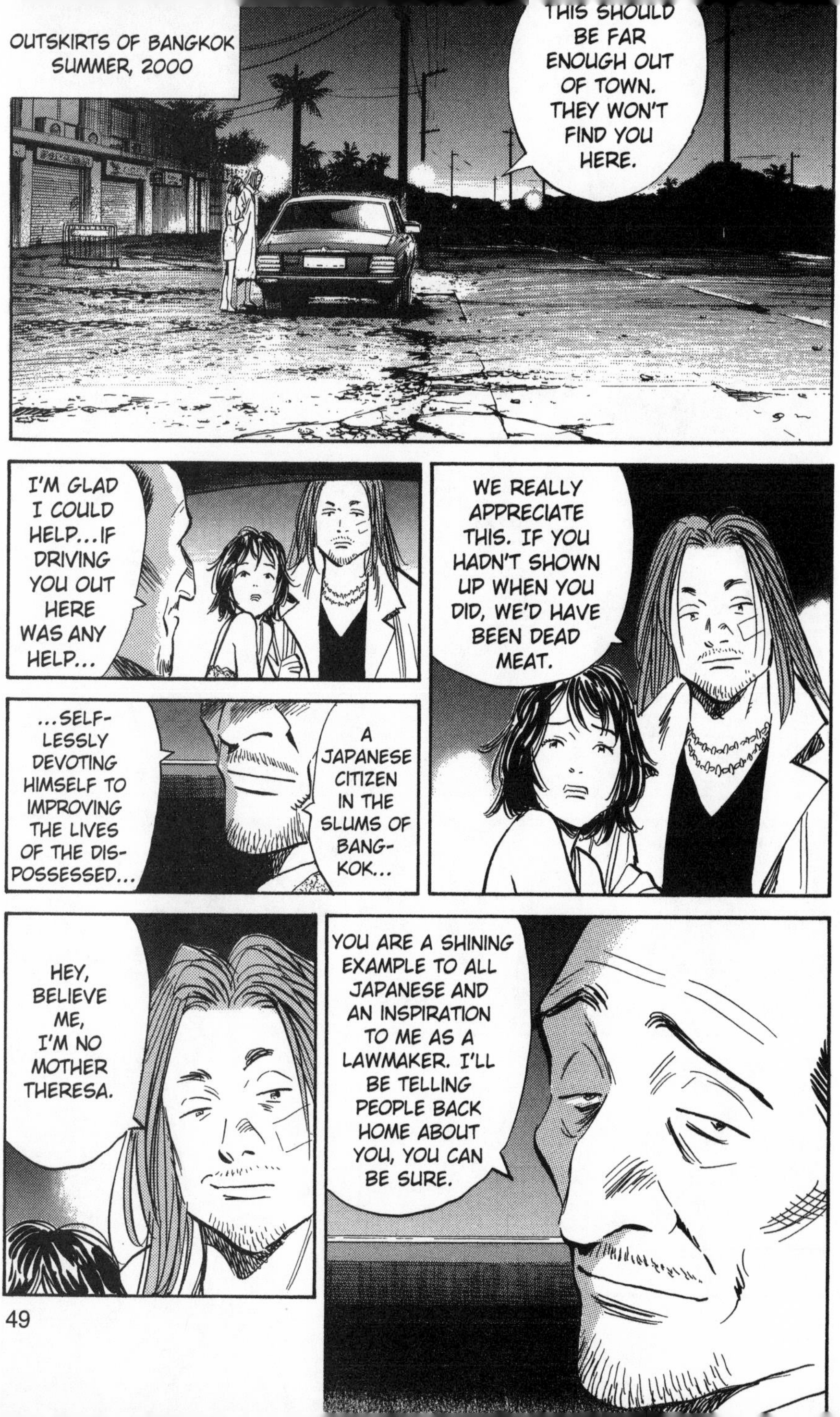
THIS SHOULD BE FAR ENOUGH OUT OF TOWN. THEY WON'T FIND YOU HERE.
OUTSKIRTS OF BANGKOK SUMMER, 2000
WE REALLY APPRECIATE THIS. IF YOU HADN'T SHOWN UP WHEN YOU DID, WE'D HAVE BEEN DEAD MEAT.
I'M GLAD I COULD HELP...IF DRIVING YOU OUT HERE WAS ANY HELP...
A JAPANESE CITIZEN IN THE SLUMS OF BANG-KOK...
...SELF-LESSLY DEVOTING HIMSELF TO IMPROVING THE LIVES OF THE DIS-POSSESSED...
YOU ARE A SHINING EXAMPLE TO ALL JAPANESE AND AN INSPIRATION TO ME AS A LAWMAKER. I'LL BE TELLING PEOPLE BACK HOME ABOUT YOU, YOU CAN BE SURE.
HEY, BELIEVE ME, I'M NO MOTHER THERESA.

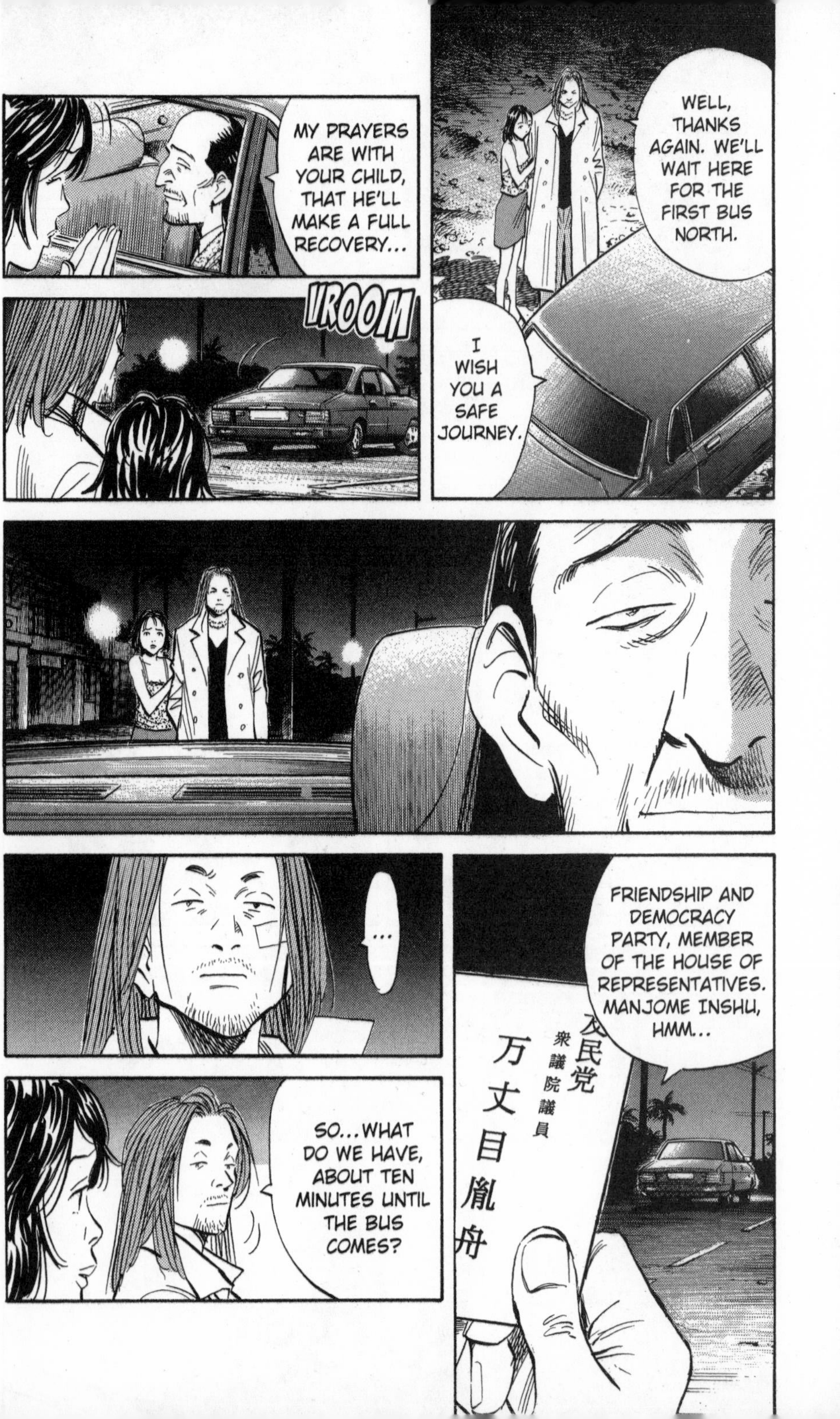

WELL, THANKS AGAIN. WE'LL WAIT HERE FOR THE FIRST BUS NORTH.
I WISH YOU A SAFE JOURNEY.
MY PRAYERS ARE WITH YOUR CHILD, THAT HE'LL MAKE A FULL RECOVERY...
VROOM
FRIENDSHIP AND DEMOCRACY PARTY, MEMBER OF THE HOUSE OF REPRESENTATIVES. MANJOME INSHU, HMM...
友民党
衆議院議員
万丈目胤舟
...
SO...WHAT DO WE HAVE, ABOUT TEN MINUTES UNTIL THE BUS COMES?

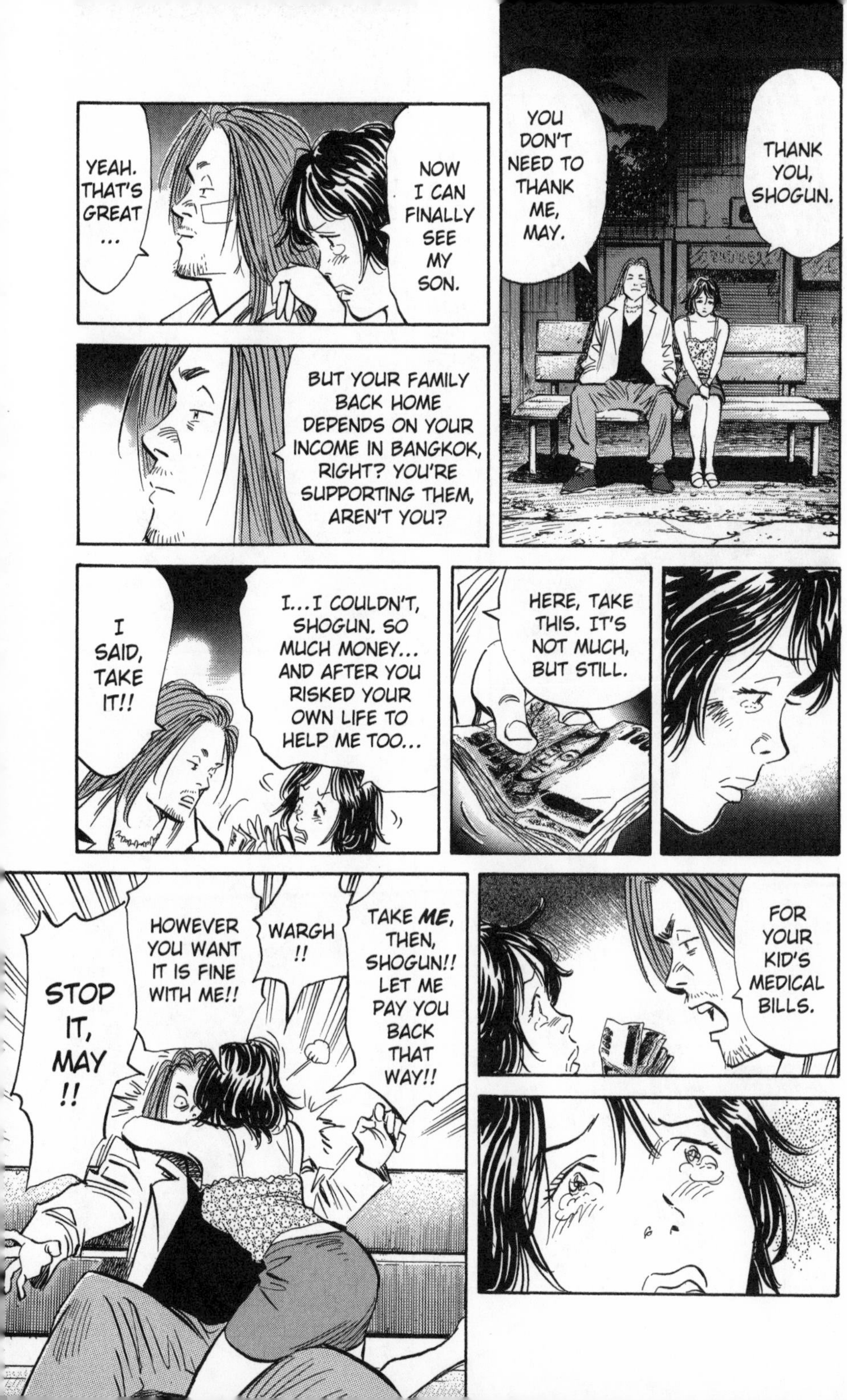
THANK YOU, SHOGUN.
YOU DON'T NEED TO THANK ME, MAY.
NOW I CAN FINALLY SEE MY SON.
YEAH. THAT'S GREAT ...
BUT YOUR FAMILY BACK HOME DEPENDS ON YOUR INCOME IN BANGKOK, RIGHT? YOU'RE SUPPORTING THEM, AREN'T YOU?
HERE, TAKE THIS. IT'S NOT MUCH, BUT STILL.
I...I COULDN'T, SHOGUN. SO MUCH MONEY... AND AFTER YOU RISKED YOUR OWN LIFE TO HELP ME TOO...
I SAID, TAKE IT!!
FOR YOUR KID'S MEDICAL BILLS.
TAKE *ME*, THEN, SHOGUN!! LET ME PAY YOU BACK THAT WAY!!
WARGH !!
HOWEVER YOU WANT IT IS FINE WITH ME!!
STOP IT, MAY !!

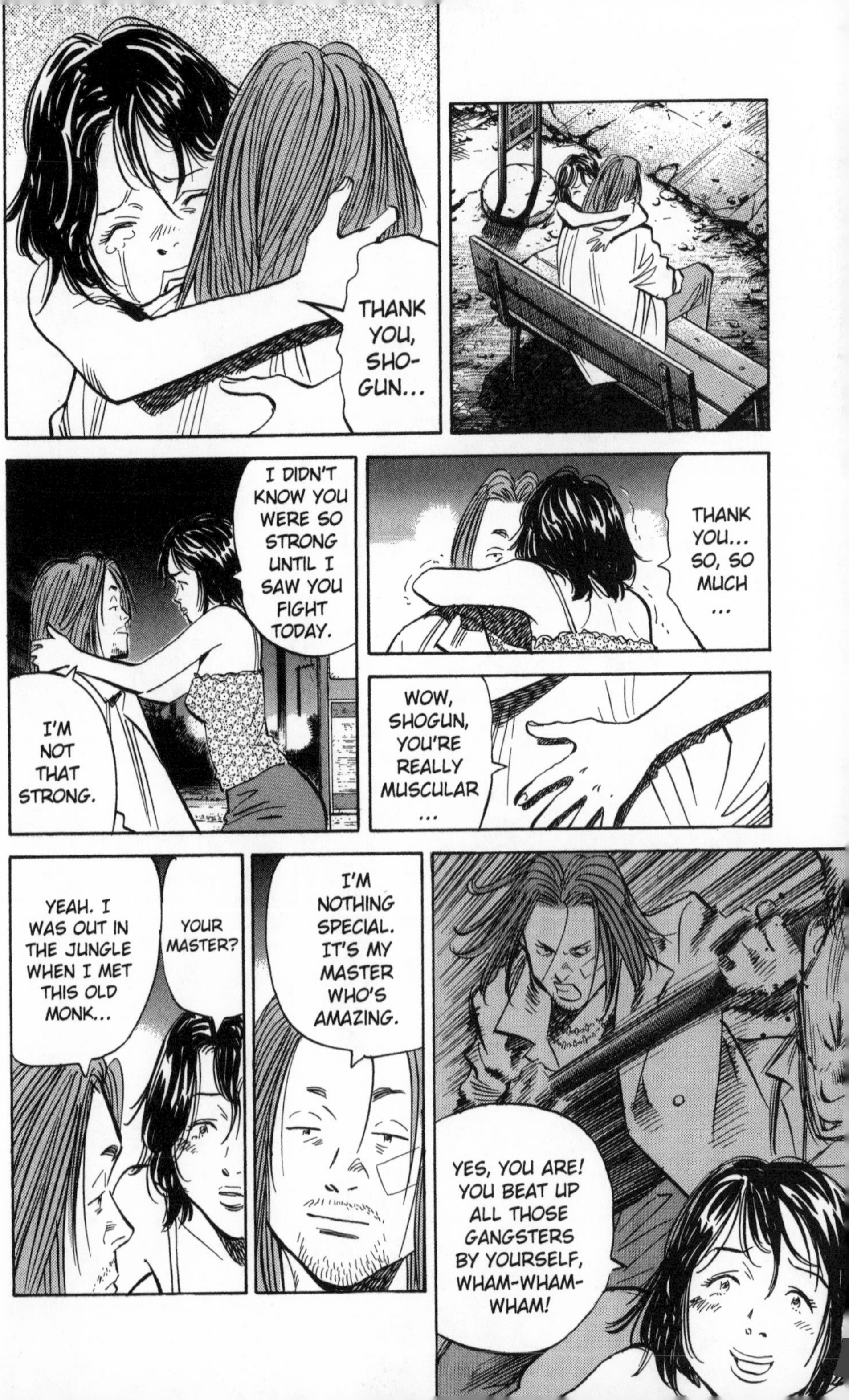
THANK YOU, SHOGUN...
THANK YOU... SO, SO MUCH ...
WOW, SHOGUN, YOU'RE REALLY MUSCULAR ...
I DIDN'T KNOW YOU WERE SO STRONG UNTIL I SAW YOU FIGHT TODAY.
I'M NOT THAT STRONG.
YES, YOU ARE! YOU BEAT UP ALL THOSE GANGSTERS BY YOURSELF, WHAM-WHAM-WHAM!
I'M NOTHING SPECIAL. IT'S MY MASTER WHO'S AMAZING.
YOUR MASTER?
YEAH. I WAS OUT IN THE JUNGLE WHEN I MET THIS OLD MONK...

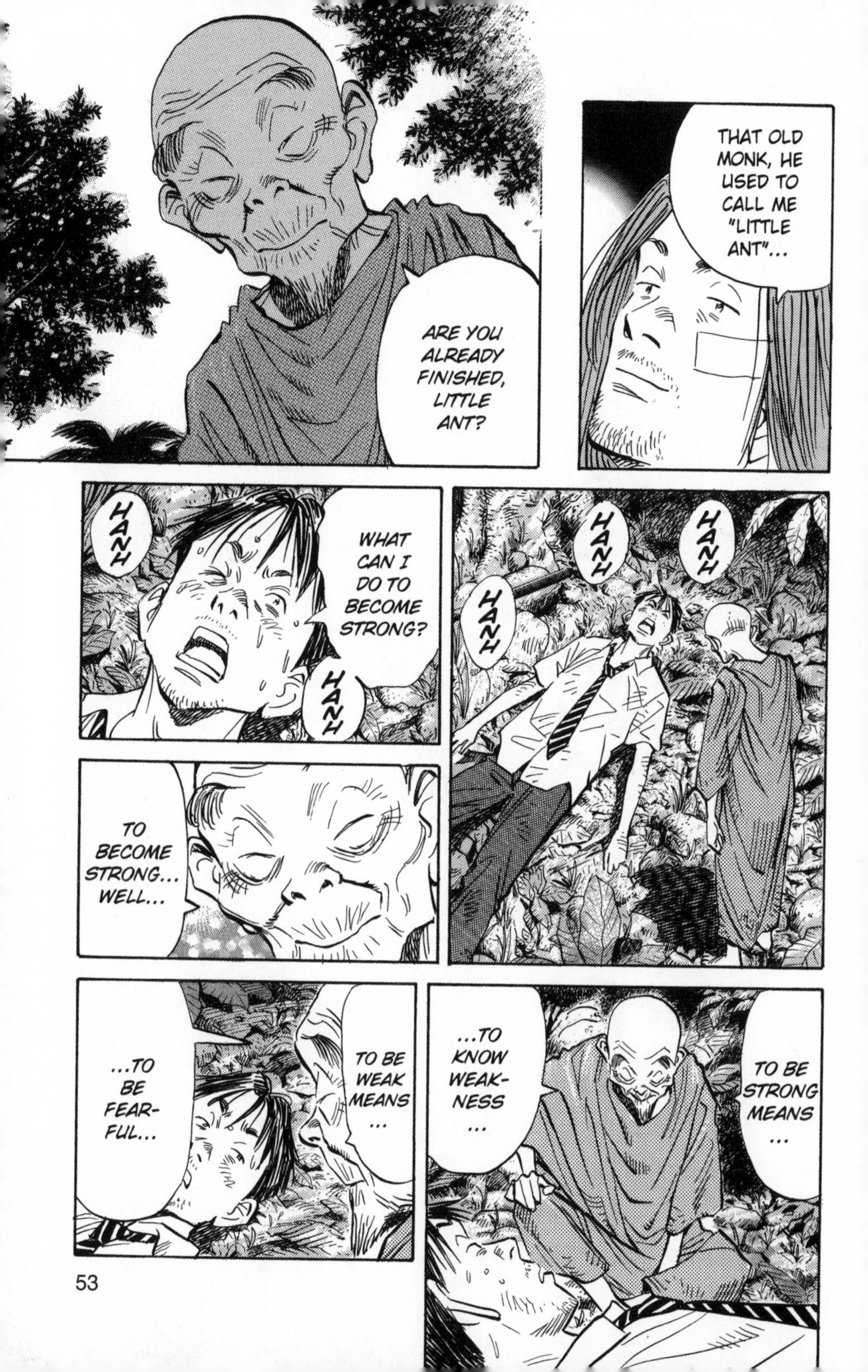
THAT OLD MONK, HE USED TO CALL ME "LITTLE ANT"...
ARE YOU ALREADY FINISHED, LITTLE ANT?
HANH
HANH
HANH
WHAT CAN I DO TO BECOME STRONG?
HANH
HANH
TO BECOME STRONG... WELL...
TO BE STRONG MEANS...
...TO KNOW WEAK-NESS...
TO BE WEAK MEANS...
...TO BE FEAR-FUL...

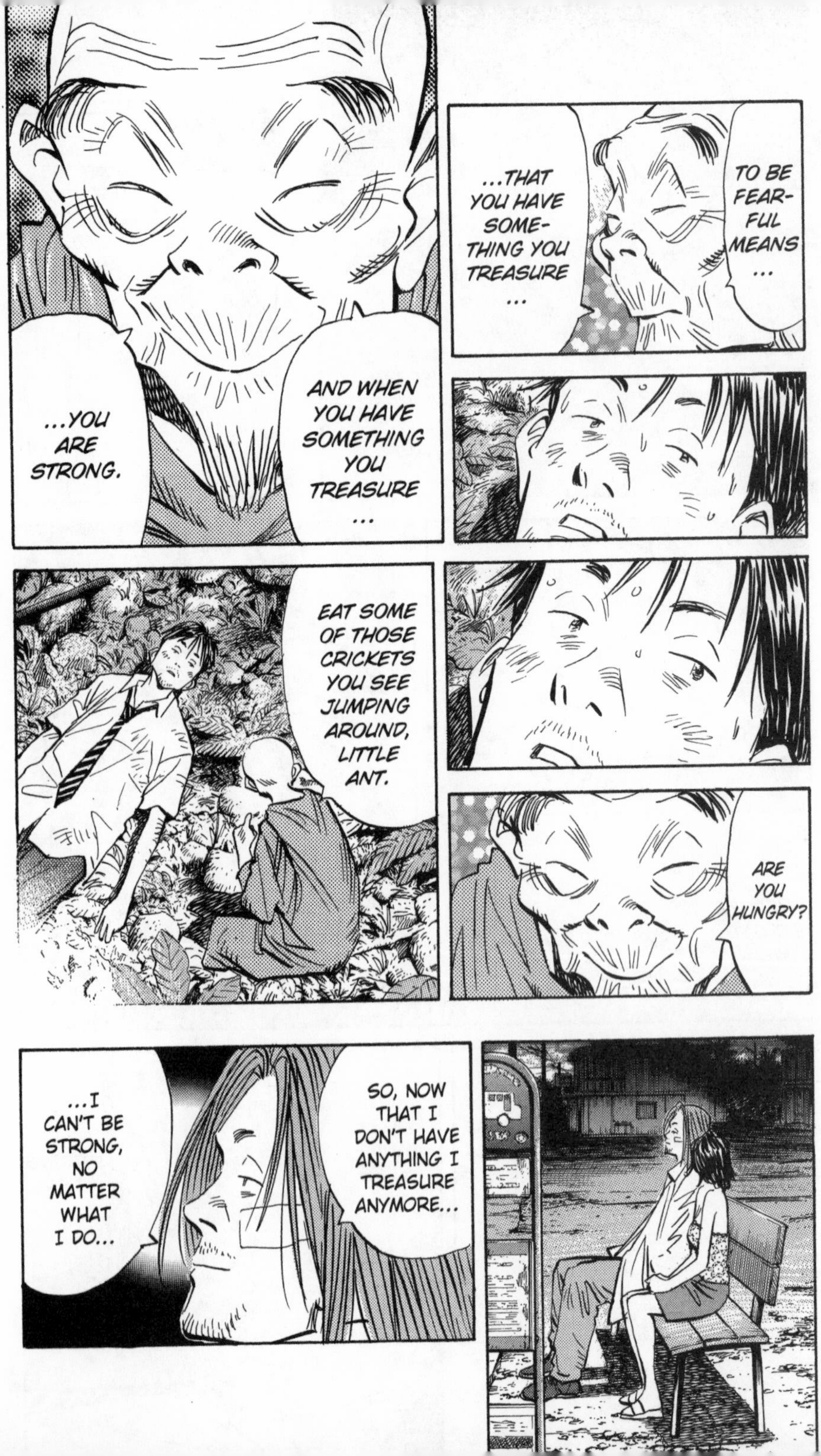
TO BE FEAR-FUL MEANS...
...THAT YOU HAVE SOME-THING YOU TREASURE...
AND WHEN YOU HAVE SOMETHING YOU TREASURE...
...YOU ARE STRONG.
ARE YOU HUNGRY?
EAT SOME OF THOSE CRICKETS YOU SEE JUMPING AROUND, LITTLE ANT.
SO, NOW THAT I DON'T HAVE ANYTHING I TREASURE ANYMORE...
...I CAN'T BE STRONG, NO MATTER WHAT I DO...

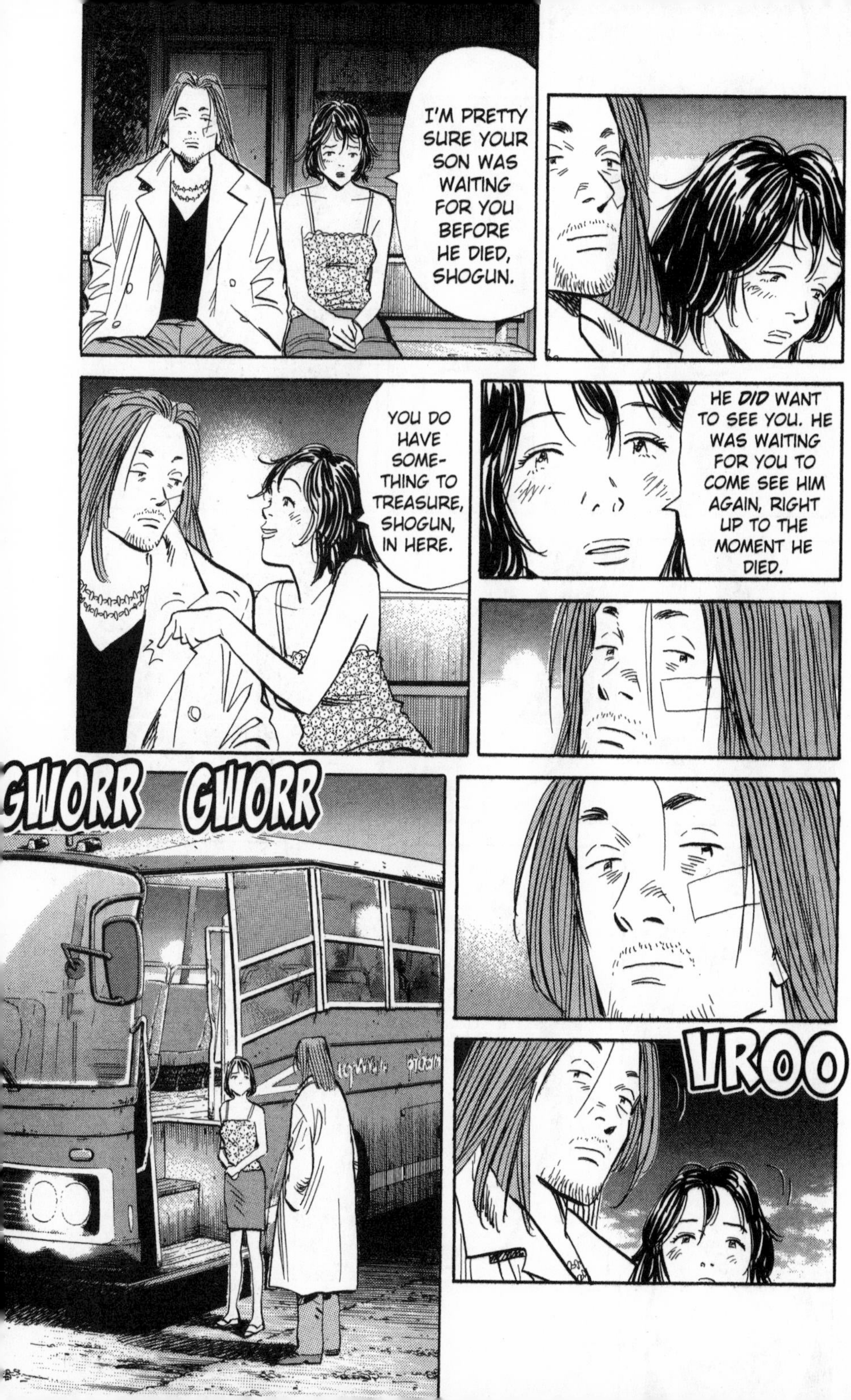
I'M PRETTY SURE YOUR SON WAS WAITING FOR YOU BEFORE HE DIED, SHOGUN.
HE *DID* WANT TO SEE YOU. HE WAS WAITING FOR YOU TO COME SEE HIM AGAIN, RIGHT UP TO THE MOMENT HE DIED.
YOU DO HAVE SOME-THING TO TREASURE, SHOGUN, IN HERE.
VROO
GWORR GWORR

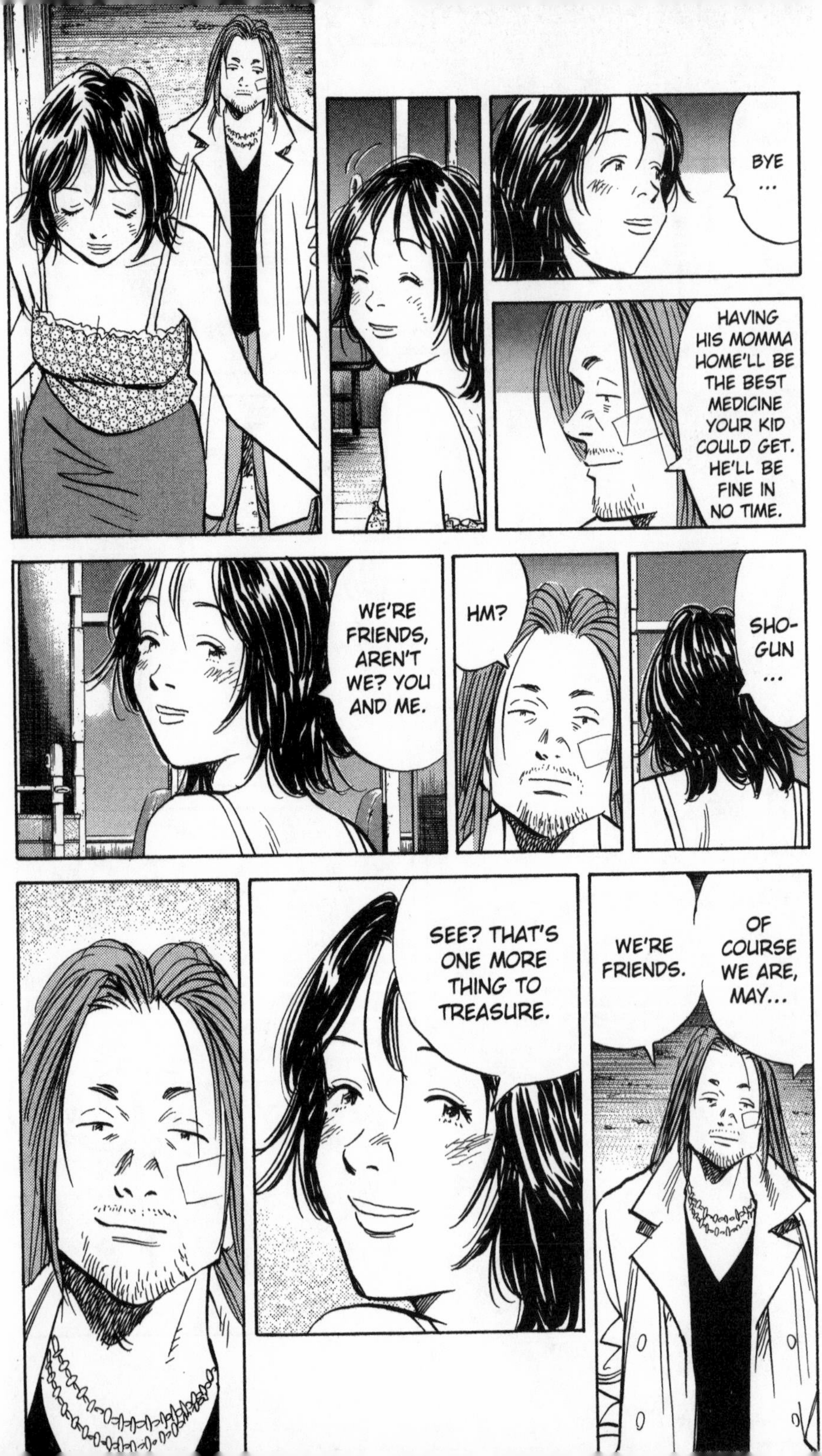
BYE ...
HAVING HIS MOMMA HOME'LL BE THE BEST MEDICINE YOUR KID COULD GET. HE'LL BE FINE IN NO TIME.
SHO-GUN ...
HM?
WE'RE FRIENDS, AREN'T WE? YOU AND ME.
OF COURSE WE ARE, MAY...
WE'RE FRIENDS.
SEE? THAT'S ONE MORE THING TO TREASURE.

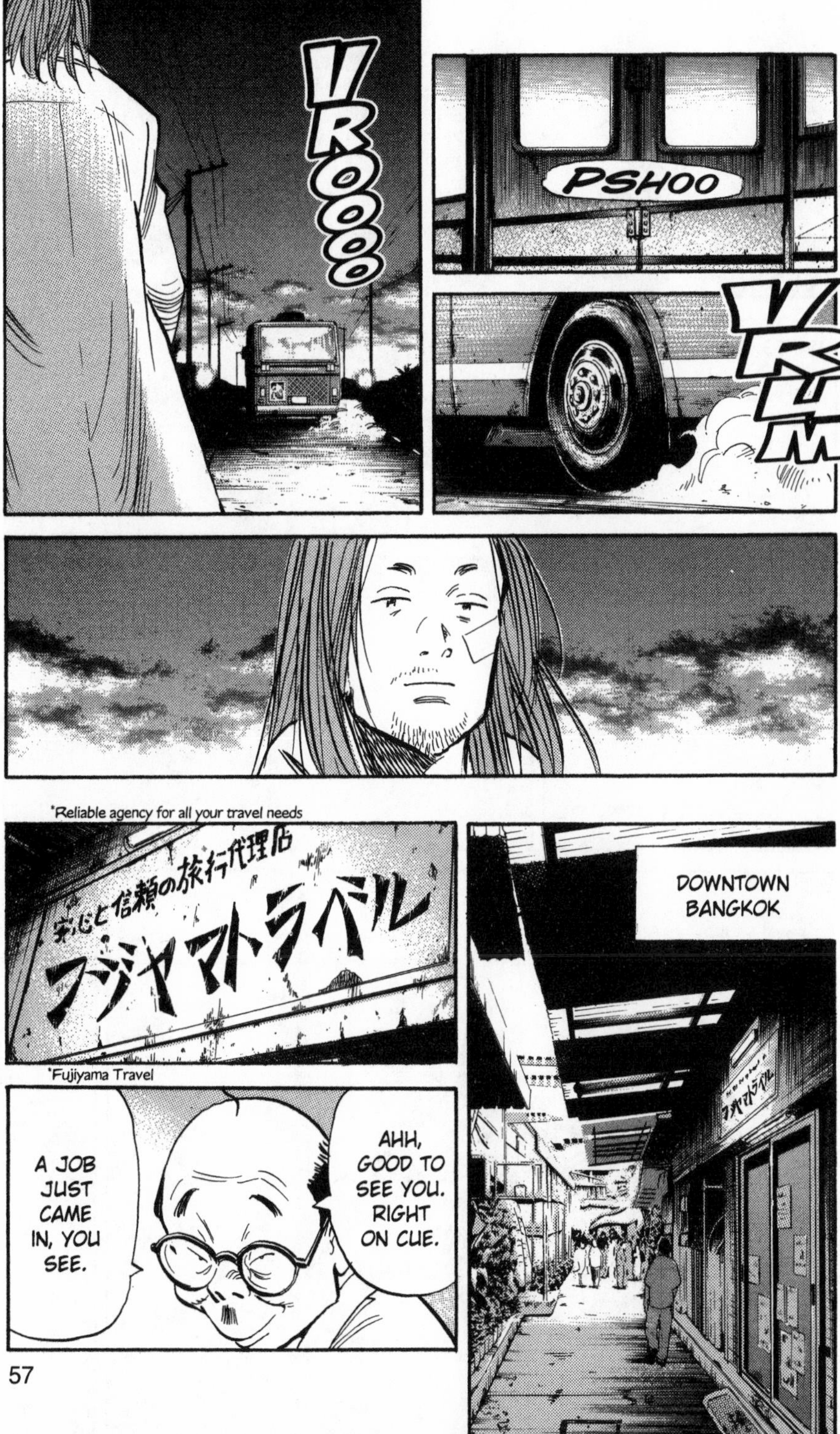
PSHOO
VRUM
VROOOOO
DOWNTOWN BANGKOK
*Reliable agency for all your travel needs
安心と信頼の旅行代理店
フジヤマトラベル
*Fujiyama Travel
AHH, GOOD TO SEE YOU. RIGHT ON CUE.
A JOB JUST CAME IN, YOU SEE.

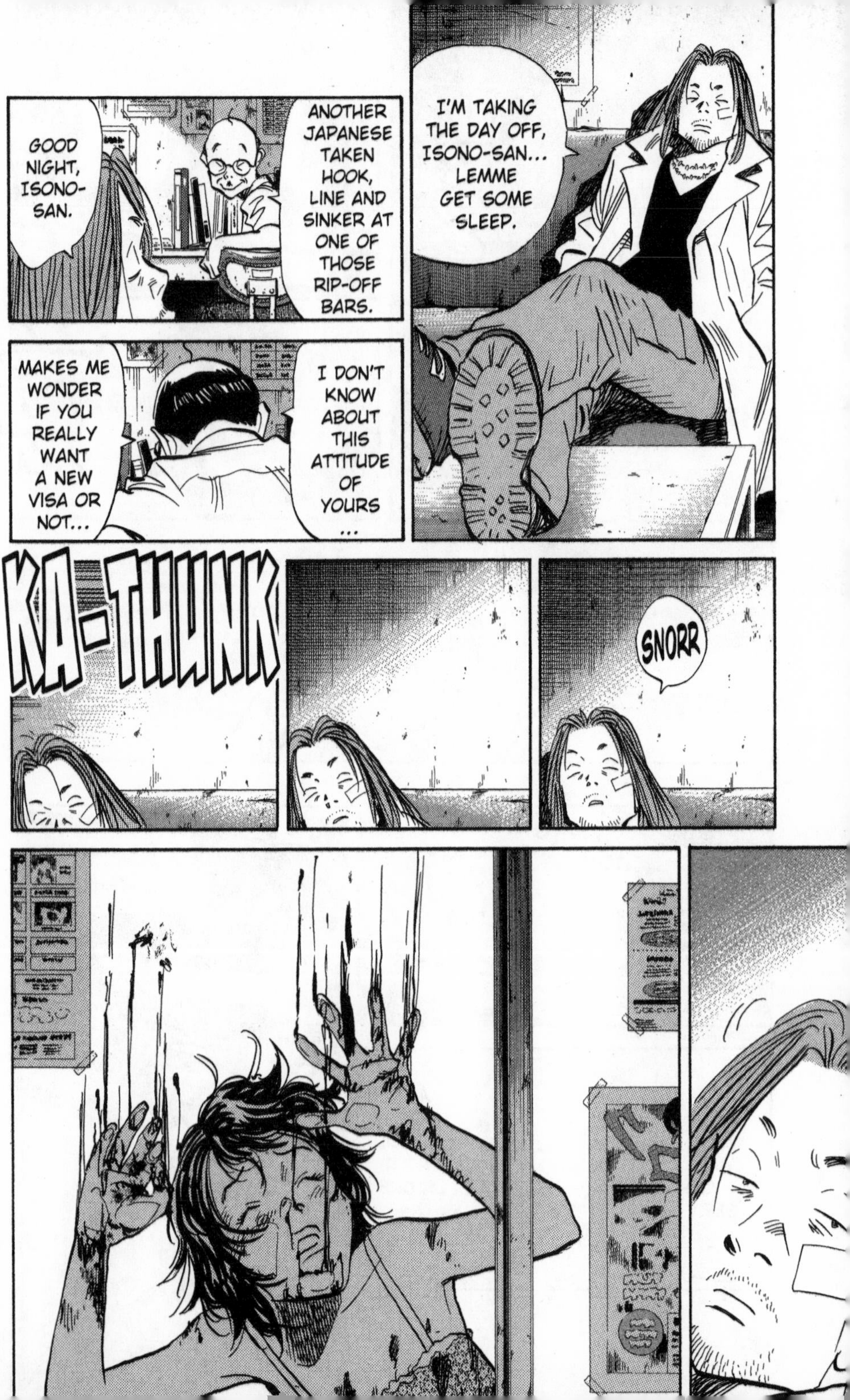
I'M TAKING THE DAY OFF, ISONO-SAN... LEMME GET SOME SLEEP.
ANOTHER JAPANESE TAKEN HOOK, LINE AND SINKER AT ONE OF THOSE RIP-OFF BARS.
GOOD NIGHT, ISONO-SAN.
I DON'T KNOW ABOUT THIS ATTITUDE OF YOURS ...
MAKES ME WONDER IF YOU REALLY WANT A NEW VISA OR NOT...
SNORR
KA-THUNK

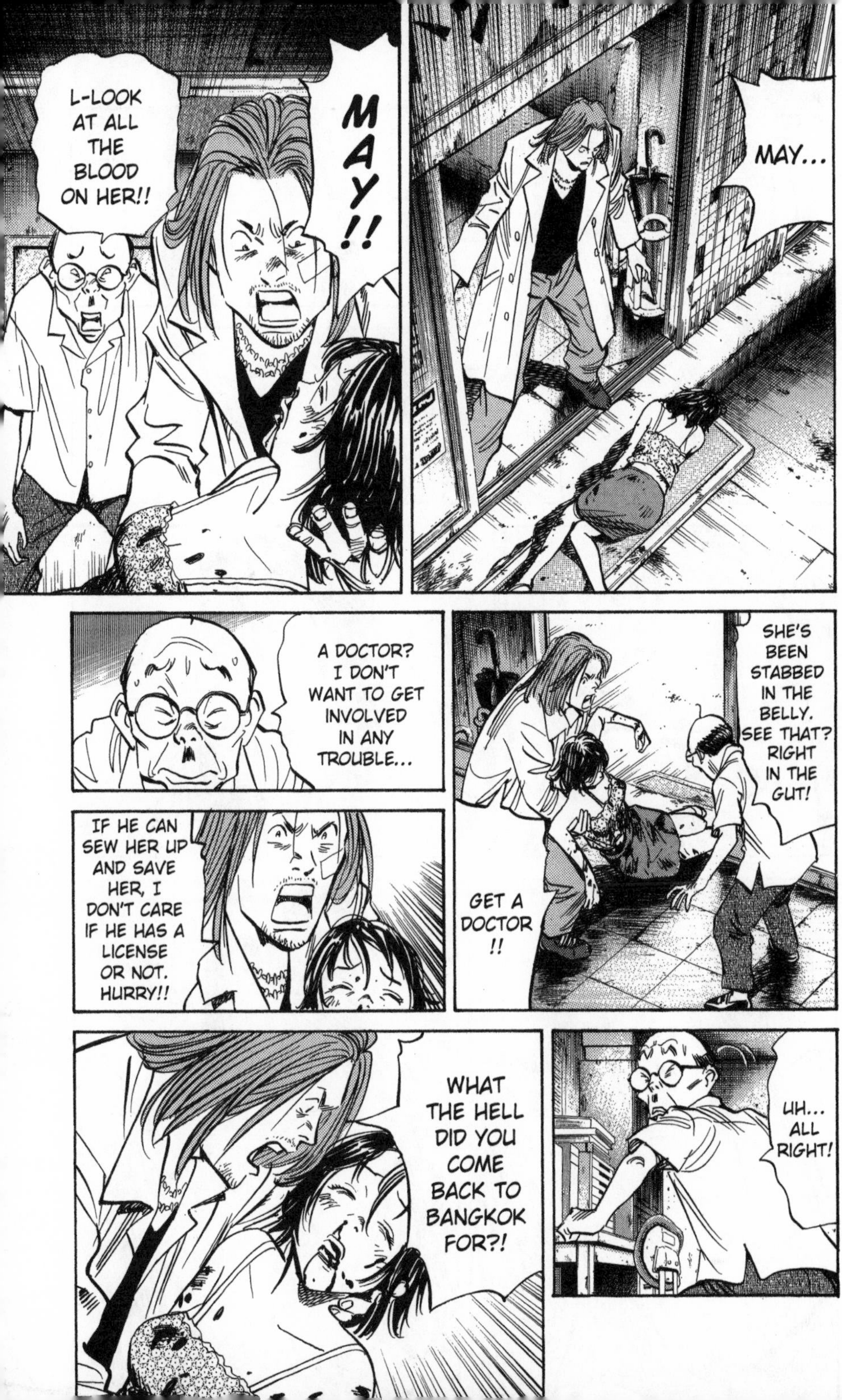
MAY...
MAY!!
L-LOOK AT ALL THE BLOOD ON HER!!
SHE'S BEEN STABBED IN THE BELLY. SEE THAT? RIGHT IN THE GUT!
GET A DOCTOR!!
A DOCTOR? I DON'T WANT TO GET INVOLVED IN ANY TROUBLE...
IF HE CAN SEW HER UP AND SAVE HER, I DON'T CARE IF HE HAS A LICENSE OR NOT. HURRY!!
UH... ALL RIGHT!
WHAT THE HELL DID YOU COME BACK TO BANGKOK FOR?!

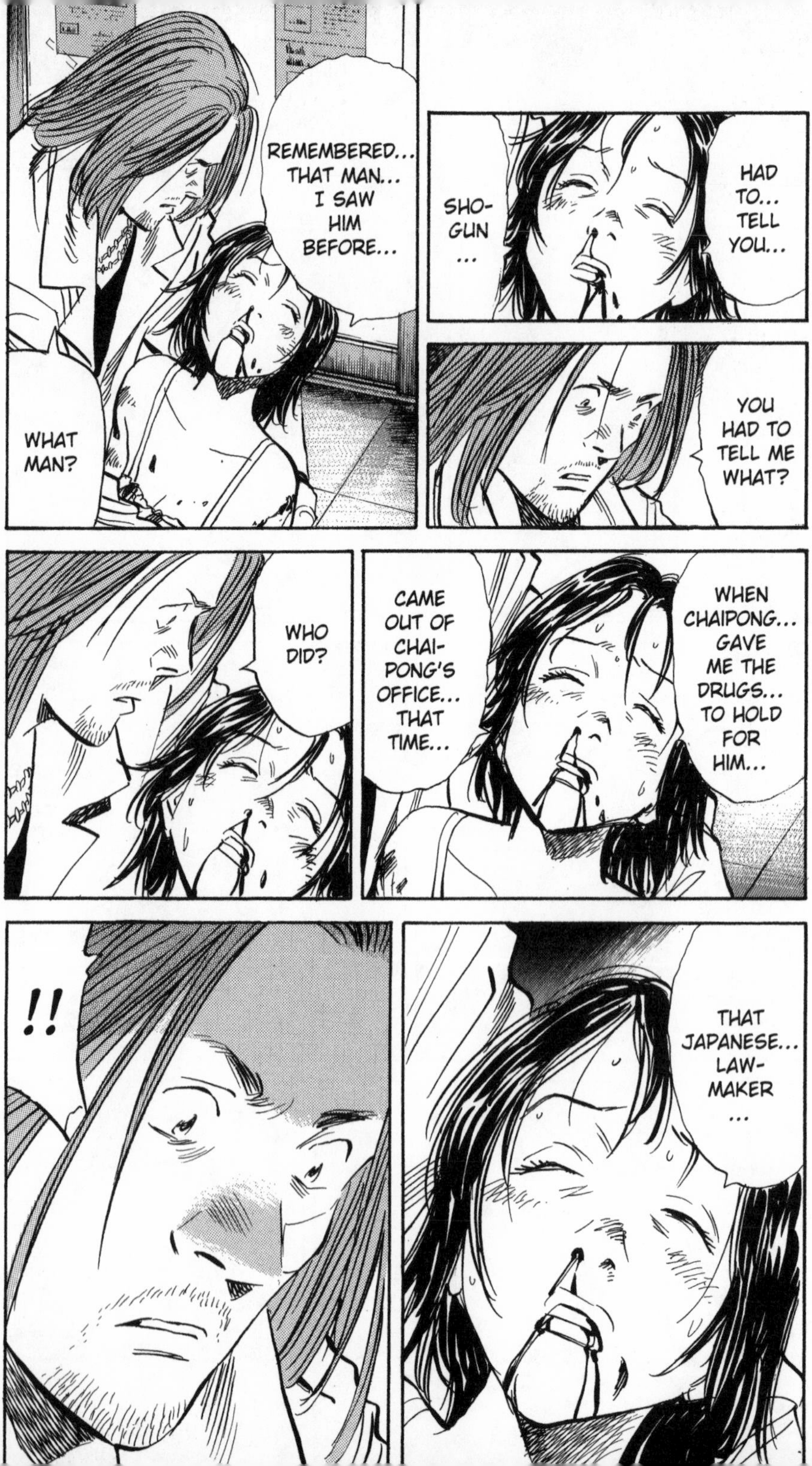
HAD TO... TELL YOU...
SHO-GUN ...
YOU HAD TO TELL ME WHAT?
REMEMBERED... THAT MAN... I SAW HIM BEFORE...
WHAT MAN?
WHEN CHAIPONG... GAVE ME THE DRUGS... TO HOLD FOR HIM...
CAME OUT OF CHAI-PONG'S OFFICE... THAT TIME...
WHO DID?
THAT JAPANESE... LAW-MAKER ...
!!

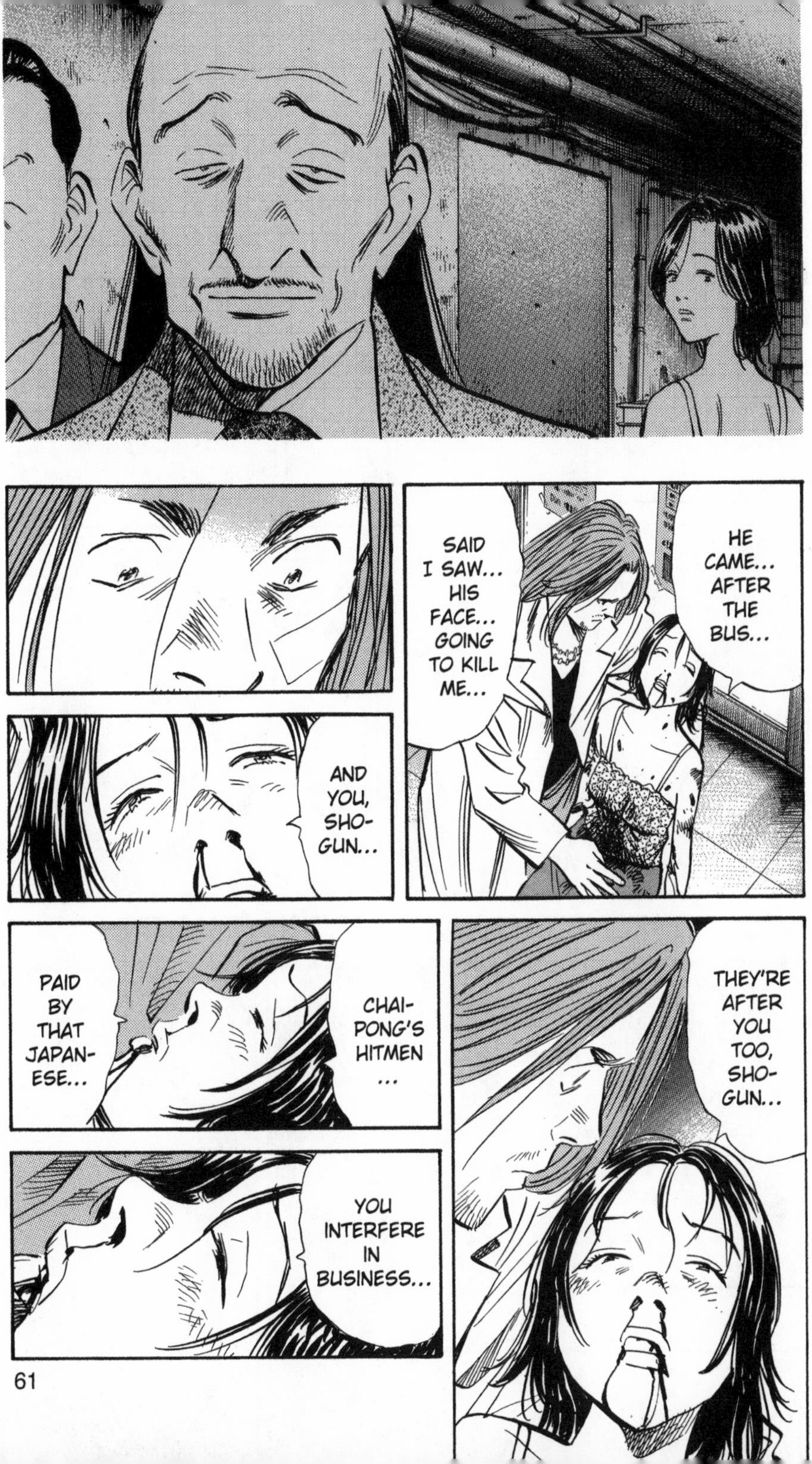
HE CAME... AFTER THE BUS...
SAID I SAW... HIS FACE... GOING TO KILL ME...
AND YOU, SHO-GUN...
THEY'RE AFTER YOU TOO, SHO-GUN...
CHAI-PONG'S HITMEN...
PAID BY THAT JAPAN-ESE...
YOU INTERFERE IN BUSINESS...

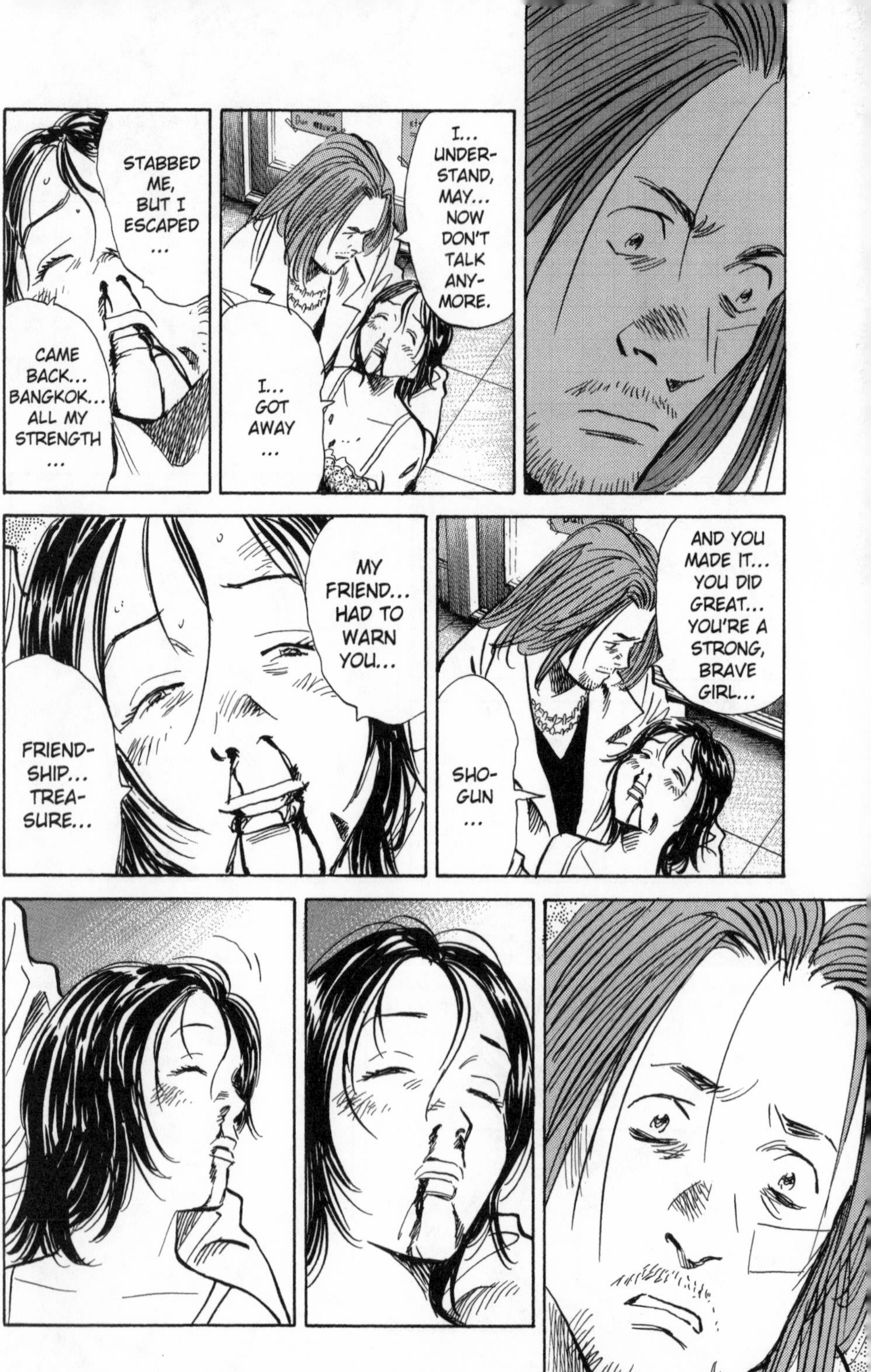
I... UNDER-STAND, MAY... NOW DON'T TALK ANY-MORE.
I... GOT AWAY ...
STABBED ME, BUT I ESCAPED ...
CAME BACK... BANGKOK... ALL MY STRENGTH ...
AND YOU MADE IT... YOU DID GREAT... YOU'RE A STRONG, BRAVE GIRL...
SHO-GUN ...
MY FRIEND... HAD TO WARN YOU...
FRIEND-SHIP... TREA-SURE...

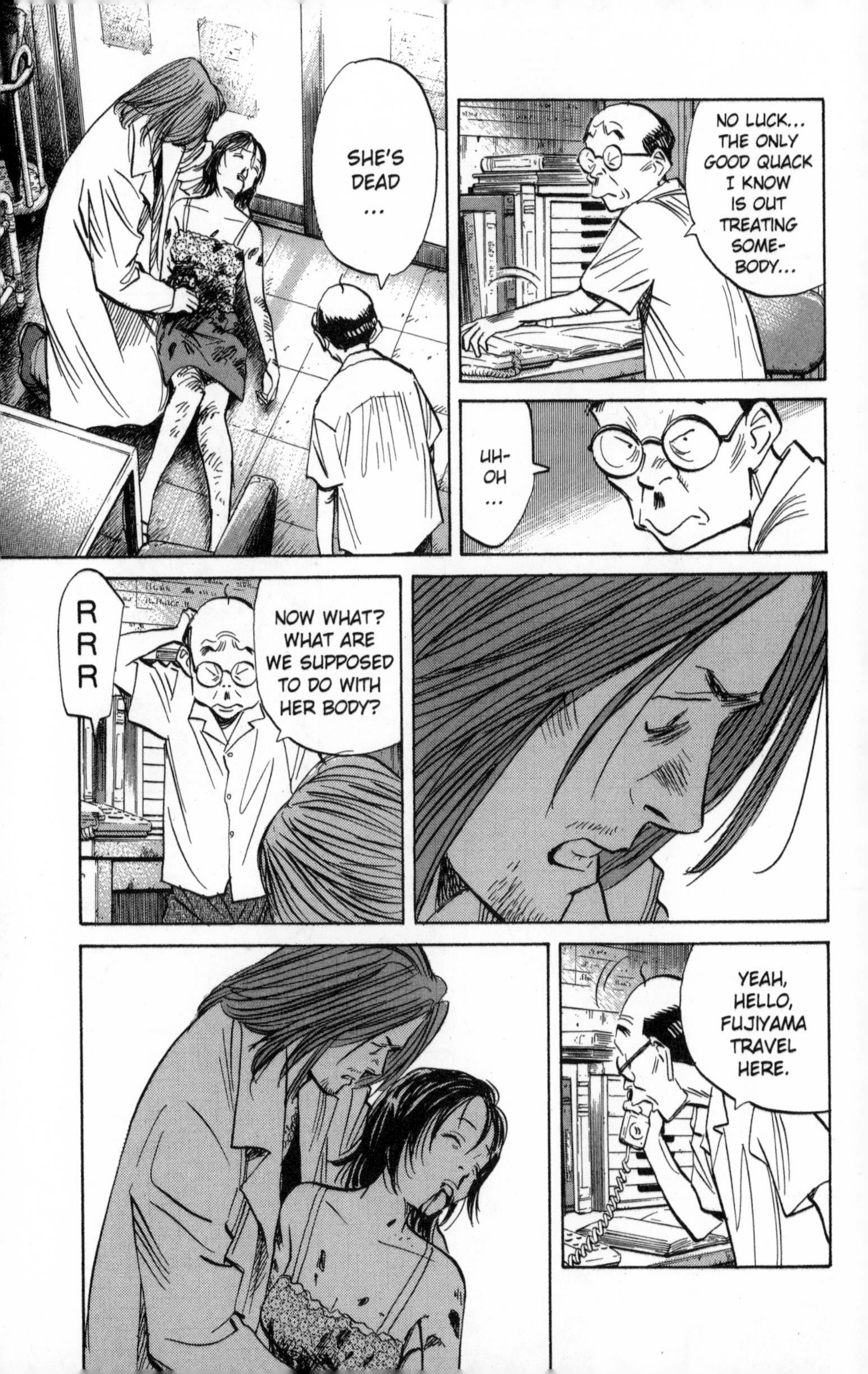
NO LUCK... THE ONLY GOOD QUACK I KNOW IS OUT TREATING SOME-BODY...
UH-OH ...
SHE'S DEAD ...
NOW WHAT? WHAT ARE WE SUPPOSED TO DO WITH HER BODY?
RRR
YEAH, HELLO, FUJIYAMA TRAVEL HERE.

HEY... IT'S FOR YOU.

TAKE IT! IT'S THE SAME FELLA WHO'S BEEN CALLING SO MUCH LATELY.

JUST FIND OUT WHAT HE WANTS! IT SEEMS TO BE PRETTY URGENT.

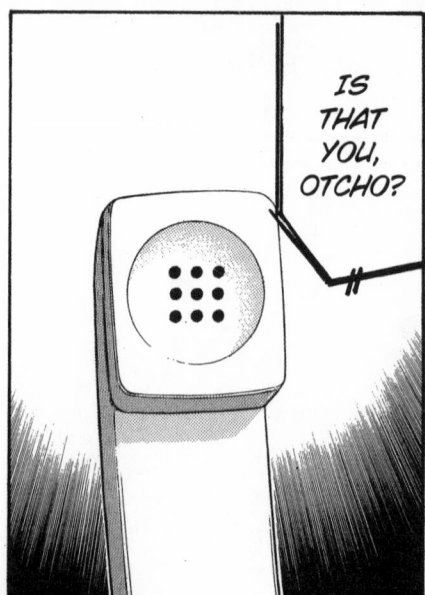

IS THAT YOU, OTCHO?

HELLO ...

WHO'S
THIS
...

IT'S
ME.

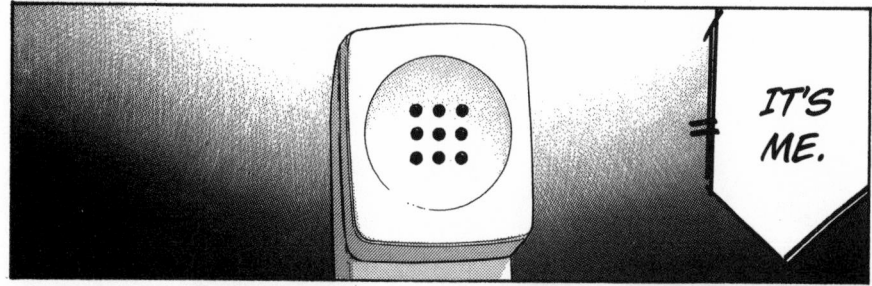

KENJI.

20世紀少年
Twentieth Century Boys

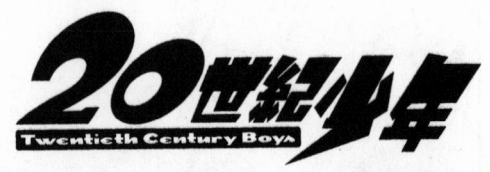

Chapter 4 Love and Peace

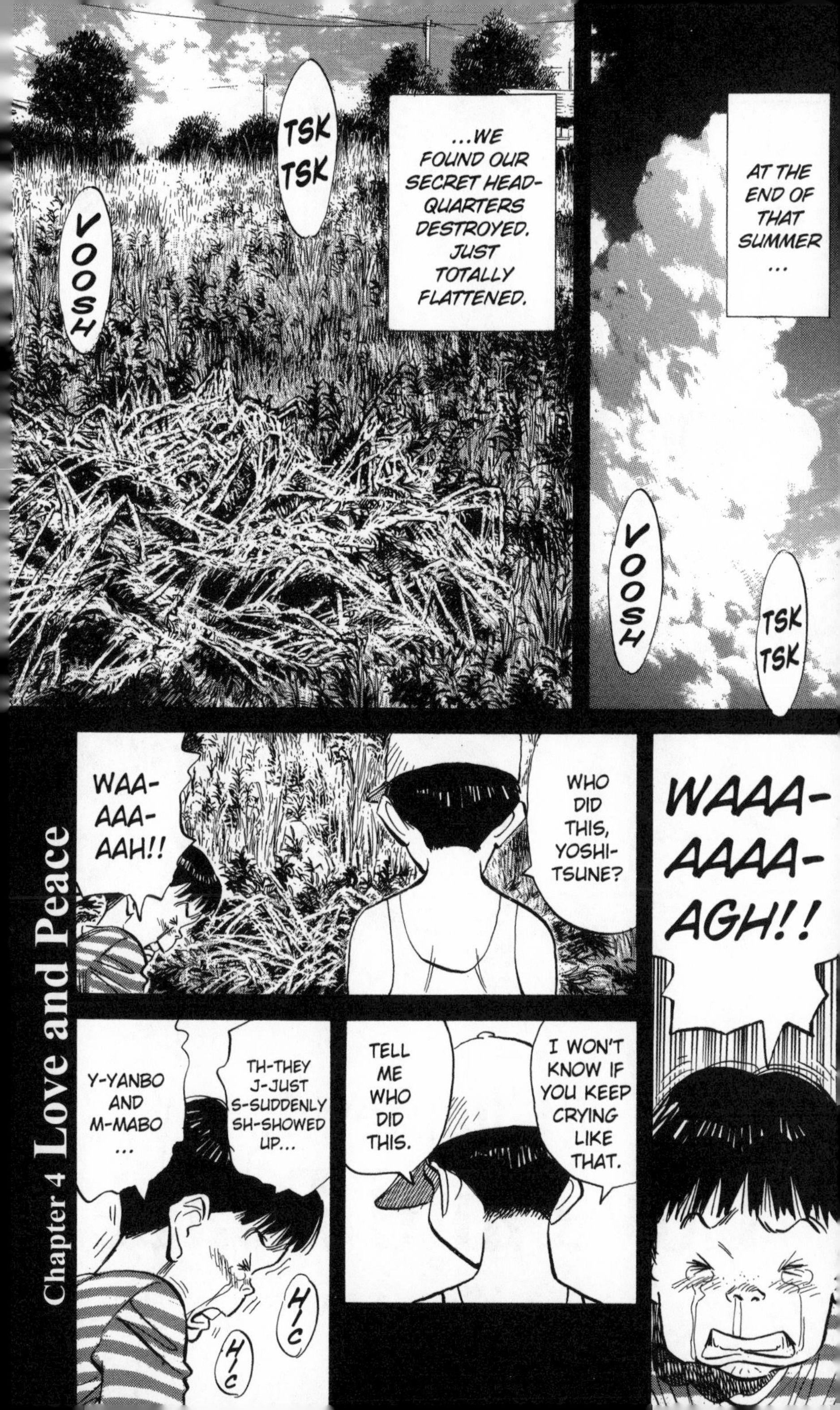
AT THE END OF THAT SUMMER...
VOOSH
TSK TSK
...WE FOUND OUR SECRET HEAD-QUARTERS DESTROYED. JUST TOTALLY FLATTENED.
TSK TSK
VOOSH
WAAAA-AAAA-AGH!!
WHO DID THIS, YOSHI-TSUNE?
WAA-AAA-AAH!!
I WON'T KNOW IF YOU KEEP CRYING LIKE THAT.
TELL ME WHO DID THIS.
TH-THEY J-JUST S-SUDDENLY SH-SHOWED UP...
Y-YANBO AND M-MABO...
HIC
HIC

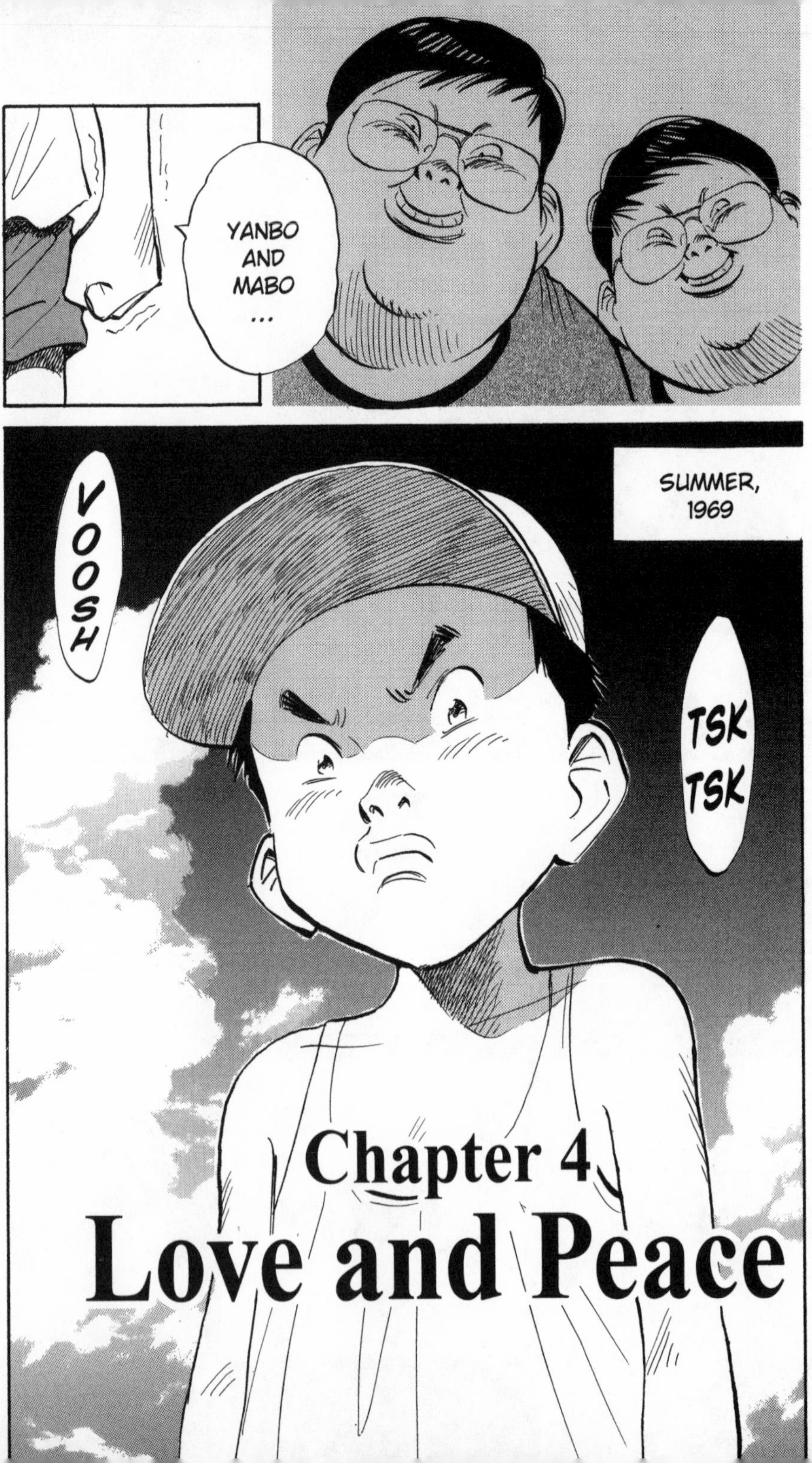
YANBO AND MABO ...
SUMMER, 1969
TSK TSK
VOOSH

Chapter 4
Love and Peace

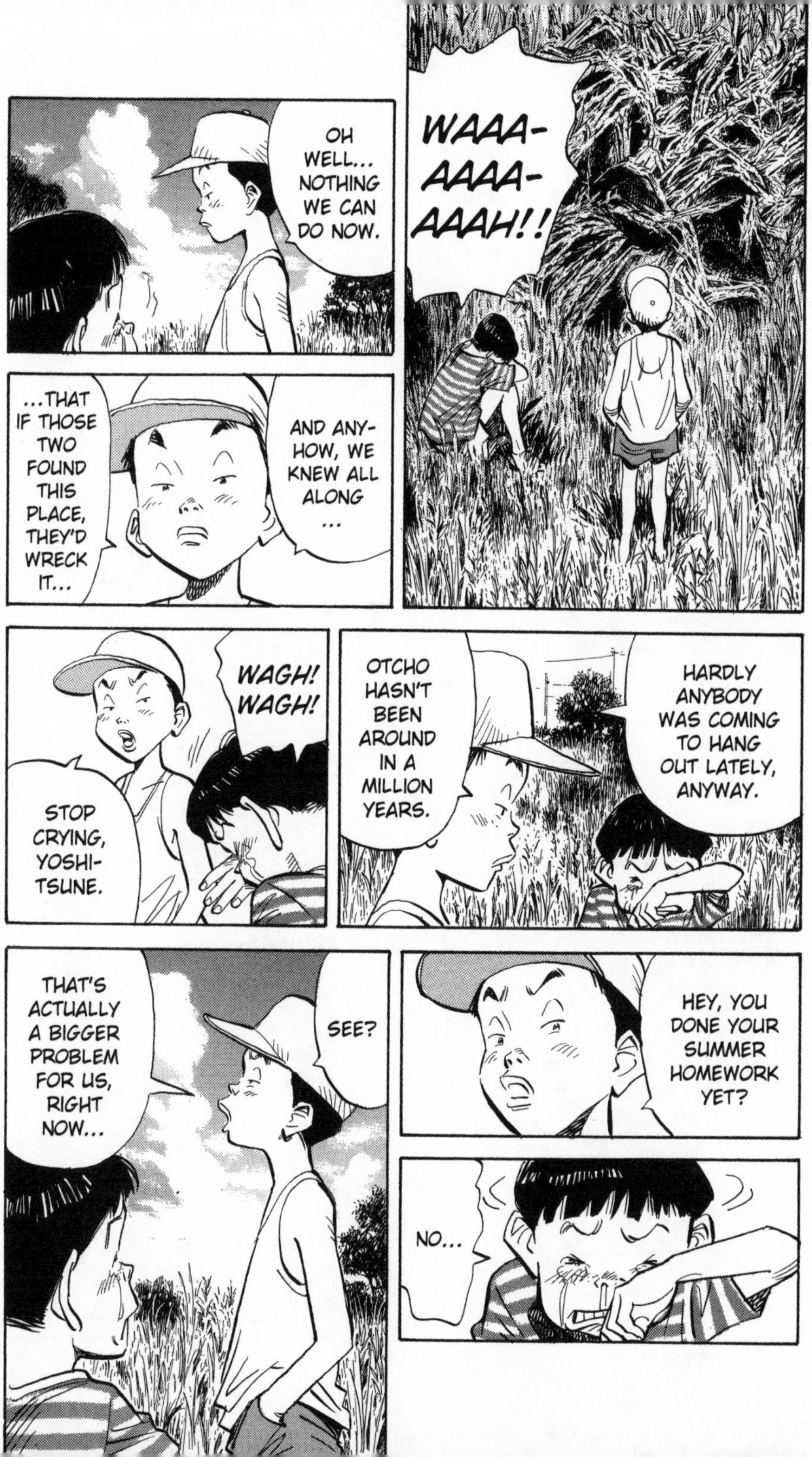
WAAAA-AAAA-AAAH!!
OH WELL... NOTHING WE CAN DO NOW.
AND ANYHOW, WE KNEW ALL ALONG...
...THAT IF THOSE TWO FOUND THIS PLACE, THEY'D WRECK IT...
HARDLY ANYBODY WAS COMING TO HANG OUT LATELY, ANYWAY.
OTCHO HASN'T BEEN AROUND IN A MILLION YEARS.
WAGH! WAGH!
STOP CRYING, YOSHI-TSUNE.
HEY, YOU DONE YOUR SUMMER HOMEWORK YET?
NO...
SEE?
THAT'S ACTUALLY A BIGGER PROBLEM FOR US, RIGHT NOW...

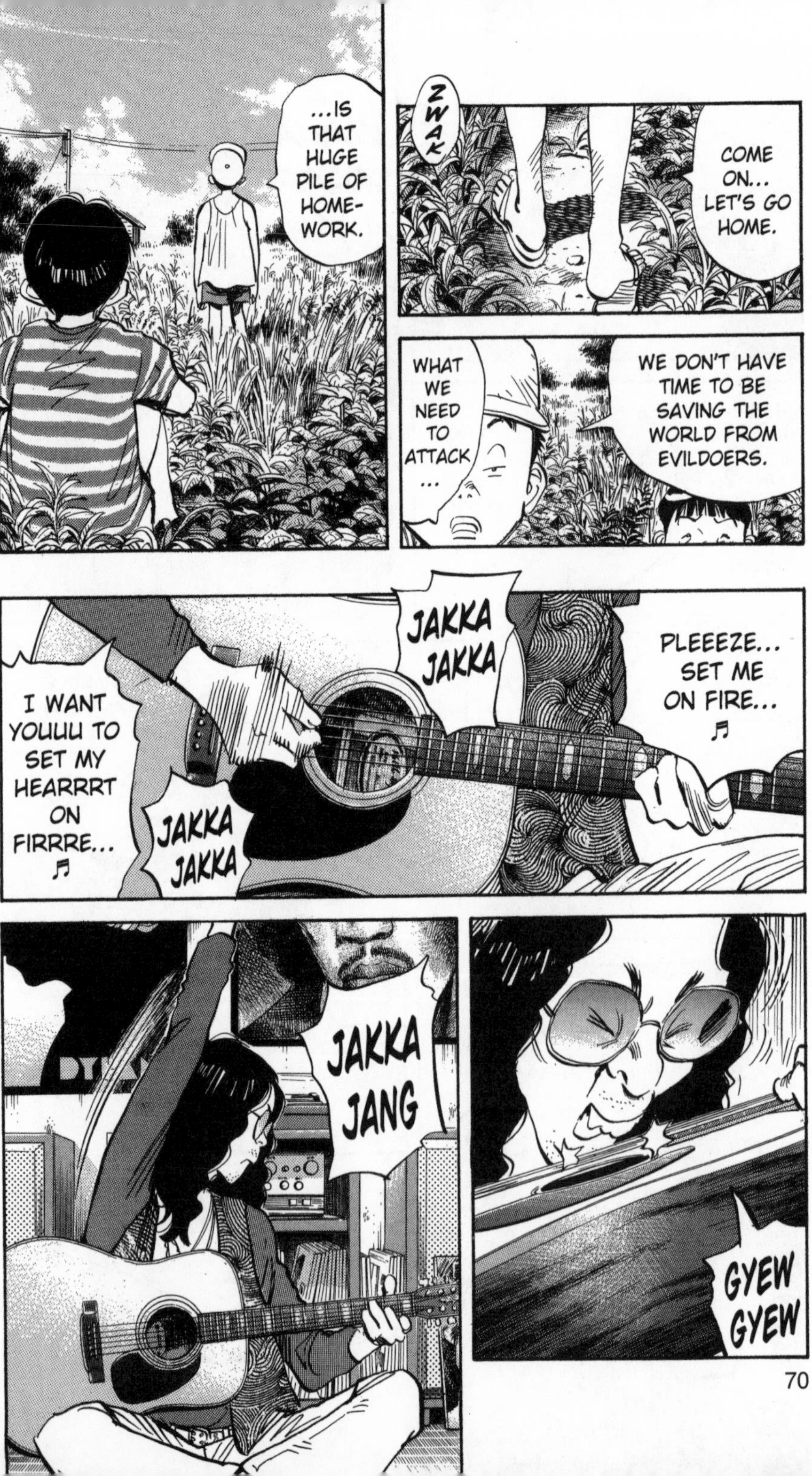
ZWAK
COME ON... LET'S GO HOME.
WE DON'T HAVE TIME TO BE SAVING THE WORLD FROM EVILDOERS.
WHAT WE NEED TO ATTACK ...
...IS THAT HUGE PILE OF HOME-WORK.
PLEEEZE... SET ME ON FIRE... ♬
JAKKA JAKKA
I WANT YOUUU TO SET MY HEARRRT ON FIRRRE... ♬
JAKKA JAKKA
GYEW GYEW
JAKKA JANG

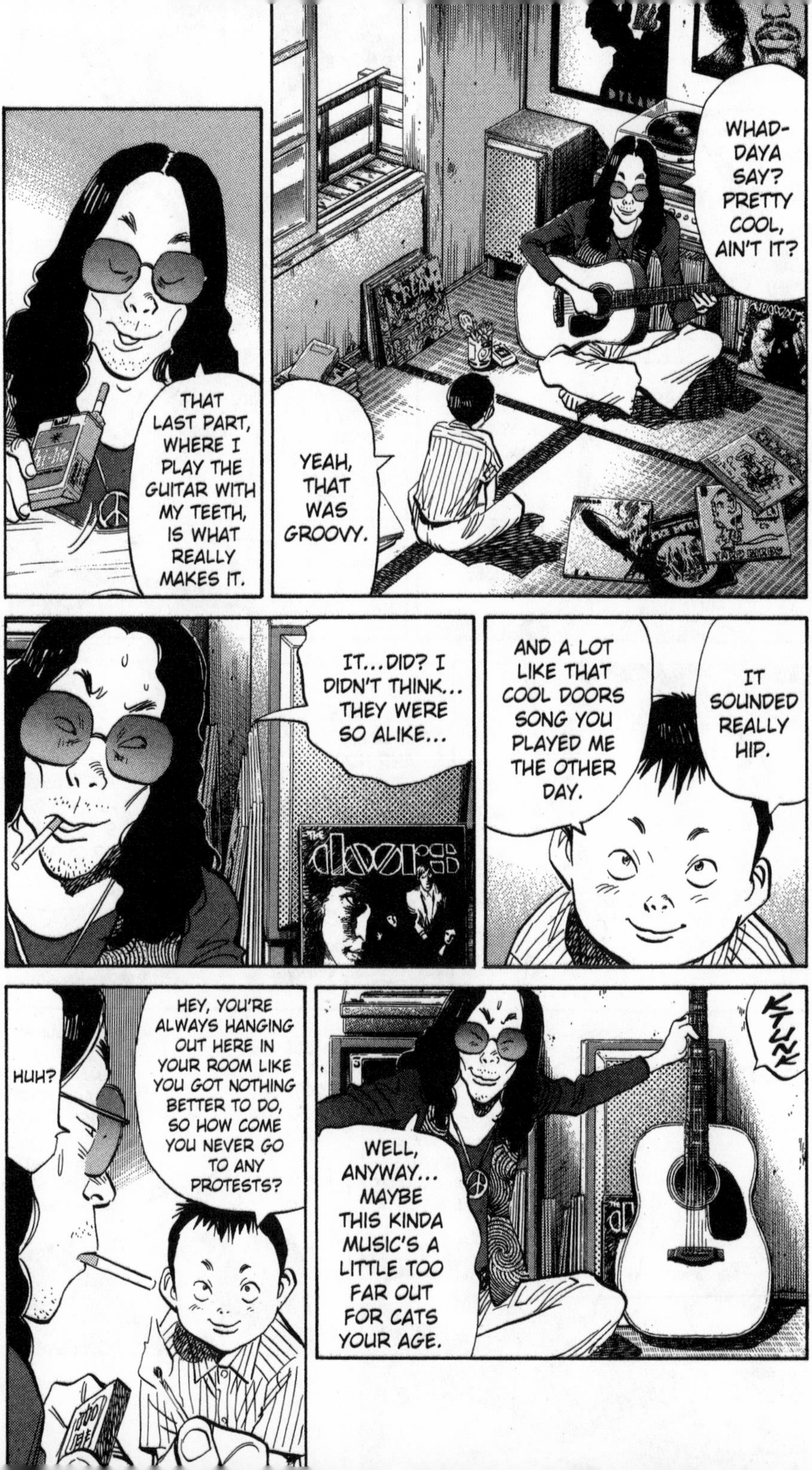
WHAD-DAYA SAY? PRETTY COOL, AIN'T IT?
YEAH, THAT WAS GROOVY.
THAT LAST PART, WHERE I PLAY THE GUITAR WITH MY TEETH, IS WHAT REALLY MAKES IT.
IT SOUNDED REALLY HIP.
AND A LOT LIKE THAT COOL DOORS SONG YOU PLAYED ME THE OTHER DAY.
IT...DID? I DIDN'T THINK... THEY WERE SO ALIKE...
KTUNK
WELL, ANYWAY... MAYBE THIS KINDA MUSIC'S A LITTLE TOO FAR OUT FOR CATS YOUR AGE.
HEY, YOU'RE ALWAYS HANGING OUT HERE IN YOUR ROOM LIKE YOU GOT NOTHING BETTER TO DO, SO HOW COME YOU NEVER GO TO ANY PROTESTS?
HUH?

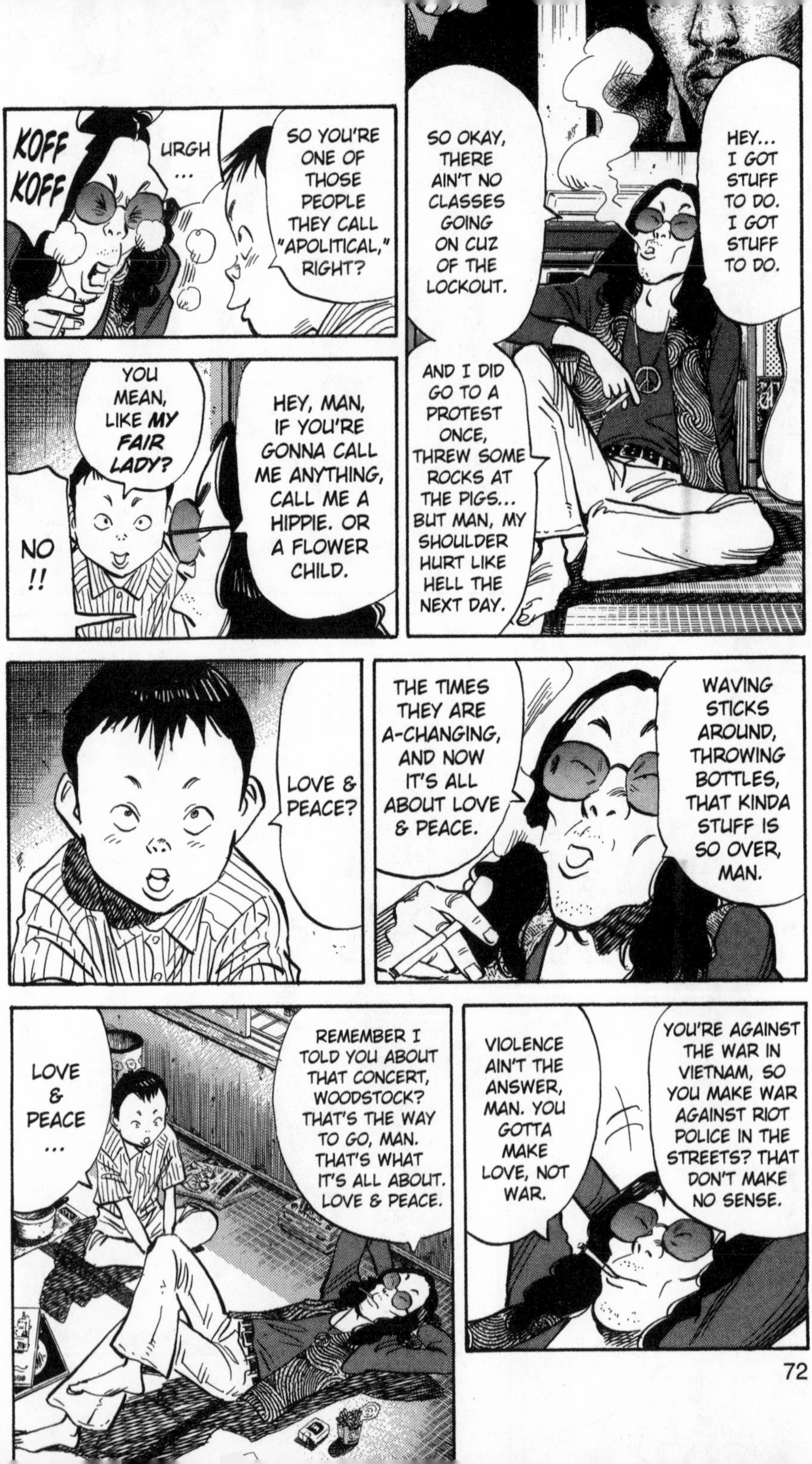
HEY... I GOT STUFF TO DO. I GOT STUFF TO DO.
SO OKAY, THERE AIN'T NO CLASSES GOING ON CUZ OF THE LOCKOUT.
AND I DID GO TO A PROTEST ONCE, THREW SOME ROCKS AT THE PIGS... BUT MAN, MY SHOULDER HURT LIKE HELL THE NEXT DAY.
SO YOU'RE ONE OF THOSE PEOPLE THEY CALL "APOLITICAL," RIGHT?
URGH ...
KOFF KOFF
HEY, MAN, IF YOU'RE GONNA CALL ME ANYTHING, CALL ME A HIPPIE. OR A FLOWER CHILD.
YOU MEAN, LIKE *MY FAIR LADY?*
NO !!
WAVING STICKS AROUND, THROWING BOTTLES, THAT KINDA STUFF IS SO OVER, MAN.
THE TIMES THEY ARE A-CHANGING, AND NOW IT'S ALL ABOUT LOVE & PEACE.
LOVE & PEACE?
YOU'RE AGAINST THE WAR IN VIETNAM, SO YOU MAKE WAR AGAINST RIOT POLICE IN THE STREETS? THAT DON'T MAKE NO SENSE.
VIOLENCE AIN'T THE ANSWER, MAN. YOU GOTTA MAKE LOVE, NOT WAR.
REMEMBER I TOLD YOU ABOUT THAT CONCERT, WOODSTOCK? THAT'S THE WAY TO GO, MAN. THAT'S WHAT IT'S ALL ABOUT. LOVE & PEACE.
LOVE & PEACE ...

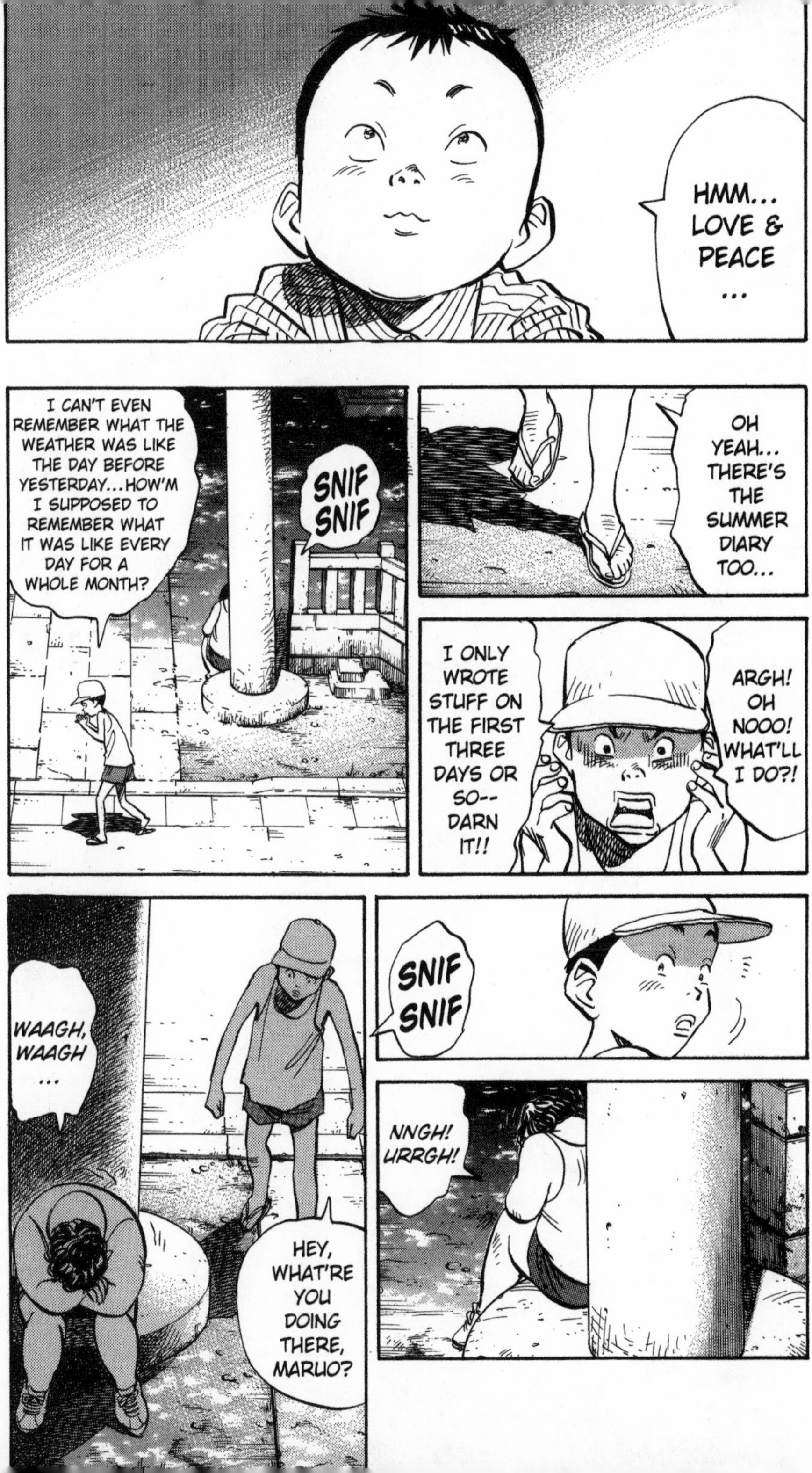
HMM... LOVE & PEACE ...
OH YEAH... THERE'S THE SUMMER DIARY TOO...
ARGH! OH NOOO! WHAT'LL I DO?!
I ONLY WROTE STUFF ON THE FIRST THREE DAYS OR SO-- DARN IT!!
I CAN'T EVEN REMEMBER WHAT THE WEATHER WAS LIKE THE DAY BEFORE YESTERDAY...HOW'M I SUPPOSED TO REMEMBER WHAT IT WAS LIKE EVERY DAY FOR A WHOLE MONTH?
SNIF SNIF
SNIF SNIF
NNGH! URRGH!
WAAGH, WAAGH ...
HEY, WHAT'RE YOU DOING THERE, MARUO?

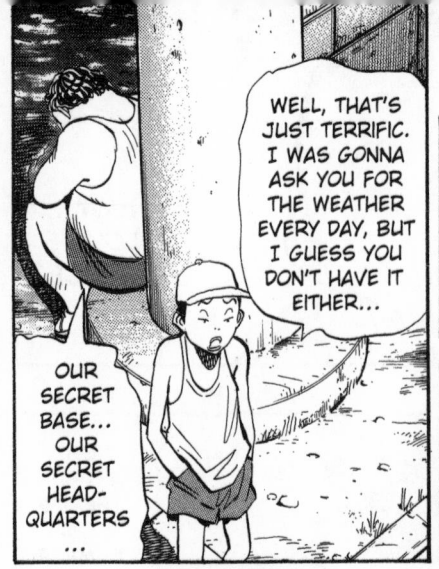

WHAT'RE YOU CRYING ABOUT?
SUDDENLY REMEMBERED ALL THE HOMEWORK WE GOTTA DO? FORGOT TO WRITE YOUR SUMMER DIARY?
WAGH ...
WAAH ...
WELL, THAT'S JUST TERRIFIC. I WAS GONNA ASK YOU FOR THE WEATHER EVERY DAY, BUT I GUESS YOU DON'T HAVE IT EITHER...
OUR SECRET BASE... OUR SECRET HEAD-QUARTERS ...
IT'S OKAY, MARUO, FORGET ABOUT IT! IT WAS KINDA OVER ALREADY, ANYWAY...
I-I'M TH-THE ONE WH-WHO D-DID IT!!
WHAT?
YANBO AND MABO SHOWED UP ALL OF A SUDDEN, AND...
HIC
HIC
COME ONNN, WHAT'RE YOU WAITING FOR?! YOU WANT ME TO PUT THE "NUMERAL FOUR LEG-LOCK" ON YOU?!
OR HOW ABOUT THE SKY-HIGH JUMP-KICK, STRAIGHT IN YOUR GUT?!

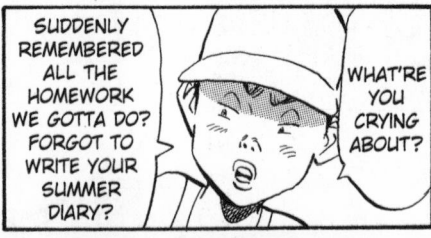

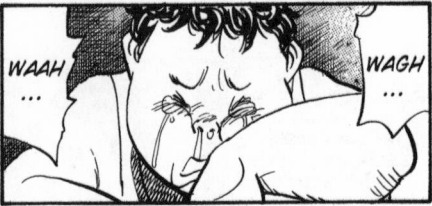

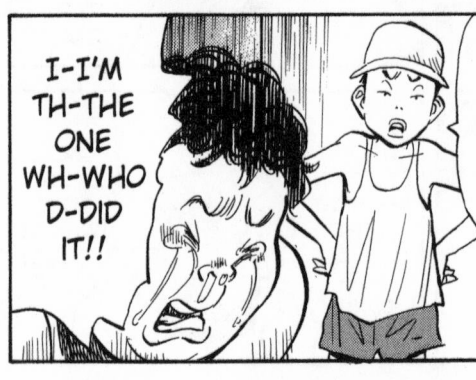

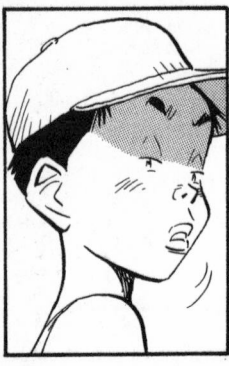

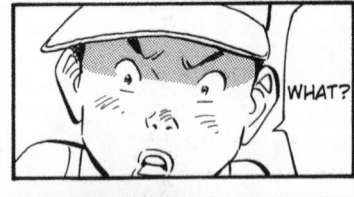

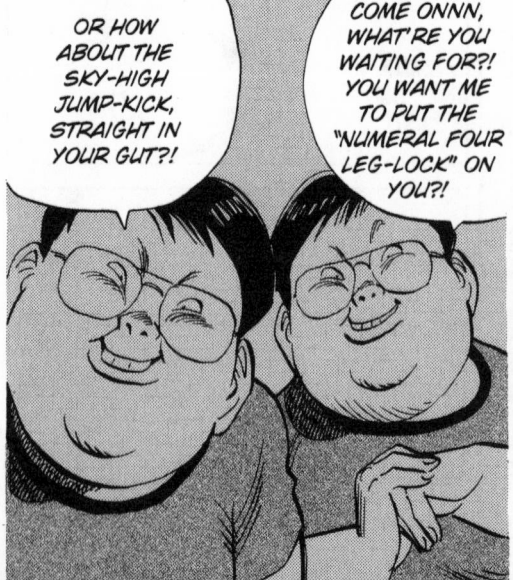

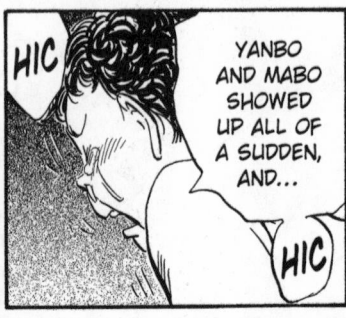

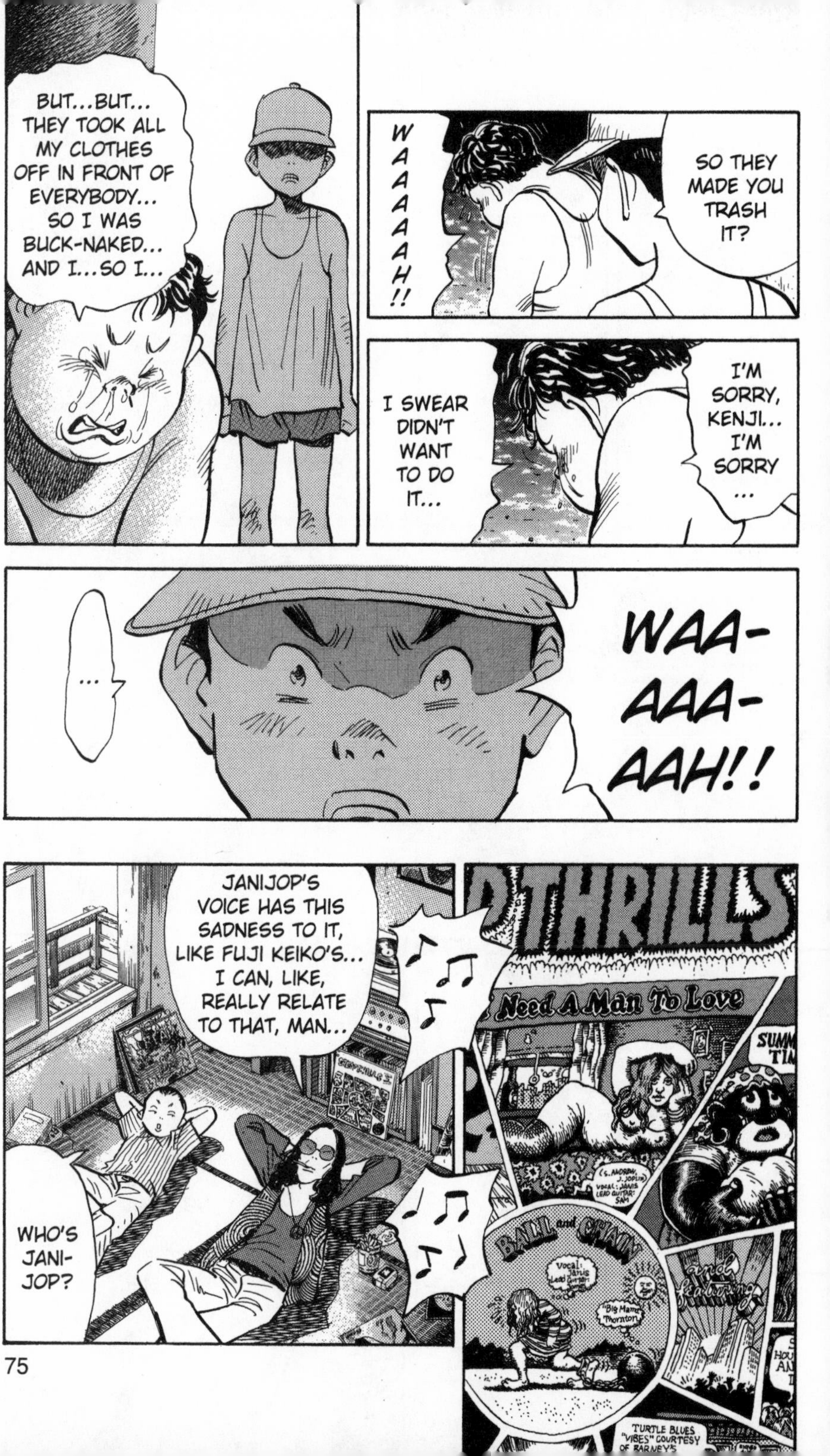
SO THEY MADE YOU TRASH IT?
WAAAAAAH!!
I'M SORRY, KENJI... I'M SORRY...
I SWEAR DIDN'T WANT TO DO IT...
BUT...BUT... THEY TOOK ALL MY CLOTHES OFF IN FRONT OF EVERYBODY... SO I WAS BUCK-NAKED... AND I...SO I...
WAA-AAA-AAH!!
...
THRILLS
Need A Man To Love
BALL and CHAIN
TURTLE BLUES "VIBES" COURTESY OF BARNEY'S
JANIJOP'S VOICE HAS THIS SADNESS TO IT, LIKE FUJI KEIKO'S... I CAN, LIKE, REALLY RELATE TO THAT, MAN...
WHO'S JANI-JOP?

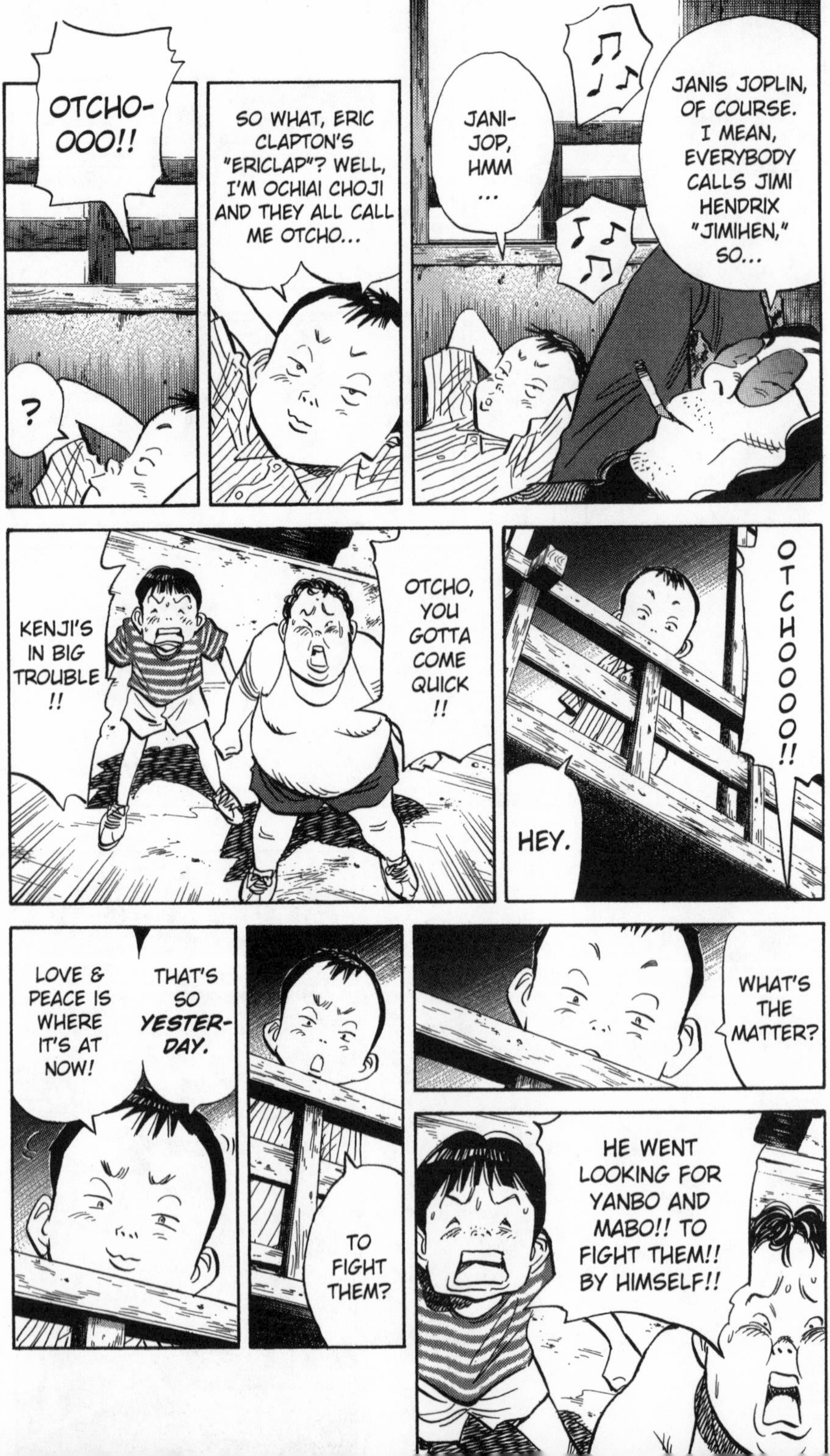

JANIS JOPLIN, OF COURSE. I MEAN, EVERYBODY CALLS JIMI HENDRIX "JIMIHEN," SO...
JANI-JOP, HMM ...
SO WHAT, ERIC CLAPTON'S "ERICLAP"? WELL, I'M OCHIAI CHOJI AND THEY ALL CALL ME OTCHO...
OTCHO-OOO!!
?
OTCHOOOOO!!
HEY.
OTCHO, YOU GOTTA COME QUICK!!
KENJI'S IN BIG TROUBLE!!
WHAT'S THE MATTER?
HE WENT LOOKING FOR YANBO AND MABO!! TO FIGHT THEM!! BY HIMSELF!!
TO FIGHT THEM?
THAT'S SO *YESTERDAY.*
LOVE & PEACE IS WHERE IT'S AT NOW!

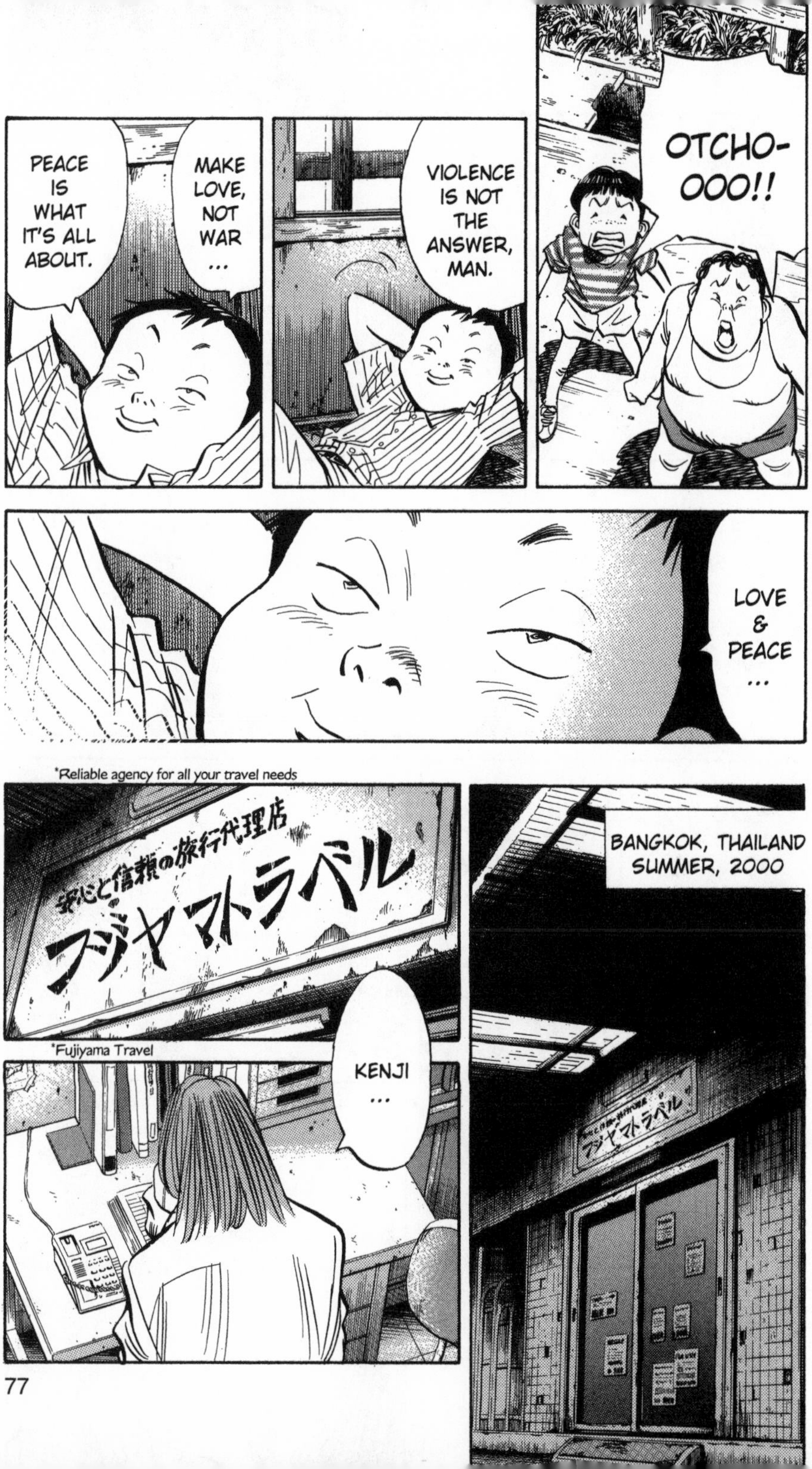
OTCHO-OOO!!
VIOLENCE IS NOT THE ANSWER, MAN.
MAKE LOVE, NOT WAR ...
PEACE IS WHAT IT'S ALL ABOUT.
LOVE & PEACE ...
BANGKOK, THAILAND SUMMER, 2000
*Reliable agency for all your travel needs
安心と信頼の旅行代理店
フジヤマトラベル
*Fujiyama Travel
KENJI ...

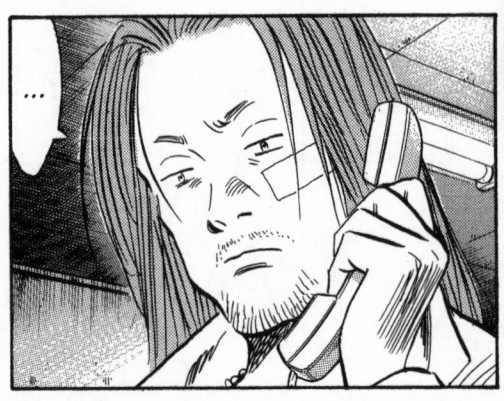

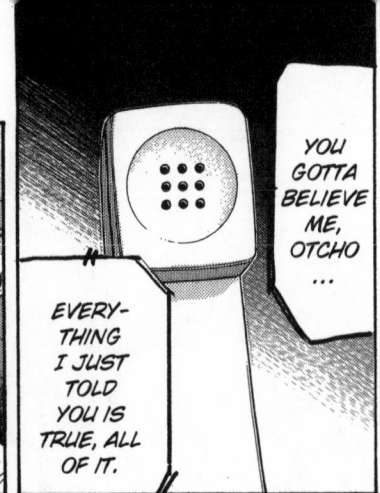

YOU GOTTA BELIEVE ME, OTCHO...
EVERYTHING I JUST TOLD YOU IS TRUE, ALL OF IT.
...
THIS COUNTRY'S SLIDING TOWARD TOTAL DISASTER.
THE FRIENDS ARE SERIOUS, THEY'RE REALLY GOING TO DO IT. AND IT'S NOT JUST JAPAN...
THEY'RE PLANNING TO DESTROY THE WHOLE WORLD.
...
WE NEED YOUR HELP, OTCHO. WE NEED YOU HERE.
YOU GOTTA COME BACK TO JAPAN, OTCHO, PLEASE...

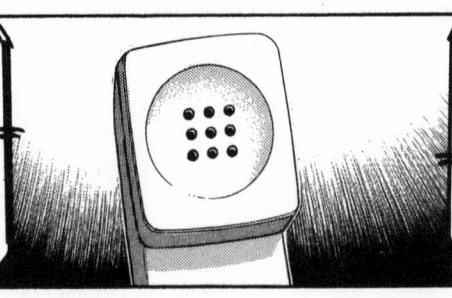

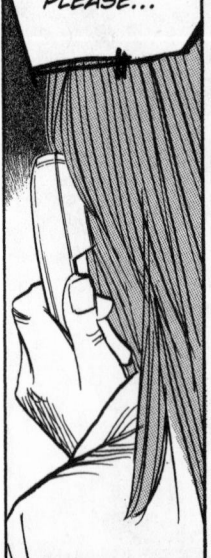

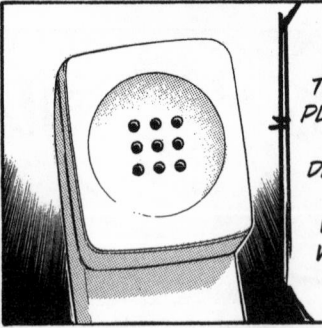

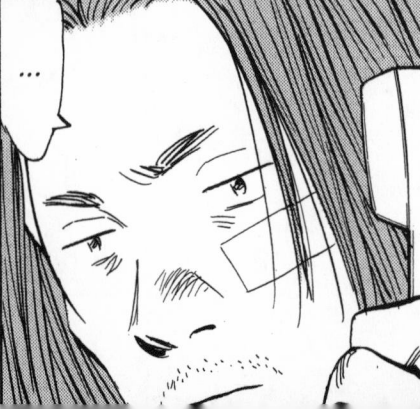

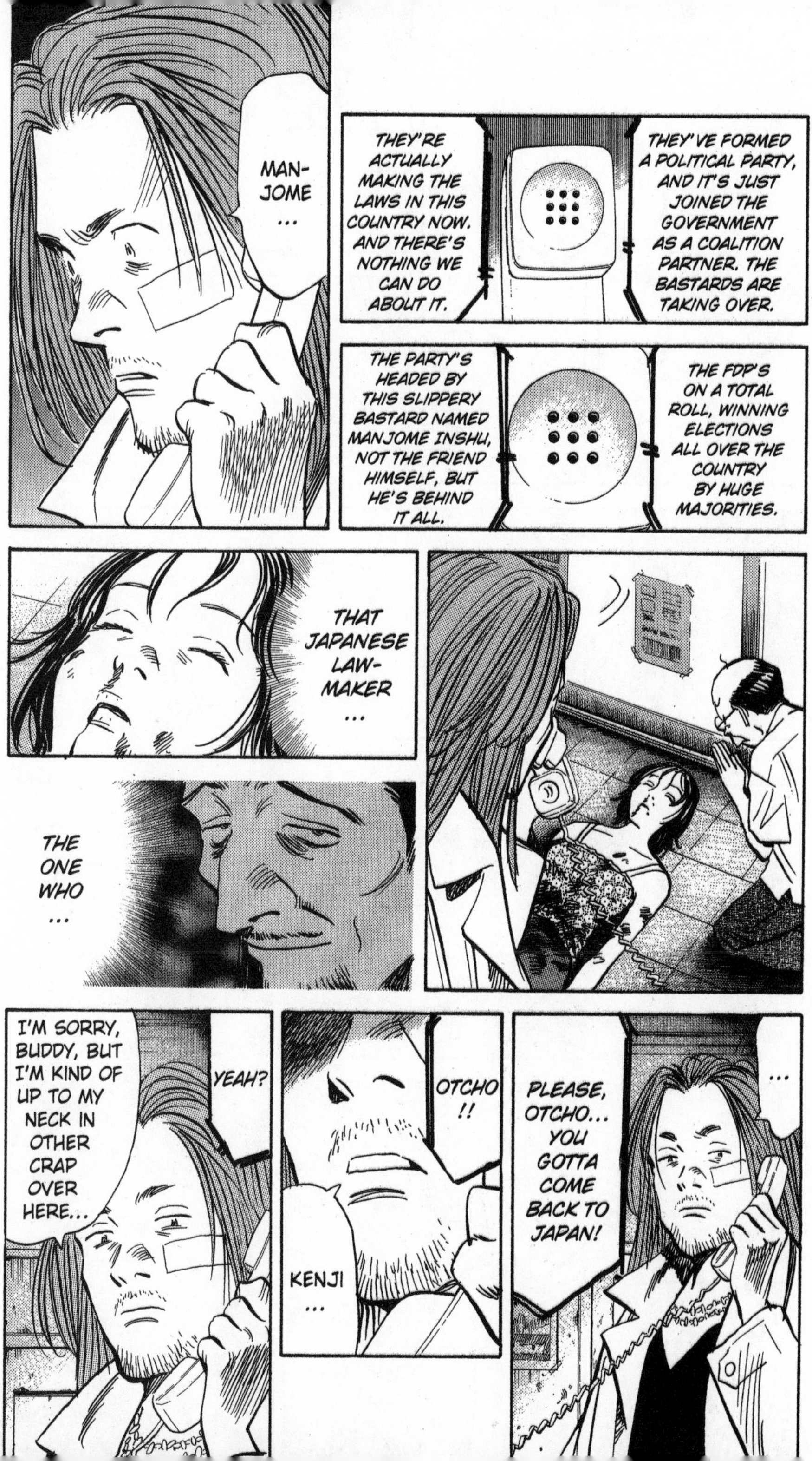
THEY'VE FORMED A POLITICAL PARTY, AND IT'S JUST JOINED THE GOVERNMENT AS A COALITION PARTNER. THE BASTARDS ARE TAKING OVER.
THEY'RE ACTUALLY MAKING THE LAWS IN THIS COUNTRY NOW. AND THERE'S NOTHING WE CAN DO ABOUT IT.
THE FDP'S ON A TOTAL ROLL, WINNING ELECTIONS ALL OVER THE COUNTRY BY HUGE MAJORITIES.
THE PARTY'S HEADED BY THIS SLIPPERY BASTARD NAMED MANJOME INSHU, NOT THE FRIEND HIMSELF, BUT HE'S BEHIND IT ALL.
MAN-JOME ...
THAT JAPANESE LAW-MAKER ...
THE ONE WHO ...
...
PLEASE, OTCHO... YOU GOTTA COME BACK TO JAPAN!
OTCHO !!
KENJI ...
YEAH?
I'M SORRY, BUDDY, BUT I'M KIND OF UP TO MY NECK IN OTHER CRAP OVER HERE...

KENJI
...

OTCHO
!!

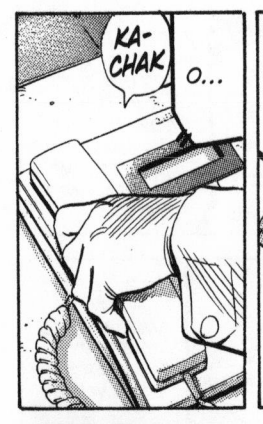

KA-CHAK

O...

HEY, OTCHO!!

OTCHO!!

IT'S BEEN A WHILE SINCE ANYBODY CALLED ME OTCHO... A LONG WHILE.

HEH HEH HEH HEH!!

WHAT'RE YOU DOING HERE ALONE? WHERE'S YOUR BUDDIES?

YEAH, COMING HERE BY YOURSELF WASN'T *BRAVE,* IT WAS *STUPID.* OR ACTUALLY, *SUICIDAL.*

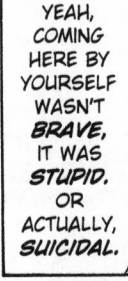

VOOSH

TSK TSK

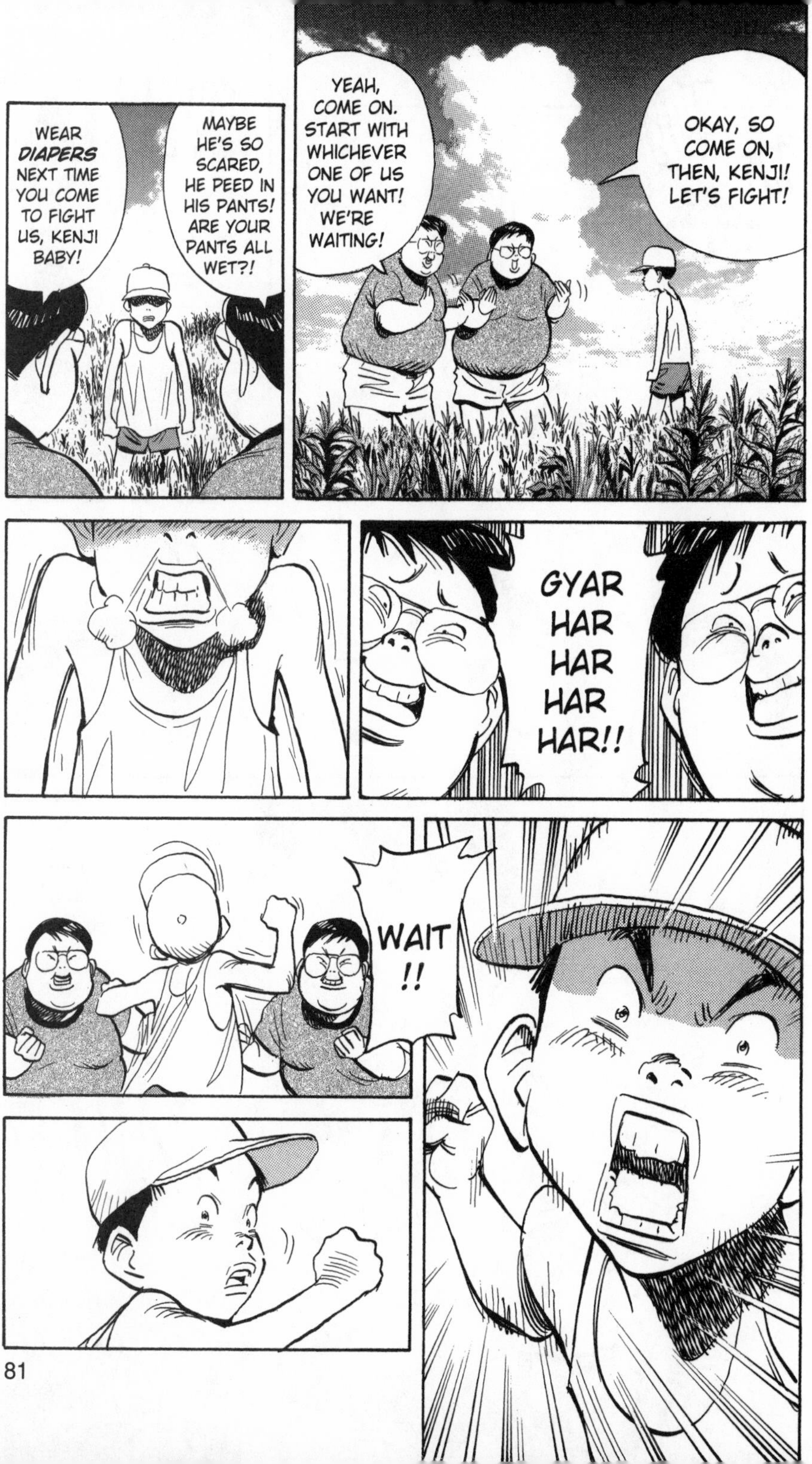
OKAY, SO COME ON, THEN, KENJI! LET'S FIGHT!
YEAH, COME ON. START WITH WHICHEVER ONE OF US YOU WANT! WE'RE WAITING!
MAYBE HE'S SO SCARED, HE PEED IN HIS PANTS! ARE YOUR PANTS ALL WET?!
WEAR DIAPERS NEXT TIME YOU COME TO FIGHT US, KENJI BABY!
GYAR HAR HAR HAR HAR!!
WAIT !!

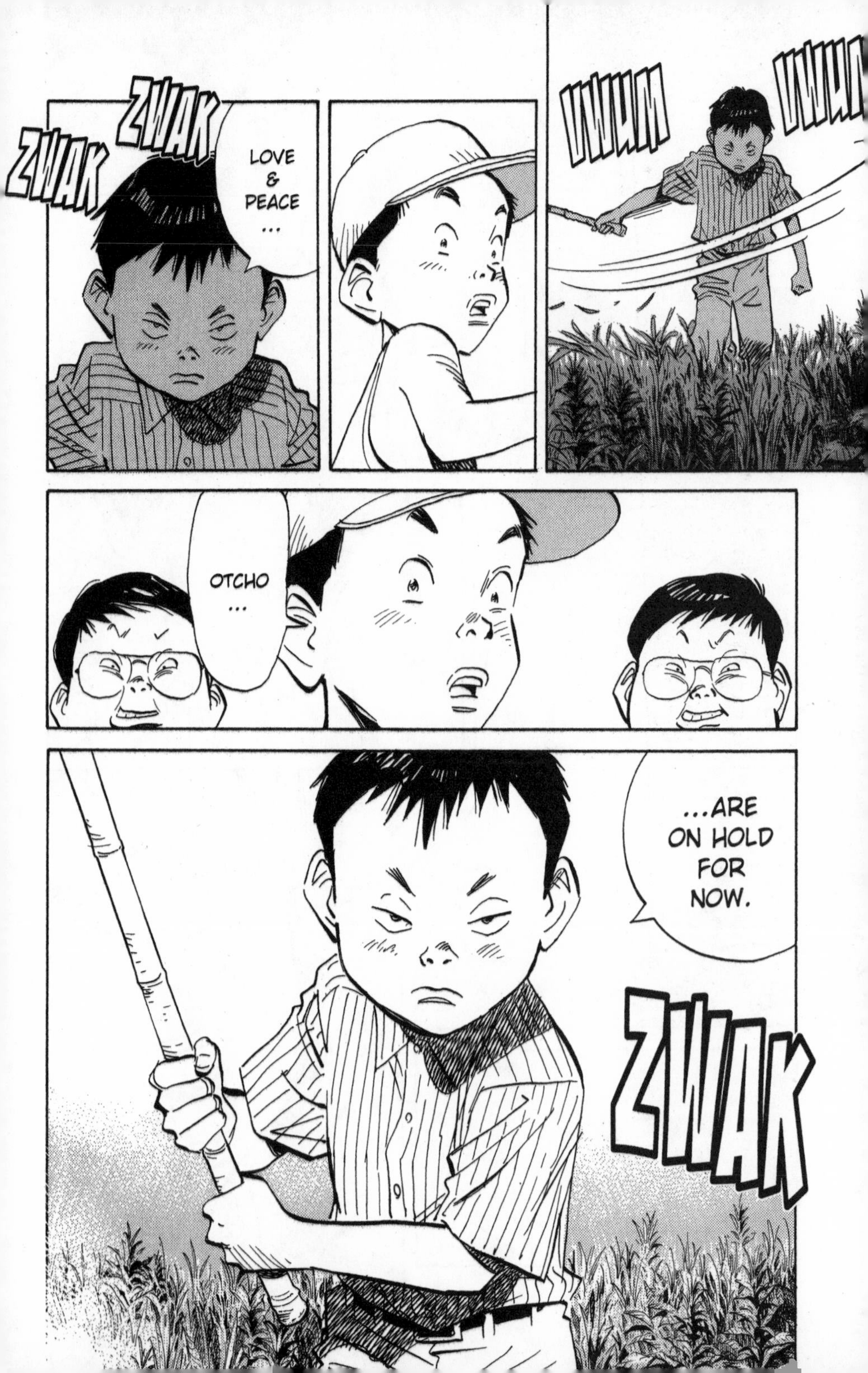
VWUM
VWUM
ZWAK
ZWAK
LOVE & PEACE ...
OTCHO ...
...ARE ON HOLD FOR NOW.
ZWAK

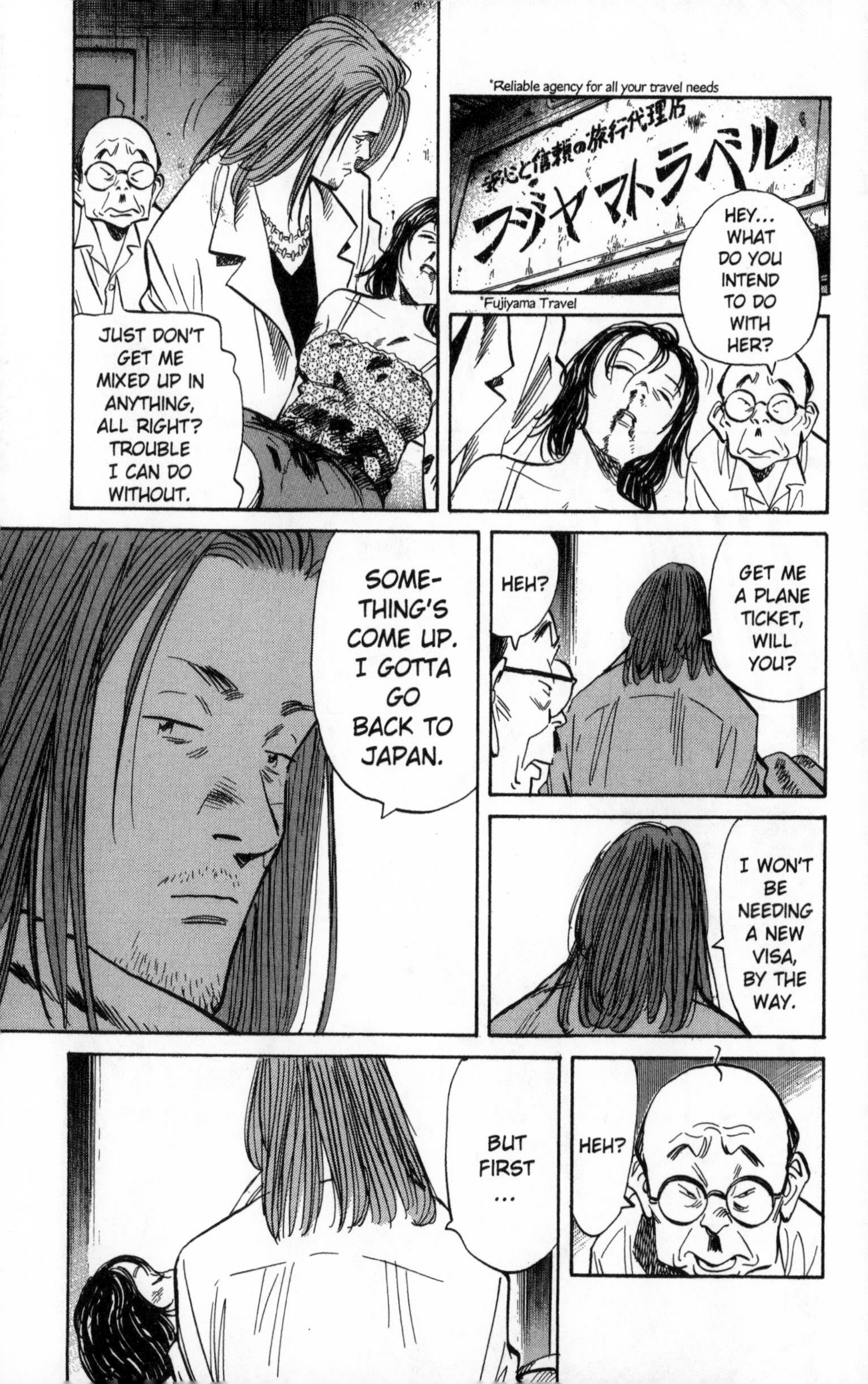
*Reliable agency for all your travel needs
安心と信頼の旅行代理店
フジヤマトラベル
*Fujiyama Travel
HEY... WHAT DO YOU INTEND TO DO WITH HER?
JUST DON'T GET ME MIXED UP IN ANYTHING, ALL RIGHT? TROUBLE I CAN DO WITHOUT.
GET ME A PLANE TICKET, WILL YOU?
HEH?
I WON'T BE NEEDING A NEW VISA, BY THE WAY.
SOME-THING'S COME UP. I GOTTA GO BACK TO JAPAN.
HEH?
BUT FIRST ...

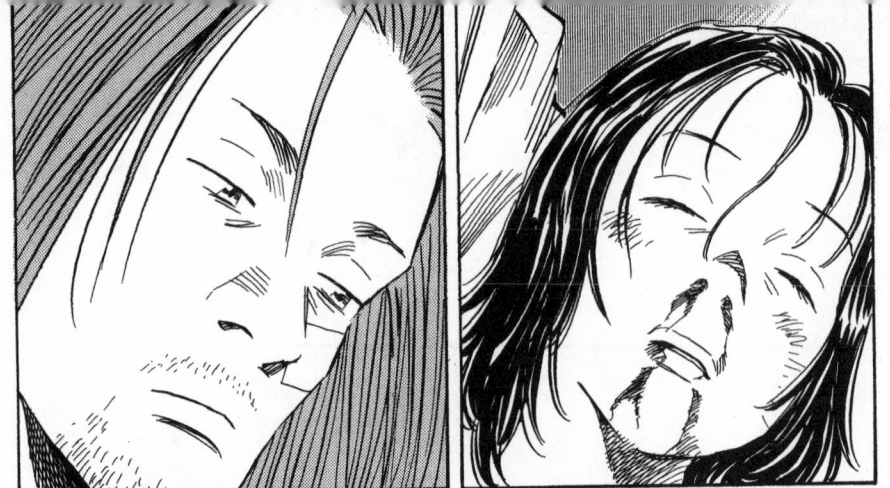

*Fujiyama Travel

ZWAK

...THERE'S A FEW THINGS I NEED TO TAKE CARE OF.

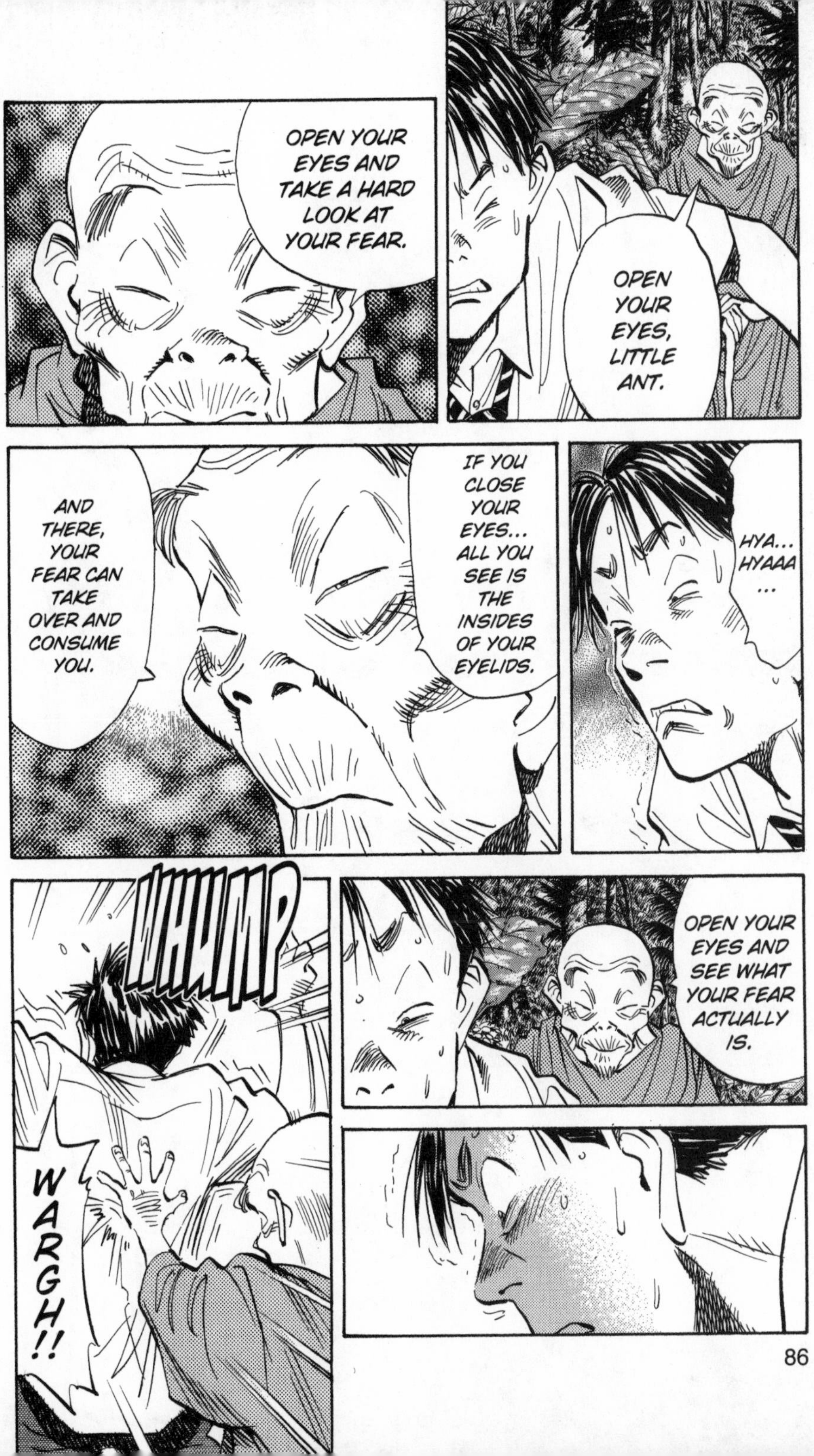
OPEN YOUR EYES, LITTLE ANT.
OPEN YOUR EYES AND TAKE A HARD LOOK AT YOUR FEAR.
HYA... HYAAA ...
IF YOU CLOSE YOUR EYES... ALL YOU SEE IS THE INSIDES OF YOUR EYELIDS.
AND THERE, YOUR FEAR CAN TAKE OVER AND CONSUME YOU.
OPEN YOUR EYES AND SEE WHAT YOUR FEAR ACTUALLY IS.
WHUMP
WARGH!!

Chapter 5 Rainbow Kid

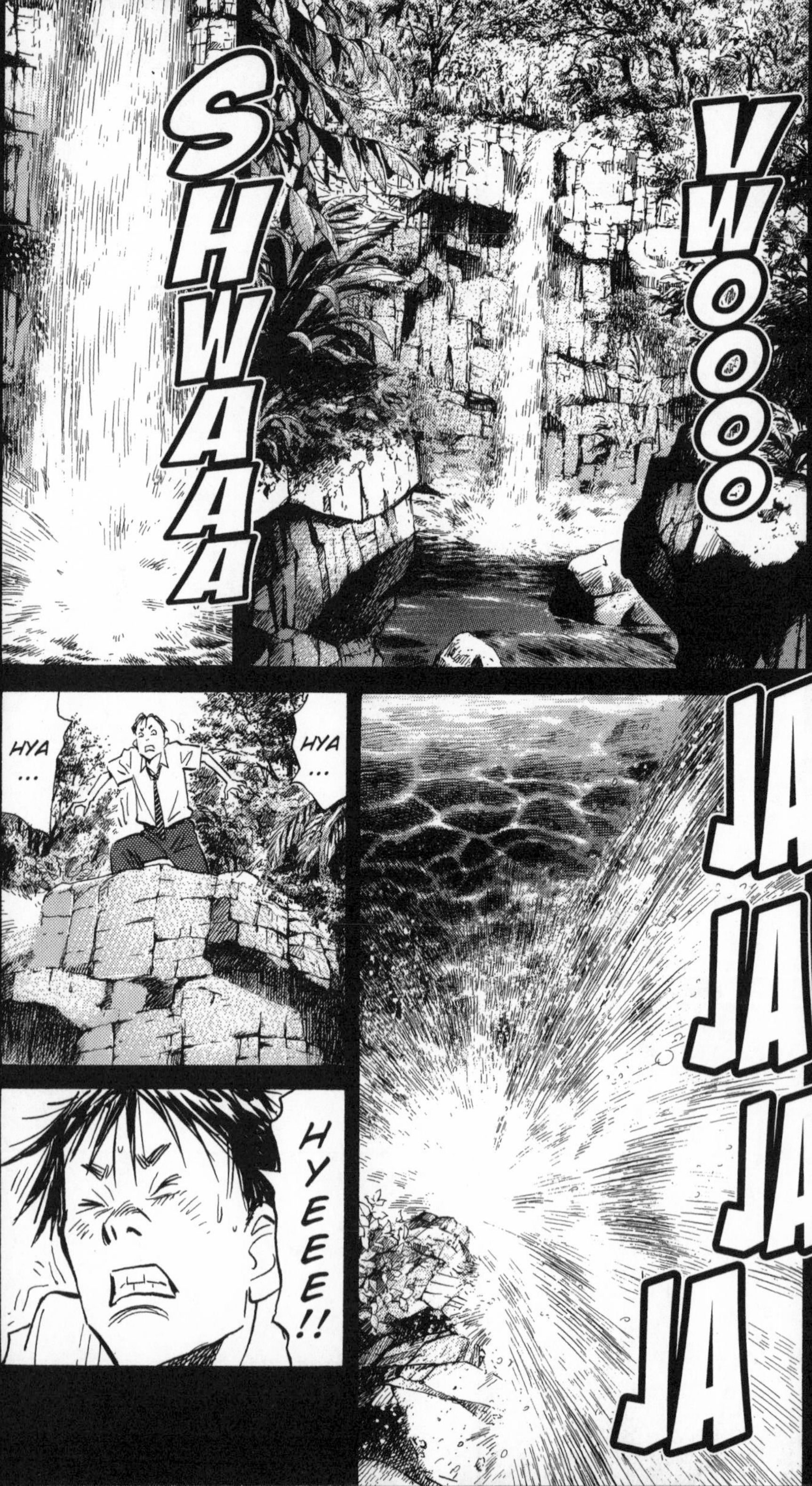
VWOOOO
SHWAAA
JA JA JA JA JA
HYA …
HYA …
HYEEE!!

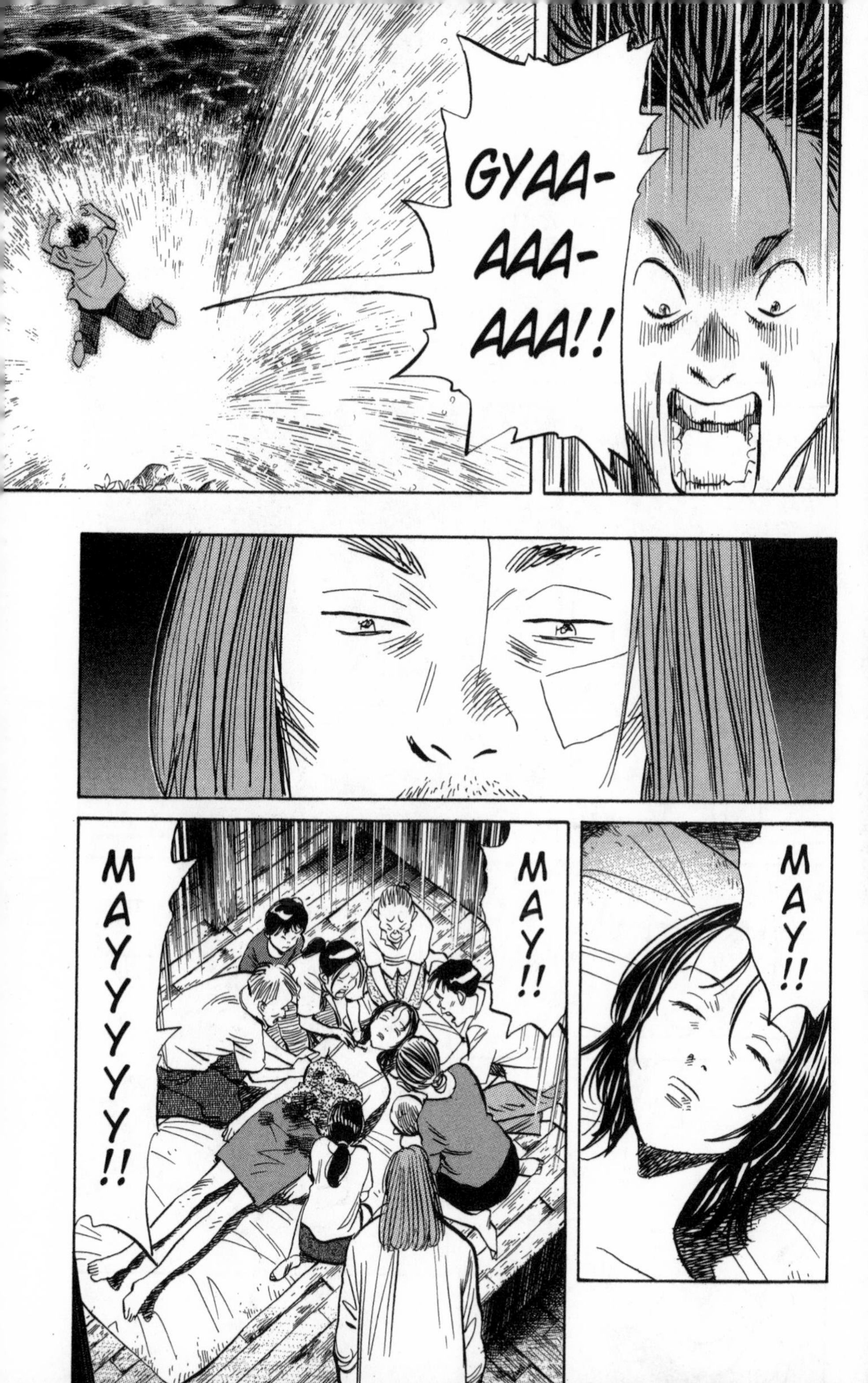
GYAA-
AAA-
AAA!!
MAY!!
MAY!!
MAYYYYYY!!

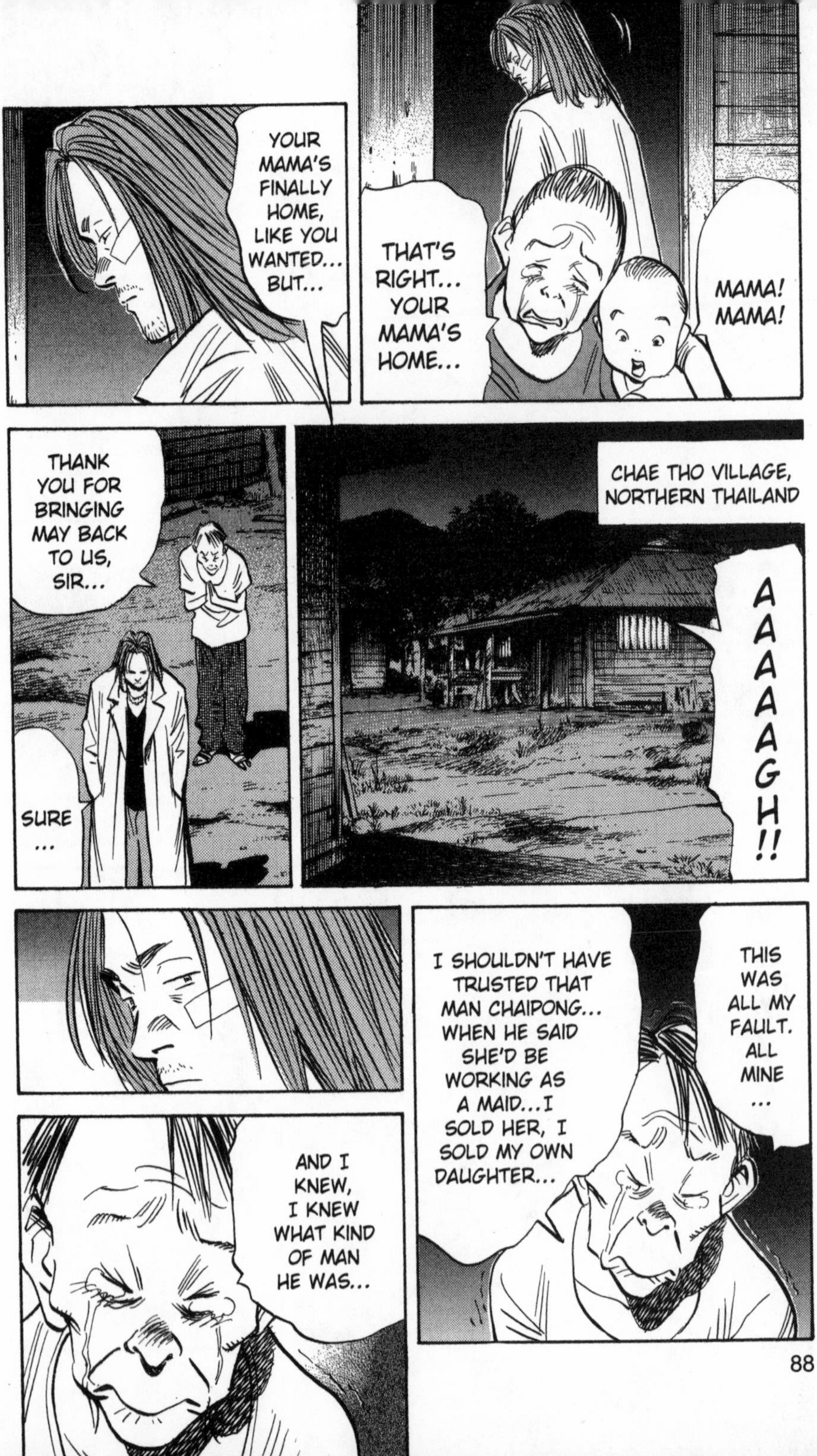
MAMA! MAMA!
THAT'S RIGHT... YOUR MAMA'S HOME...
YOUR MAMA'S FINALLY HOME, LIKE YOU WANTED... BUT...
CHAE THO VILLAGE, NORTHERN THAILAND
AAAAAAGH!!
THANK YOU FOR BRINGING MAY BACK TO US, SIR...
SURE...
THIS WAS ALL MY FAULT. ALL MINE...
I SHOULDN'T HAVE TRUSTED THAT MAN CHAIPONG... WHEN HE SAID SHE'D BE WORKING AS A MAID... I SOLD HER, I SOLD MY OWN DAUGHTER...
AND I KNEW, I KNEW WHAT KIND OF MAN HE WAS...

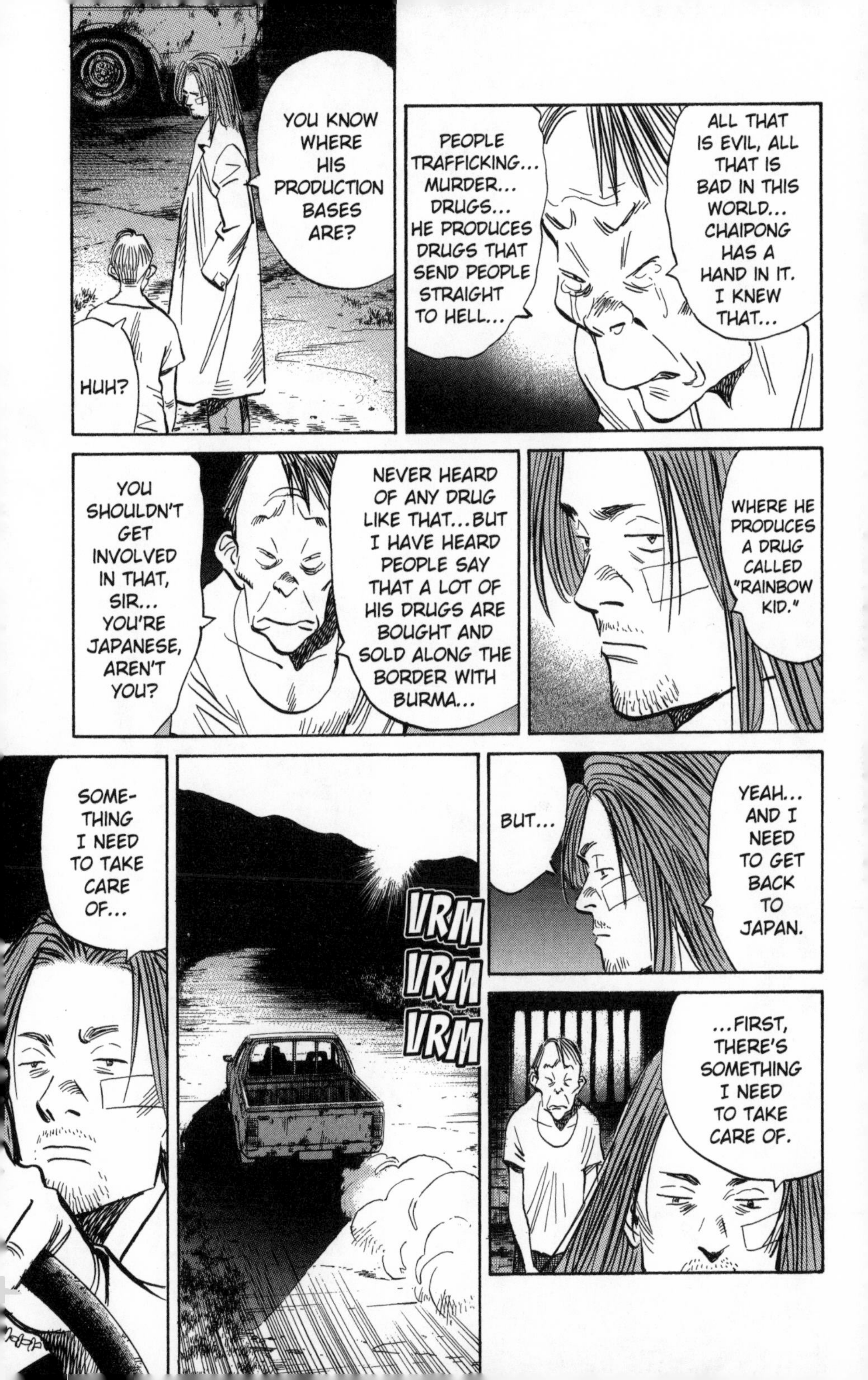
ALL THAT IS EVIL, ALL THAT IS BAD IN THIS WORLD... CHAIPONG HAS A HAND IN IT. I KNEW THAT...
PEOPLE TRAFFICKING... MURDER... DRUGS... HE PRODUCES DRUGS THAT SEND PEOPLE STRAIGHT TO HELL...
YOU KNOW WHERE HIS PRODUCTION BASES ARE?
HUH?
WHERE HE PRODUCES A DRUG CALLED "RAINBOW KID."
NEVER HEARD OF ANY DRUG LIKE THAT...BUT I HAVE HEARD PEOPLE SAY THAT A LOT OF HIS DRUGS ARE BOUGHT AND SOLD ALONG THE BORDER WITH BURMA...
YOU SHOULDN'T GET INVOLVED IN THAT, SIR... YOU'RE JAPANESE, AREN'T YOU?
YEAH... AND I NEED TO GET BACK TO JAPAN.
BUT...
...FIRST, THERE'S SOMETHING I NEED TO TAKE CARE OF.
VRM
VRM
VRM
SOME-THING I NEED TO TAKE CARE OF...

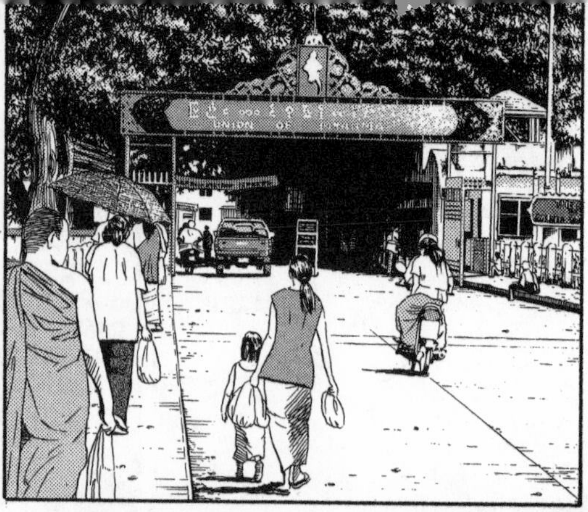

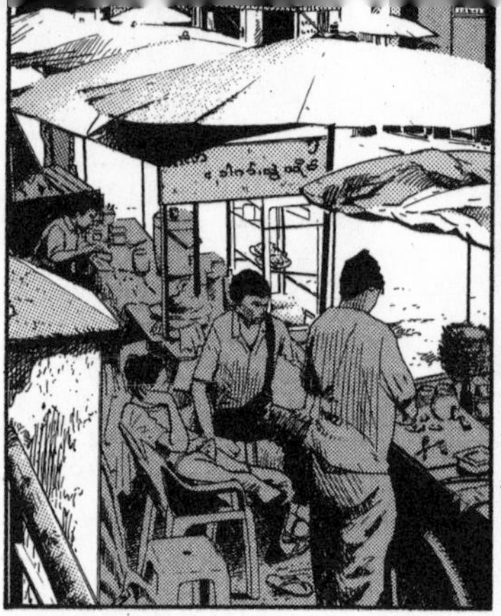

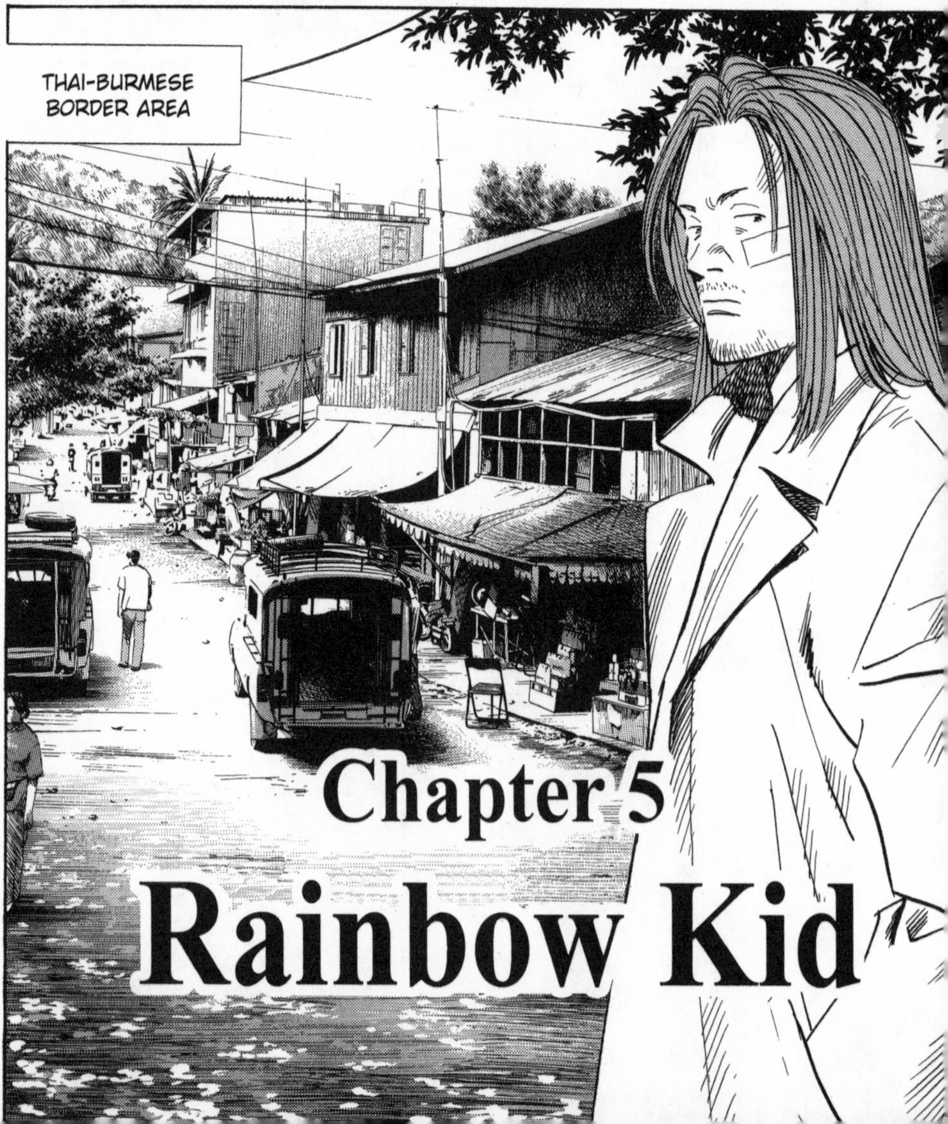
THAI-BURMESE BORDER AREA

Chapter 5
Rainbow Kid

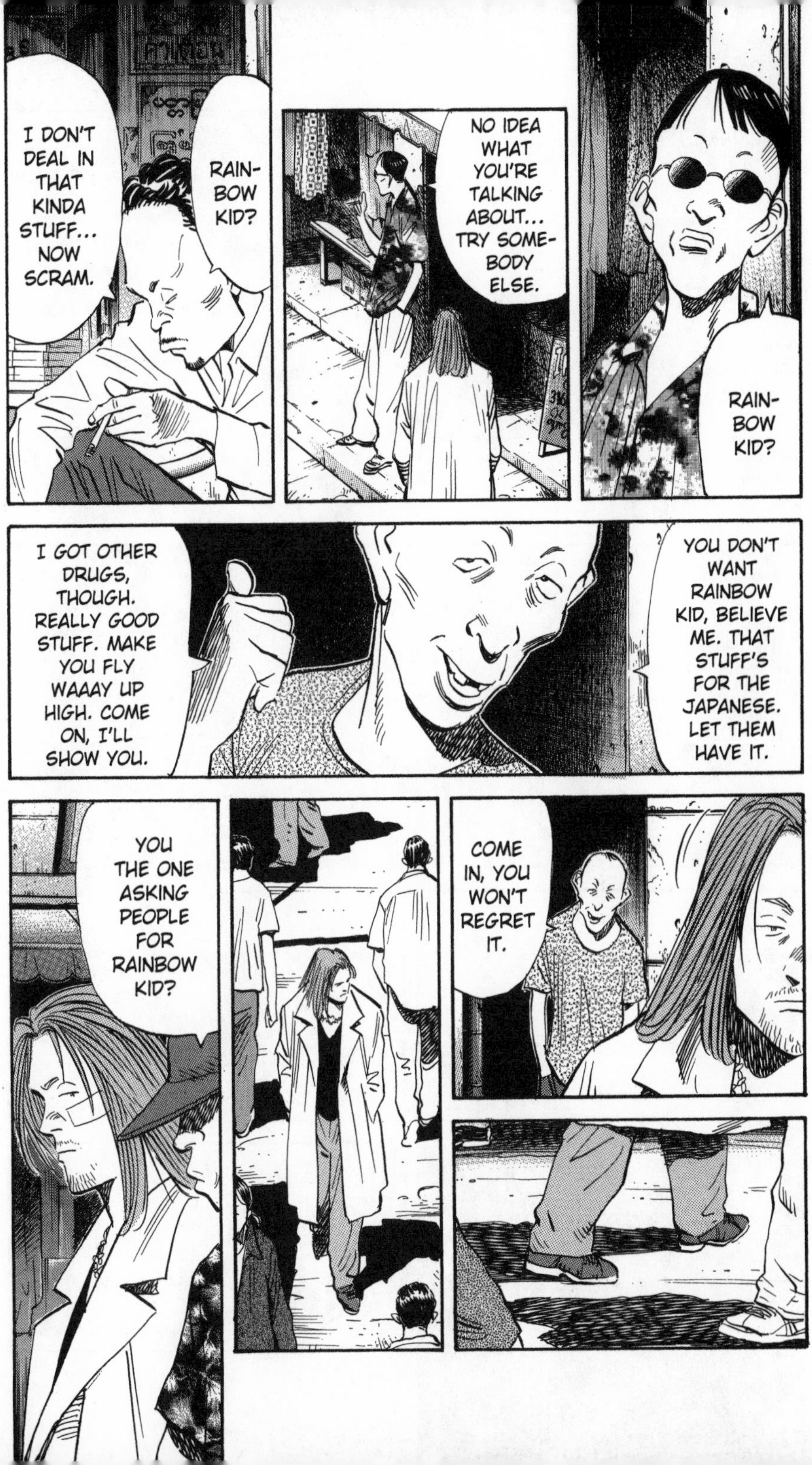
RAINBOW KID?
NO IDEA WHAT YOU'RE TALKING ABOUT... TRY SOMEBODY ELSE.
RAINBOW KID?
I DON'T DEAL IN THAT KINDA STUFF... NOW SCRAM.
YOU DON'T WANT RAINBOW KID, BELIEVE ME. THAT STUFF'S FOR THE JAPANESE. LET THEM HAVE IT.
I GOT OTHER DRUGS, THOUGH. REALLY GOOD STUFF. MAKE YOU FLY WAAAY UP HIGH. COME ON, I'LL SHOW YOU.
COME IN, YOU WON'T REGRET IT.
YOU THE ONE ASKING PEOPLE FOR RAINBOW KID?

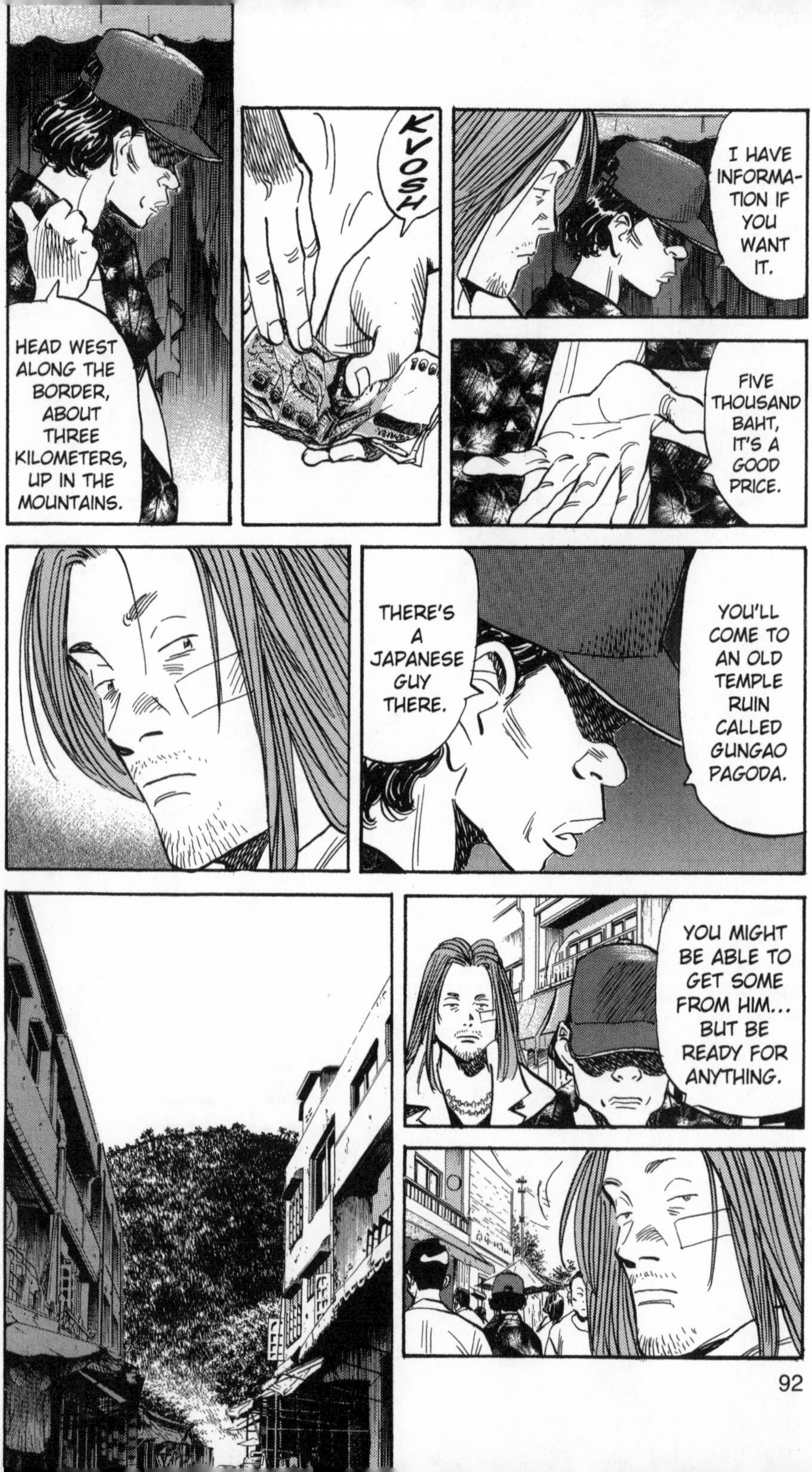
I HAVE INFORMATION IF YOU WANT IT.
FIVE THOUSAND BAHT, IT'S A GOOD PRICE.
KVOSH
HEAD WEST ALONG THE BORDER, ABOUT THREE KILOMETERS, UP IN THE MOUNTAINS.
YOU'LL COME TO AN OLD TEMPLE RUIN CALLED GUNGAO PAGODA.
THERE'S A JAPANESE GUY THERE.
YOU MIGHT BE ABLE TO GET SOME FROM HIM... BUT BE READY FOR ANYTHING.

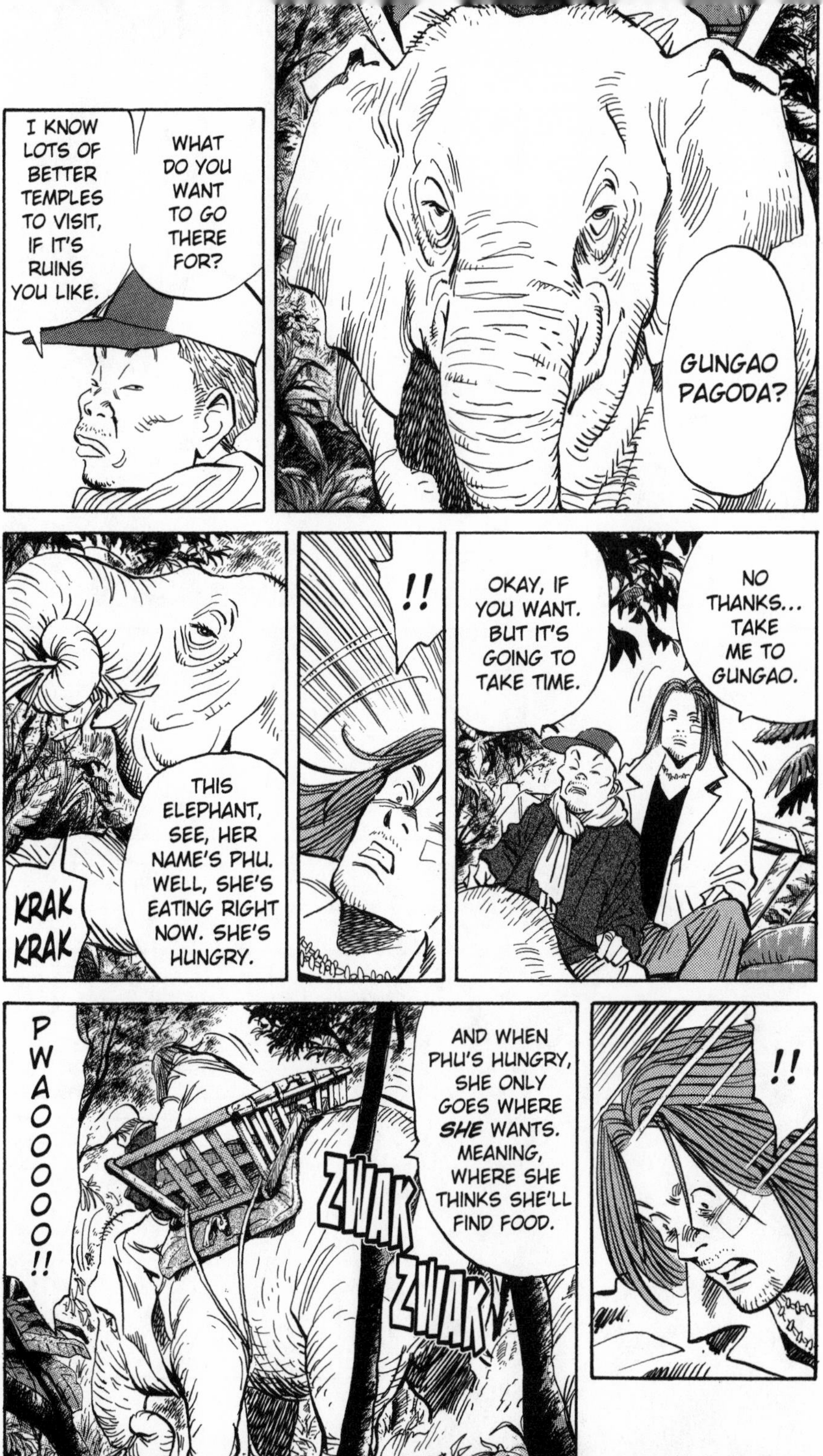
GUNGAO PAGODA?
WHAT DO YOU WANT TO GO THERE FOR?
I KNOW LOTS OF BETTER TEMPLES TO VISIT, IF IT'S RUINS YOU LIKE.
NO THANKS... TAKE ME TO GUNGAO.
OKAY, IF YOU WANT. BUT IT'S GOING TO TAKE TIME.
!!
THIS ELEPHANT, SEE, HER NAME'S PHU. WELL, SHE'S EATING RIGHT NOW. SHE'S HUNGRY.
KRAK KRAK
!!
AND WHEN PHU'S HUNGRY, SHE ONLY GOES WHERE *SHE* WANTS. MEANING, WHERE SHE THINKS SHE'LL FIND FOOD.
ZWAK ZWAK
PWAOOOOOO!!

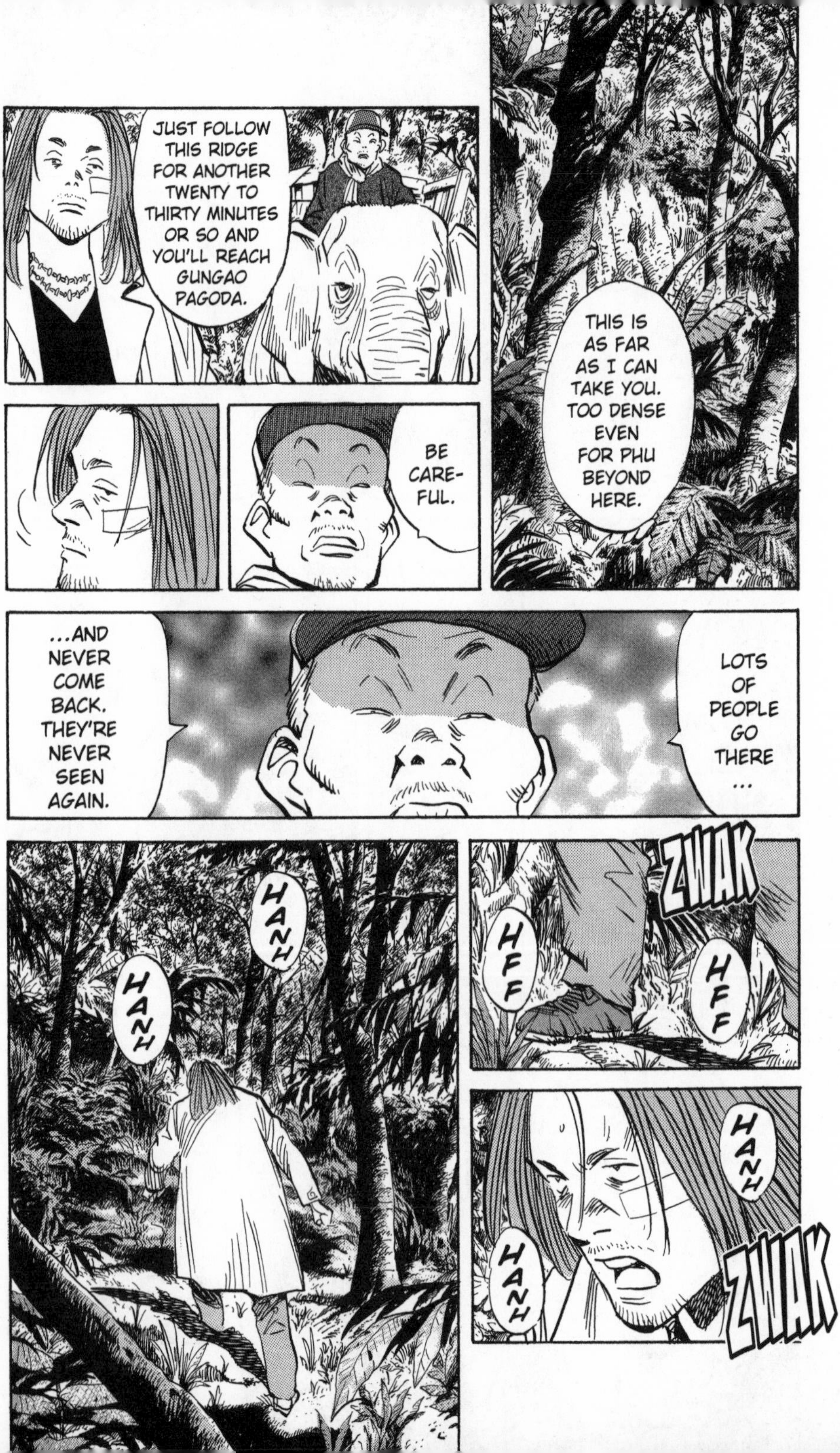
THIS IS AS FAR AS I CAN TAKE YOU. TOO DENSE EVEN FOR PHU BEYOND HERE.
JUST FOLLOW THIS RIDGE FOR ANOTHER TWENTY TO THIRTY MINUTES OR SO AND YOU'LL REACH GUNGAO PAGODA.
BE CAREFUL.
LOTS OF PEOPLE GO THERE...
...AND NEVER COME BACK. THEY'RE NEVER SEEN AGAIN.
ZWAK
HFF
HFF
HANH
HANH
ZWAK
HANH
HANH

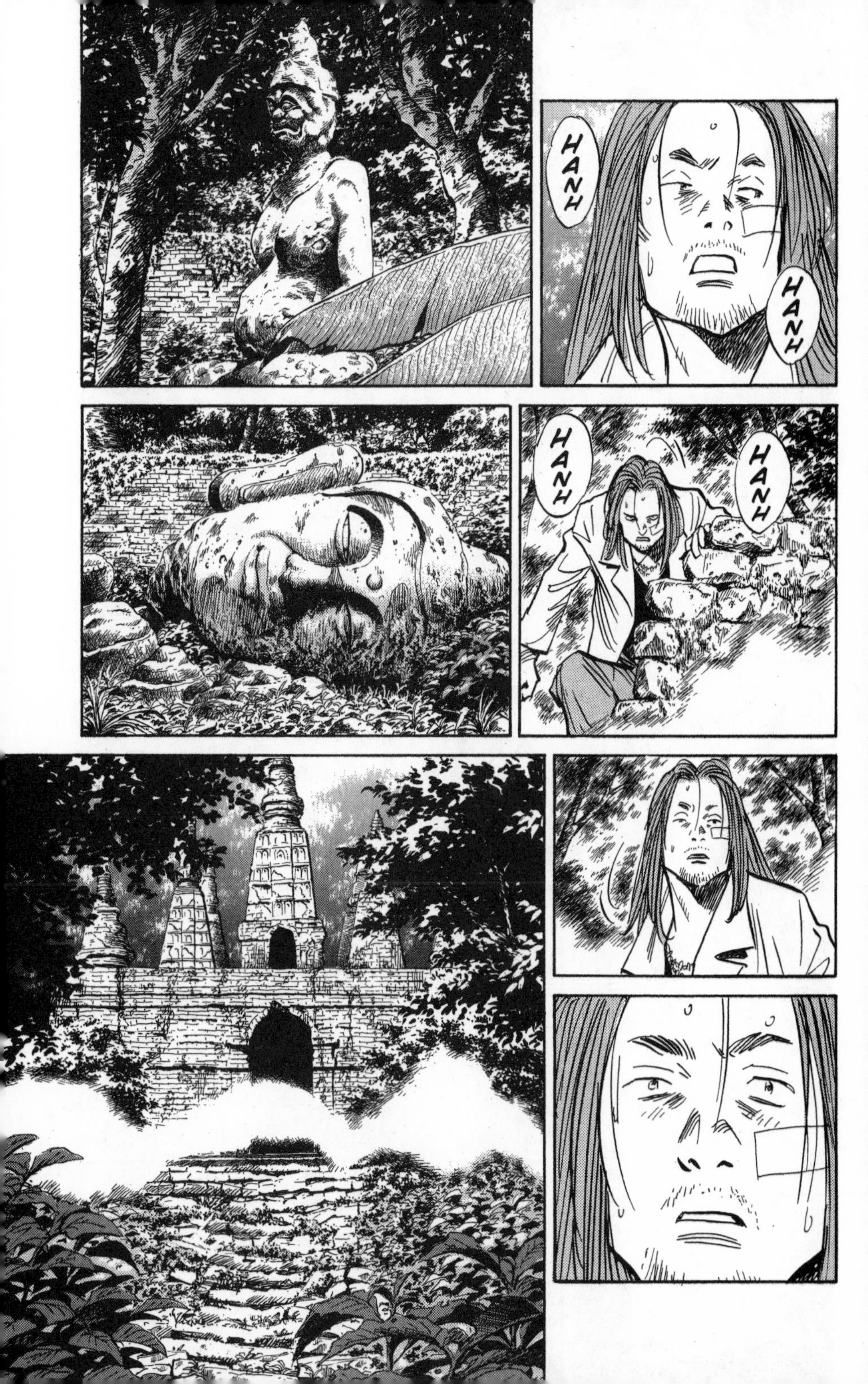
HANH
HANH
HANH
HANH

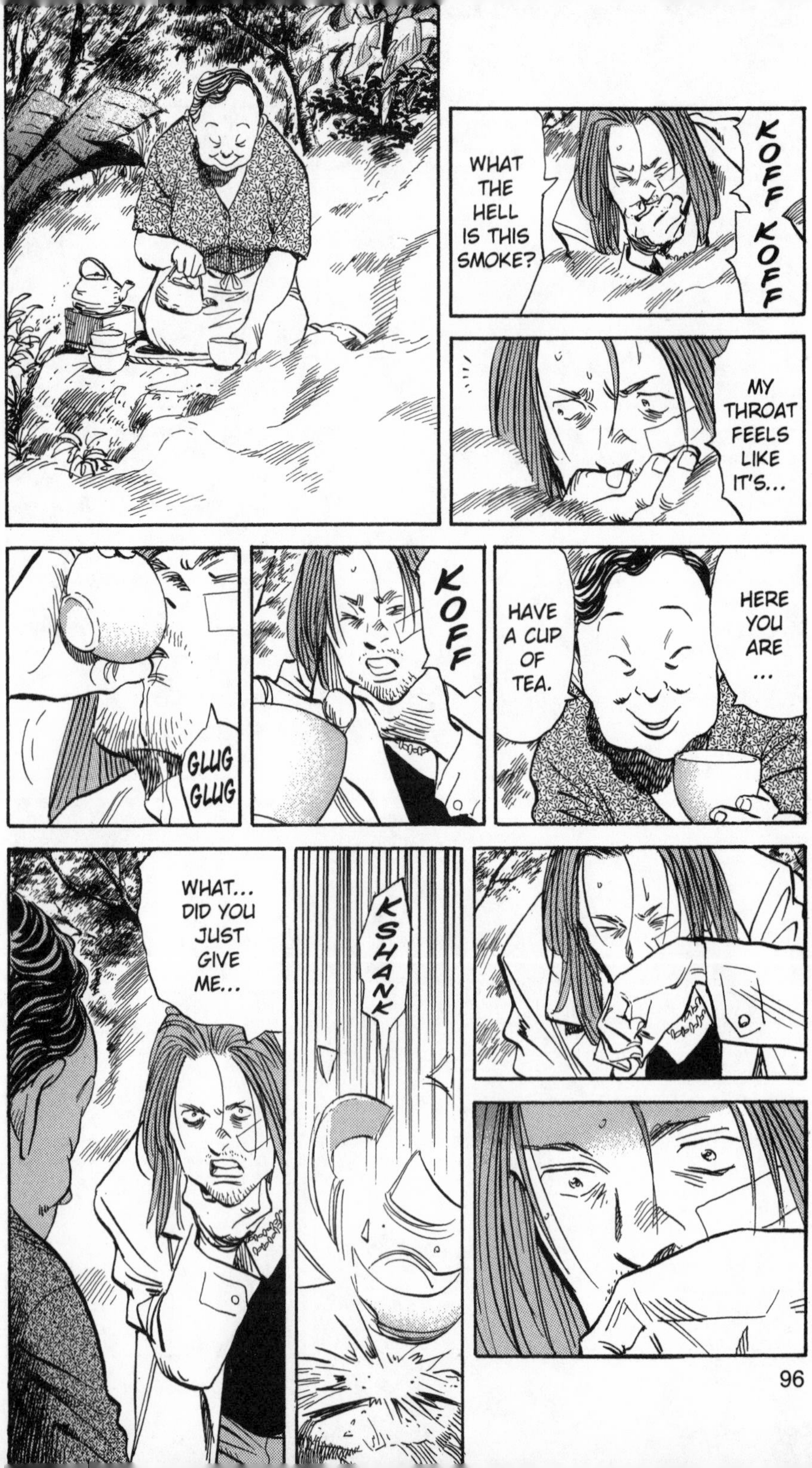
KOFF KOFF
WHAT THE HELL IS THIS SMOKE?
MY THROAT FEELS LIKE IT'S...
HERE YOU ARE ...
HAVE A CUP OF TEA.
KOFF
GLUG GLUG
KSHANK
WHAT... DID YOU JUST GIVE ME...

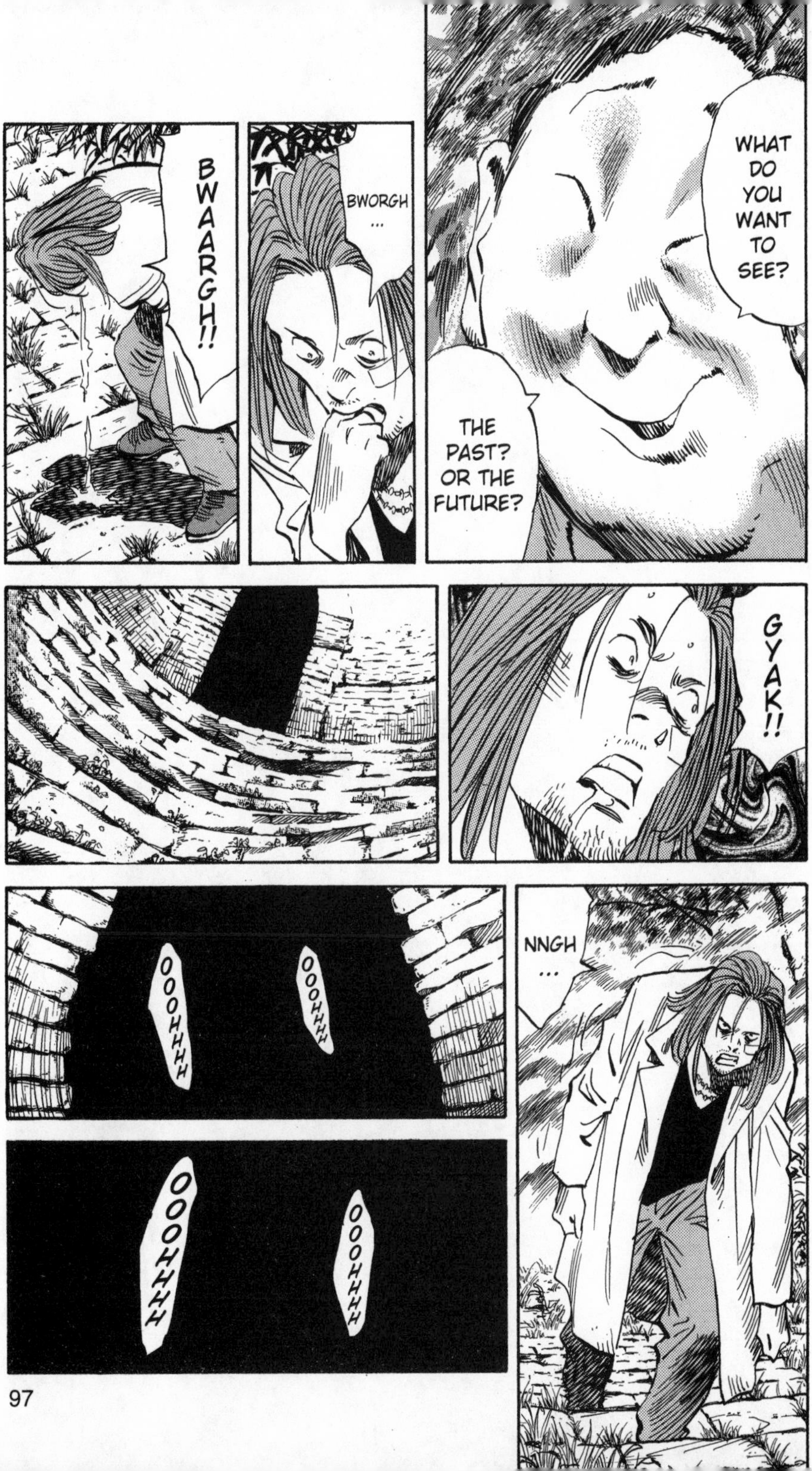
WHAT DO YOU WANT TO SEE?
THE PAST? OR THE FUTURE?
BWORGH ...
BWAARGH!!
GYAK!!
NNGH ...
OOOHHHH
OOOHHHH
OOOHHHH
OOOHHHH

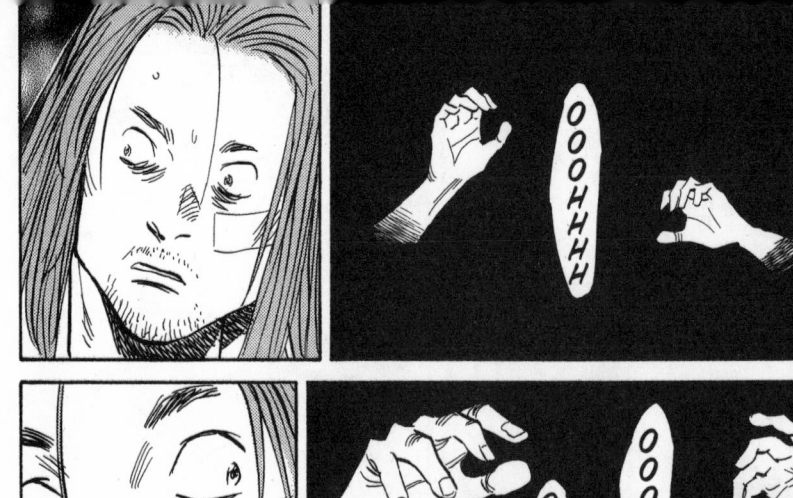
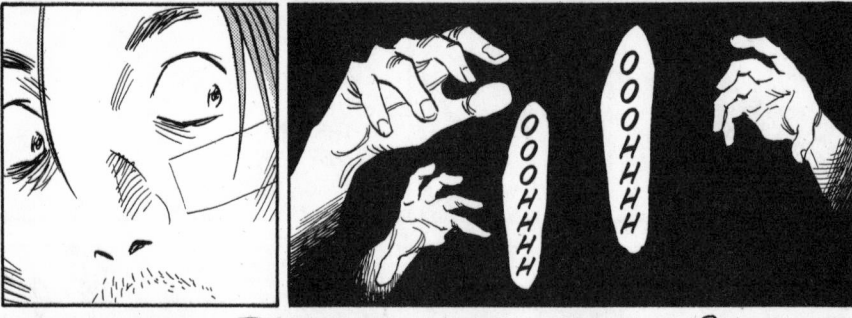

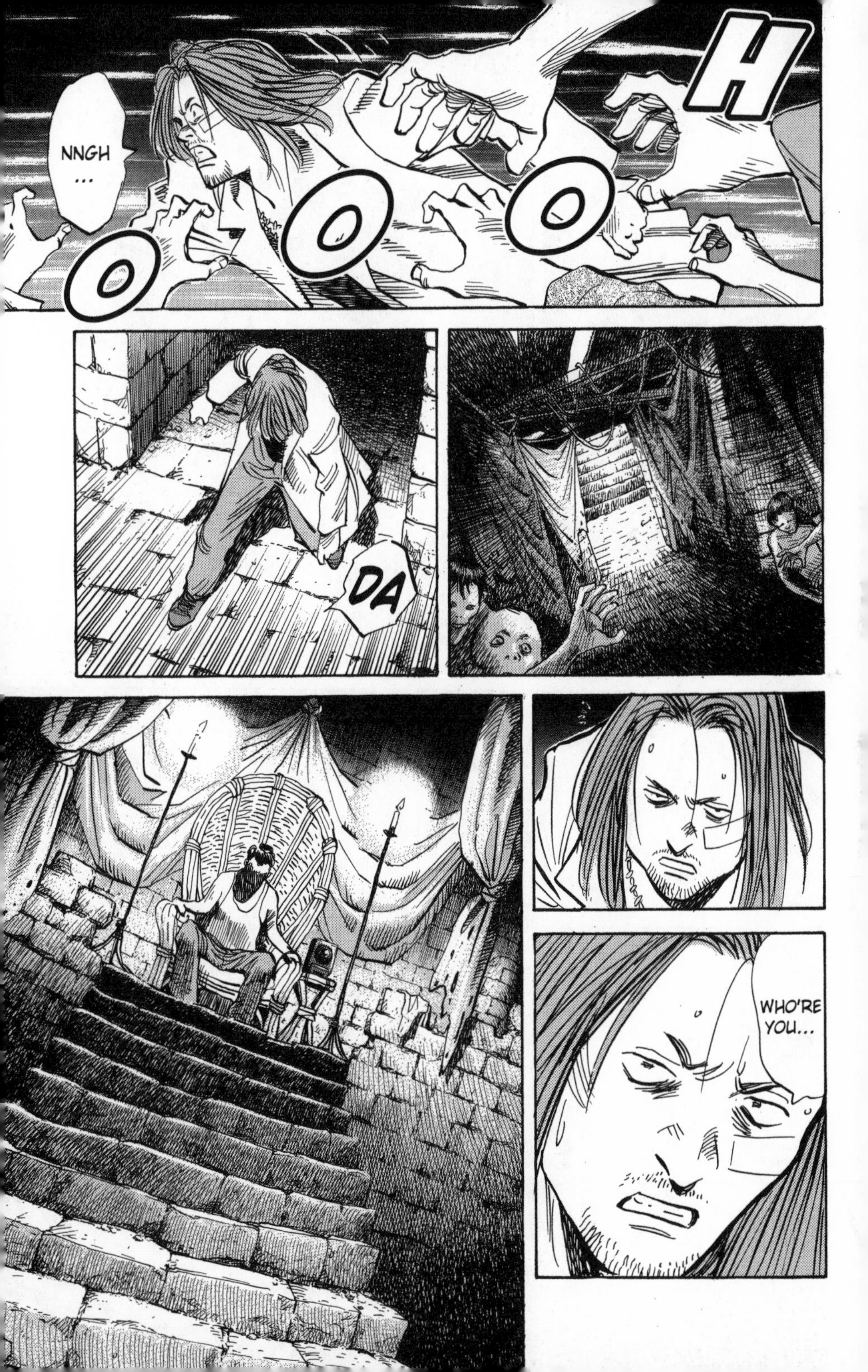
OOOH
NNGH ...
DA
WHO'RE YOU...

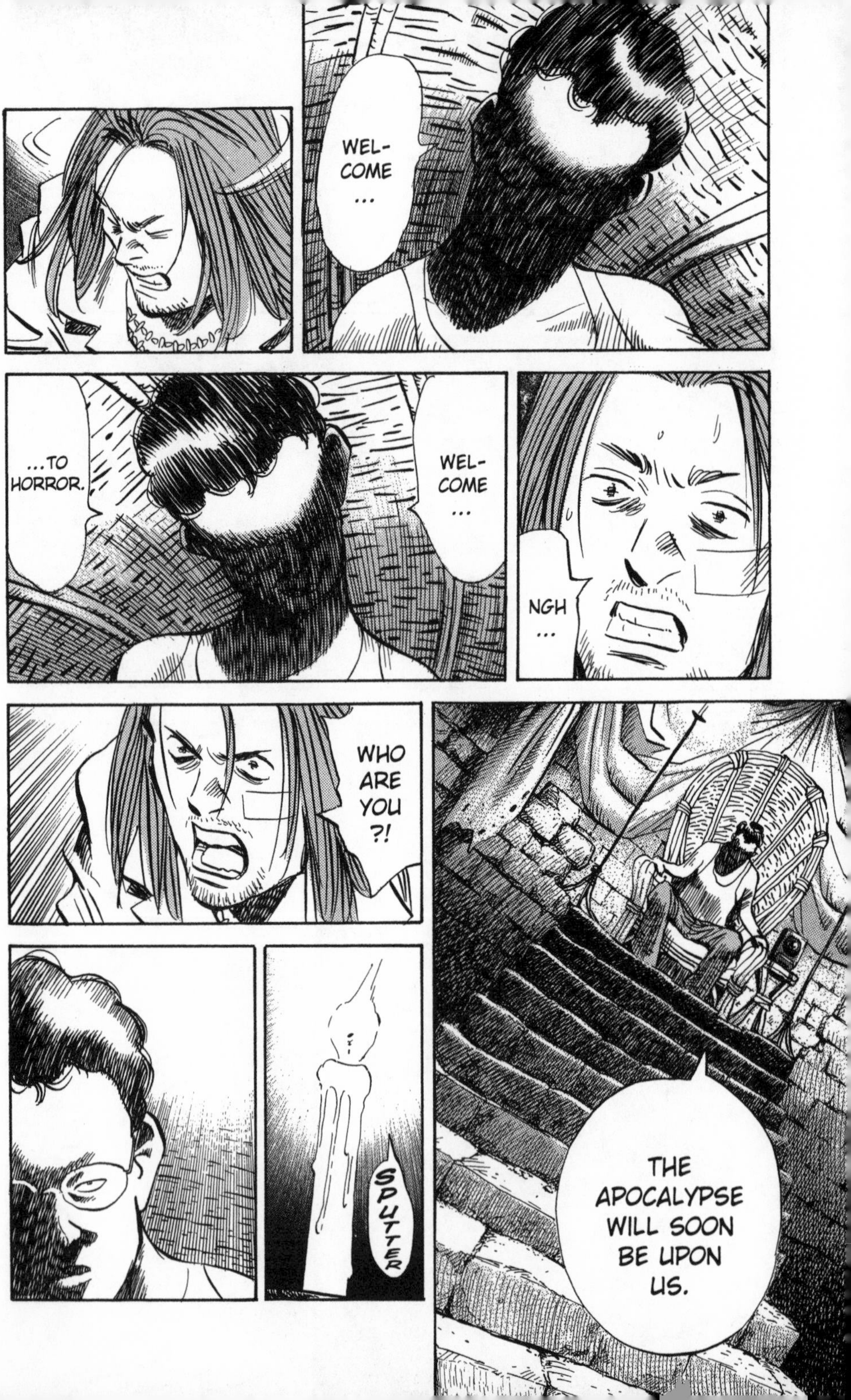
WEL- COME ...
NGH ...
WEL- COME ...
...TO HORROR.
THE APOCALYPSE WILL SOON BE UPON US.
WHO ARE YOU ?!
SPUTTER

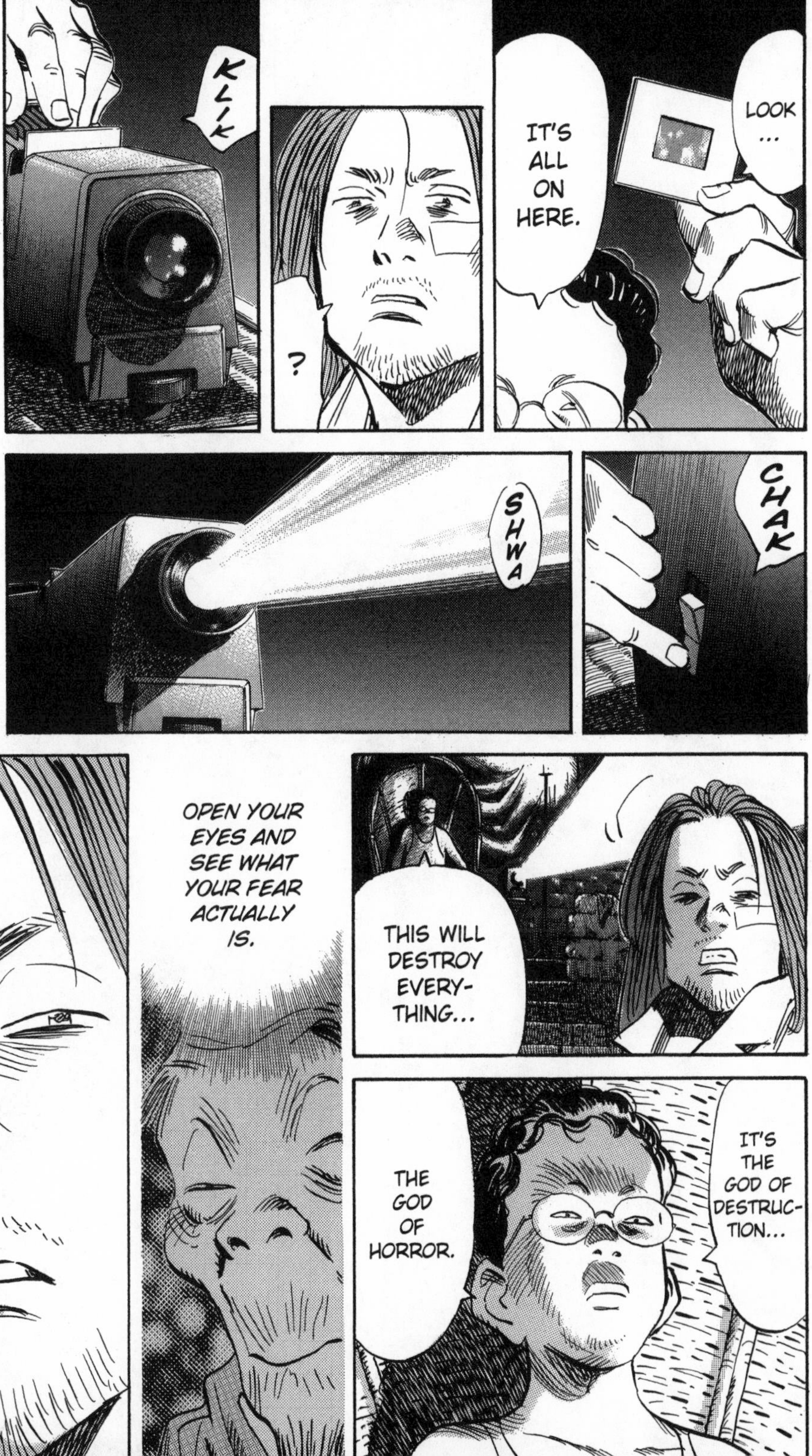
LOOK...
IT'S ALL ON HERE.
?
KLIK
CHAK
SHWA
THIS WILL DESTROY EVERY-THING...
IT'S THE GOD OF DESTRUC-TION...
THE GOD OF HORROR.
OPEN YOUR EYES AND SEE WHAT YOUR FEAR ACTUALLY IS.

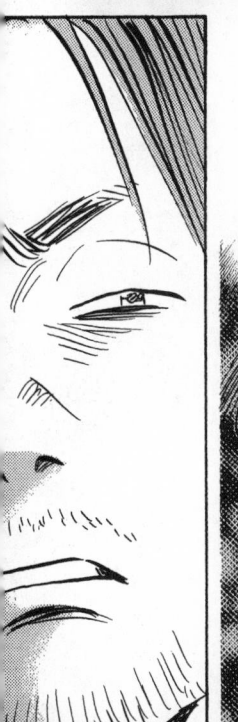

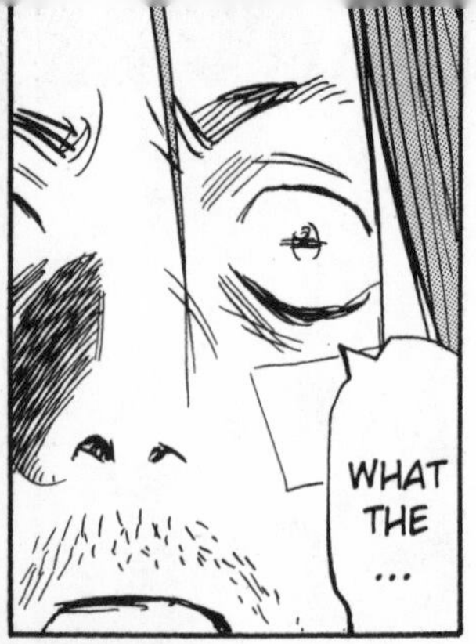
WHAT THE ...
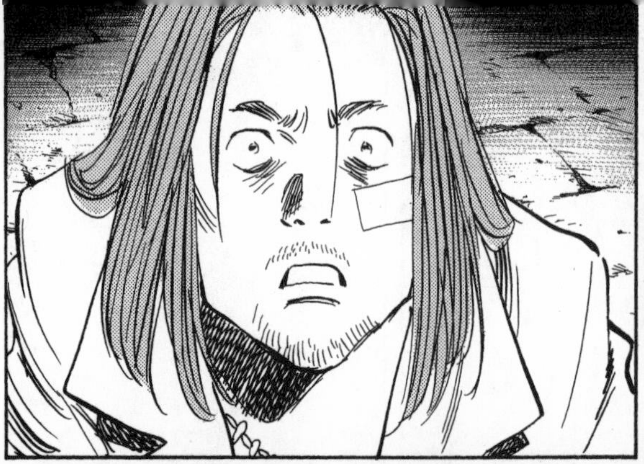
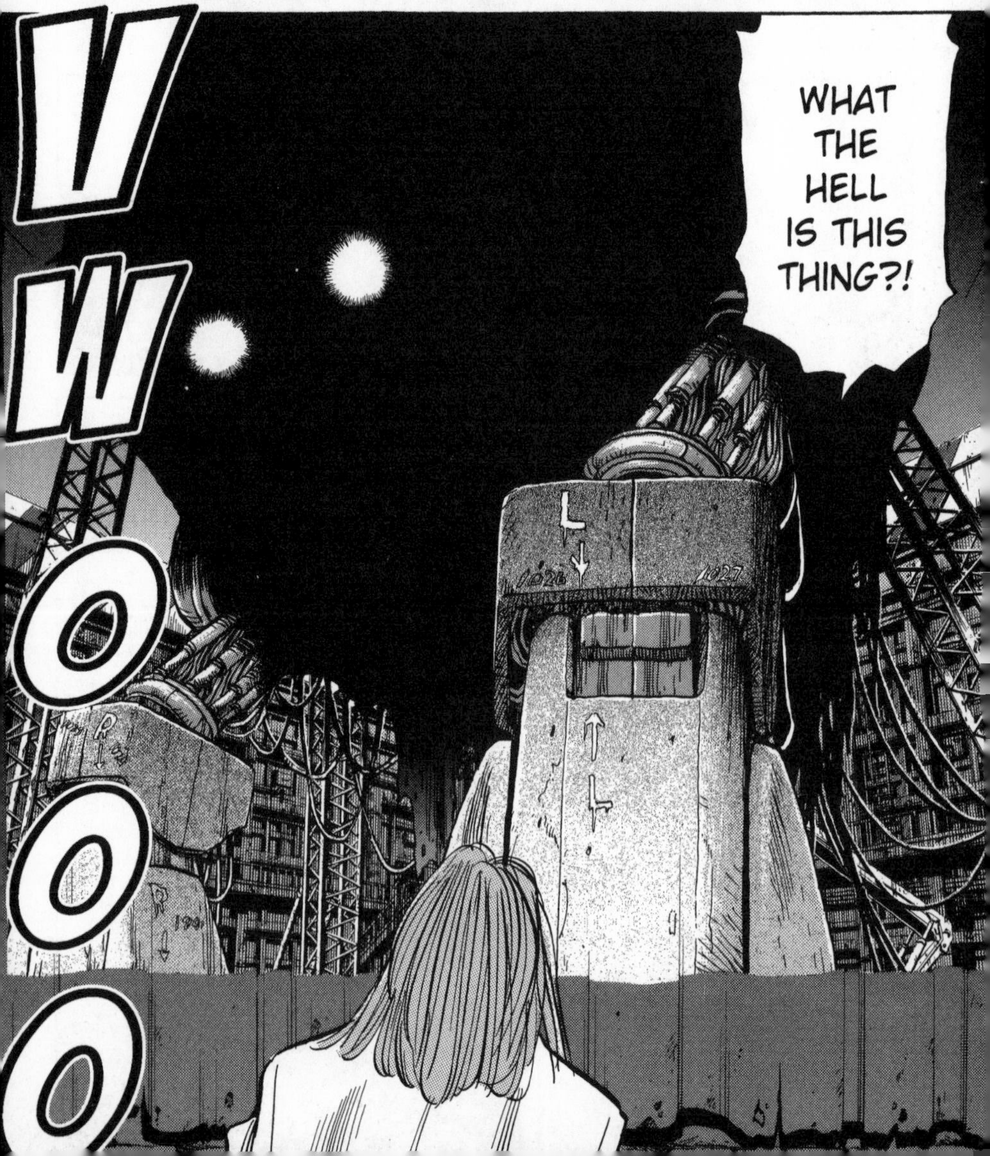
VWOOO
WHAT THE HELL IS THIS THING?!

Chapter 6 Light

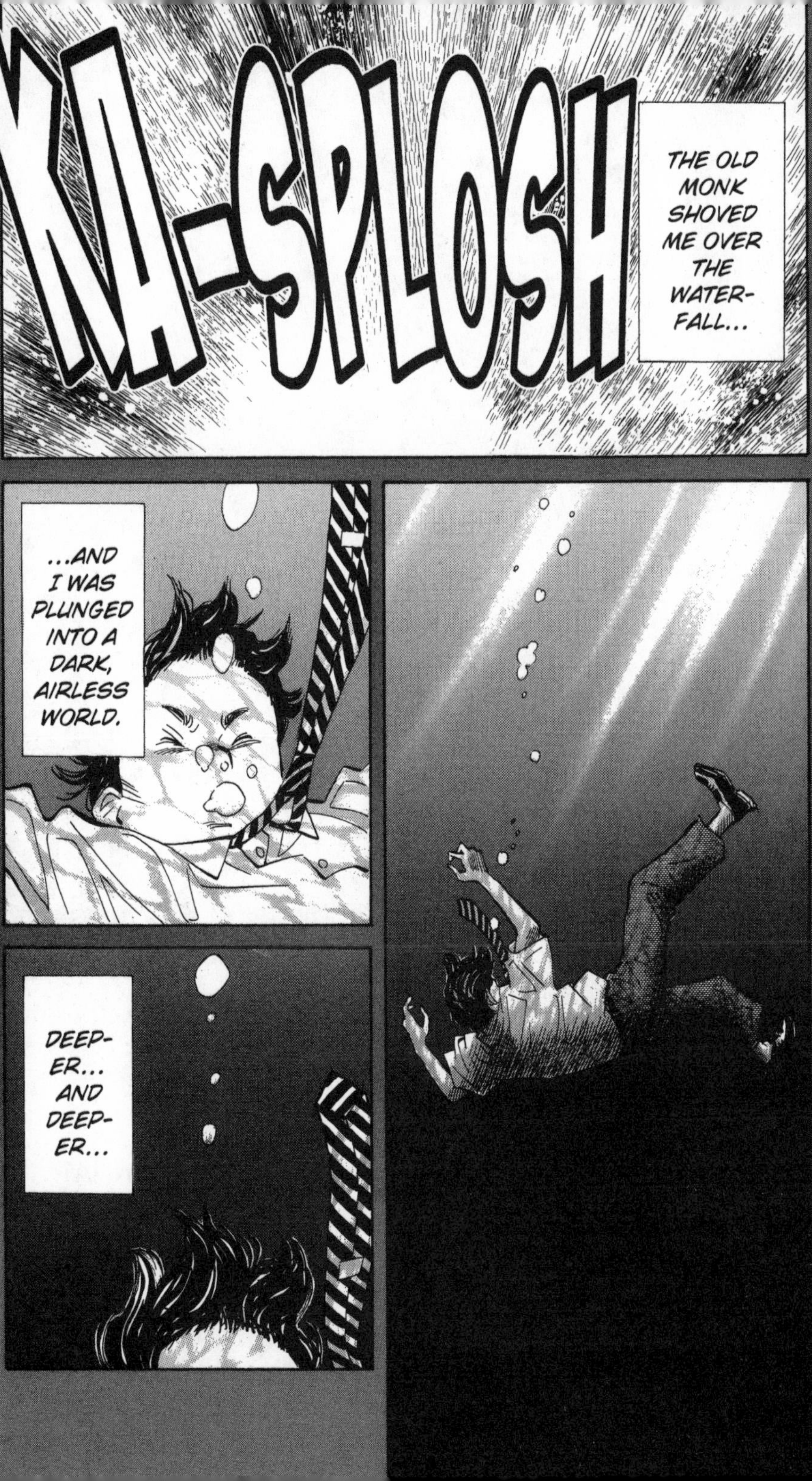
THE OLD MONK SHOVED ME OVER THE WATER-FALL...
KA-SPLOSH
...AND I WAS PLUNGED INTO A DARK, AIRLESS WORLD.
DEEP-ER... AND DEEP-ER...

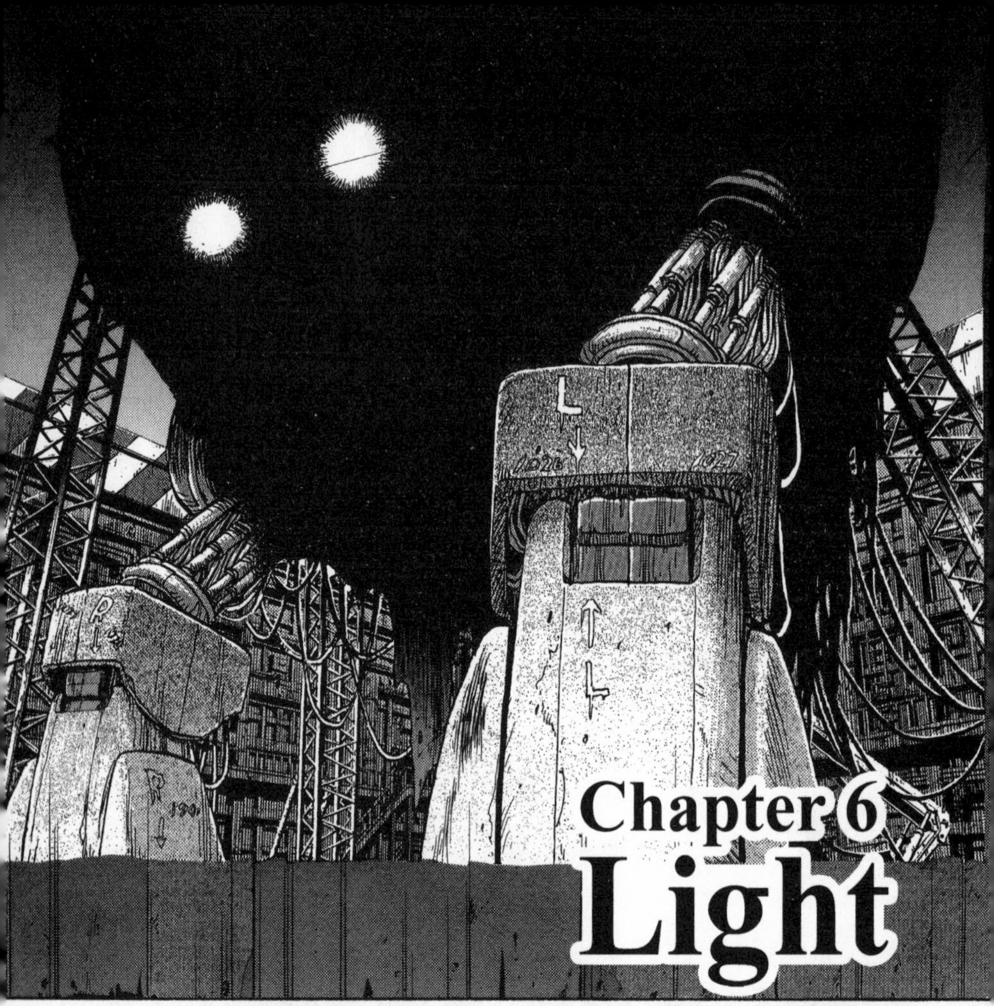
Chapter 6
Light

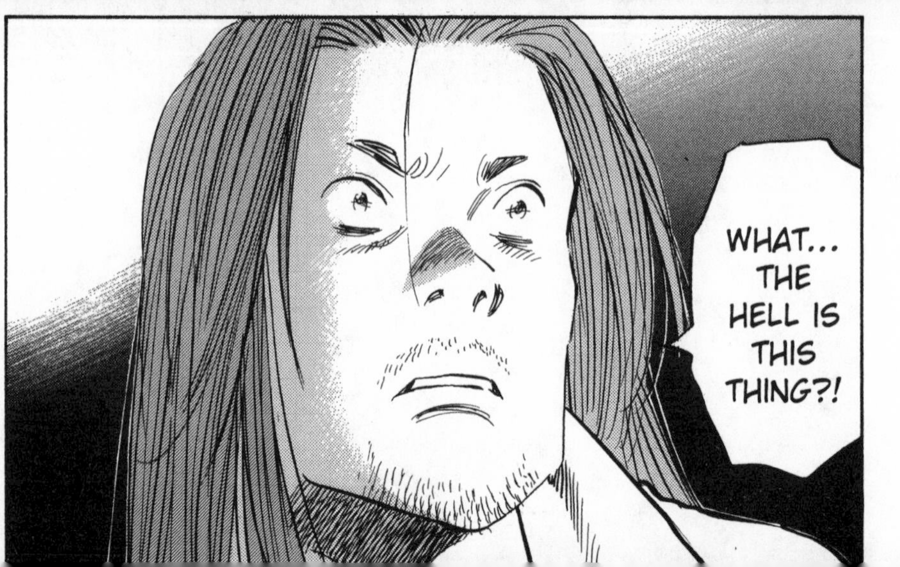
WHAT... THE HELL IS THIS THING?!

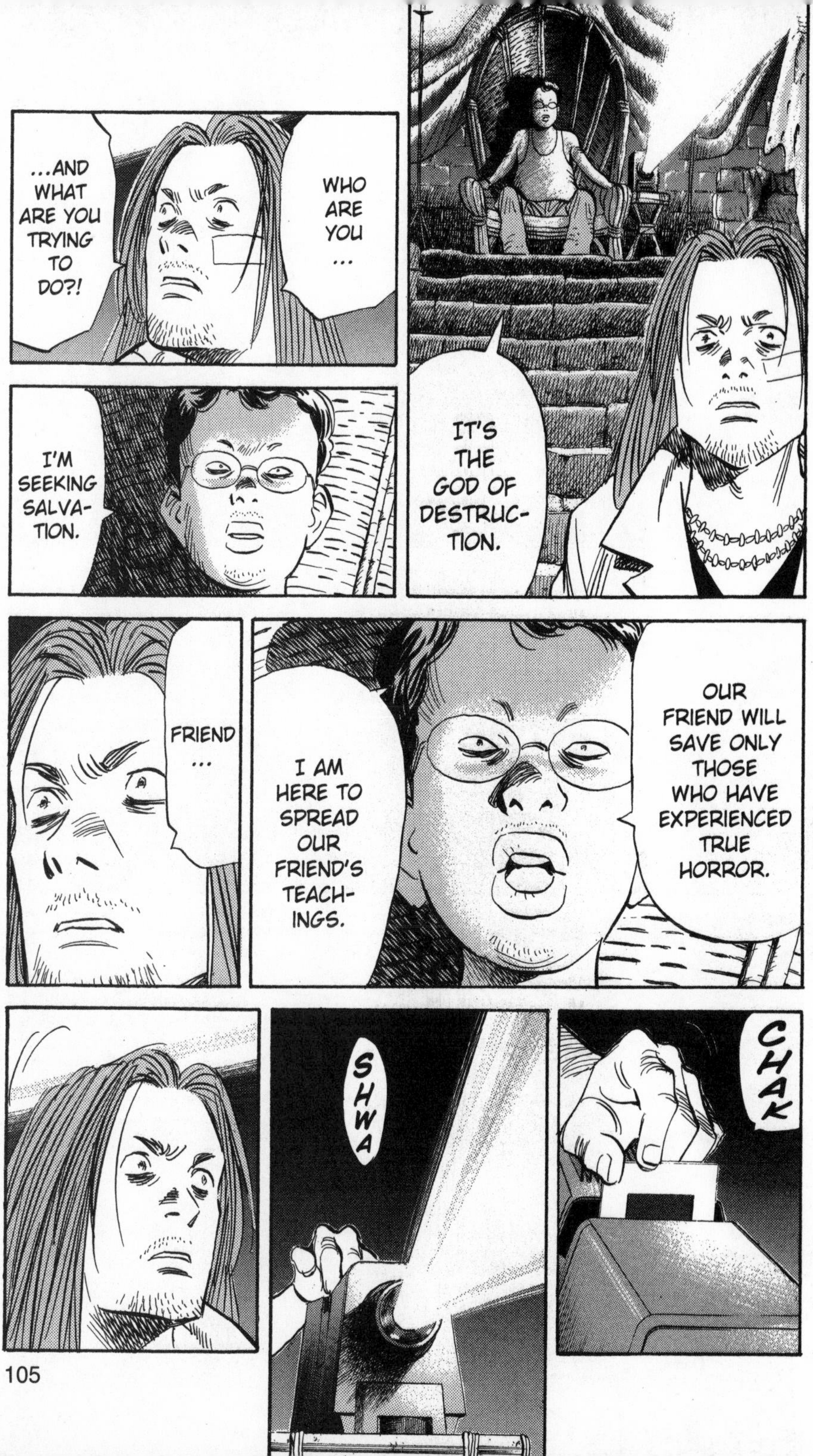
IT'S THE GOD OF DESTRUCTION.
WHO ARE YOU ...
...AND WHAT ARE YOU TRYING TO DO?!
I'M SEEKING SALVATION.
OUR FRIEND WILL SAVE ONLY THOSE WHO HAVE EXPERIENCED TRUE HORROR.
I AM HERE TO SPREAD OUR FRIEND'S TEACHINGS.
FRIEND ...
CHAK
SHWA

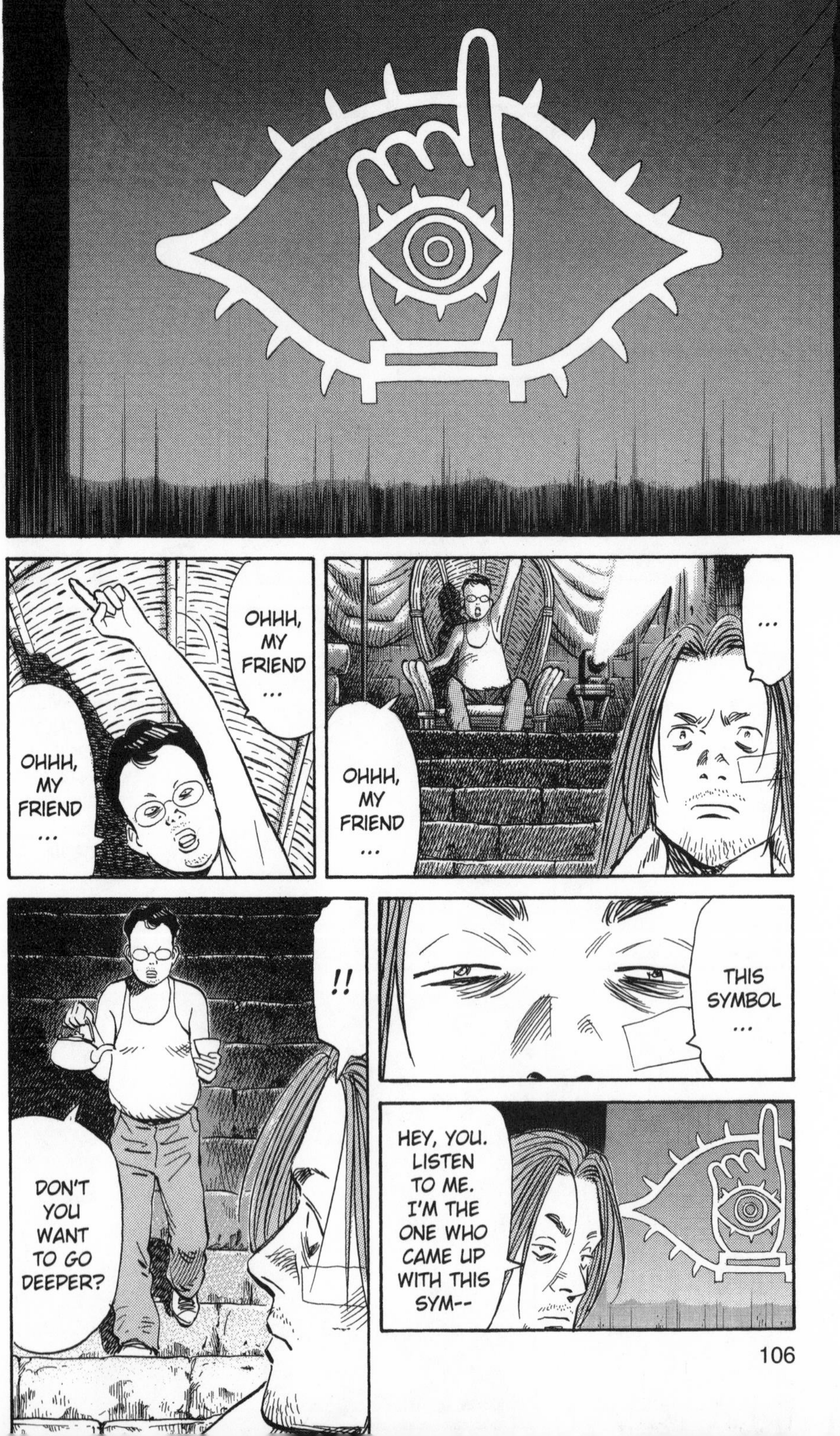
...
OHHH, MY FRIEND ...
OHHH, MY FRIEND ...
OHHH, MY FRIEND ...
THIS SYMBOL ...
HEY, YOU. LISTEN TO ME. I'M THE ONE WHO CAME UP WITH THIS SYM--
!!
DON'T YOU WANT TO GO DEEPER?

RAIN-
BOW
KID...

GWUP

GET TO
KNOW
TRUE
HORROR
...

THIS
STUFF
WORKS!

ZWOK

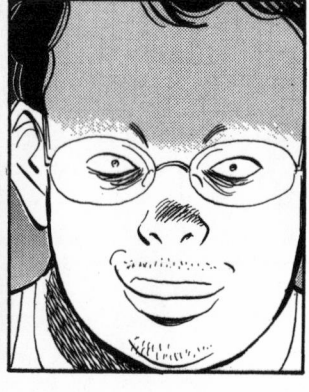

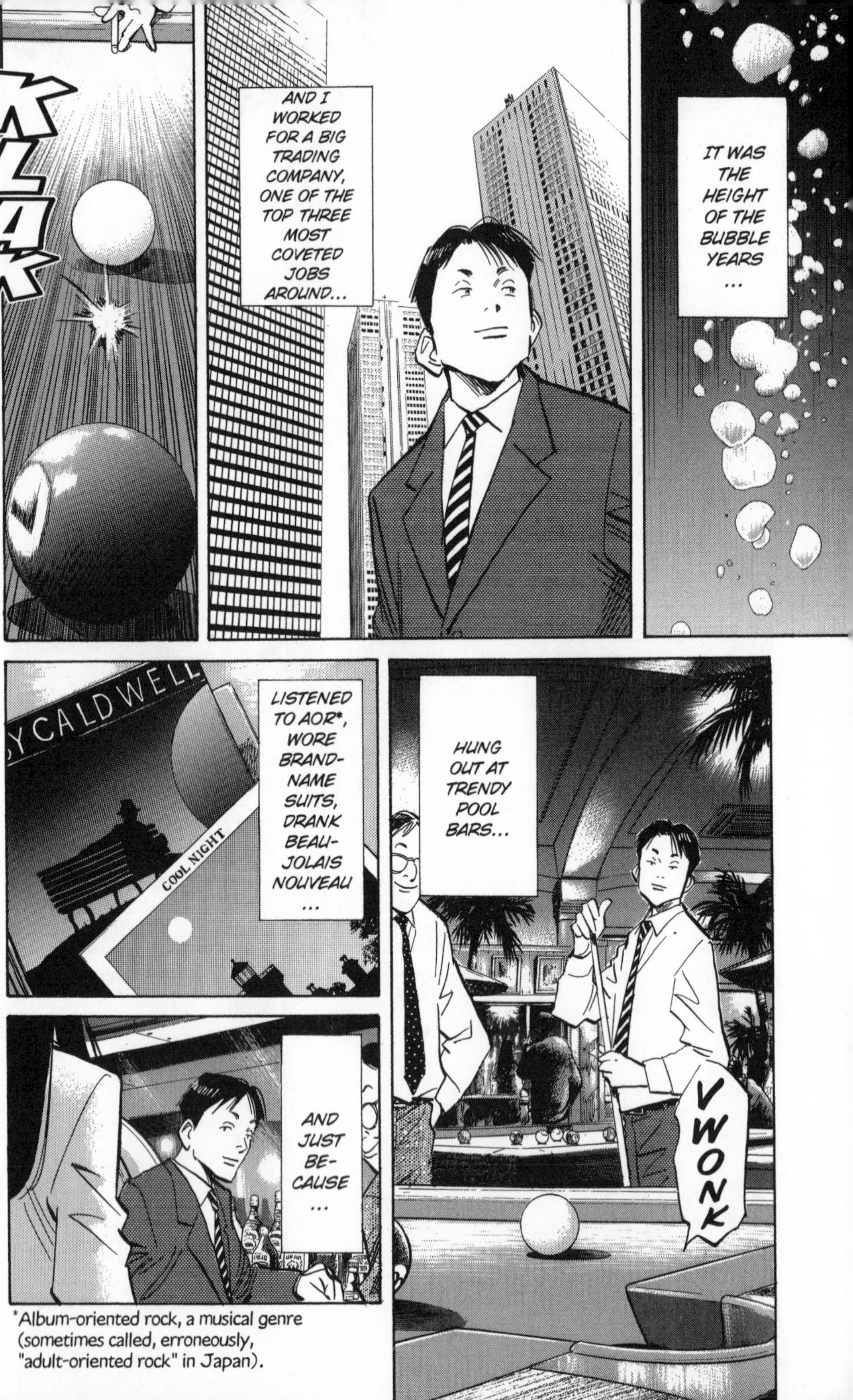
IT WAS THE HEIGHT OF THE BUBBLE YEARS ...
AND I WORKED FOR A BIG TRADING COMPANY, ONE OF THE TOP THREE MOST COVETED JOBS AROUND...
KLAK
HUNG OUT AT TRENDY POOL BARS...
VWONK
CALDWELL
COOL NIGHT
LISTENED TO AOR*, WORE BRAND-NAME SUITS, DRANK BEAU-JOLAIS NOUVEAU ...
AND JUST BE-CAUSE ...

*Album-oriented rock, a musical genre (sometimes called, erroneously, "adult-oriented rock" in Japan).

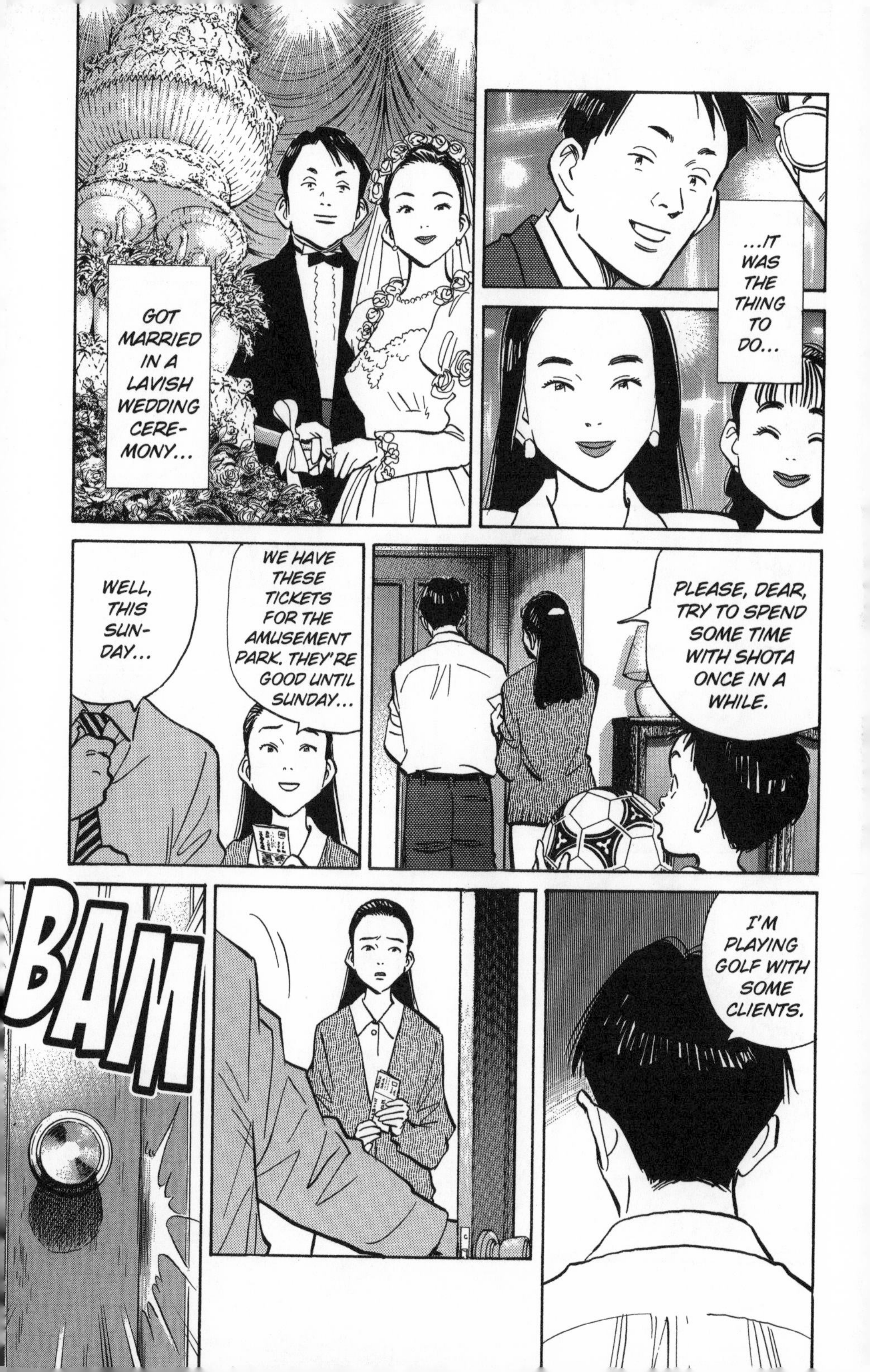
...IT WAS THE THING TO DO...
GOT MARRIED IN A LAVISH WEDDING CERE-MONY...
PLEASE, DEAR, TRY TO SPEND SOME TIME WITH SHOTA ONCE IN A WHILE.
WE HAVE THESE TICKETS FOR THE AMUSEMENT PARK. THEY'RE GOOD UNTIL SUNDAY...
WELL, THIS SUN-DAY...
I'M PLAYING GOLF WITH SOME CLIENTS.
BAM

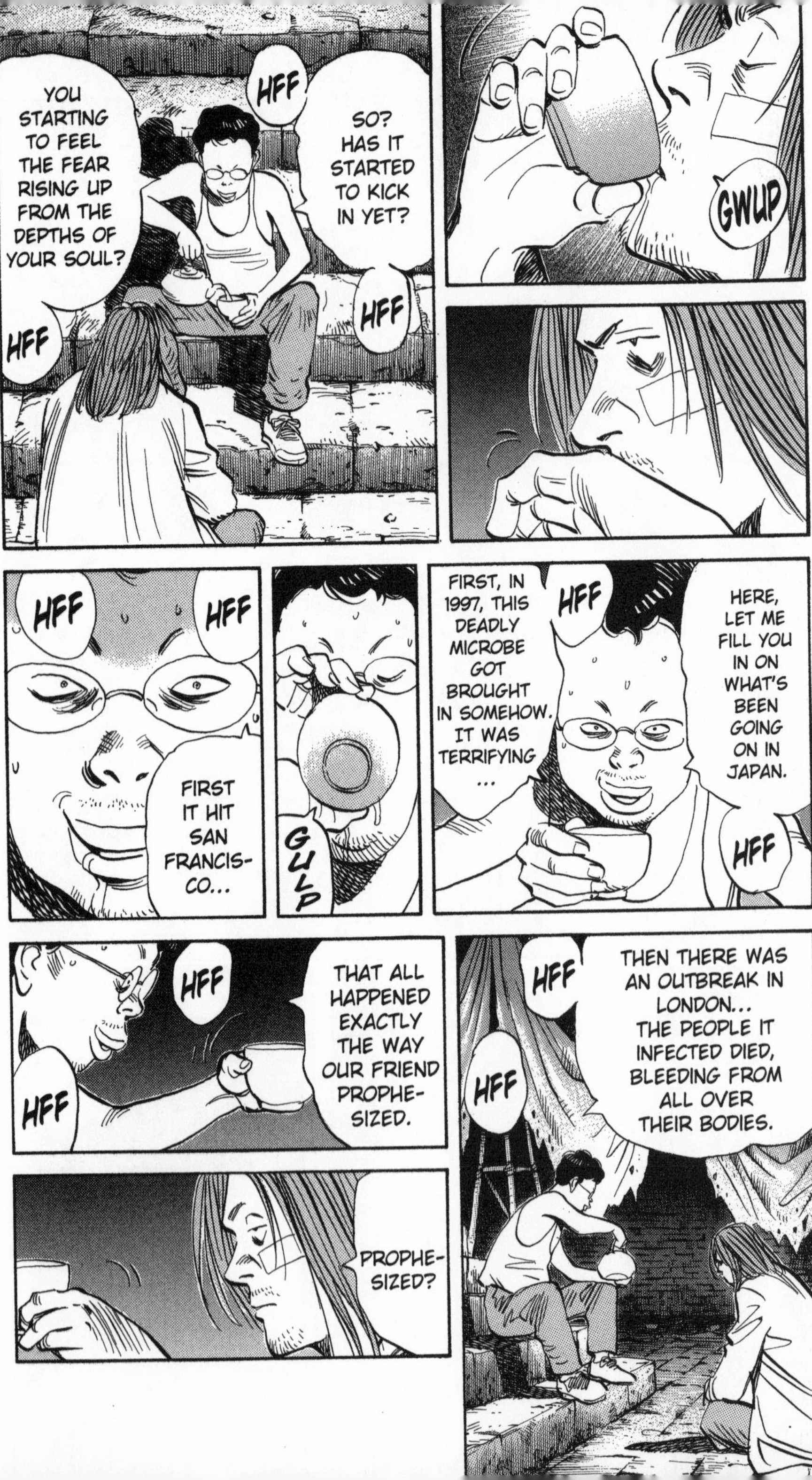
GWUP
HFF
SO? HAS IT STARTED TO KICK IN YET?
HFF
YOU STARTING TO FEEL THE FEAR RISING UP FROM THE DEPTHS OF YOUR SOUL?
HFF
HERE, LET ME FILL YOU IN ON WHAT'S BEEN GOING ON IN JAPAN.
HFF
FIRST, IN 1997, THIS DEADLY MICROBE GOT BROUGHT IN SOMEHOW. IT WAS TERRIFYING ...
HFF
GULP
HFF
HFF
FIRST IT HIT SAN FRANCISCO...
THEN THERE WAS AN OUTBREAK IN LONDON... THE PEOPLE IT INFECTED DIED, BLEEDING FROM ALL OVER THEIR BODIES.
HFF
HFF
THAT ALL HAPPENED EXACTLY THE WAY OUR FRIEND PROPHESIZED.
HFF
HFF
PROPHESIZED?

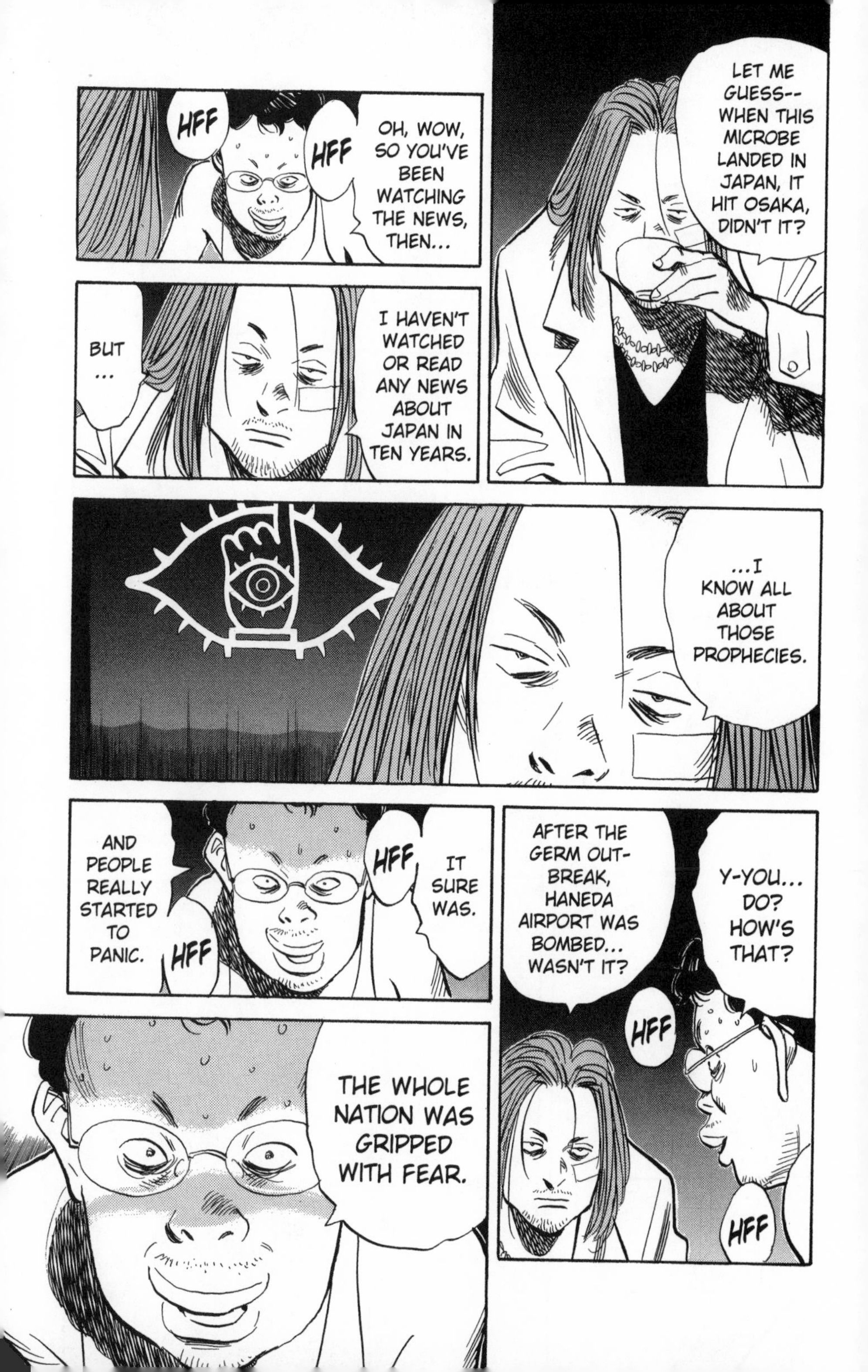
LET ME GUESS-- WHEN THIS MICROBE LANDED IN JAPAN, IT HIT OSAKA, DIDN'T IT?
OH, WOW, SO YOU'VE BEEN WATCHING THE NEWS, THEN...
HFF
HFF
I HAVEN'T WATCHED OR READ ANY NEWS ABOUT JAPAN IN TEN YEARS.
BUT ...
...I KNOW ALL ABOUT THOSE PROPHECIES.
Y-YOU... DO? HOW'S THAT?
AFTER THE GERM OUT-BREAK, HANEDA AIRPORT WAS BOMBED... WASN'T IT?
HFF
HFF
IT SURE WAS.
HFF
AND PEOPLE REALLY STARTED TO PANIC.
HFF
THE WHOLE NATION WAS GRIPPED WITH FEAR.

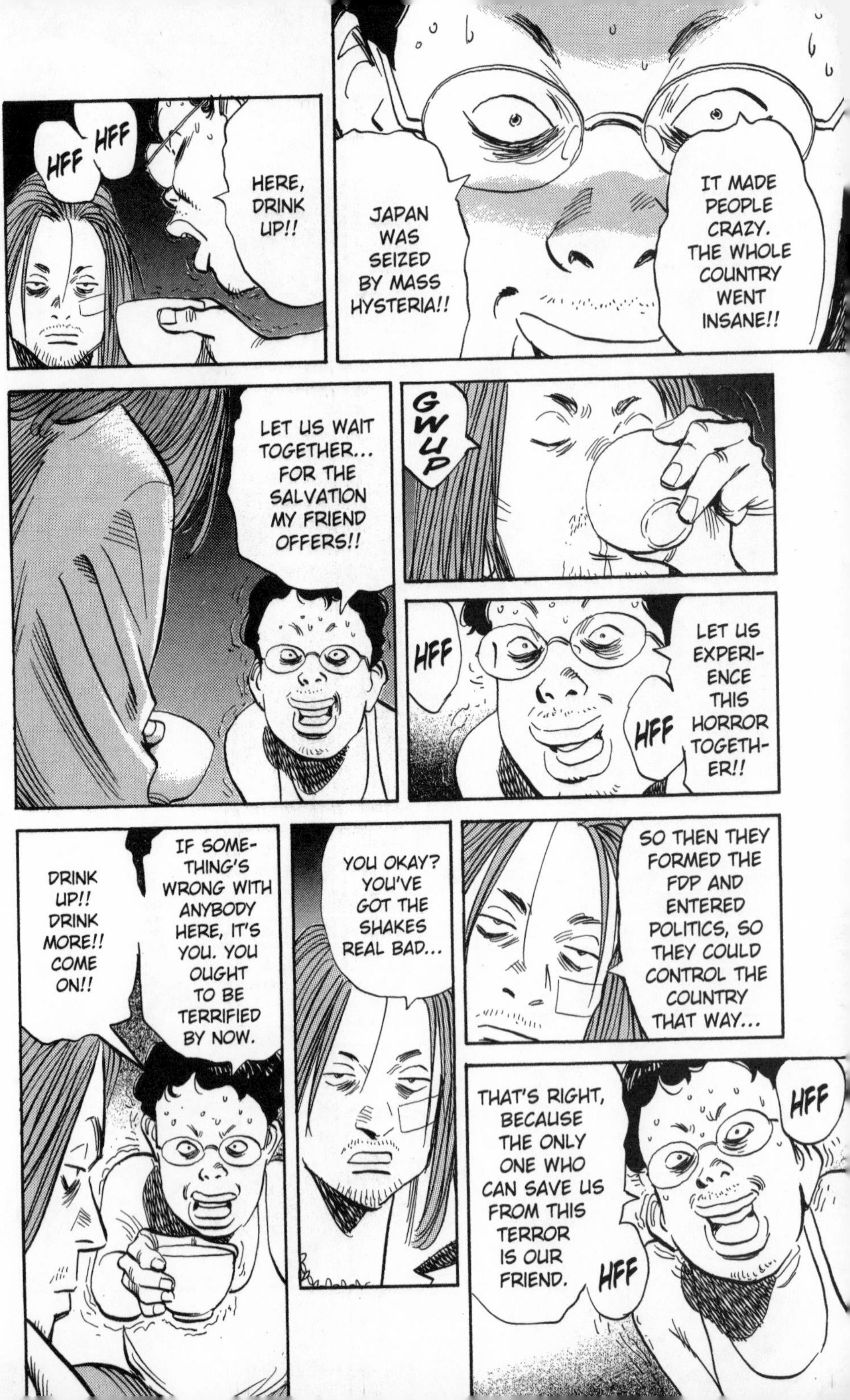
JAPAN WAS SEIZED BY MASS HYSTERIA!!
IT MADE PEOPLE CRAZY. THE WHOLE COUNTRY WENT INSANE!!
HFF HFF
HERE, DRINK UP!!
GWUP
LET US EXPERIENCE THIS HORROR TOGETHER!!
HFF
HFF
LET US WAIT TOGETHER... FOR THE SALVATION MY FRIEND OFFERS!!
SO THEN THEY FORMED THE FDP AND ENTERED POLITICS, SO THEY COULD CONTROL THE COUNTRY THAT WAY...
HFF
THAT'S RIGHT, BECAUSE THE ONLY ONE WHO CAN SAVE US FROM THIS TERROR IS OUR FRIEND.
HFF
YOU OKAY? YOU'VE GOT THE SHAKES REAL BAD...
IF SOMETHING'S WRONG WITH ANYBODY HERE, IT'S YOU. YOU OUGHT TO BE TERRIFIED BY NOW.
DRINK UP!! DRINK MORE!! COME ON!!

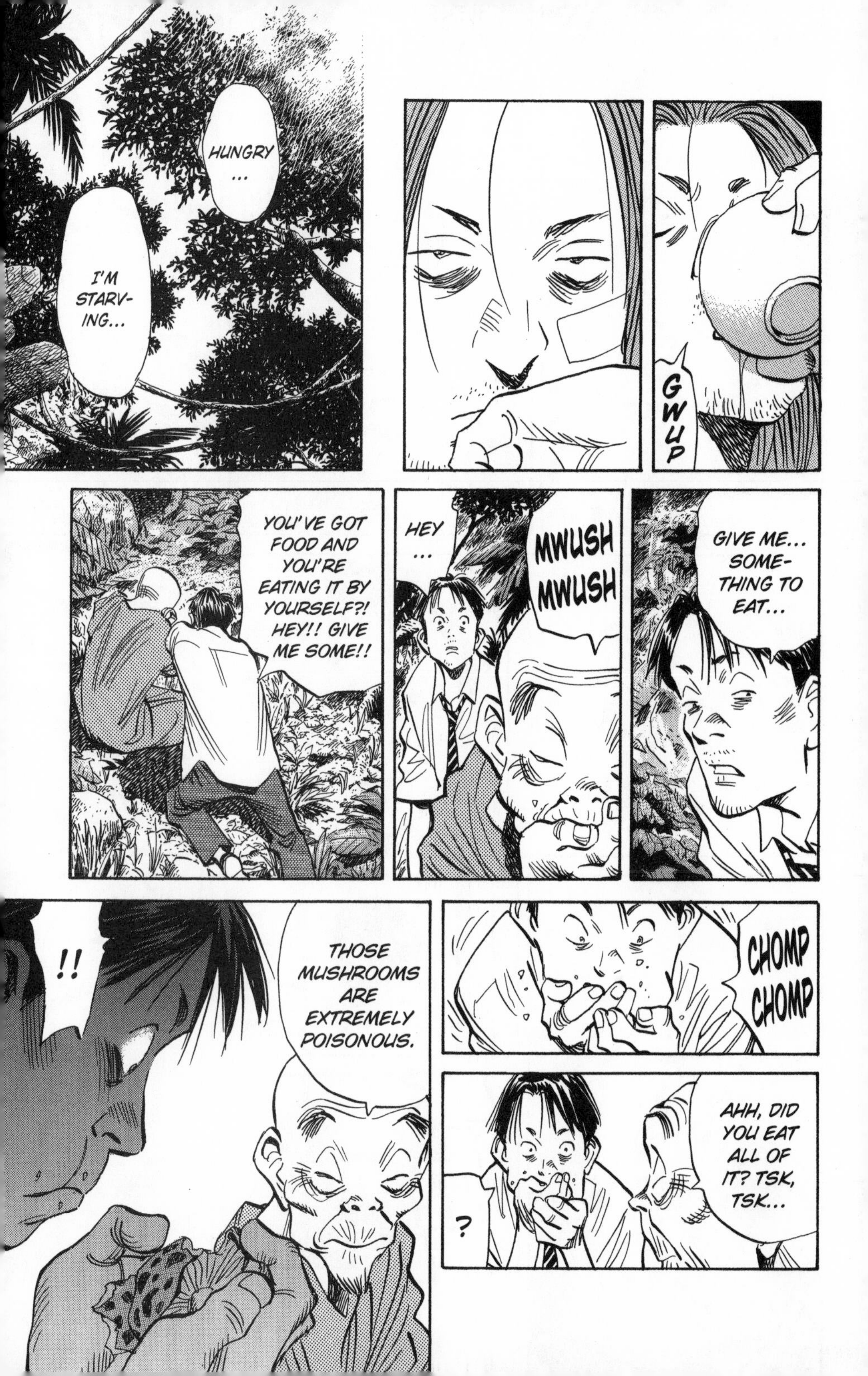
GWUP
HUNGRY...
I'M STARVING...
GIVE ME... SOMETHING TO EAT...
MWUSH MWUSH
HEY...
YOU'VE GOT FOOD AND YOU'RE EATING IT BY YOURSELF?! HEY!! GIVE ME SOME!!
CHOMP CHOMP
AHH, DID YOU EAT ALL OF IT? TSK, TSK...
?
THOSE MUSHROOMS ARE EXTREMELY POISONOUS.
!!

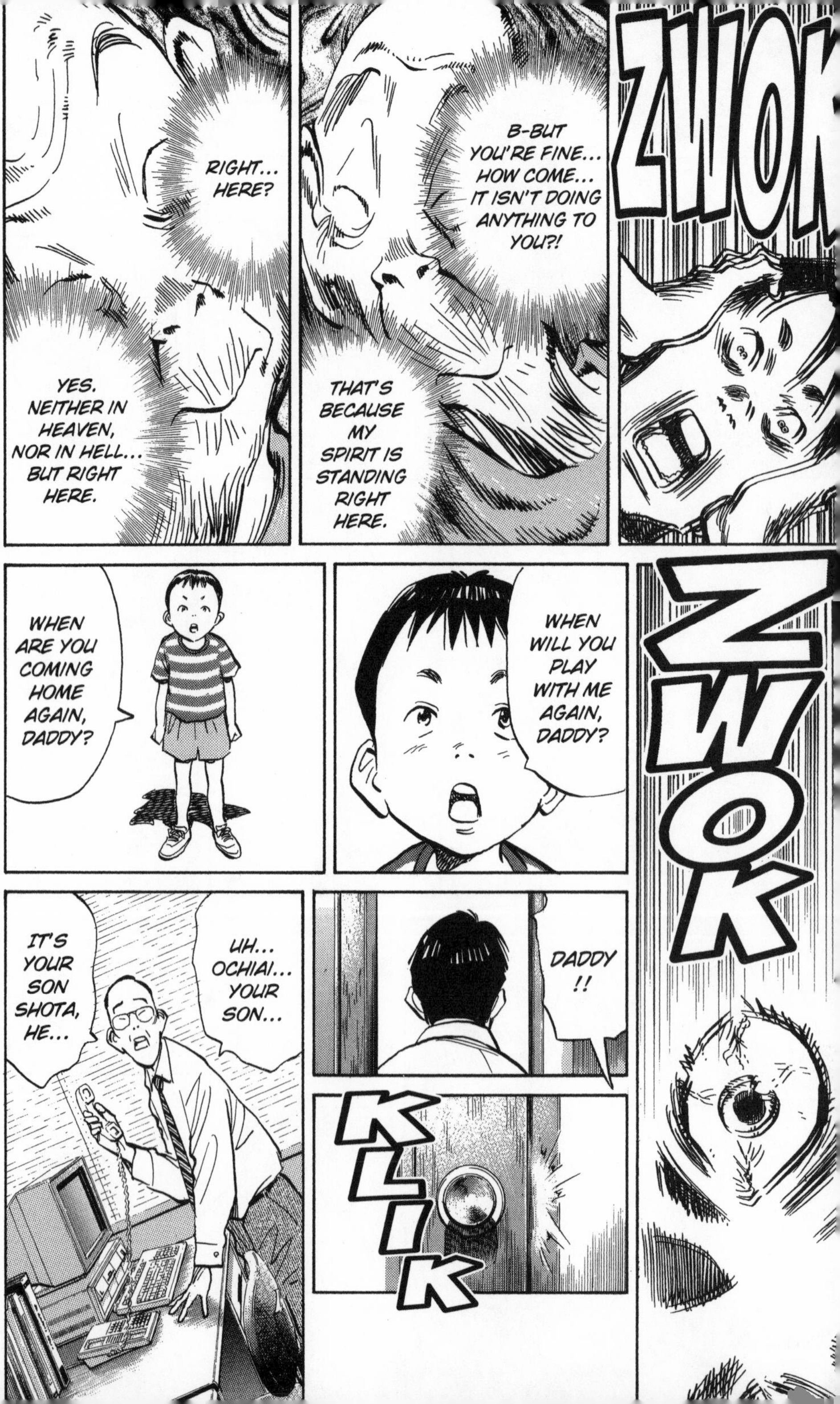
ZWOK
B-BUT YOU'RE FINE... HOW COME... IT ISN'T DOING ANYTHING TO YOU?!
THAT'S BECAUSE MY SPIRIT IS STANDING RIGHT HERE.
RIGHT... HERE?
YES. NEITHER IN HEAVEN, NOR IN HELL... BUT RIGHT HERE.
ZWOK
WHEN WILL YOU PLAY WITH ME AGAIN, DADDY?
WHEN ARE YOU COMING HOME AGAIN, DADDY?
DADDY !!
KLIK
UH... OCHIAI... YOUR SON...
IT'S YOUR SON SHOTA, HE...

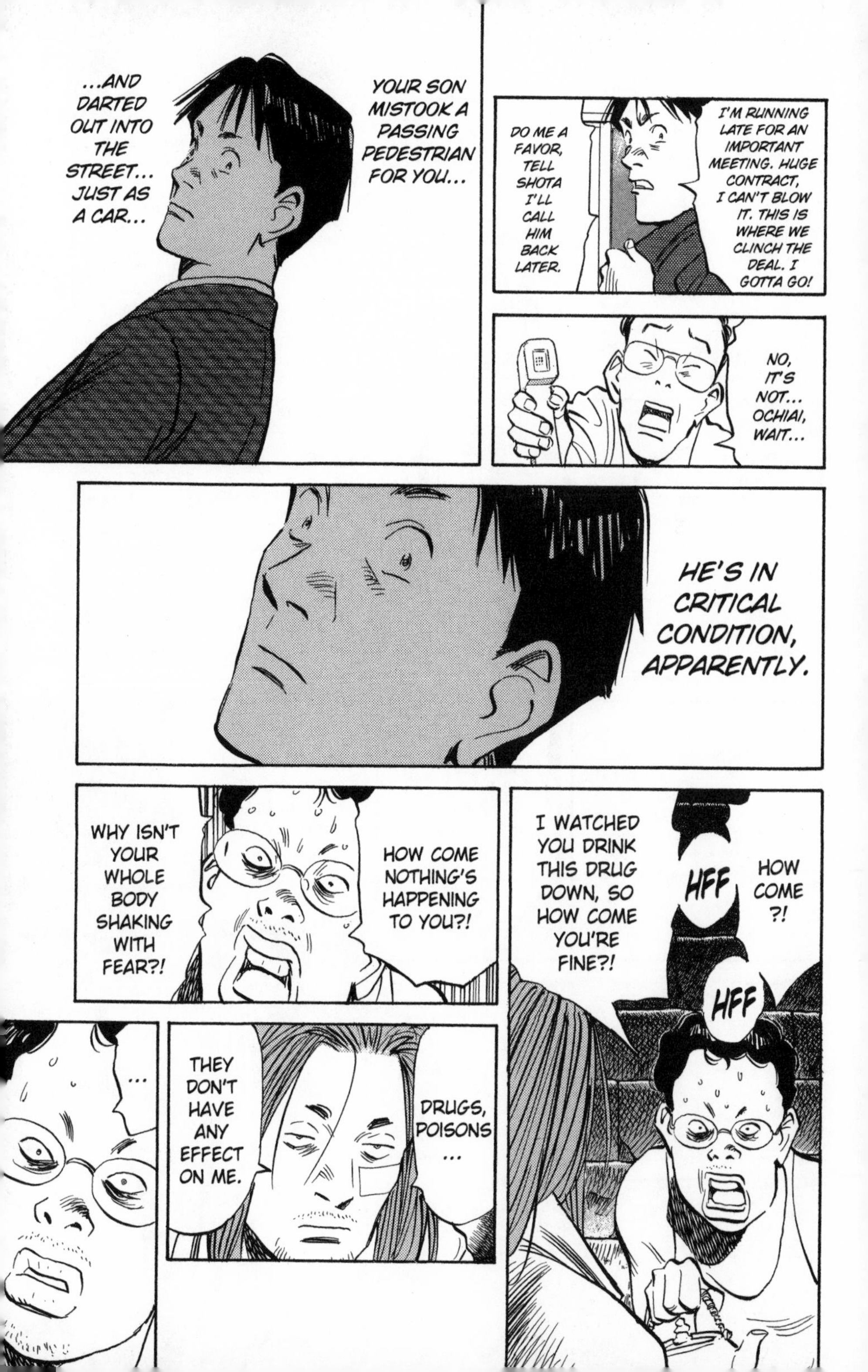
I'M RUNNING LATE FOR AN IMPORTANT MEETING. HUGE CONTRACT, I CAN'T BLOW IT. THIS IS WHERE WE CLINCH THE DEAL. I GOTTA GO!
DO ME A FAVOR, TELL SHOTA I'LL CALL HIM BACK LATER.
NO, IT'S NOT... OCHIAI, WAIT...
YOUR SON MISTOOK A PASSING PEDESTRIAN FOR YOU...
...AND DARTED OUT INTO THE STREET... JUST AS A CAR...
HE'S IN CRITICAL CONDITION, APPARENTLY.
HOW COME ?!
HFF
I WATCHED YOU DRINK THIS DRUG DOWN, SO HOW COME YOU'RE FINE?!
HFF
HOW COME NOTHING'S HAPPENING TO YOU?!
WHY ISN'T YOUR WHOLE BODY SHAKING WITH FEAR?!
DRUGS, POISONS...
THEY DON'T HAVE ANY EFFECT ON ME.
...

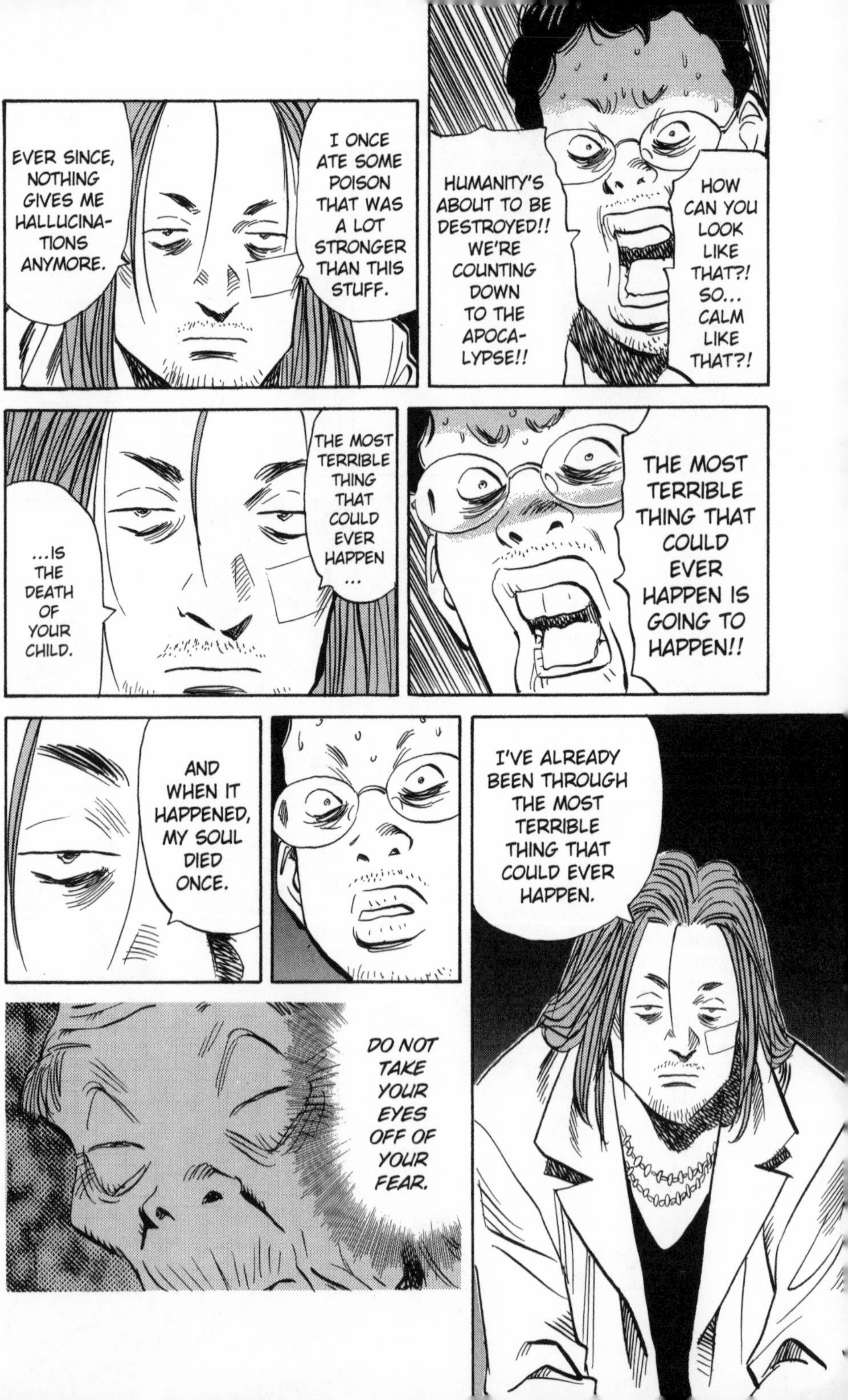
HOW CAN YOU LOOK LIKE THAT?! SO... CALM LIKE THAT?!
HUMANITY'S ABOUT TO BE DESTROYED!! WE'RE COUNTING DOWN TO THE APOCA-LYPSE!!
I ONCE ATE SOME POISON THAT WAS A LOT STRONGER THAN THIS STUFF.
EVER SINCE, NOTHING GIVES ME HALLUCINA-TIONS ANYMORE.
THE MOST TERRIBLE THING THAT COULD EVER HAPPEN IS GOING TO HAPPEN!!
THE MOST TERRIBLE THING THAT COULD EVER HAPPEN...
...IS THE DEATH OF YOUR CHILD.
I'VE ALREADY BEEN THROUGH THE MOST TERRIBLE THING THAT COULD EVER HAPPEN.
AND WHEN IT HAPPENED, MY SOUL DIED ONCE.
DO NOT TAKE YOUR EYES OFF OF YOUR FEAR.

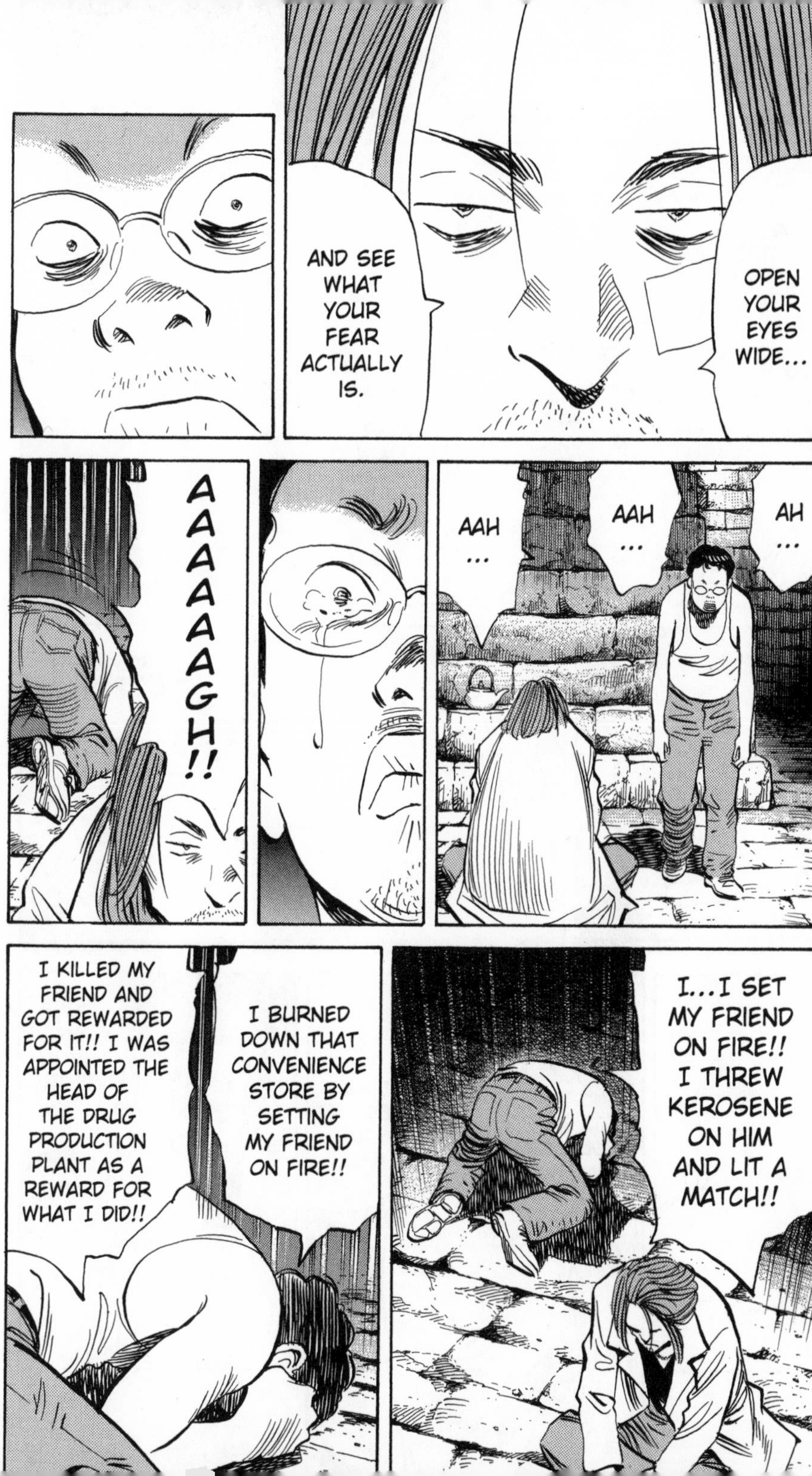
OPEN YOUR EYES WIDE...
AND SEE WHAT YOUR FEAR ACTUALLY IS.
AH ...
AAH ...
AAH ...
AAAAAAGH!!
I...I SET MY FRIEND ON FIRE!! I THREW KEROSENE ON HIM AND LIT A MATCH!!
I BURNED DOWN THAT CONVENIENCE STORE BY SETTING MY FRIEND ON FIRE!!
I KILLED MY FRIEND AND GOT REWARDED FOR IT!! I WAS APPOINTED THE HEAD OF THE DRUG PRODUCTION PLANT AS A REWARD FOR WHAT I DID!!

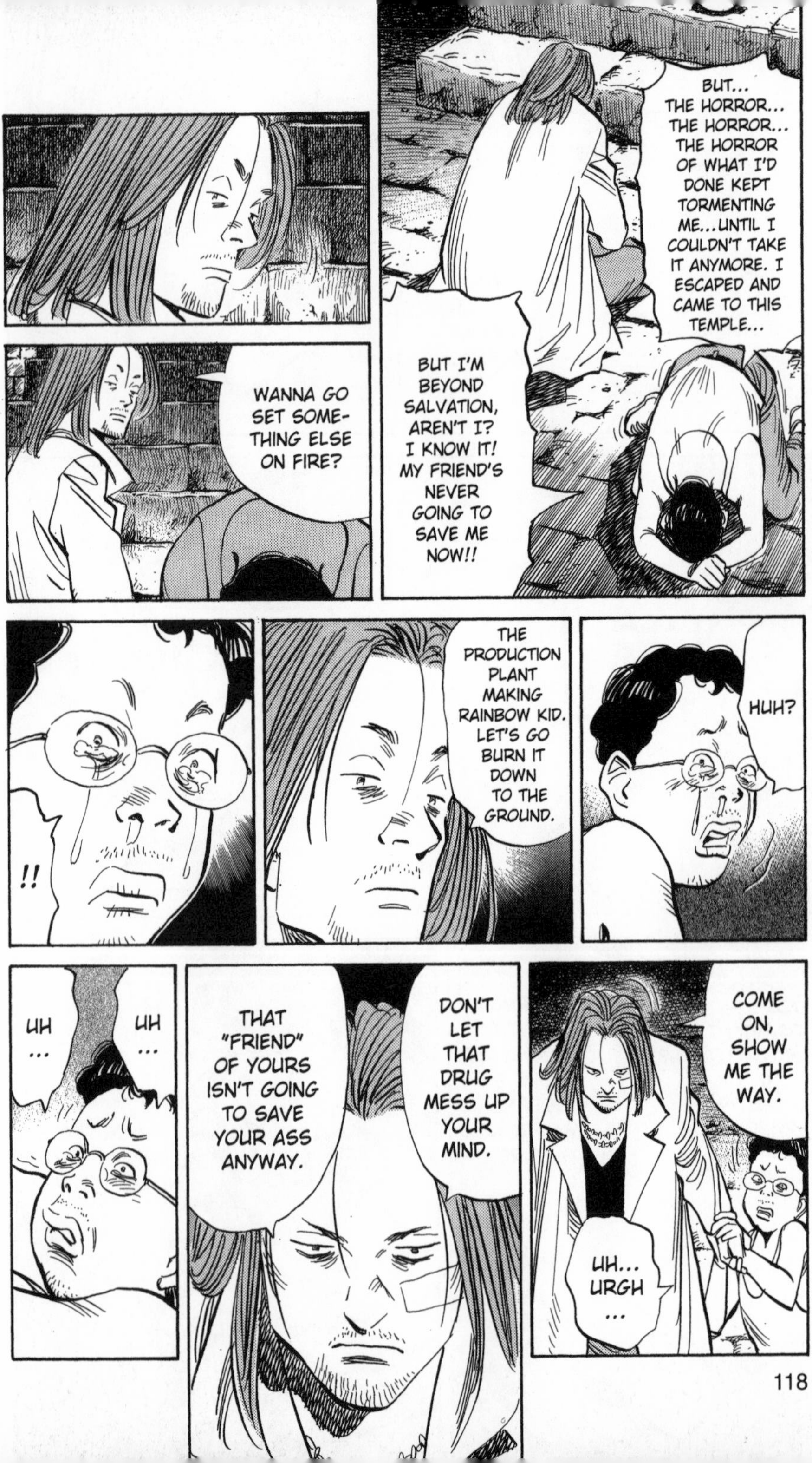
BUT... THE HORROR... THE HORROR... THE HORROR OF WHAT I'D DONE KEPT TORMENTING ME...UNTIL I COULDN'T TAKE IT ANYMORE. I ESCAPED AND CAME TO THIS TEMPLE...
BUT I'M BEYOND SALVATION, AREN'T I? I KNOW IT! MY FRIEND'S NEVER GOING TO SAVE ME NOW!!
WANNA GO SET SOME-THING ELSE ON FIRE?
HUH?
THE PRODUCTION PLANT MAKING RAINBOW KID. LET'S GO BURN IT DOWN TO THE GROUND.
!!
COME ON, SHOW ME THE WAY.
UH... URGH ...
DON'T LET THAT DRUG MESS UP YOUR MIND.
THAT "FRIEND" OF YOURS ISN'T GOING TO SAVE YOUR ASS ANYWAY.
UH ...
UH ...

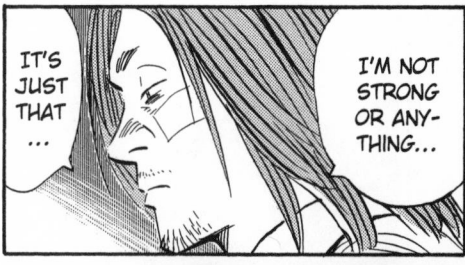

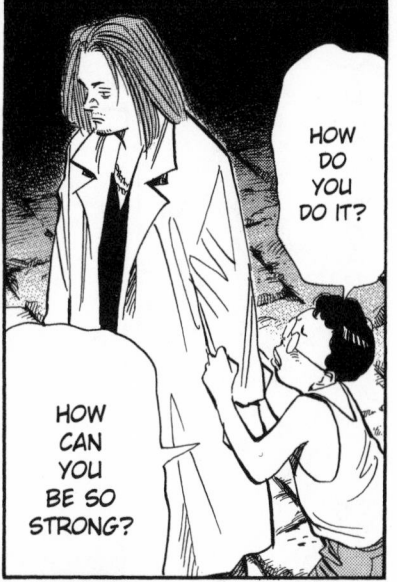

HOW DO YOU DO IT?
HOW CAN YOU BE SO STRONG?
I'M NOT STRONG OR ANY-THING...
IT'S JUST THAT ...
THAT TIME... WHEN I WAS TRYING TO CONQUER MY FEAR AND GOT PUSHED OVER THE WATER-FALL...
...I WAS PLUNGED INTO THIS DARK, AIRLESS WORLD, SINKING DEEPER AND DEEPER...
AND I THOUGHT I'D KEEP SINKING FOREVER, ALL THE WAY DOWN TO HELL...
BUT I LOOKED UP-WARD ...
AND I SAW LIGHT SHINING.

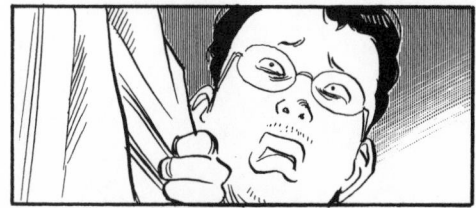

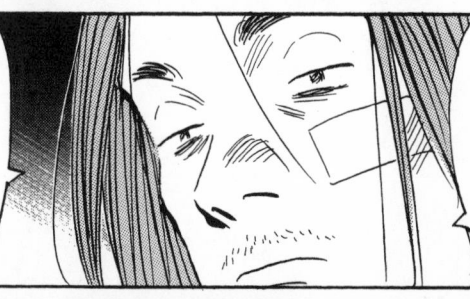

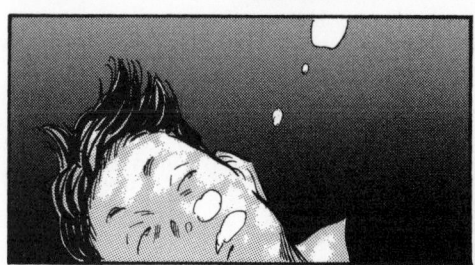

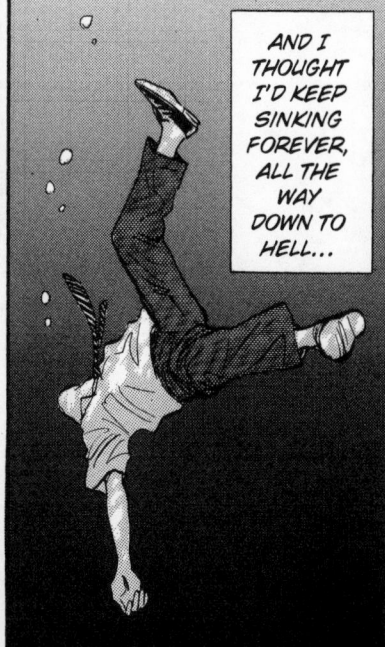

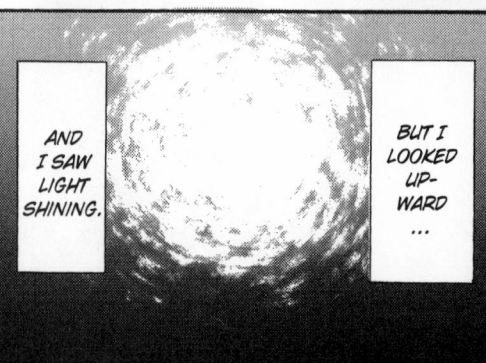

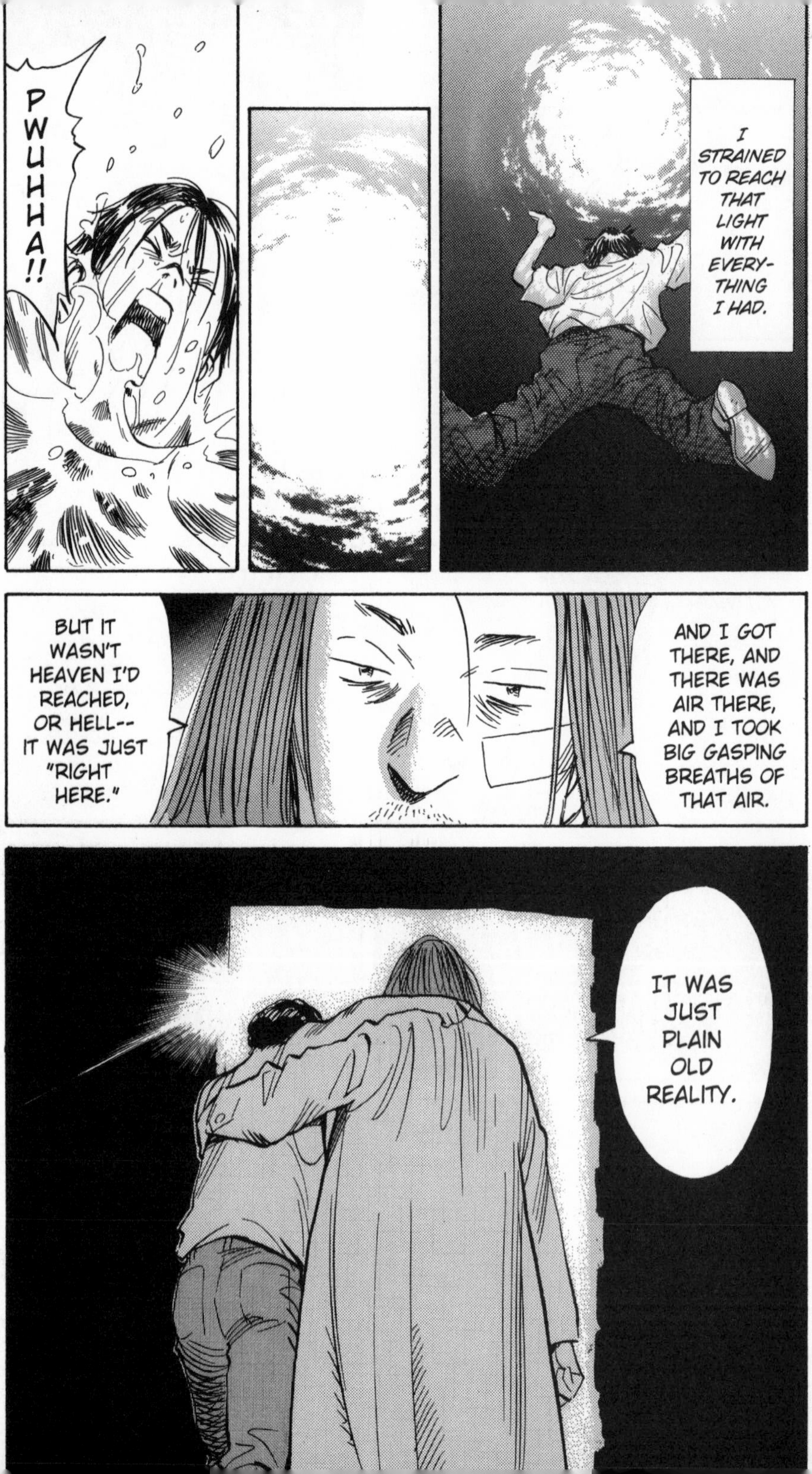
I STRAINED TO REACH THAT LIGHT WITH EVERY-THING I HAD.
PWUHHA!!
AND I GOT THERE, AND THERE WAS AIR THERE, AND I TOOK BIG GASPING BREATHS OF THAT AIR.
BUT IT WASN'T HEAVEN I'D REACHED, OR HELL-- IT WAS JUST "RIGHT HERE."
IT WAS JUST PLAIN OLD REALITY.

Chapter 7 Blowup

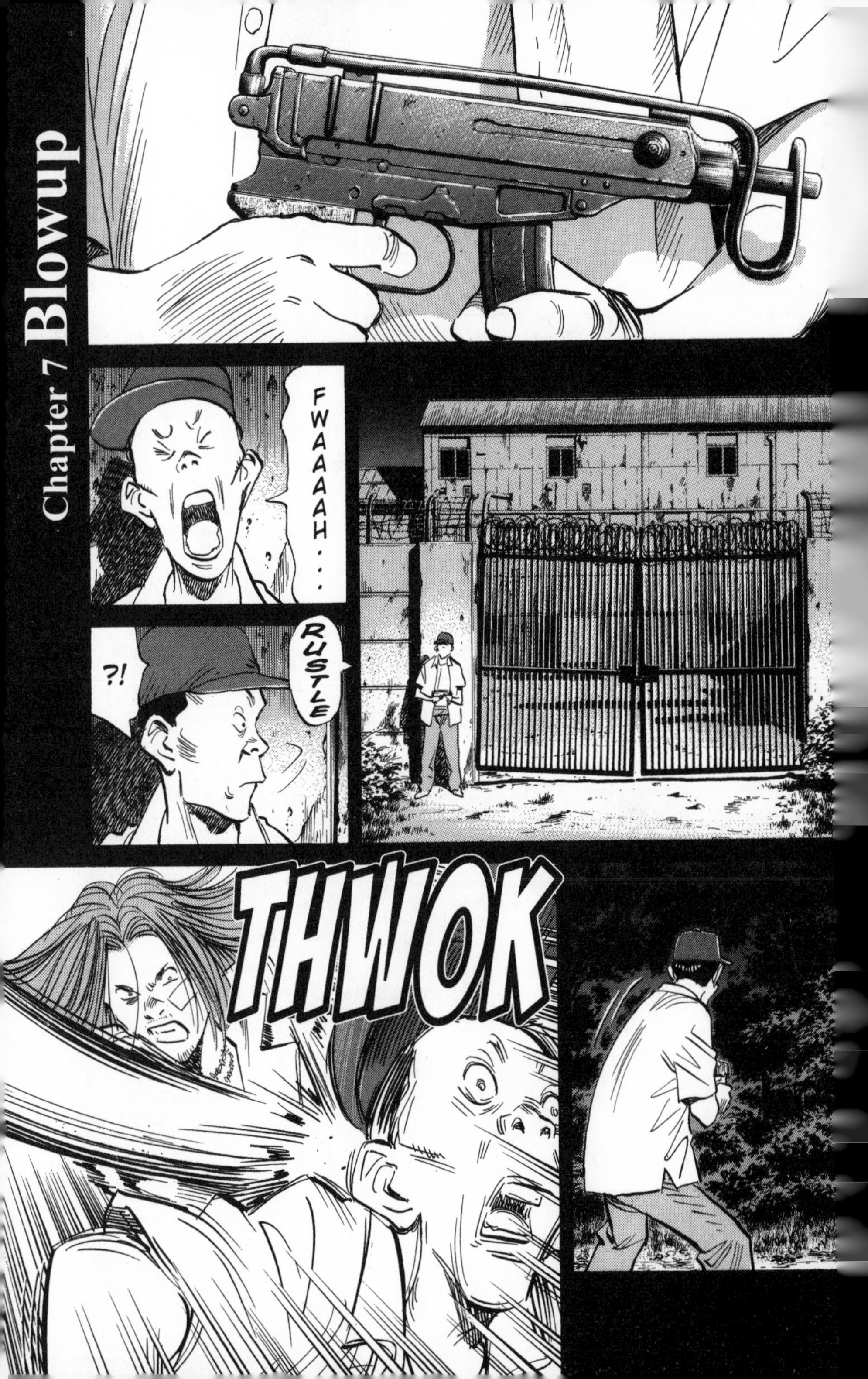
FWAAAAH...
RUSTLE
?!
THWOK

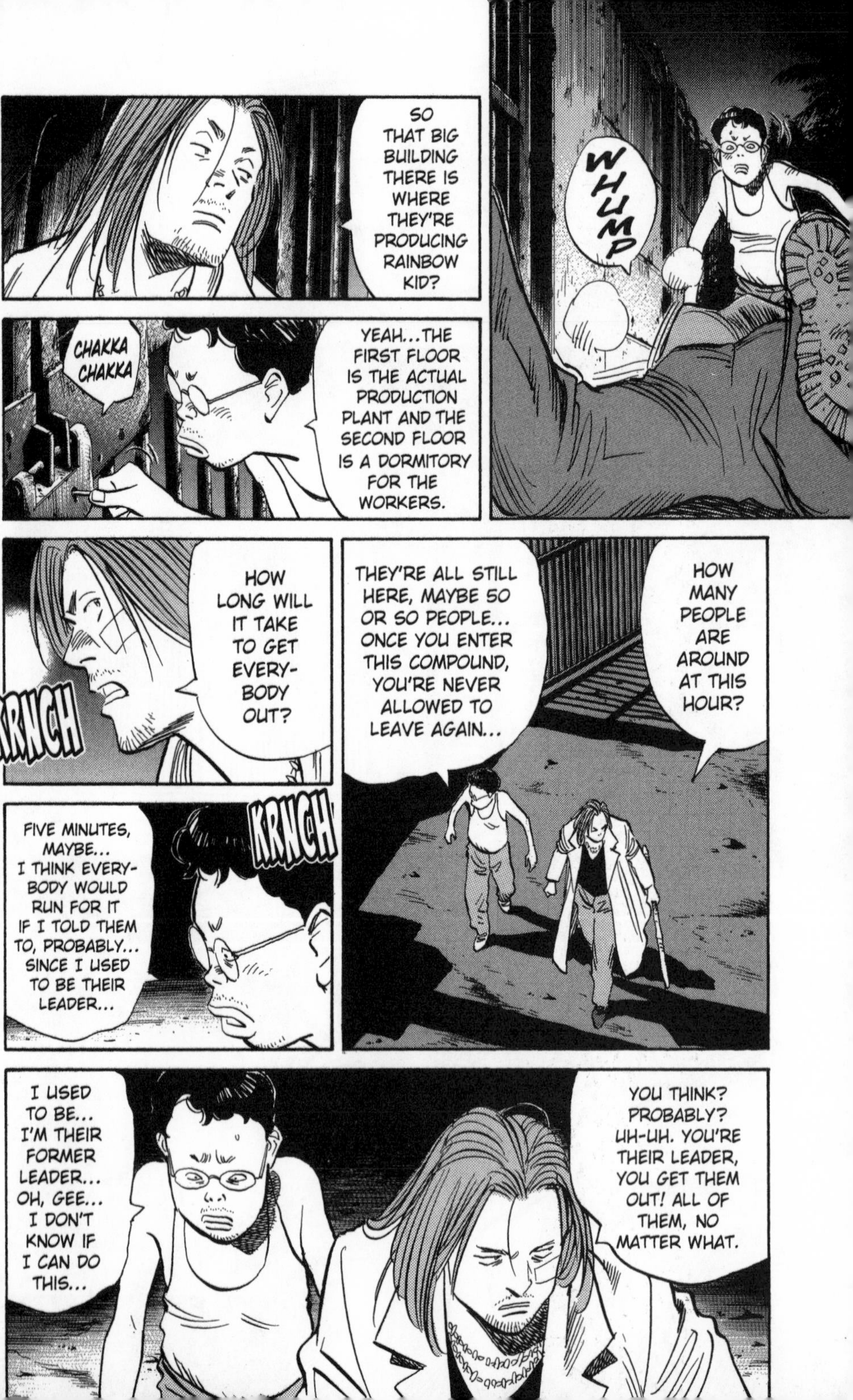
WHUMP
SO THAT BIG BUILDING THERE IS WHERE THEY'RE PRODUCING RAINBOW KID?
YEAH...THE FIRST FLOOR IS THE ACTUAL PRODUCTION PLANT AND THE SECOND FLOOR IS A DORMITORY FOR THE WORKERS.
CHAKKA CHAKKA
HOW MANY PEOPLE ARE AROUND AT THIS HOUR?
THEY'RE ALL STILL HERE, MAYBE 50 OR SO PEOPLE... ONCE YOU ENTER THIS COMPOUND, YOU'RE NEVER ALLOWED TO LEAVE AGAIN...
HOW LONG WILL IT TAKE TO GET EVERY-BODY OUT?
KRNCH
KRNCH
FIVE MINUTES, MAYBE... I THINK EVERY-BODY WOULD RUN FOR IT IF I TOLD THEM TO, PROBABLY... SINCE I USED TO BE THEIR LEADER...
YOU THINK? PROBABLY? UH-UH. YOU'RE THEIR LEADER, YOU GET THEM OUT! ALL OF THEM, NO MATTER WHAT.
I USED TO BE... I'M THEIR FORMER LEADER... OH, GEE... I DON'T KNOW IF I CAN DO THIS...

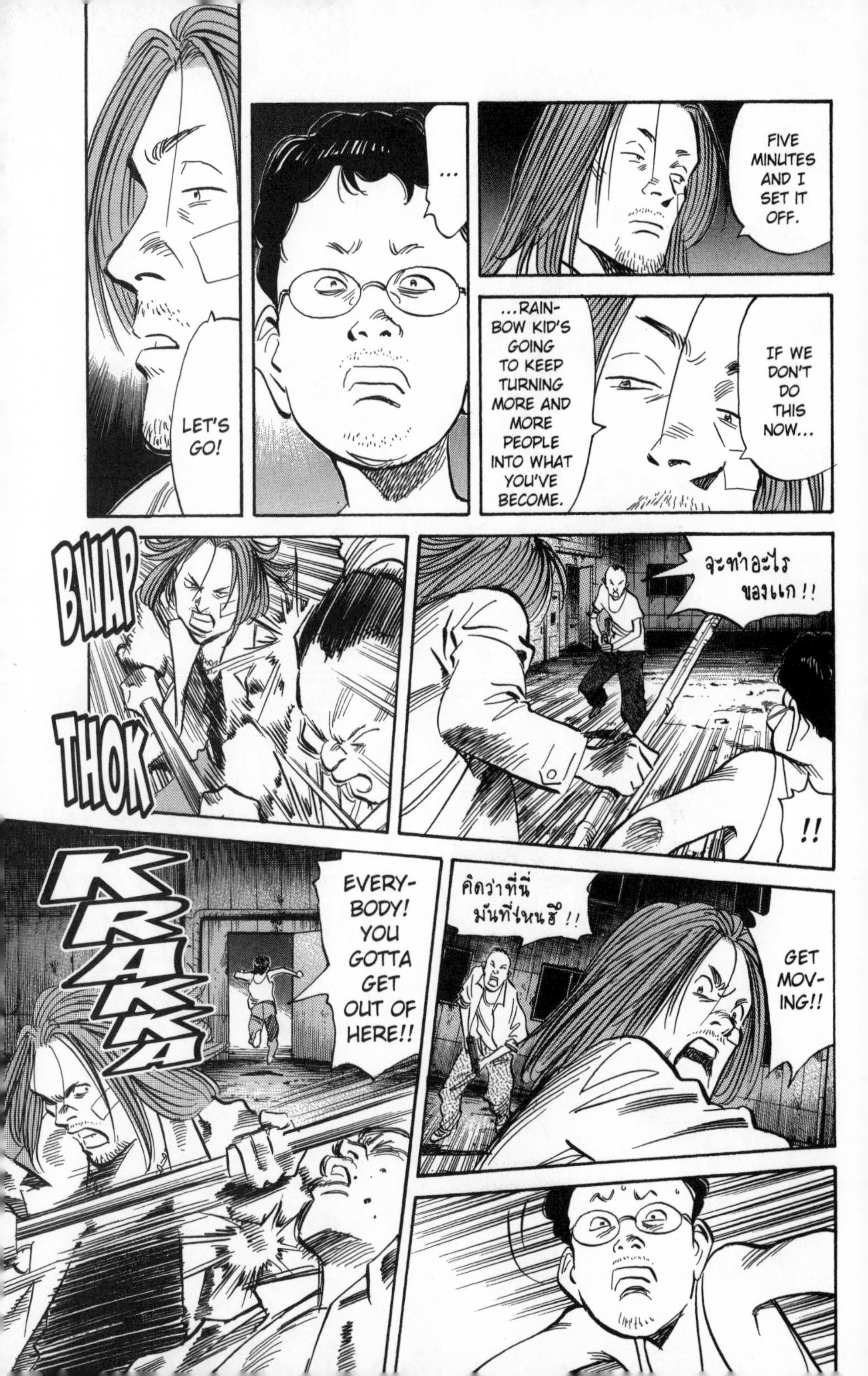
FIVE MINUTES AND I SET IT OFF.
IF WE DON'T DO THIS NOW...
...RAIN-BOW KID'S GOING TO KEEP TURNING MORE AND MORE PEOPLE INTO WHAT YOU'VE BECOME.
...
LET'S GO!
จะทำอะไรของแก !!
!!
BWAP
THOK
คิดว่าที่นี่มันที่ไหนฮึ !!
GET MOV-ING!!
EVERY-BODY! YOU GOTTA GET OUT OF HERE!!
KRAKKA

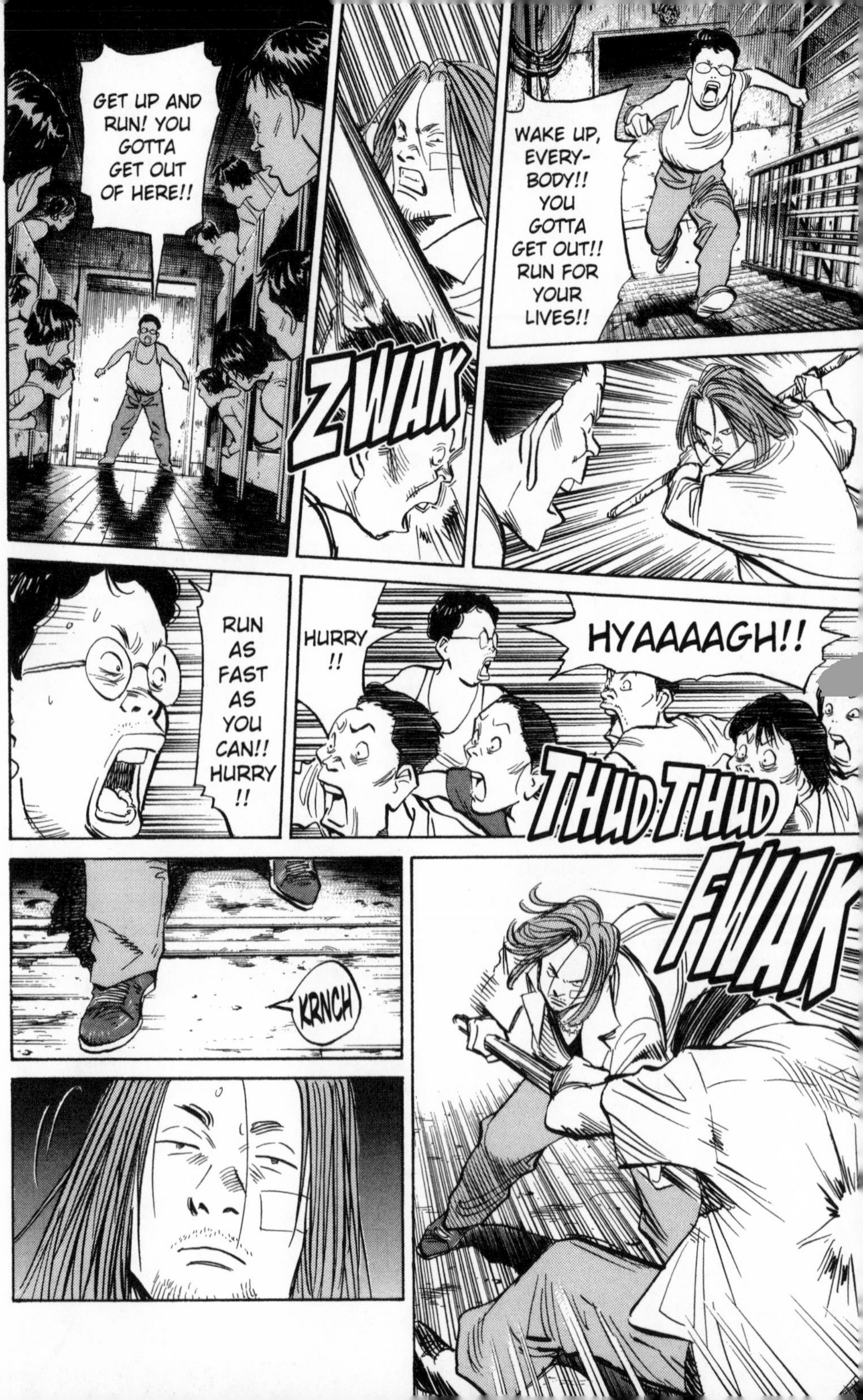
WAKE UP, EVERY-BODY!! YOU GOTTA GET OUT!! RUN FOR YOUR LIVES!!
ZWAK
GET UP AND RUN! YOU GOTTA GET OUT OF HERE!!
HYAAAAGH!!
HURRY!!
THUD THUD
RUN AS FAST AS YOU CAN!! HURRY!!
FWAK
KRNCH

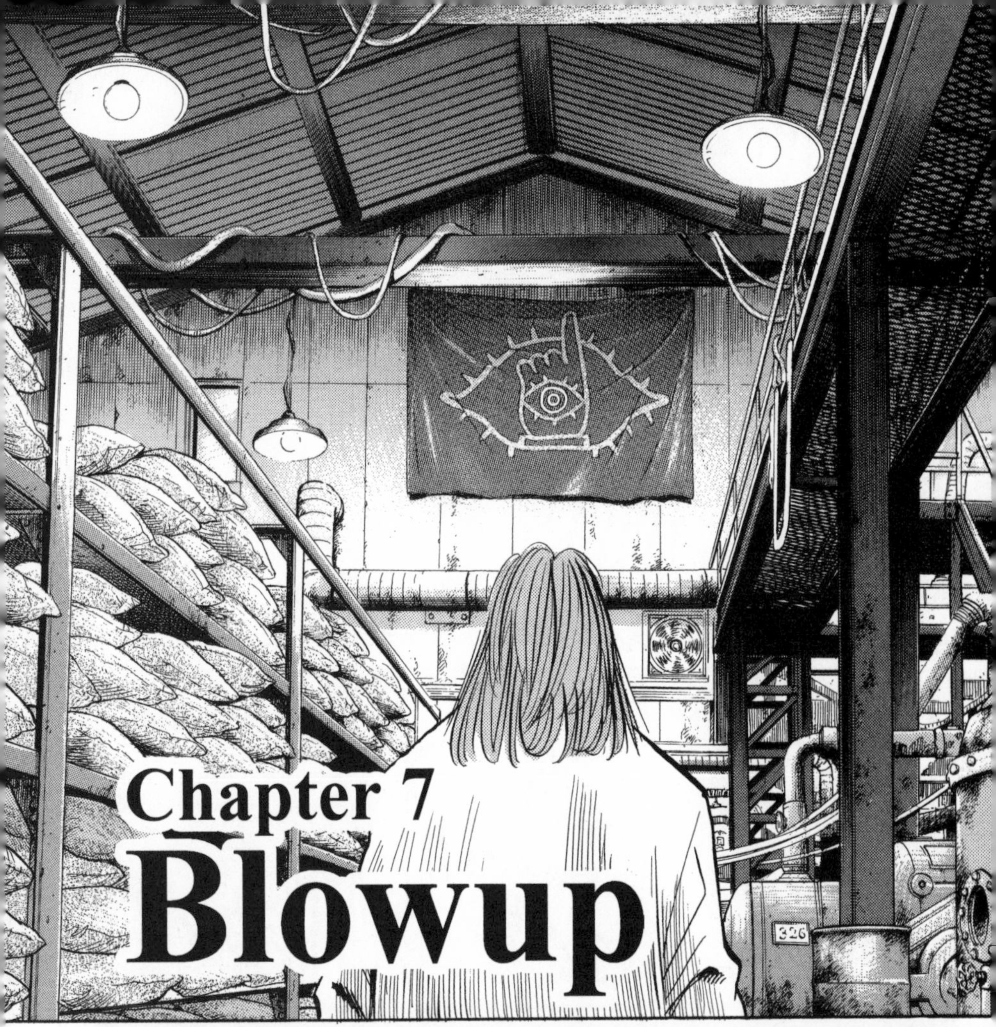
Chapter 7
Blowup
326

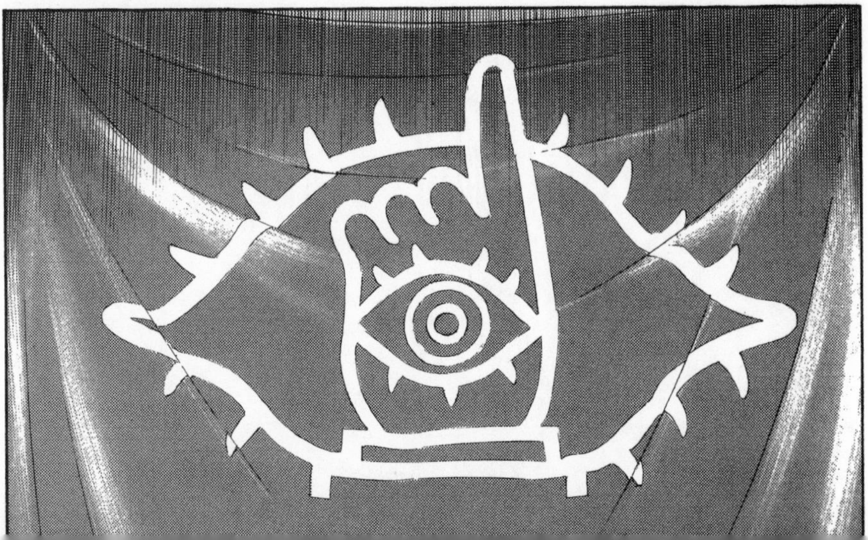

ZWAK

ZWAK

CRAZY. FUNNY HOW A KID'S MIND WORKS ...

THWOP THWOP

ZWAK

VWOOMPH

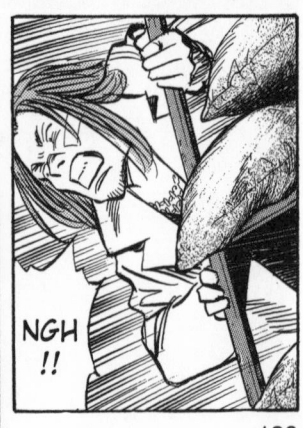

NGH !!

126

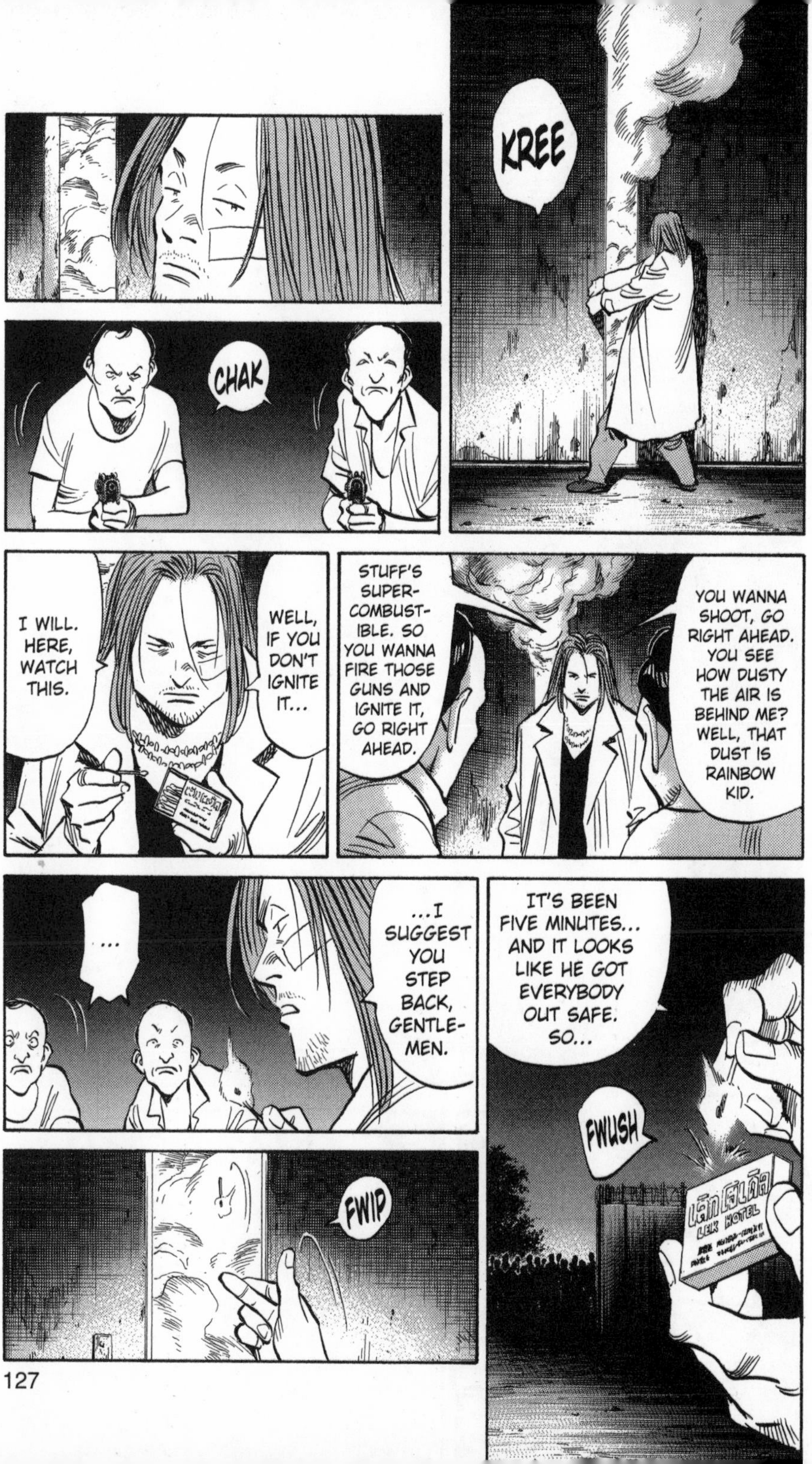
KREE
CHAK
YOU WANNA SHOOT, GO RIGHT AHEAD. YOU SEE HOW DUSTY THE AIR IS BEHIND ME? WELL, THAT DUST IS RAINBOW KID.
STUFF'S SUPER-COMBUSTIBLE. SO YOU WANNA FIRE THOSE GUNS AND IGNITE IT, GO RIGHT AHEAD.
WELL, IF YOU DON'T IGNITE IT...
I WILL. HERE, WATCH THIS.
IT'S BEEN FIVE MINUTES... AND IT LOOKS LIKE HE GOT EVERYBODY OUT SAFE. SO...
FWUSH
LEK HOTEL
...I SUGGEST YOU STEP BACK, GENTLEMEN.
...
FWIP

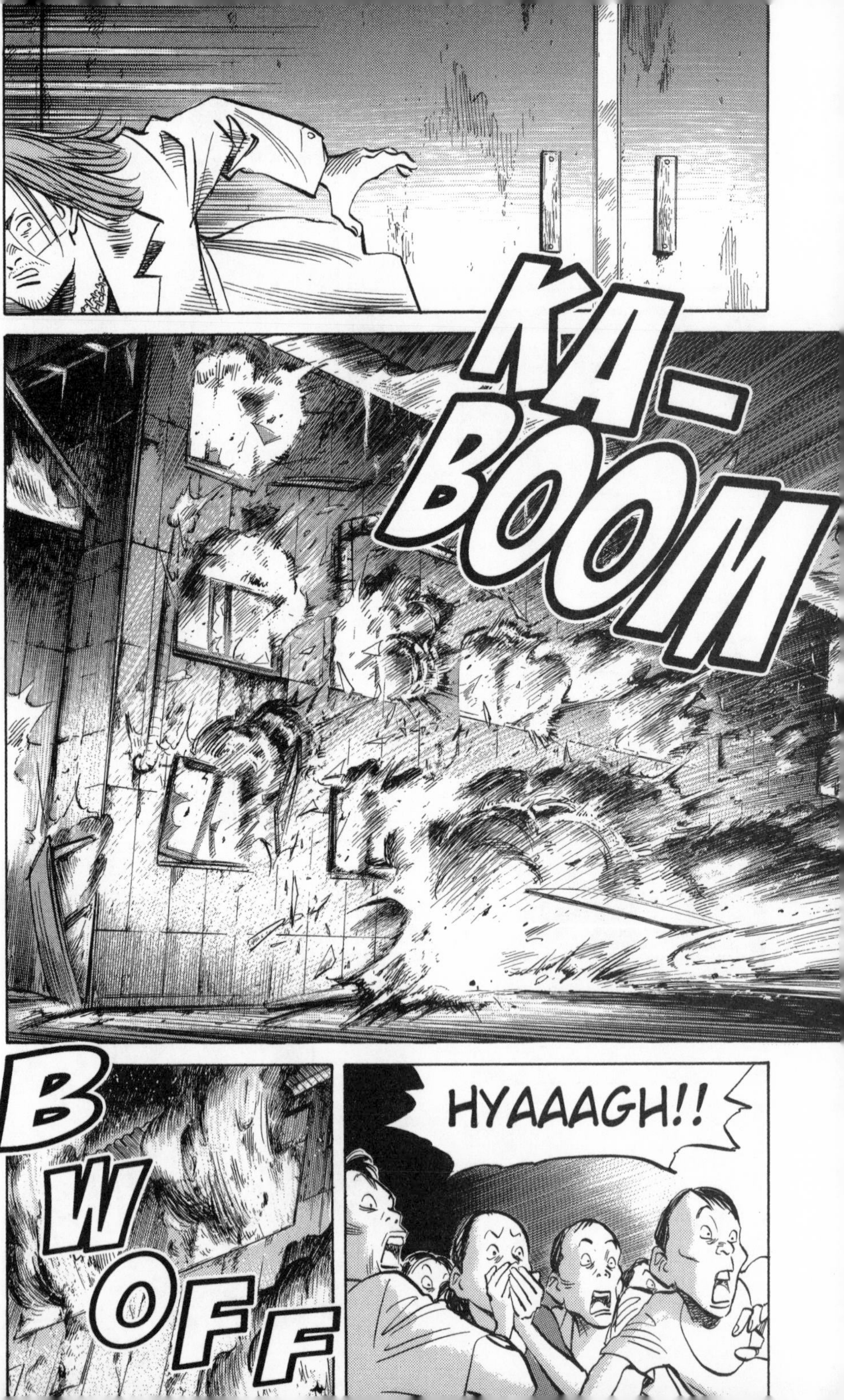
KA-BOOM
HYAAAGH!!
BWOFF

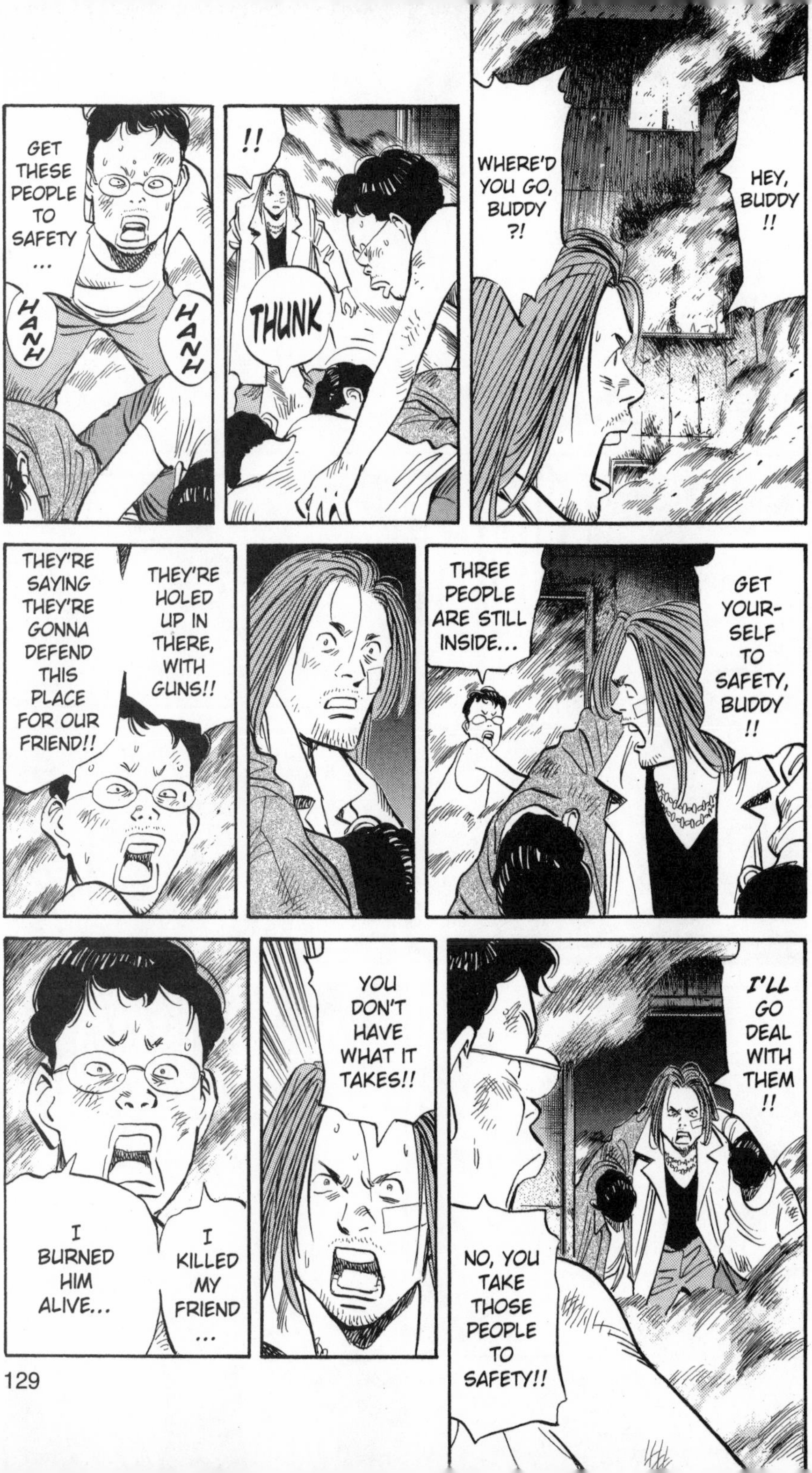
HEY, BUDDY!!
WHERE'D YOU GO, BUDDY?!
!!
THUNK
GET THESE PEOPLE TO SAFETY...
HANH
HANH
GET YOURSELF TO SAFETY, BUDDY!!
THREE PEOPLE ARE STILL INSIDE...
THEY'RE HOLED UP IN THERE, WITH GUNS!!
THEY'RE SAYING THEY'RE GONNA DEFEND THIS PLACE FOR OUR FRIEND!!
I'LL GO DEAL WITH THEM!!
NO, YOU TAKE THOSE PEOPLE TO SAFETY!!
YOU DON'T HAVE WHAT IT TAKES!!
I KILLED MY FRIEND...
I BURNED HIM ALIVE...

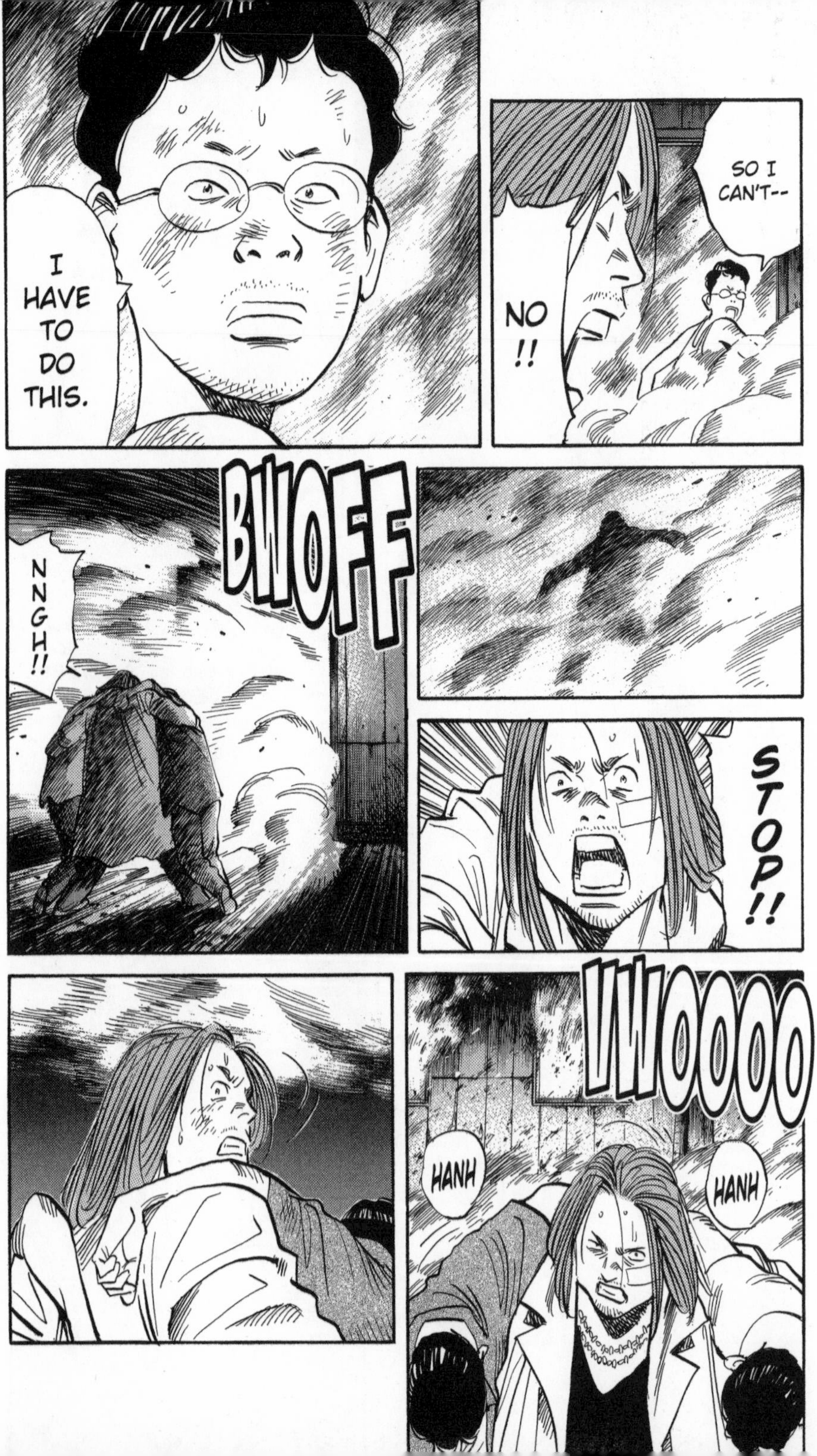
SO I CAN'T--
NO !!
I HAVE TO DO THIS.
STOP!!
BWOFF
NNGH!!
VWOOOO
HANH
HANH

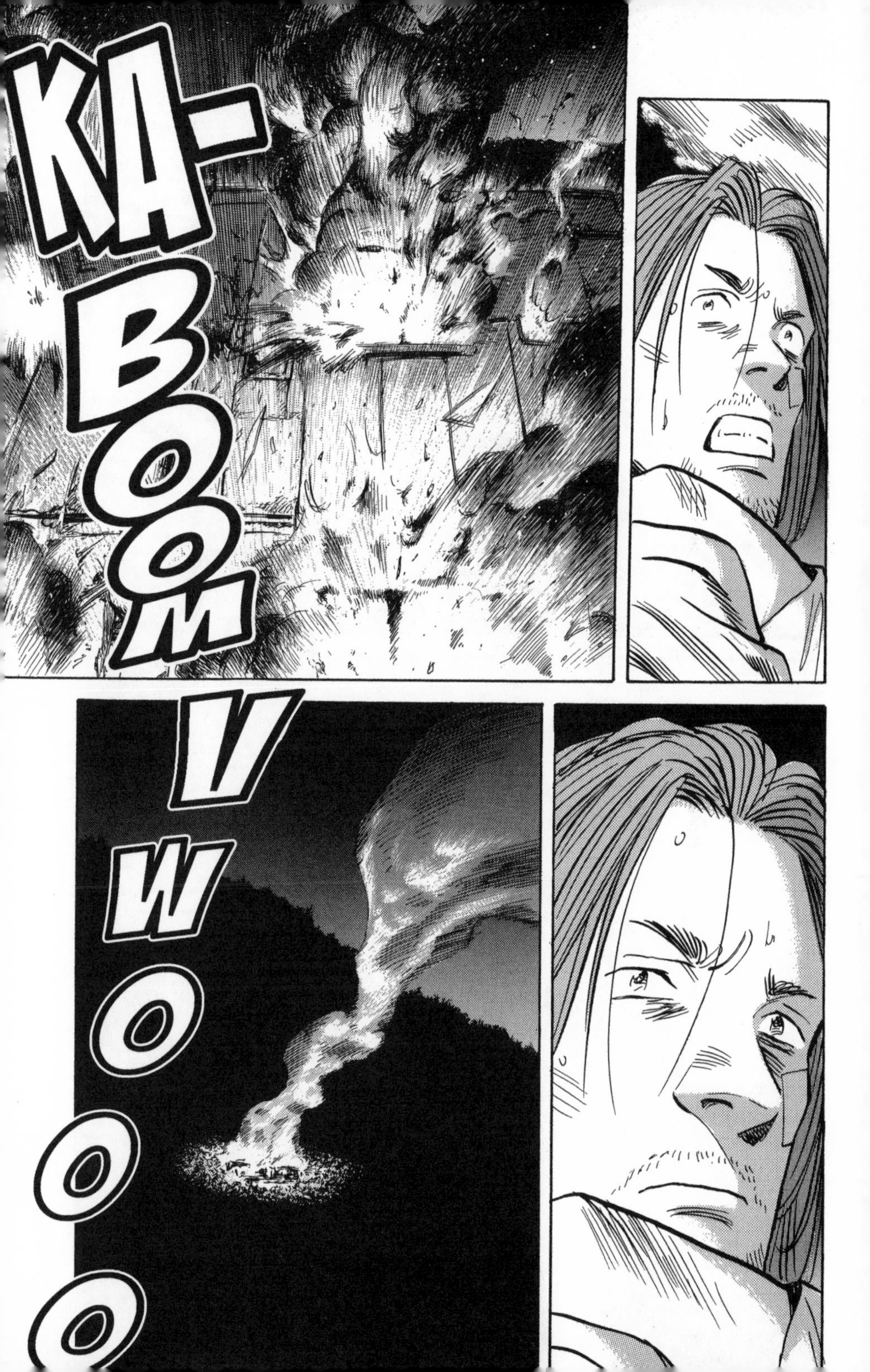
KA-BOOM
VWOOOO

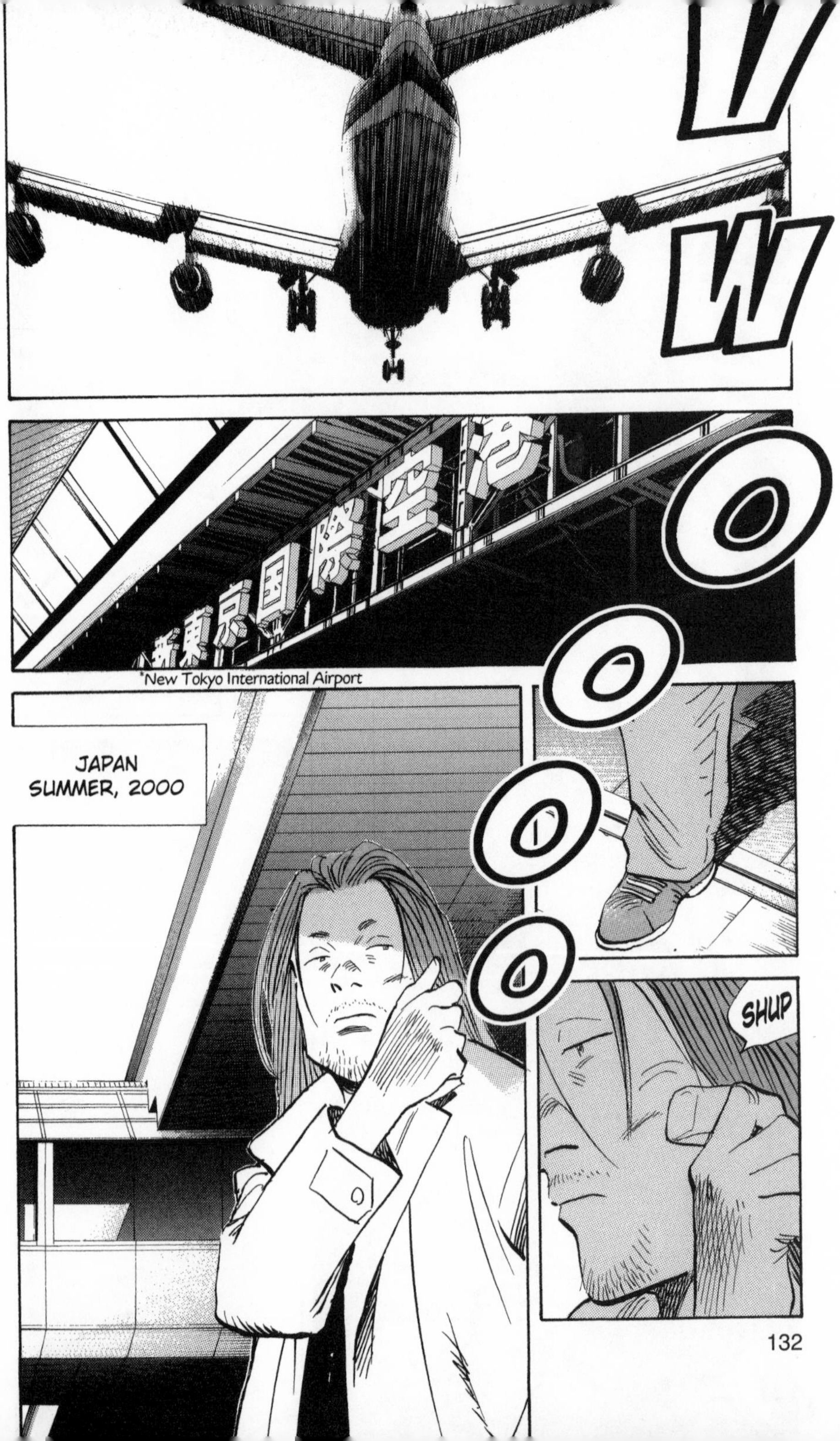
VWOOOOO
新東京国際空港
*New Tokyo International Airport
SHUP
JAPAN
SUMMER, 2000

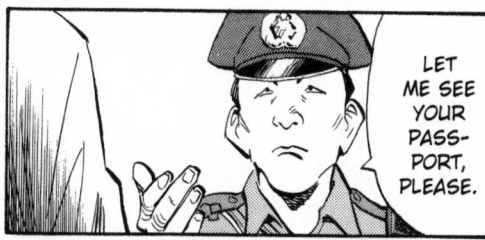

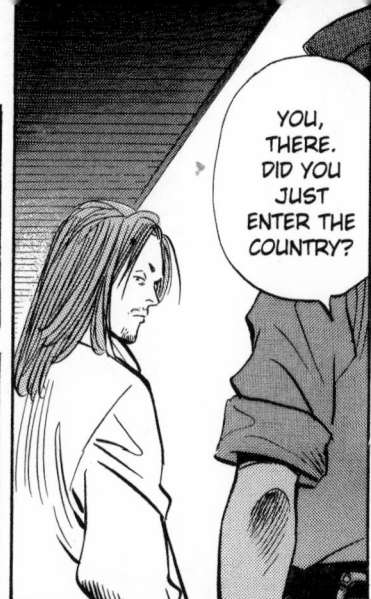

YOU, THERE. DID YOU JUST ENTER THE COUNTRY?
LET ME SEE YOUR PASSPORT, PLEASE.
I ALREADY SHOWED MY PASSPORT AT IMMIGRATION, INSIDE.
THERE'S A SUMMIT TAKING PLACE IN OKINAWA. LOTS OF DIGNITARIES HERE IN TOKYO AS WELL. I JUST NEED TO SEE YOUR ID.
WHAT FOR? WHAT THE HELL DID I DO?
LET ME SEE YOUR PASSPORT, PLEASE.
WELL, I'M ASKING YOU WHAT FOR!
LOOK, JUST SHOW ME YOUR PASSPORT!!
KLINK

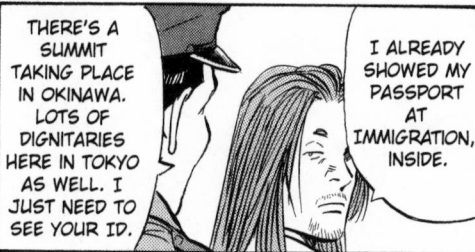

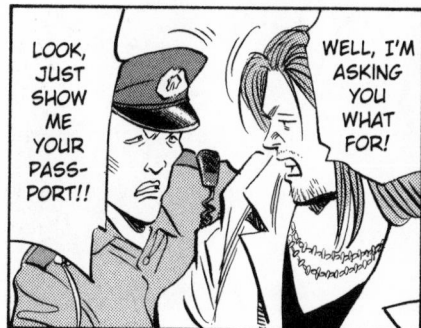

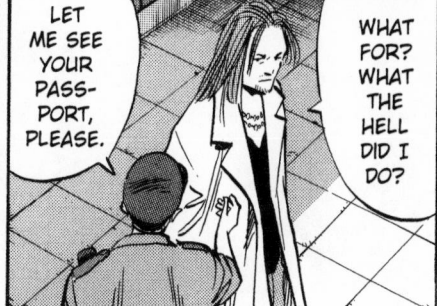

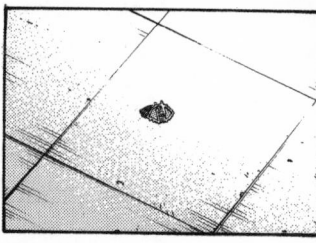

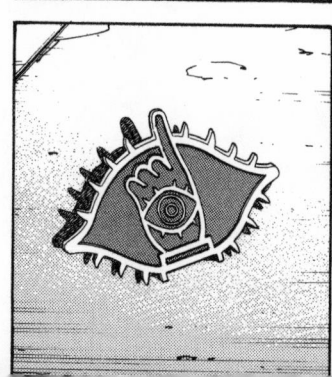

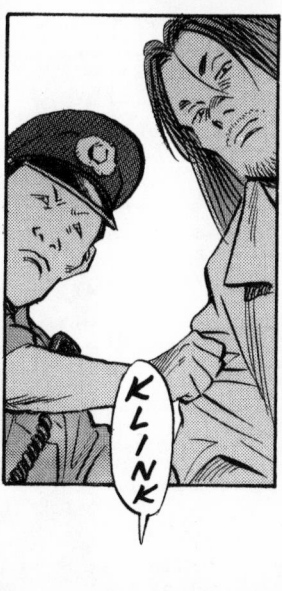

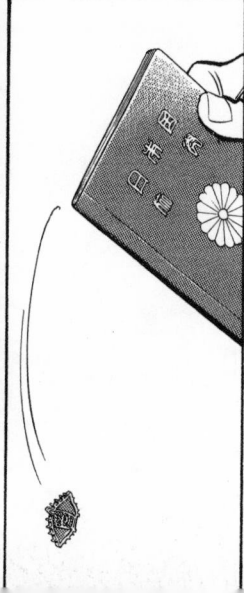

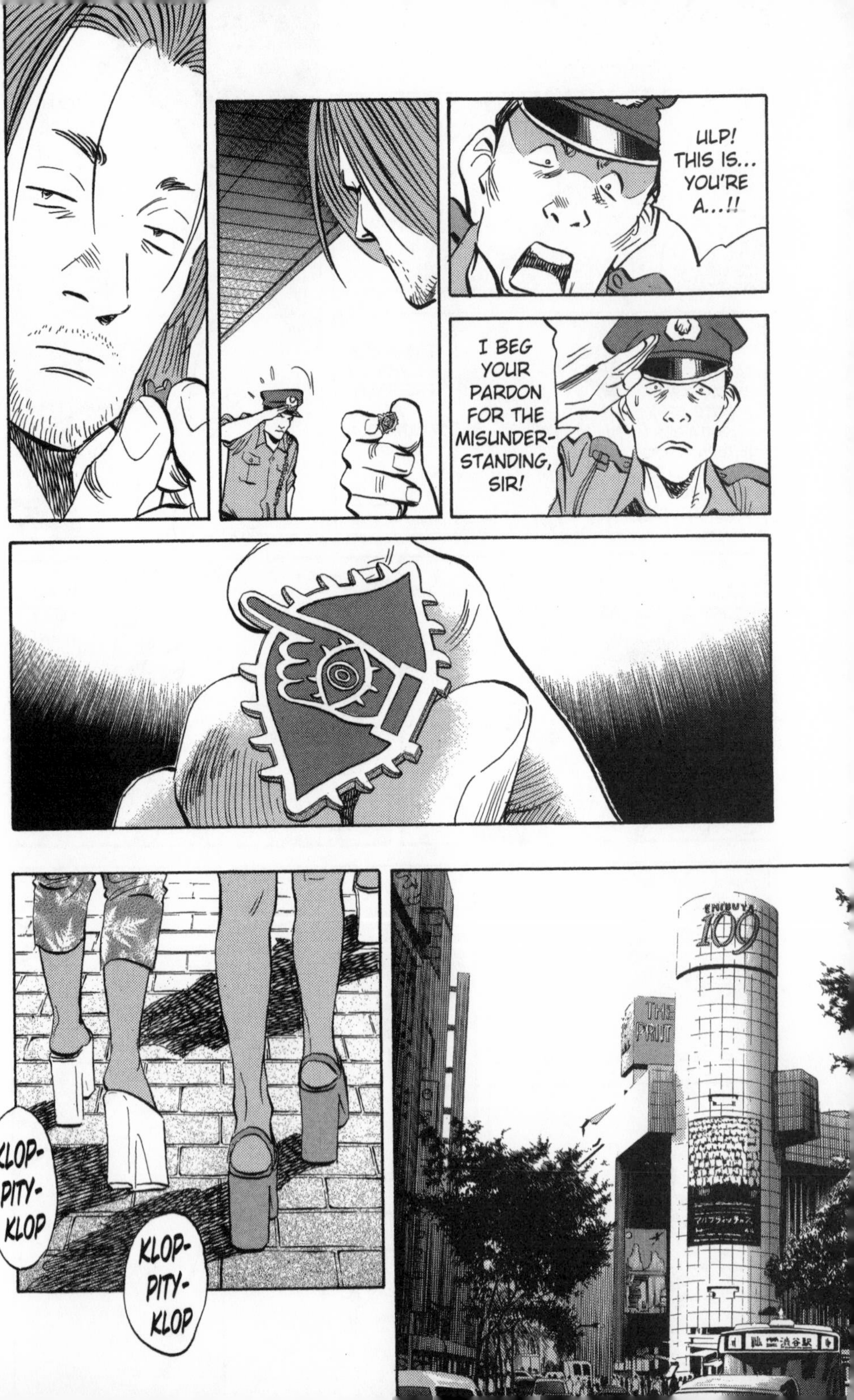
ULP! THIS IS... YOU'RE A...!!
I BEG YOUR PARDON FOR THE MISUNDER-STANDING, SIR!
109
KLOP-PITY-KLOP
KLOP-PITY-KLOP

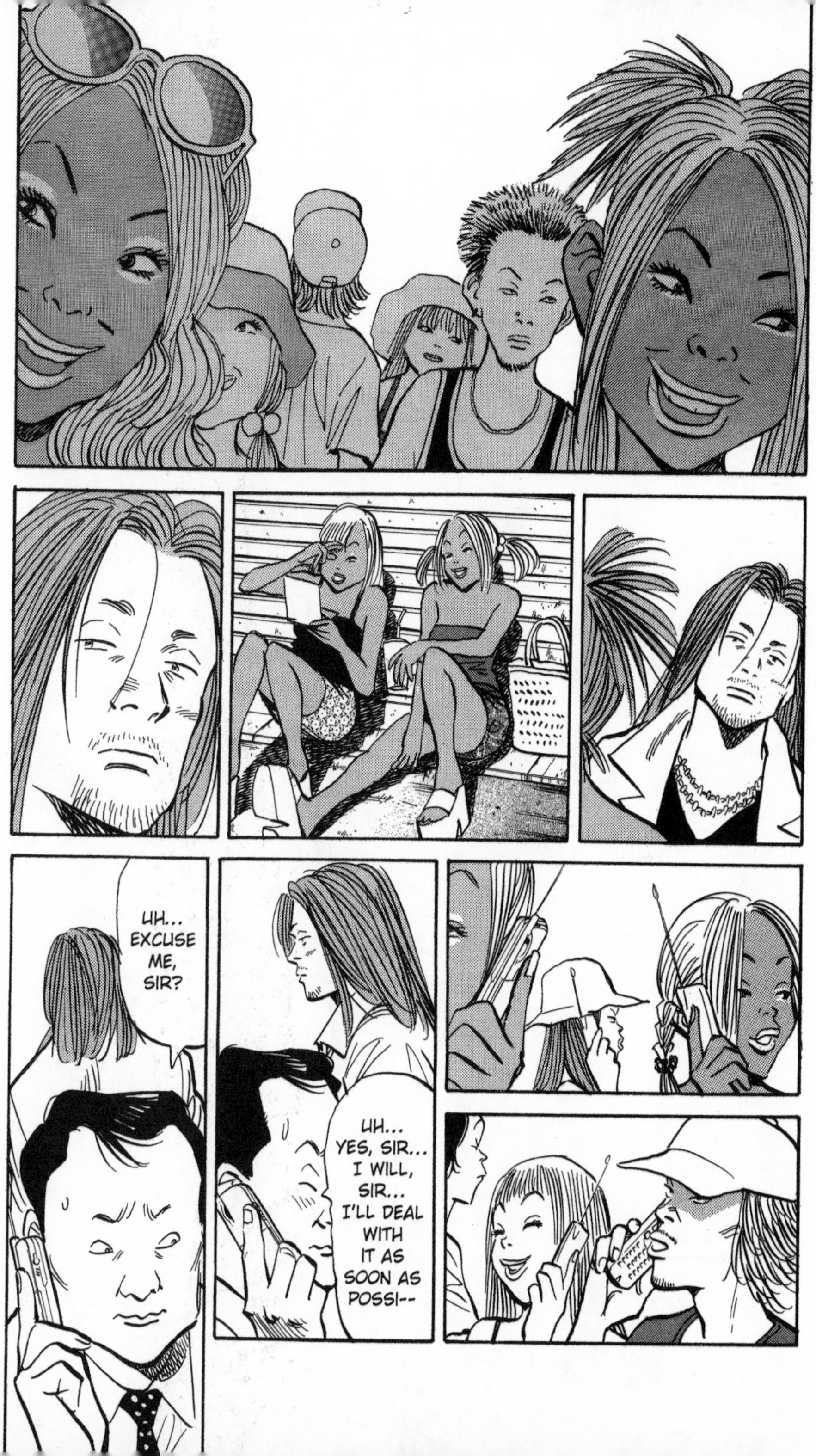
UH... YES, SIR... I WILL, SIR... I'LL DEAL WITH IT AS SOON AS POSSI--
UH... EXCUSE ME, SIR?

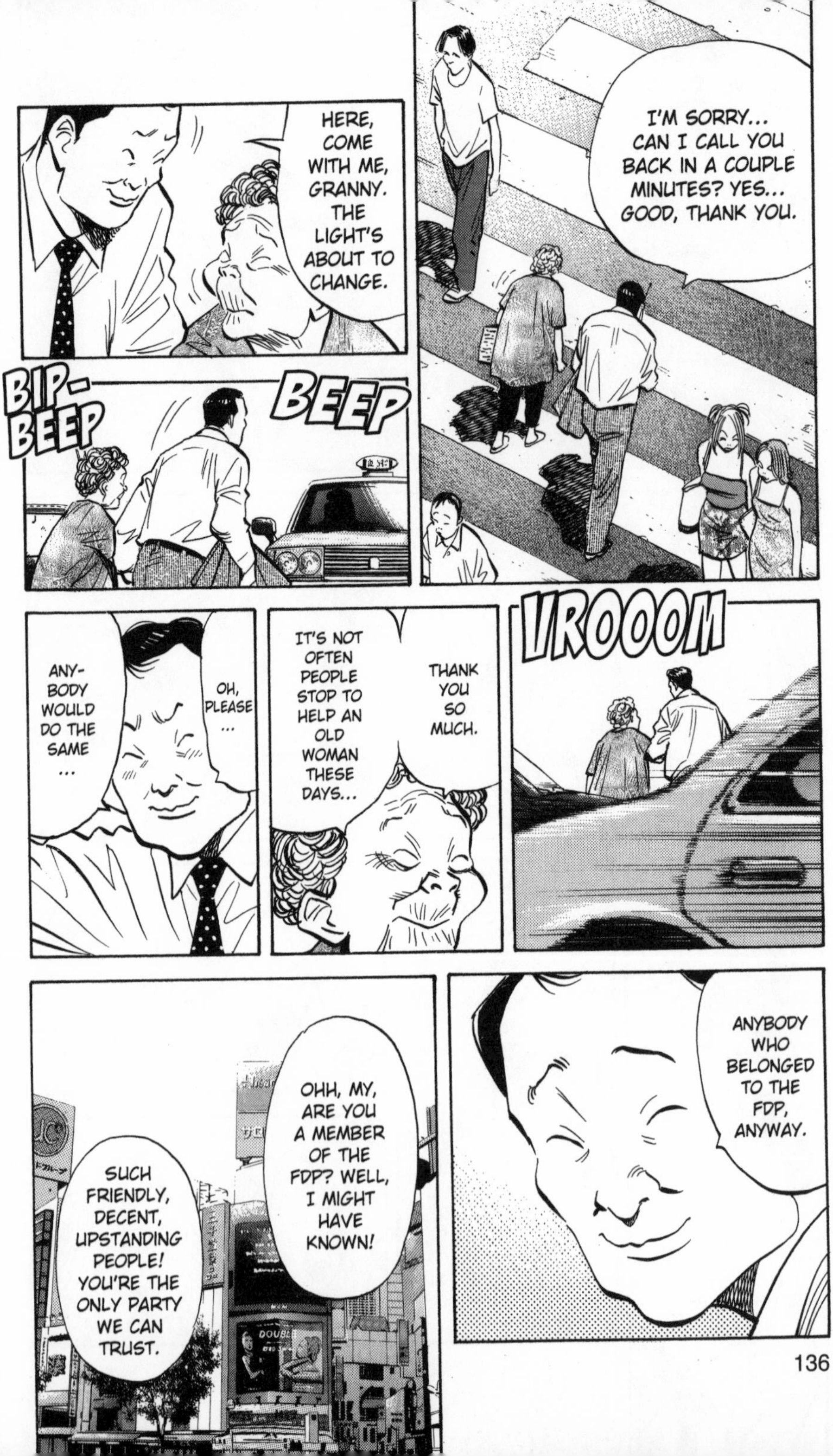
I'M SORRY... CAN I CALL YOU BACK IN A COUPLE MINUTES? YES... GOOD, THANK YOU.
HERE, COME WITH ME, GRANNY. THE LIGHT'S ABOUT TO CHANGE.
BEEP
BIP-BEEP
VROOOM
THANK YOU SO MUCH.
IT'S NOT OFTEN PEOPLE STOP TO HELP AN OLD WOMAN THESE DAYS...
OH, PLEASE...
ANY-BODY WOULD DO THE SAME...
ANYBODY WHO BELONGED TO THE FDP, ANYWAY.
OHH, MY, ARE YOU A MEMBER OF THE FDP? WELL, I MIGHT HAVE KNOWN!
SUCH FRIENDLY, DECENT, UPSTANDING PEOPLE! YOU'RE THE ONLY PARTY WE CAN TRUST.

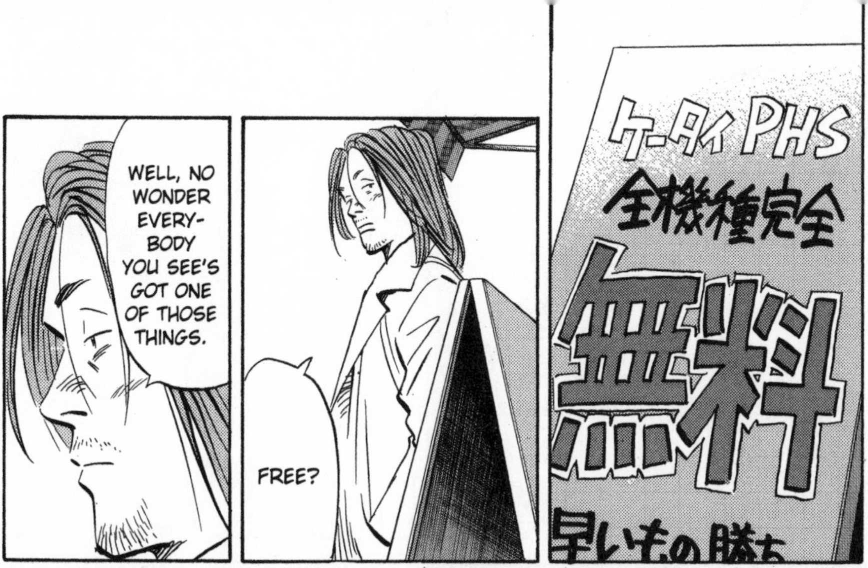
ケータイ PHS
全機種完全
無料
早いもの勝ち
FREE?
WELL, NO WONDER EVERY-BODY YOU SEE'S GOT ONE OF THOSE THINGS.

*Cell phones, All models totally FREE, Hurry before we run out!

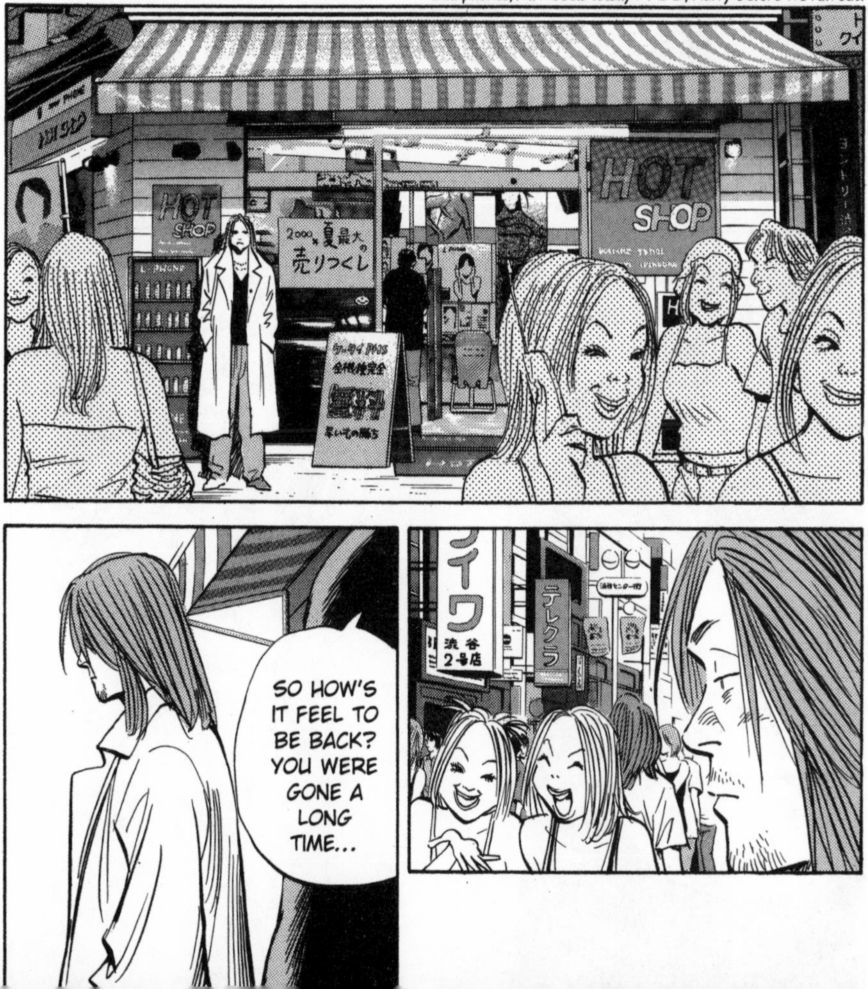
HOT SHOP
HOT SHOP
2000年夏最大の売りつくし
テレクラ
SO HOW'S IT FEEL TO BE BACK? YOU WERE GONE A LONG TIME...

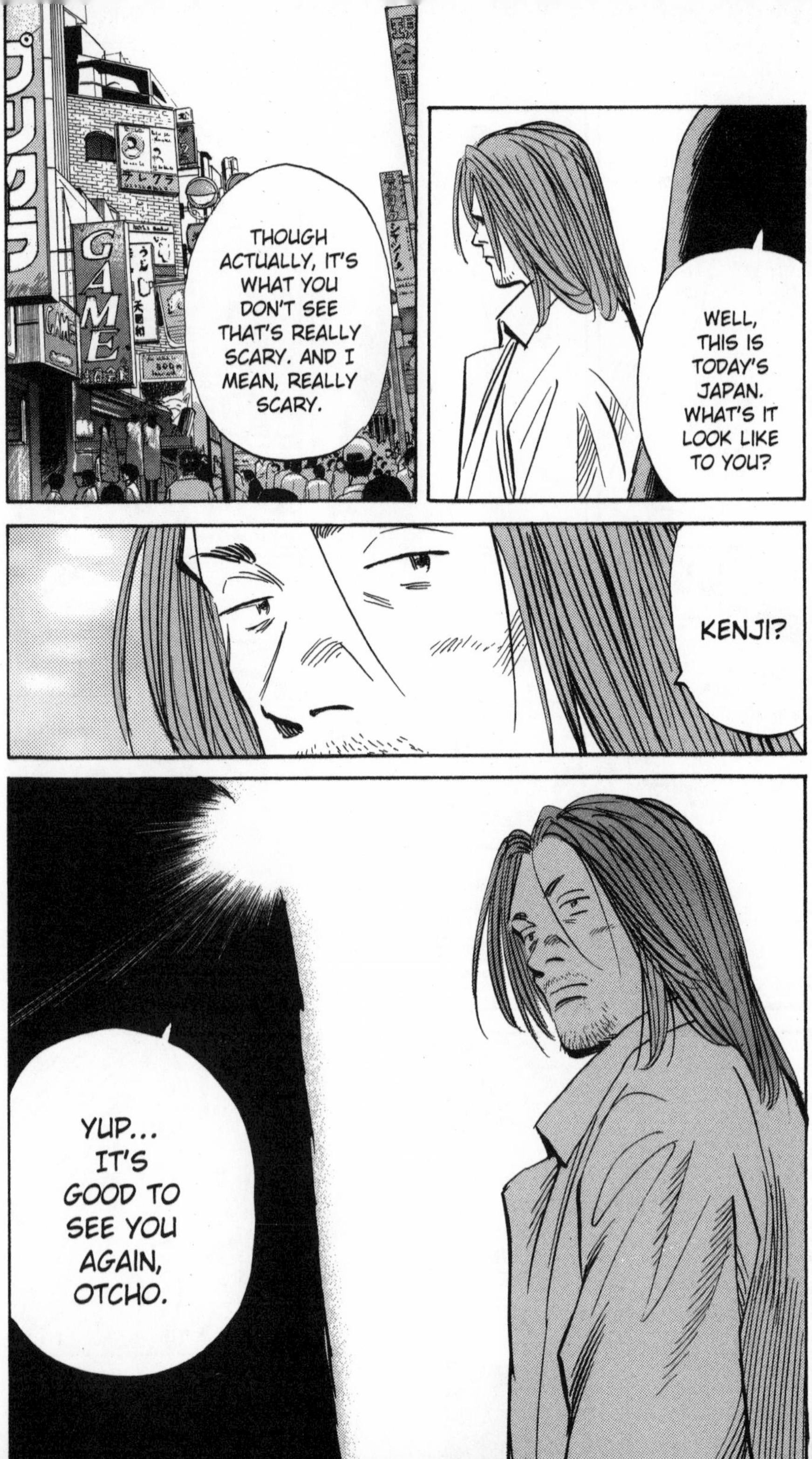
WELL, THIS IS TODAY'S JAPAN. WHAT'S IT LOOK LIKE TO YOU?
THOUGH ACTUALLY, IT'S WHAT YOU DON'T SEE THAT'S REALLY SCARY. AND I MEAN, REALLY SCARY.
GAME
GAME
KENJI?
YUP... IT'S GOOD TO SEE YOU AGAIN, OTCHO.

Chapter 8 Secret Headquarters

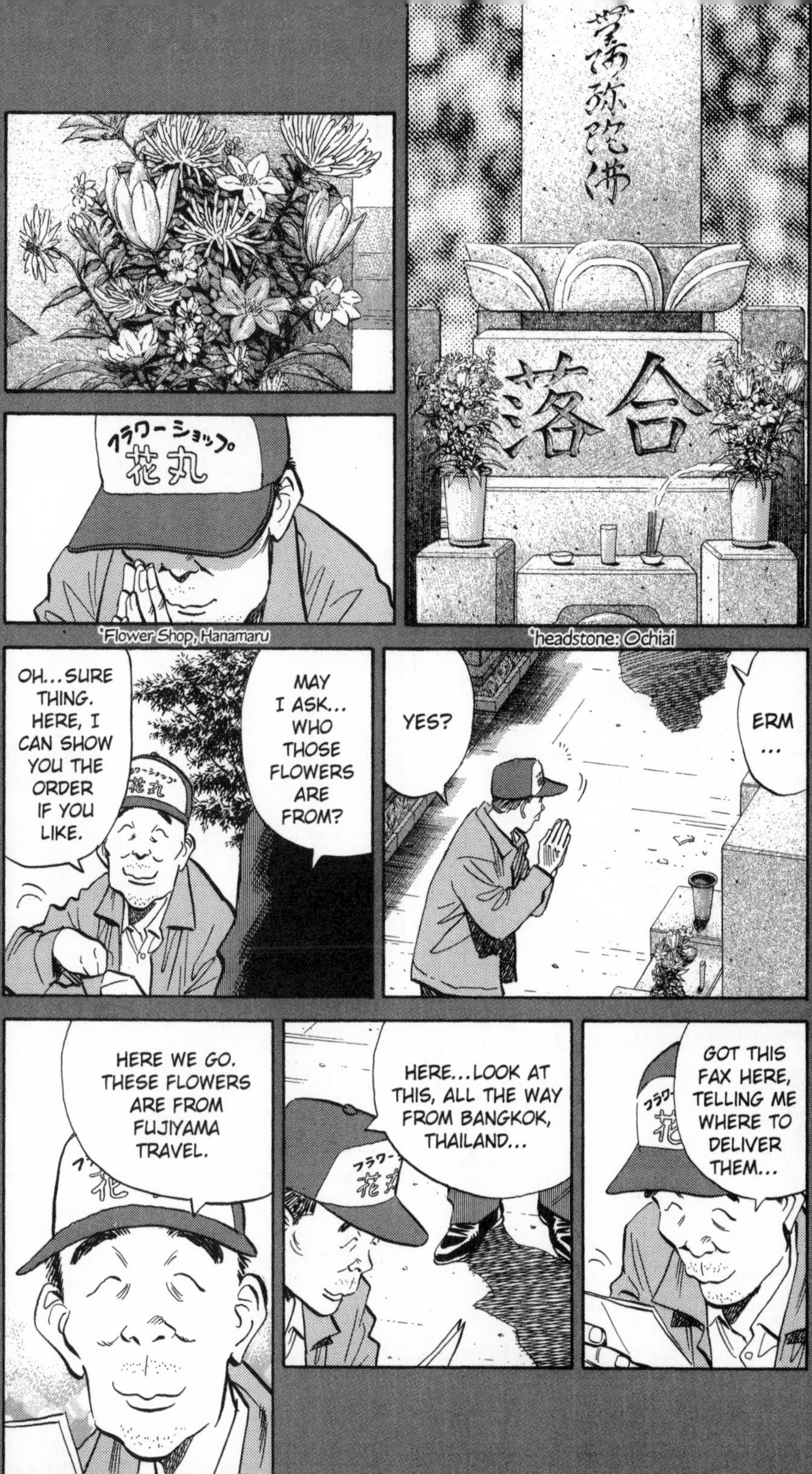
*headstone: Ochiai
*Flower Shop, Hanamaru
ERM ...
YES?
MAY I ASK... WHO THOSE FLOWERS ARE FROM?
OH...SURE THING. HERE, I CAN SHOW YOU THE ORDER IF YOU LIKE.
GOT THIS FAX HERE, TELLING ME WHERE TO DELIVER THEM...
HERE...LOOK AT THIS, ALL THE WAY FROM BANGKOK, THAILAND...
HERE WE GO. THESE FLOWERS ARE FROM FUJIYAMA TRAVEL.

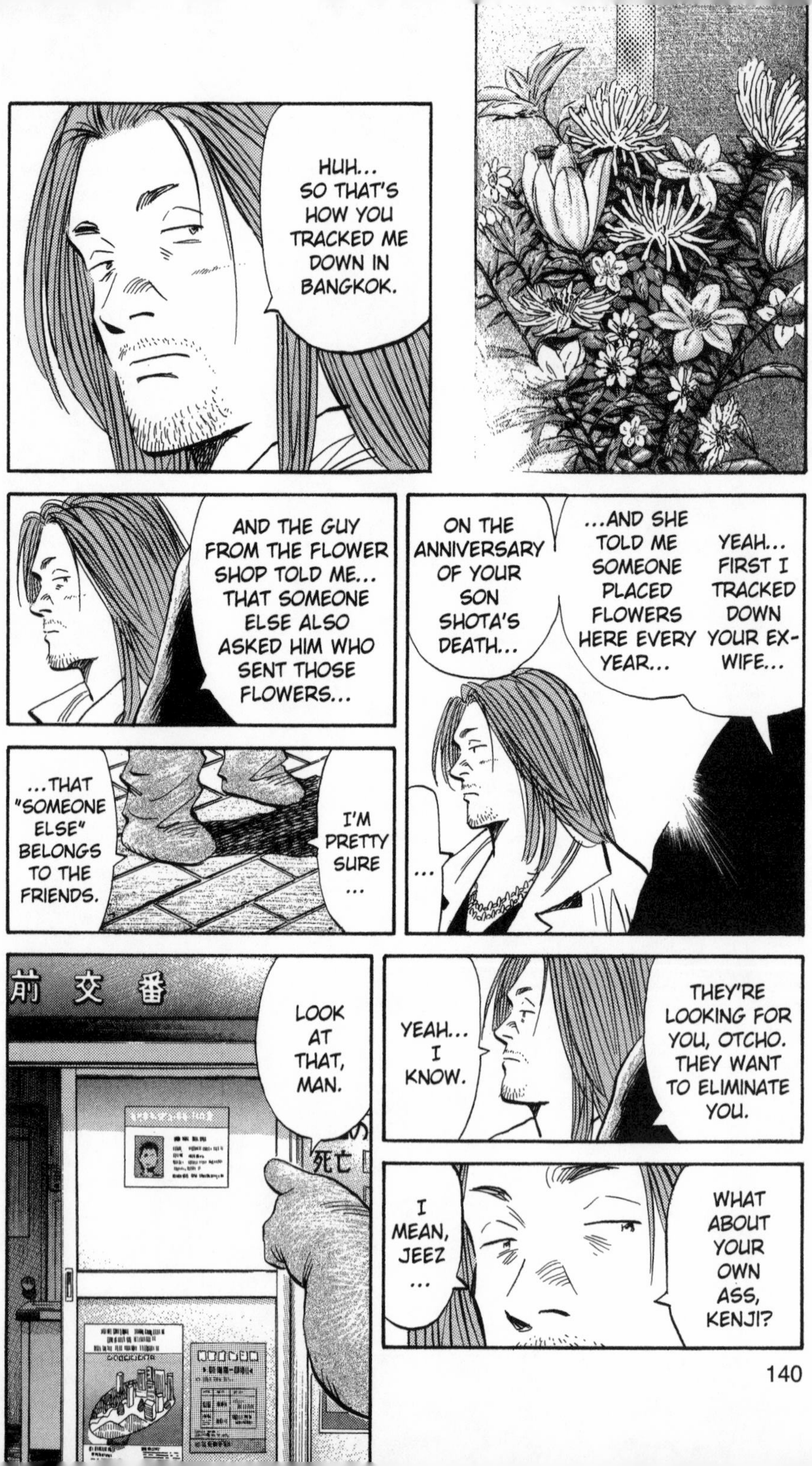

HUH... SO THAT'S HOW YOU TRACKED ME DOWN IN BANGKOK.
YEAH... FIRST I TRACKED DOWN YOUR EX-WIFE...
...AND SHE TOLD ME SOMEONE PLACED FLOWERS HERE EVERY YEAR...
ON THE ANNIVERSARY OF YOUR SON SHOTA'S DEATH...
...
AND THE GUY FROM THE FLOWER SHOP TOLD ME... THAT SOMEONE ELSE ALSO ASKED HIM WHO SENT THOSE FLOWERS...
I'M PRETTY SURE...
...THAT "SOMEONE ELSE" BELONGS TO THE FRIENDS.
THEY'RE LOOKING FOR YOU, OTCHO. THEY WANT TO ELIMINATE YOU.
YEAH... I KNOW.
WHAT ABOUT YOUR OWN ASS, KENJI?
I MEAN, JEEZ...
前 交 番
LOOK AT THAT, MAN.

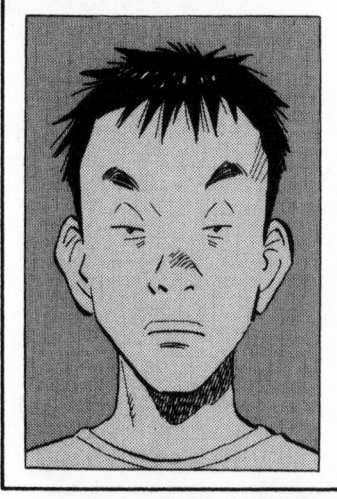

Have you seen this man?

Endo Kenji

Height: about 175cm Medium build
Long narrow face, sharp-eyed expression

Wanted in connection with:

Bombing of Jonan Medical College
Attack on FDP headquarters
Obstructing officers in the line of
duty and numerous other offenses.

If you have any information that could lead
to his arrest, please contact your nearest
police station. Thank you for your cooperation.

WANTED IN CONNECTION WITH BOMBING OF JONAN MEDICAL COLLEGE... ATTACK ON FDP HEAD-QUARTERS...

YOU'RE A BONA FIDE TERRORIST, MAN.

HMPH...FIRST TIME I SEE MY CHILDHOOD BUDDY'S FACE IN I DON'T KNOW HOW LONG AND IT'S ON A GOD-DAMN WANTED POSTER...

YEAH... AND LOOK AT MY MUG ON THAT THING. BUT YOU KNOW WHAT, OTCHO? THIS IS REALITY.

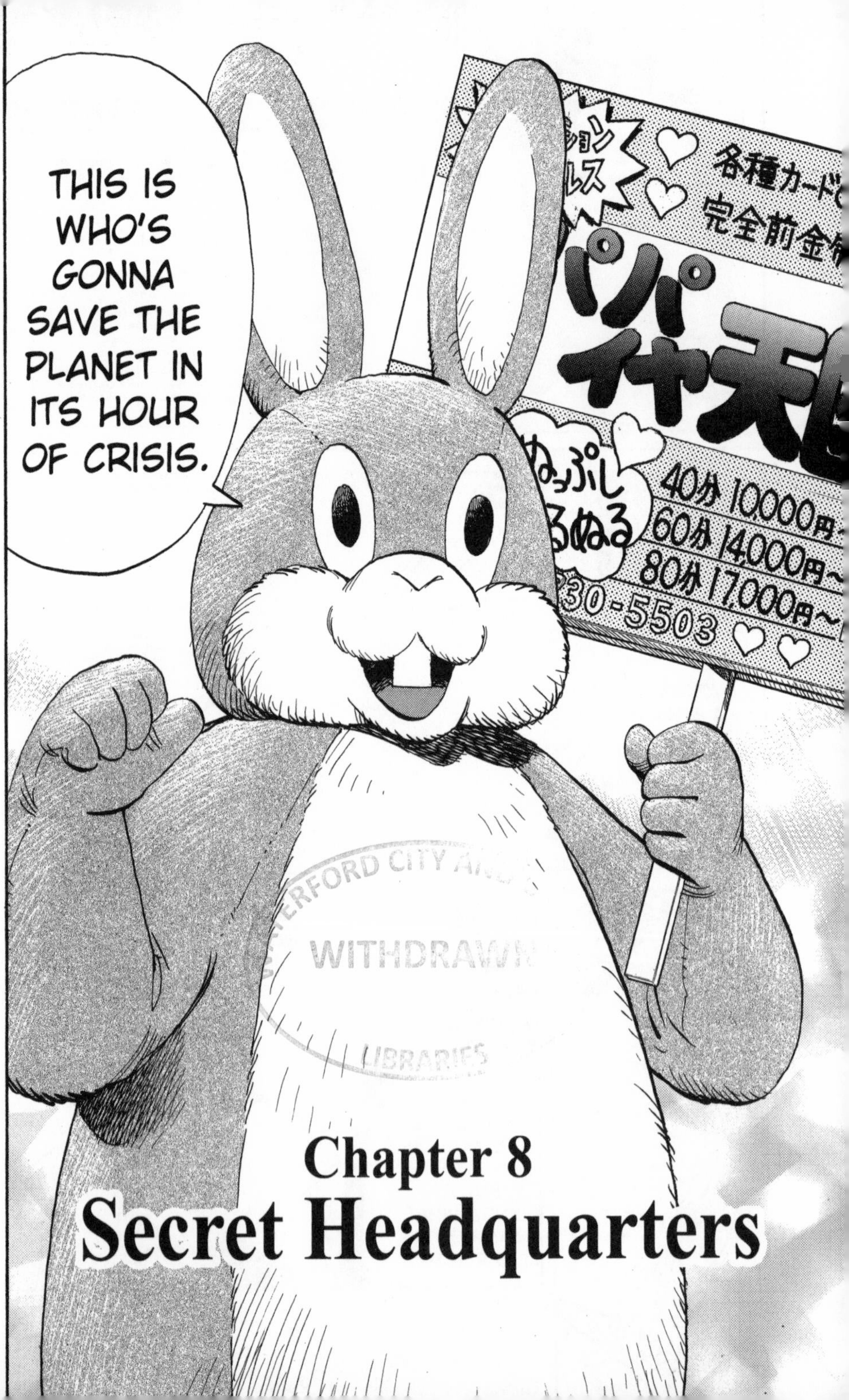
THIS IS WHO'S GONNA SAVE THE PLANET IN ITS HOUR OF CRISIS.
各種カード
40分 10,000円
60分 14,000円
80分 17,000円~
30-5503

Chapter 8
Secret Headquarters

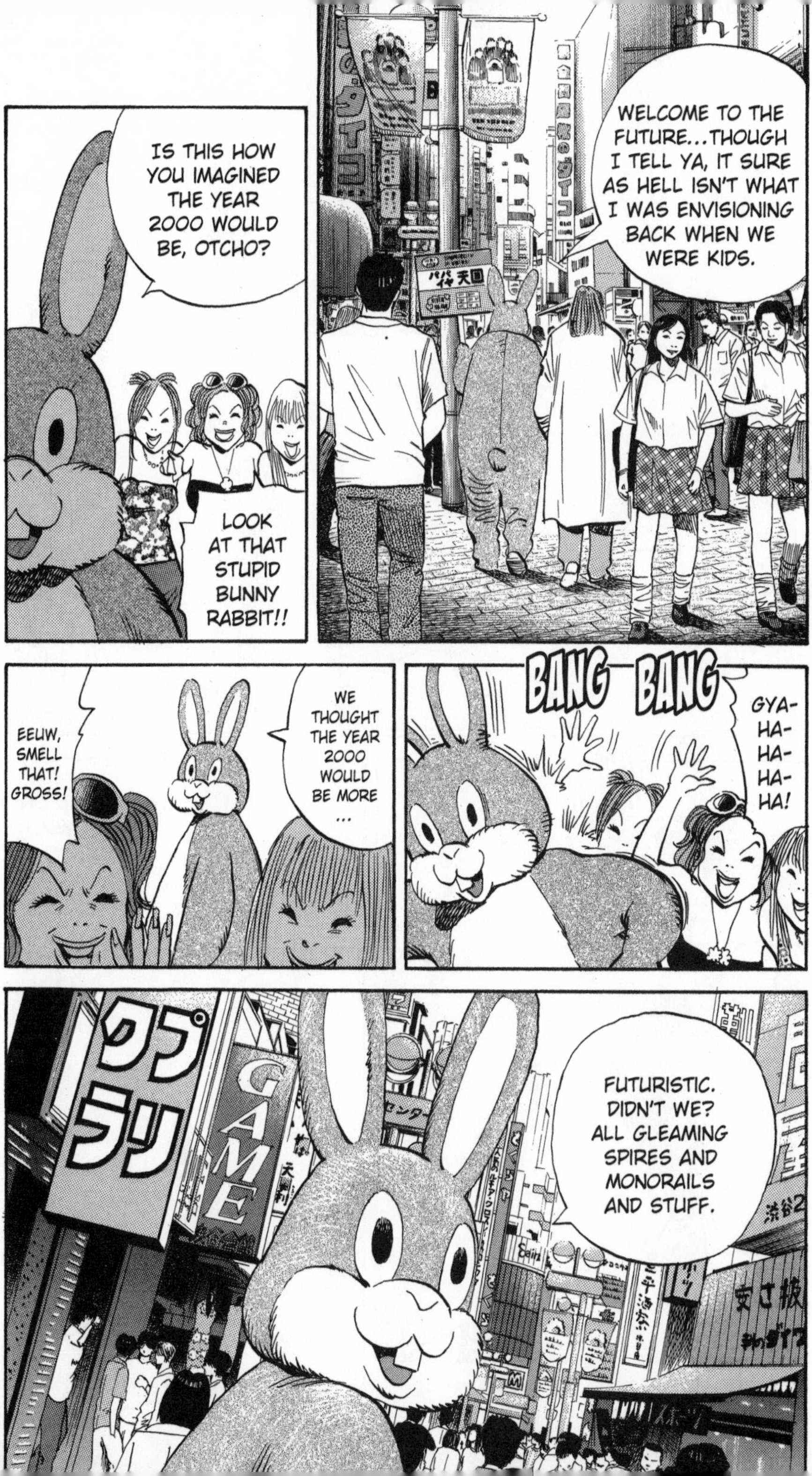
WELCOME TO THE FUTURE...THOUGH I TELL YA, IT SURE AS HELL ISN'T WHAT I WAS ENVISIONING BACK WHEN WE WERE KIDS.
IS THIS HOW YOU IMAGINED THE YEAR 2000 WOULD BE, OTCHO?
LOOK AT THAT STUPID BUNNY RABBIT!!
BANG BANG
GYA-HA-HA-HA-HA!
WE THOUGHT THE YEAR 2000 WOULD BE MORE ...
EEUW, SMELL THAT! GROSS!
GAME
FUTURISTIC. DIDN'T WE? ALL GLEAMING SPIRES AND MONORAILS AND STUFF.

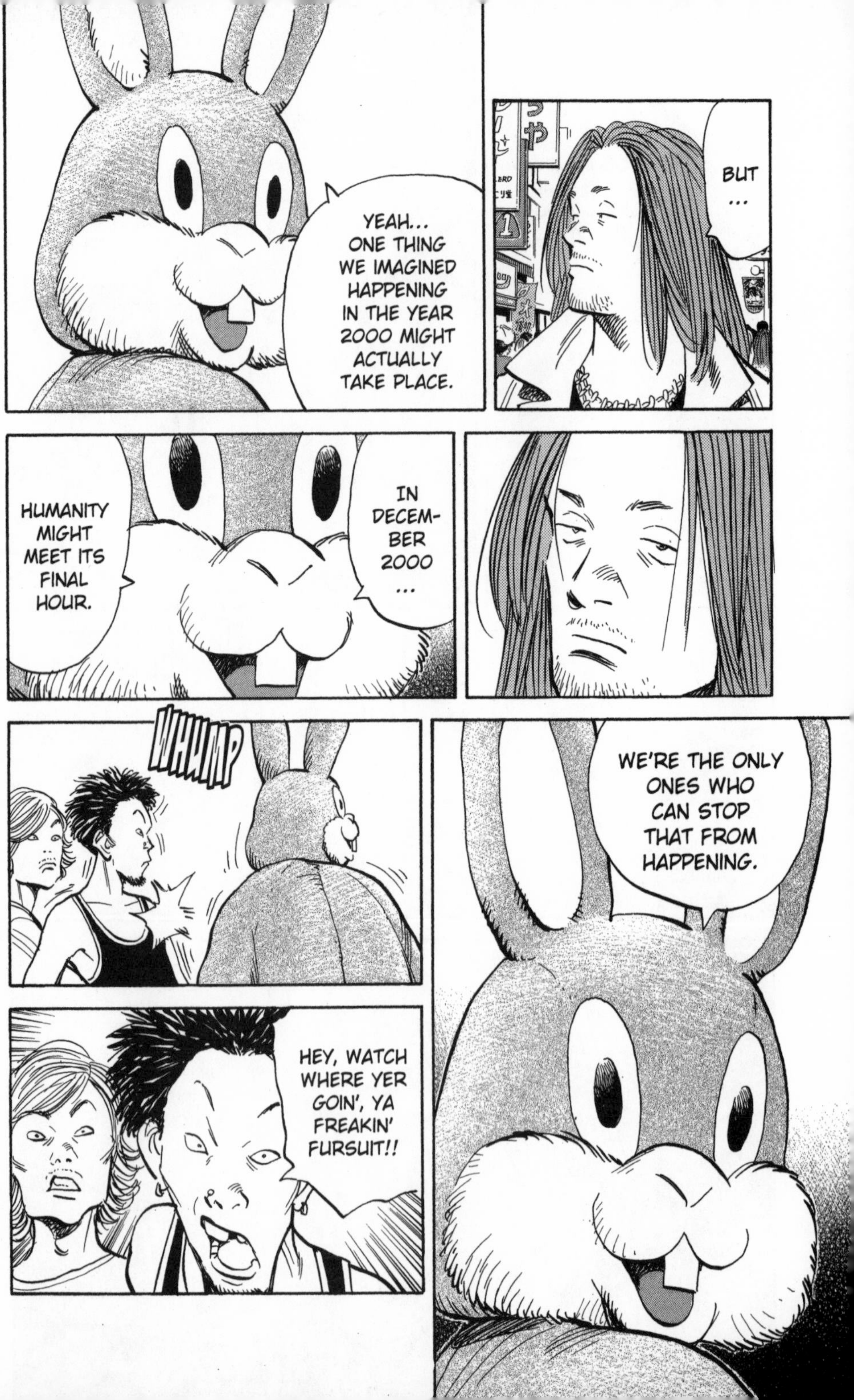
BUT ...
YEAH... ONE THING WE IMAGINED HAPPENING IN THE YEAR 2000 MIGHT ACTUALLY TAKE PLACE.
IN DECEMBER 2000 ...
HUMANITY MIGHT MEET ITS FINAL HOUR.
WE'RE THE ONLY ONES WHO CAN STOP THAT FROM HAPPENING.
WHUMP
HEY, WATCH WHERE YER GOIN', YA FREAKIN' FURSUIT!!

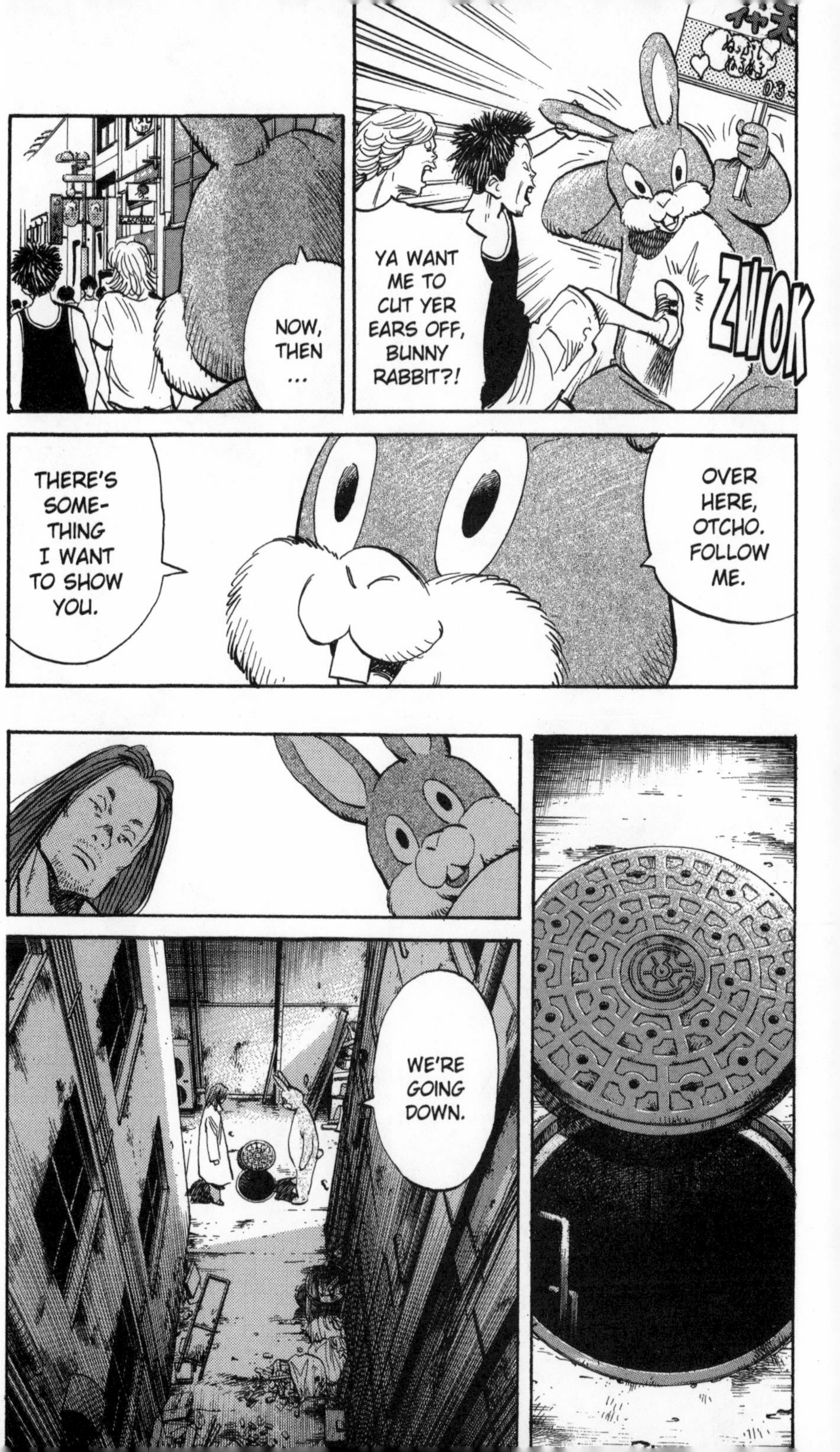
YA WANT ME TO CUT YER EARS OFF, BUNNY RABBIT?!
ZWOK
NOW, THEN ...
OVER HERE, OTCHO. FOLLOW ME.
THERE'S SOME-THING I WANT TO SHOW YOU.
WE'RE GOING DOWN.

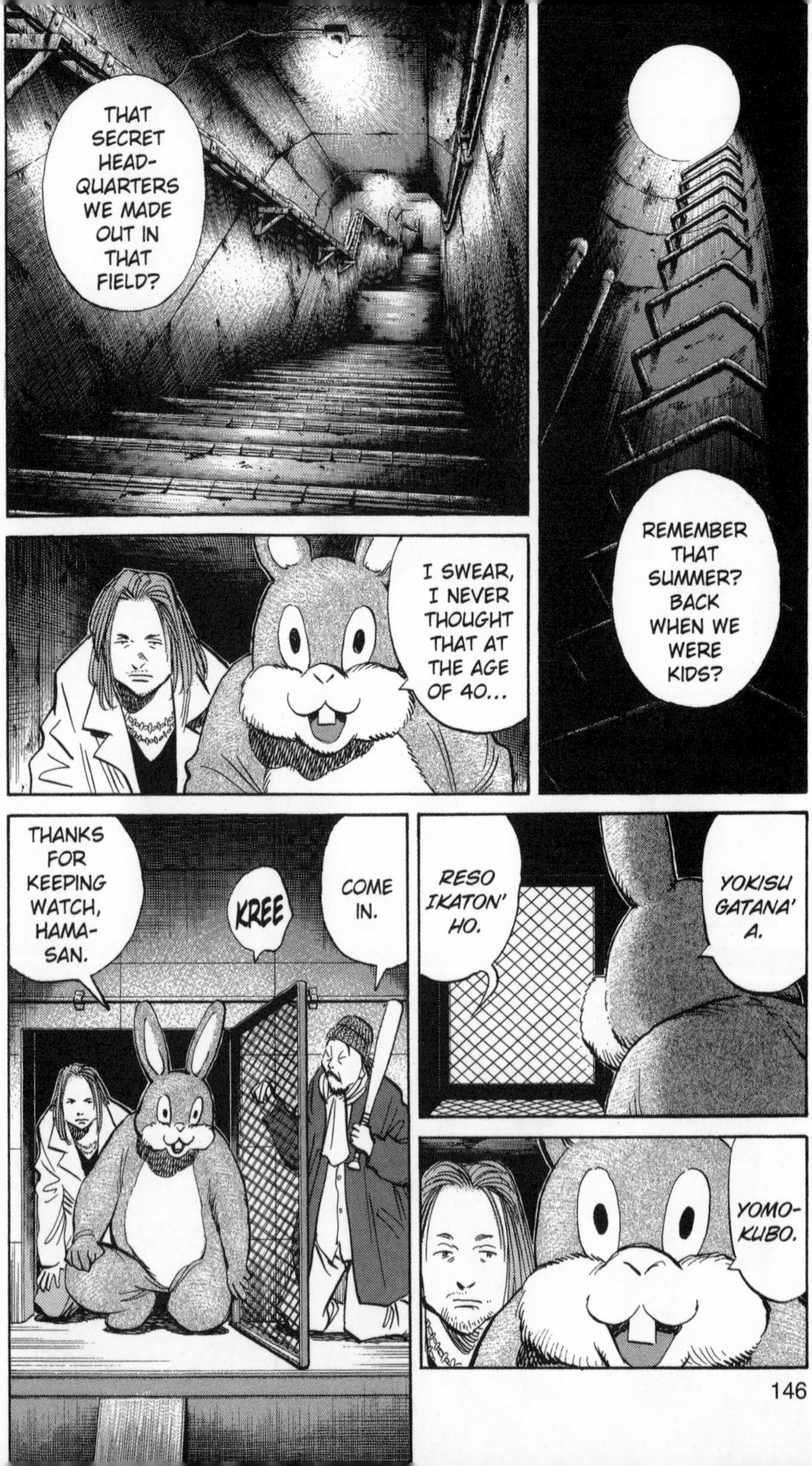
REMEMBER THAT SUMMER? BACK WHEN WE WERE KIDS?
THAT SECRET HEAD-QUARTERS WE MADE OUT IN THAT FIELD?
I SWEAR, I NEVER THOUGHT THAT AT THE AGE OF 40...
YOKISU GATANA' A.
RESO IKATON' HO.
YOMO-KUBO.
COME IN.
KREE
THANKS FOR KEEPING WATCH, HAMA-SAN.

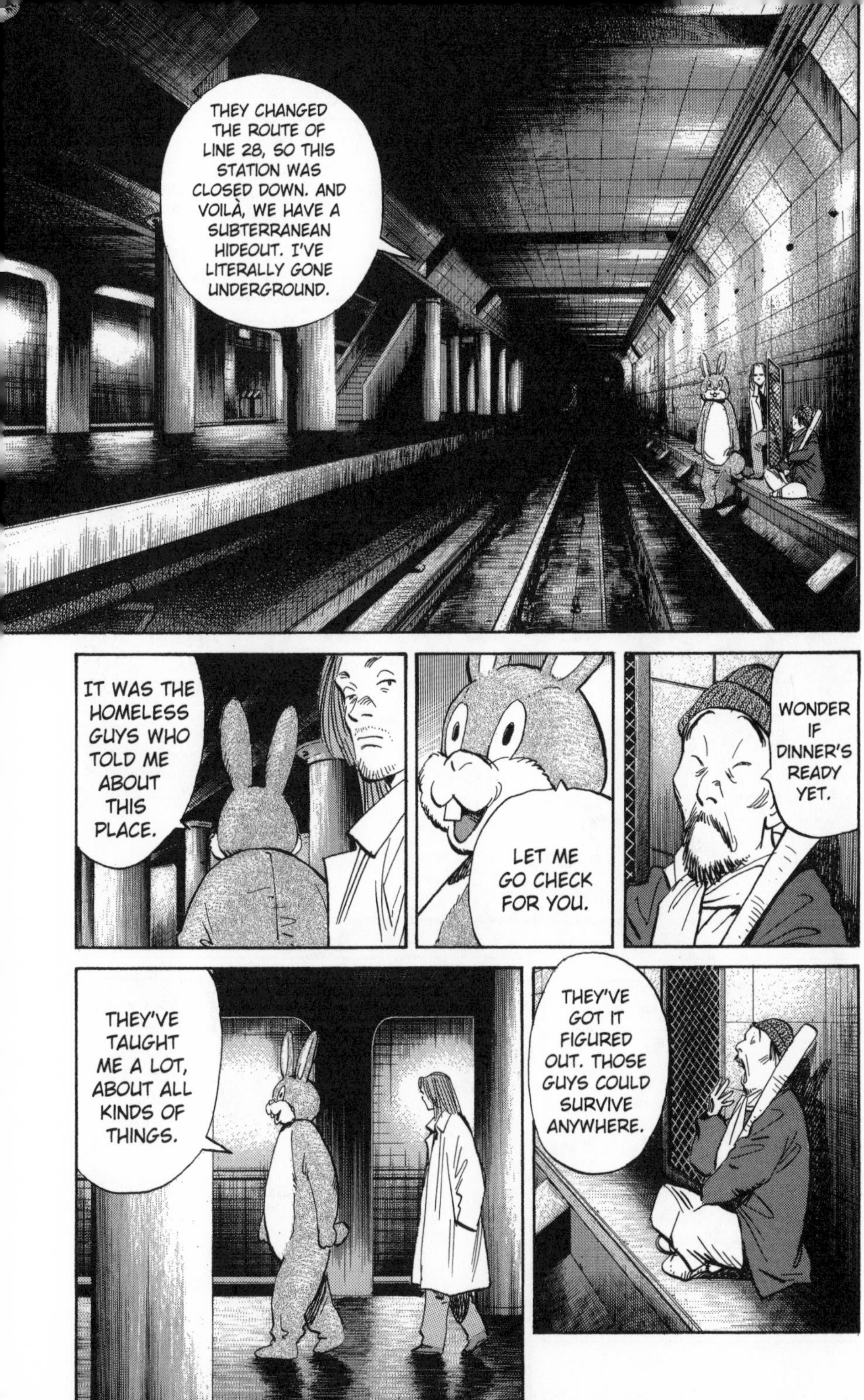
THEY CHANGED THE ROUTE OF LINE 28, SO THIS STATION WAS CLOSED DOWN. AND VOILÀ, WE HAVE A SUBTERRANEAN HIDEOUT. I'VE LITERALLY GONE UNDERGROUND.
WONDER IF DINNER'S READY YET.
LET ME GO CHECK FOR YOU.
IT WAS THE HOMELESS GUYS WHO TOLD ME ABOUT THIS PLACE.
THEY'VE GOT IT FIGURED OUT. THOSE GUYS COULD SURVIVE ANYWHERE.
THEY'VE TAUGHT ME A LOT, ABOUT ALL KINDS OF THINGS.

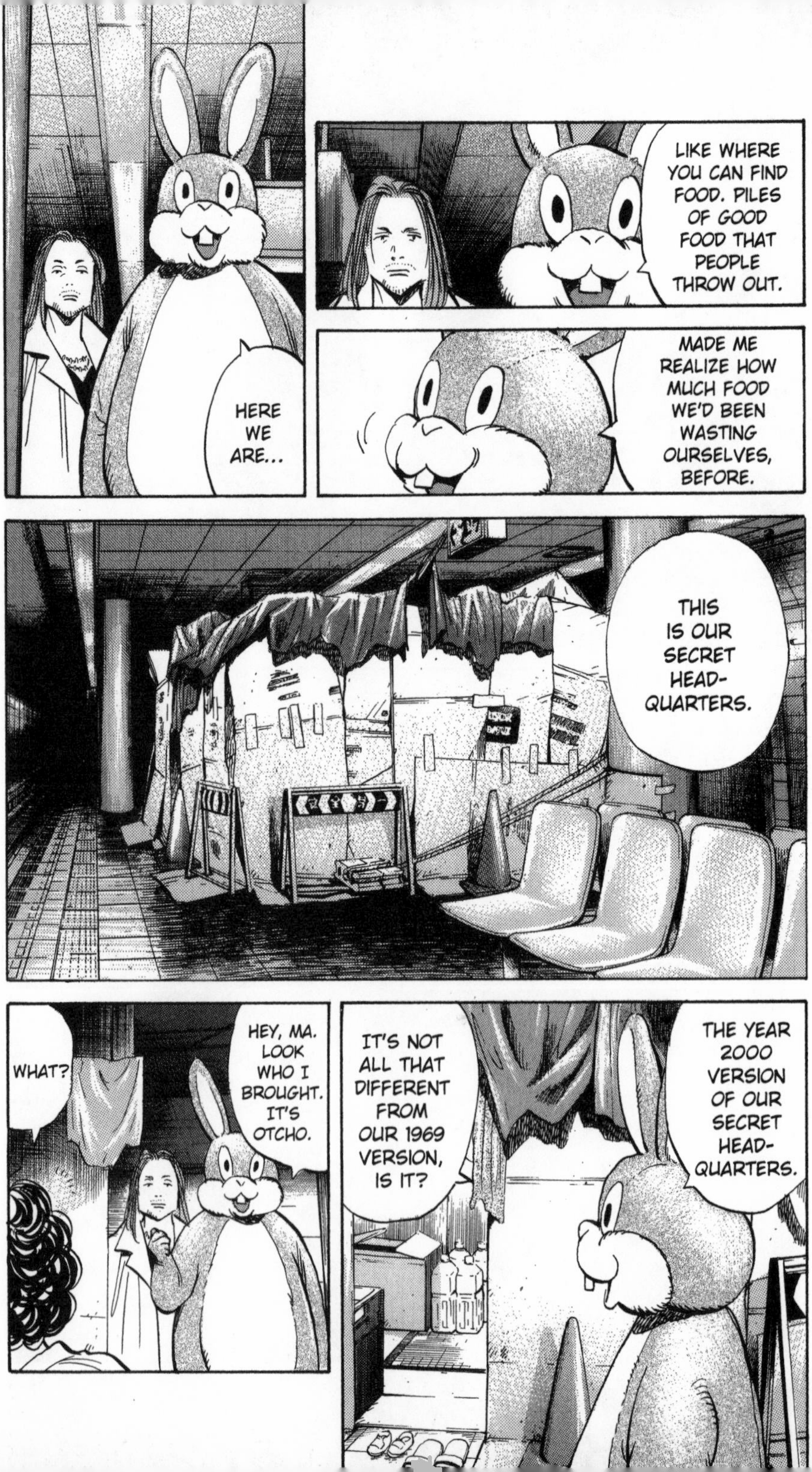
LIKE WHERE YOU CAN FIND FOOD. PILES OF GOOD FOOD THAT PEOPLE THROW OUT.
MADE ME REALIZE HOW MUCH FOOD WE'D BEEN WASTING OURSELVES, BEFORE.
HERE WE ARE...
THIS IS OUR SECRET HEAD-QUARTERS.
THE YEAR 2000 VERSION OF OUR SECRET HEAD-QUARTERS.
IT'S NOT ALL THAT DIFFERENT FROM OUR 1969 VERSION, IS IT?
HEY, MA. LOOK WHO I BROUGHT. IT'S OTCHO.
WHAT?

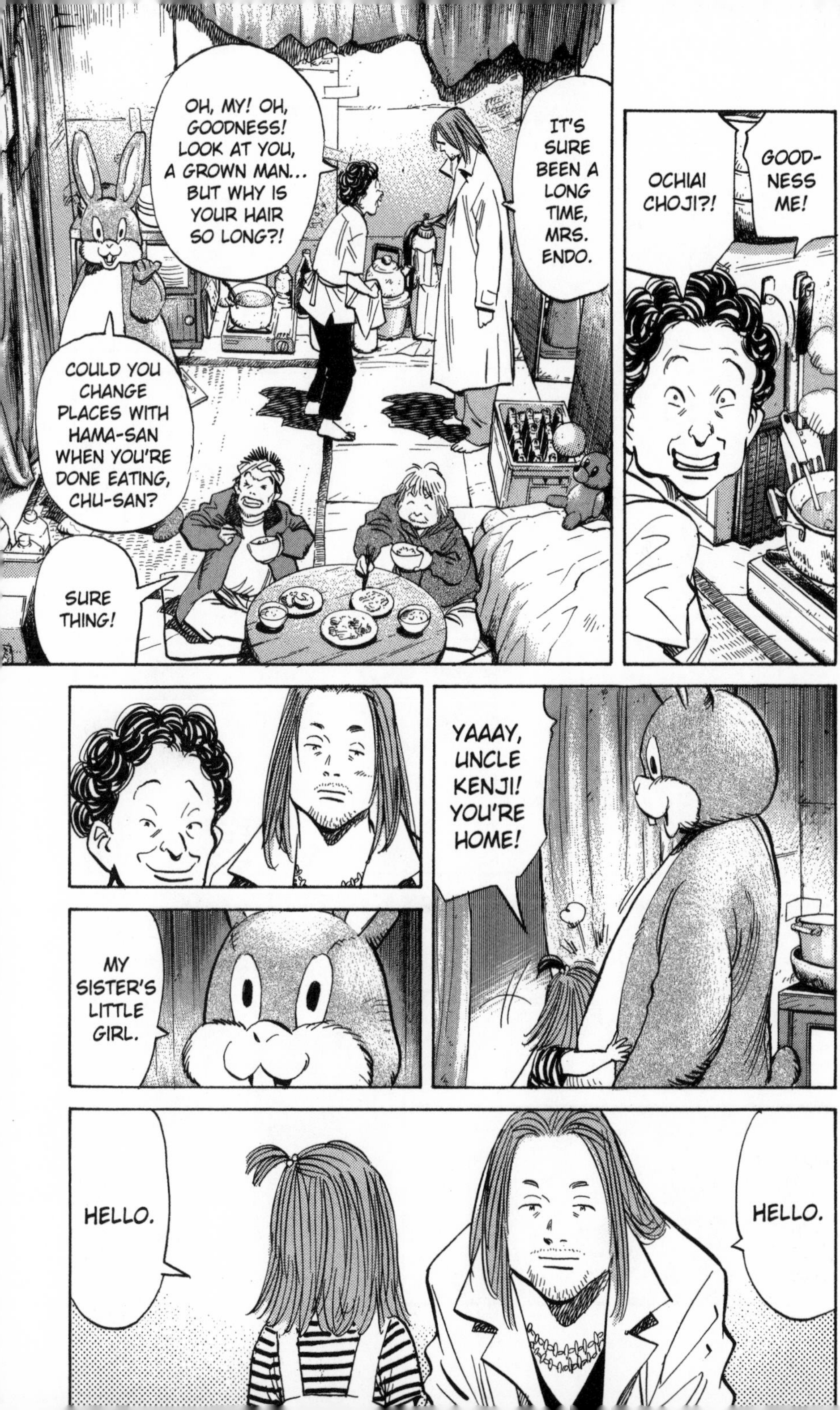
GOOD-NESS ME!
OCHIAI CHOJI?!
IT'S SURE BEEN A LONG TIME, MRS. ENDO.
OH, MY! OH, GOODNESS! LOOK AT YOU, A GROWN MAN... BUT WHY IS YOUR HAIR SO LONG?!
COULD YOU CHANGE PLACES WITH HAMA-SAN WHEN YOU'RE DONE EATING, CHU-SAN?
SURE THING!
YAAAY, UNCLE KENJI! YOU'RE HOME!
MY SISTER'S LITTLE GIRL.
HELLO.
HELLO.

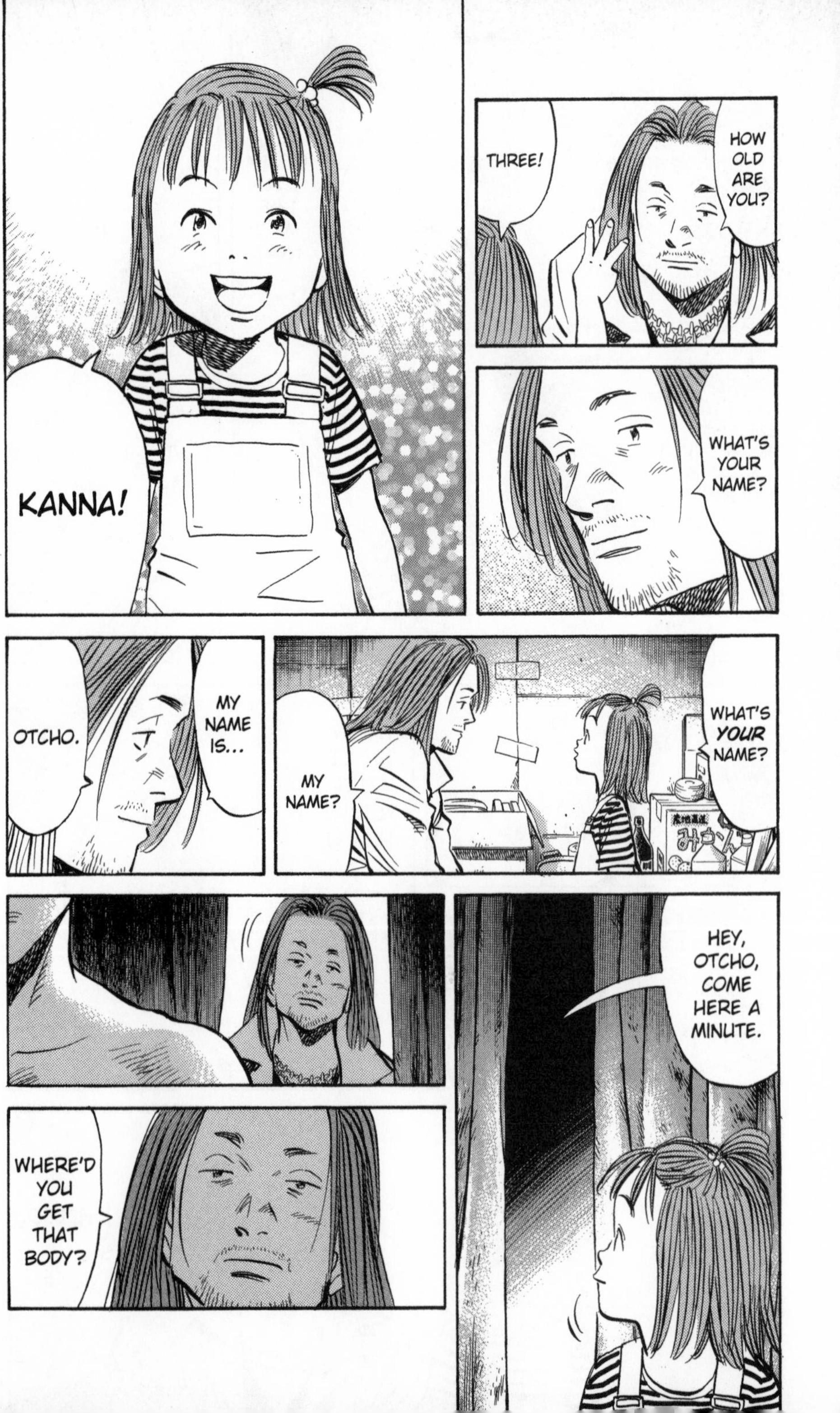
HOW OLD ARE YOU?
THREE!
WHAT'S YOUR NAME?
KANNA!
WHAT'S *YOUR* NAME?
MY NAME?
MY NAME IS...
OTCHO.
HEY, OTCHO, COME HERE A MINUTE.
WHERE'D YOU GET THAT BODY?

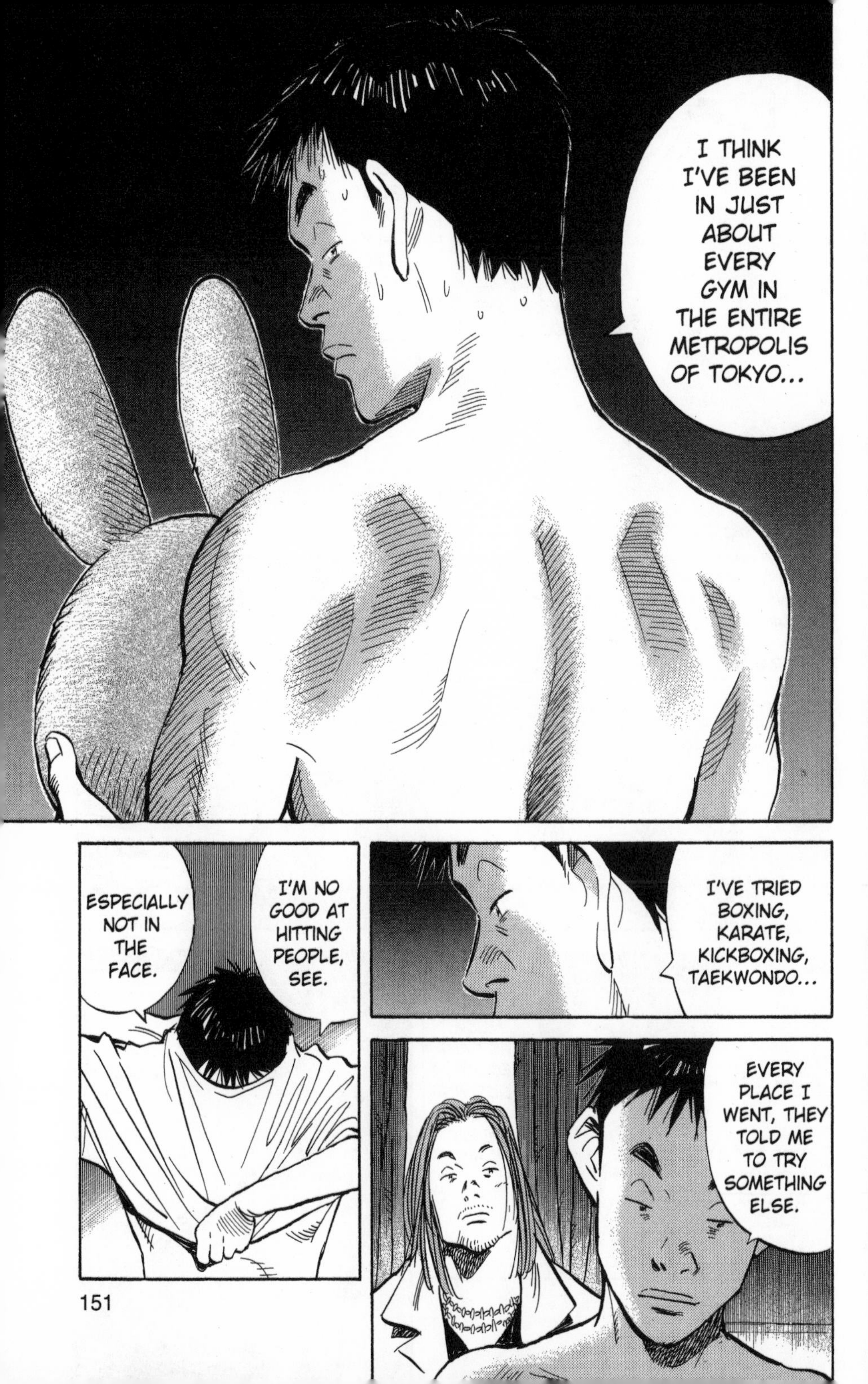
I THINK I'VE BEEN IN JUST ABOUT EVERY GYM IN THE ENTIRE METROPOLIS OF TOKYO...
I'VE TRIED BOXING, KARATE, KICKBOXING, TAEKWONDO...
EVERY PLACE I WENT, THEY TOLD ME TO TRY SOMETHING ELSE.
I'M NO GOOD AT HITTING PEOPLE, SEE.
ESPECIALLY NOT IN THE FACE.

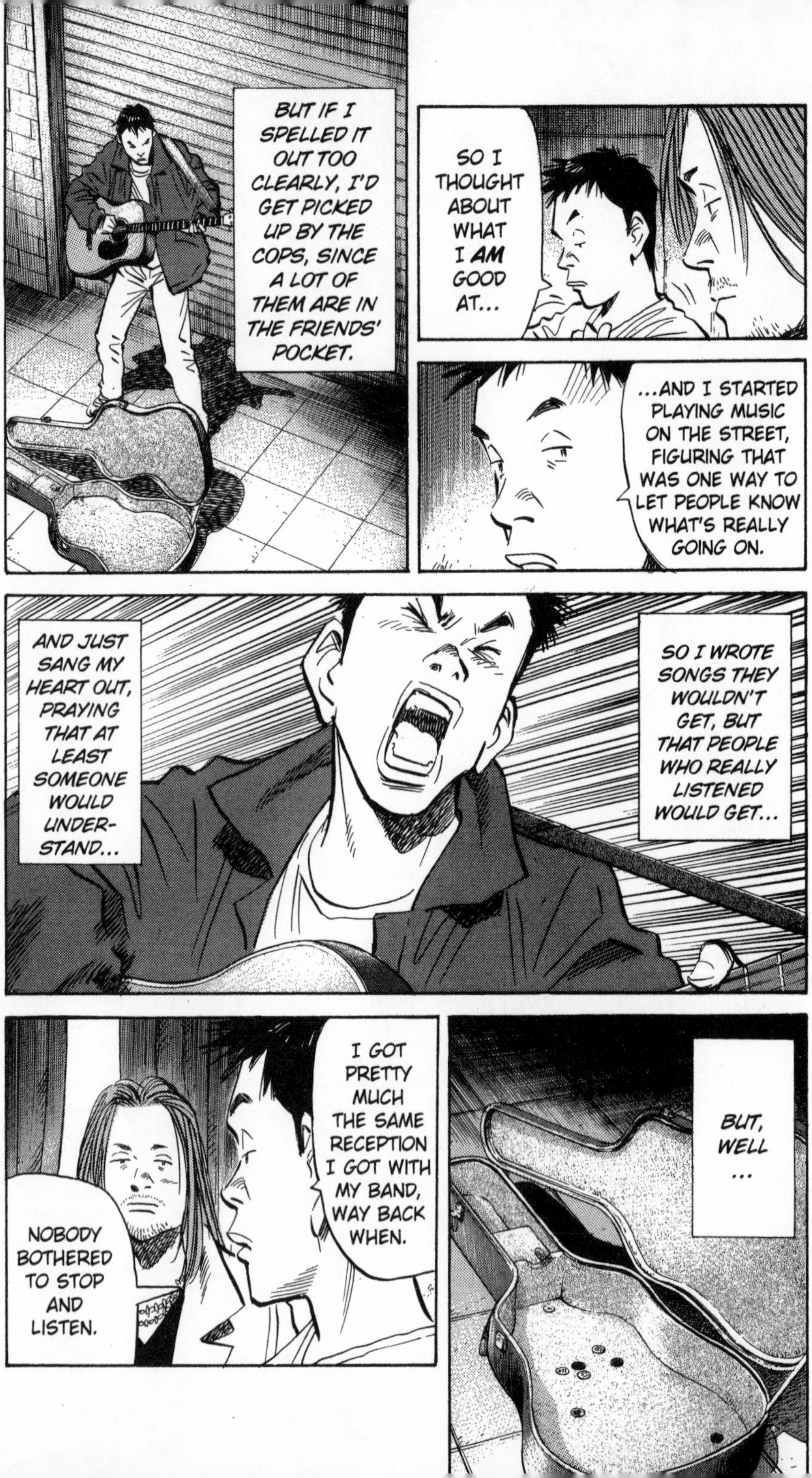
SO I THOUGHT ABOUT WHAT I **AM** GOOD AT...
...AND I STARTED PLAYING MUSIC ON THE STREET, FIGURING THAT WAS ONE WAY TO LET PEOPLE KNOW WHAT'S REALLY GOING ON.
BUT IF I SPELLED IT OUT TOO CLEARLY, I'D GET PICKED UP BY THE COPS, SINCE A LOT OF THEM ARE IN THE FRIENDS' POCKET.
SO I WROTE SONGS THEY WOULDN'T GET, BUT THAT PEOPLE WHO REALLY LISTENED WOULD GET...
AND JUST SANG MY HEART OUT, PRAYING THAT AT LEAST SOMEONE WOULD UNDER-STAND...
BUT, WELL ...
I GOT PRETTY MUCH THE SAME RECEPTION I GOT WITH MY BAND, WAY BACK WHEN.
NOBODY BOTHERED TO STOP AND LISTEN.

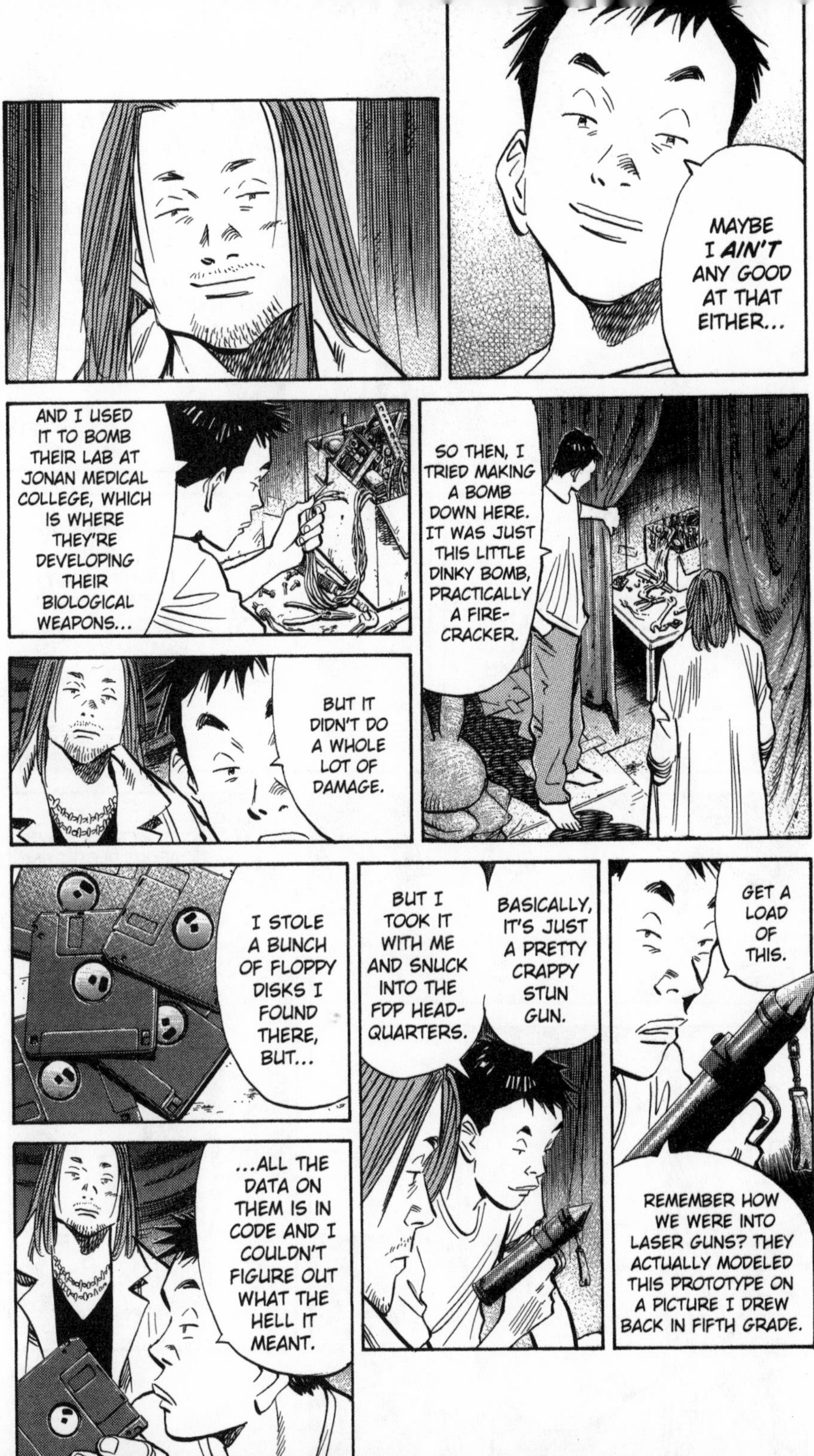
MAYBE I ***AIN'T*** ANY GOOD AT THAT EITHER...
SO THEN, I TRIED MAKING A BOMB DOWN HERE. IT WAS JUST THIS LITTLE DINKY BOMB, PRACTICALLY A FIRE-CRACKER.
AND I USED IT TO BOMB THEIR LAB AT JONAN MEDICAL COLLEGE, WHICH IS WHERE THEY'RE DEVELOPING THEIR BIOLOGICAL WEAPONS...
BUT IT DIDN'T DO A WHOLE LOT OF DAMAGE.
GET A LOAD OF THIS.
REMEMBER HOW WE WERE INTO LASER GUNS? THEY ACTUALLY MODELED THIS PROTOTYPE ON A PICTURE I DREW BACK IN FIFTH GRADE.
BASICALLY, IT'S JUST A PRETTY CRAPPY STUN GUN.
BUT I TOOK IT WITH ME AND SNUCK INTO THE FDP HEAD-QUARTERS.
I STOLE A BUNCH OF FLOPPY DISKS I FOUND THERE, BUT...
...ALL THE DATA ON THEM IS IN CODE AND I COULDN'T FIGURE OUT WHAT THE HELL IT MEANT.

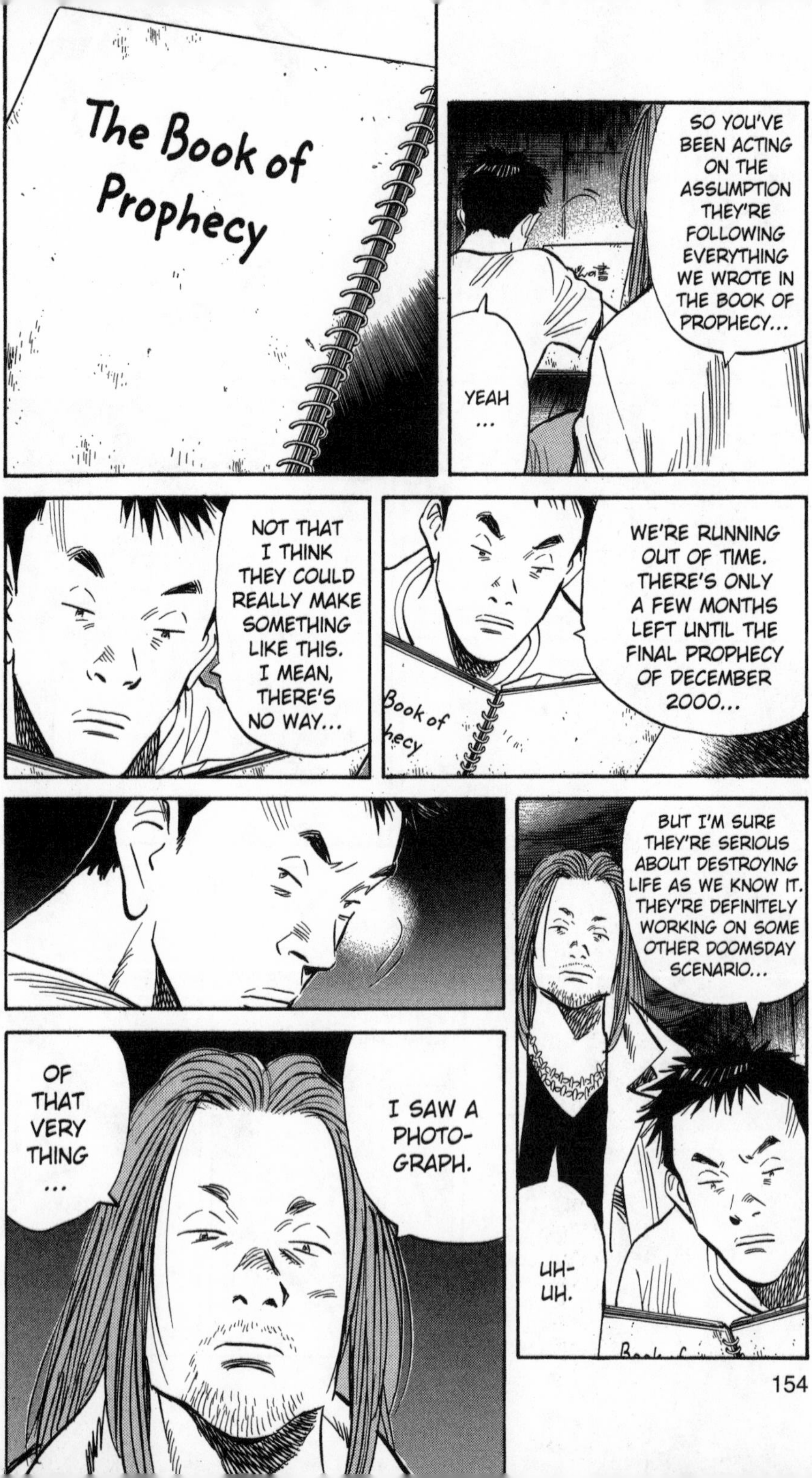
SO YOU'VE BEEN ACTING ON THE ASSUMPTION THEY'RE FOLLOWING EVERYTHING WE WROTE IN THE BOOK OF PROPHECY...
YEAH ...
The Book of Prophecy
WE'RE RUNNING OUT OF TIME. THERE'S ONLY A FEW MONTHS LEFT UNTIL THE FINAL PROPHECY OF DECEMBER 2000...
NOT THAT I THINK THEY COULD REALLY MAKE SOMETHING LIKE THIS. I MEAN, THERE'S NO WAY...
BUT I'M SURE THEY'RE SERIOUS ABOUT DESTROYING LIFE AS WE KNOW IT. THEY'RE DEFINITELY WORKING ON SOME OTHER DOOMSDAY SCENARIO...
UH-UH.
I SAW A PHOTOGRAPH.
OF THAT VERY THING ...

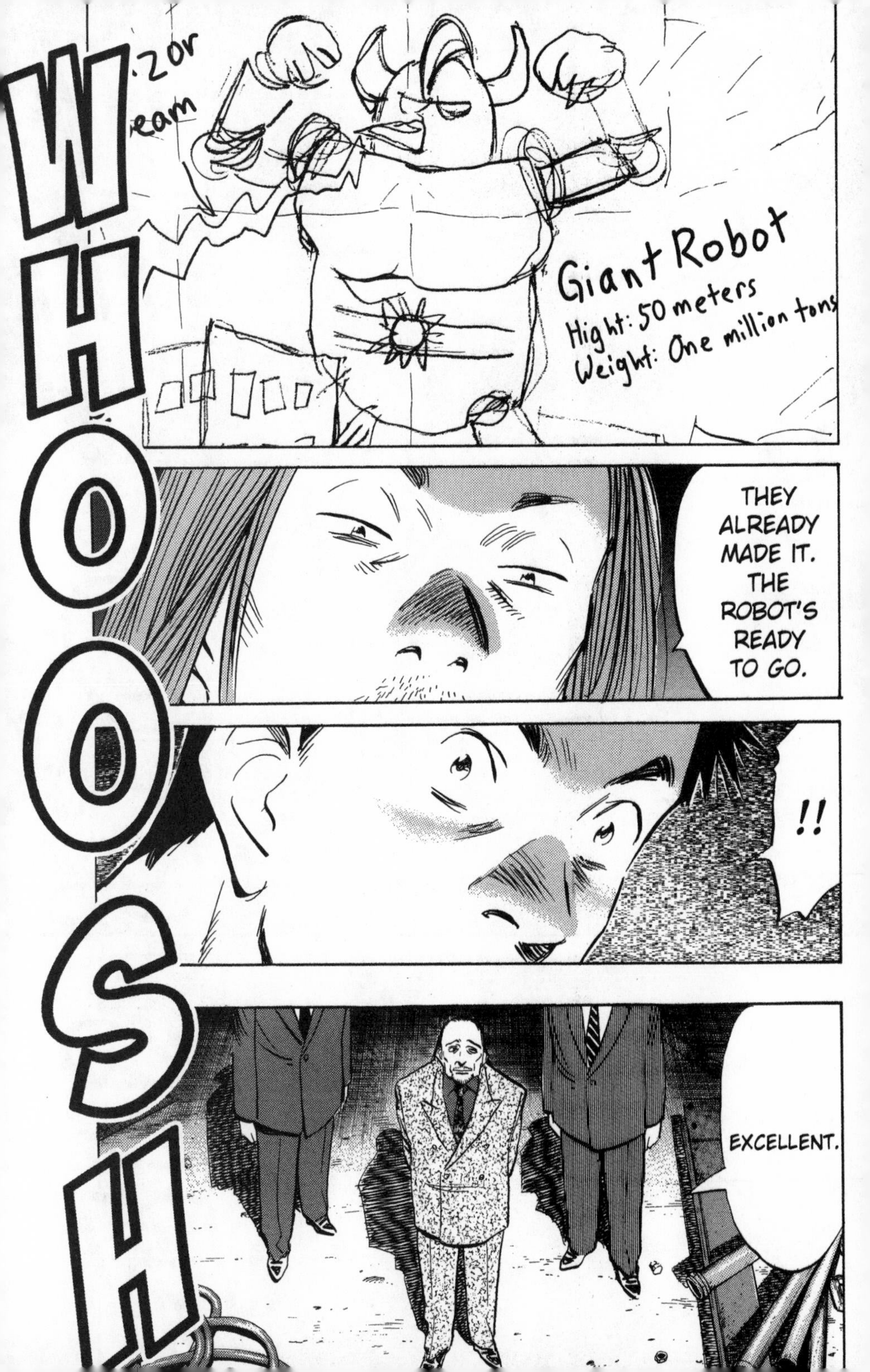
Giant Robot
Hight: 50 meters
Weight: One million tons
WHOOSH
THEY ALREADY MADE IT. THE ROBOT'S READY TO GO.
!!
EXCELLENT.

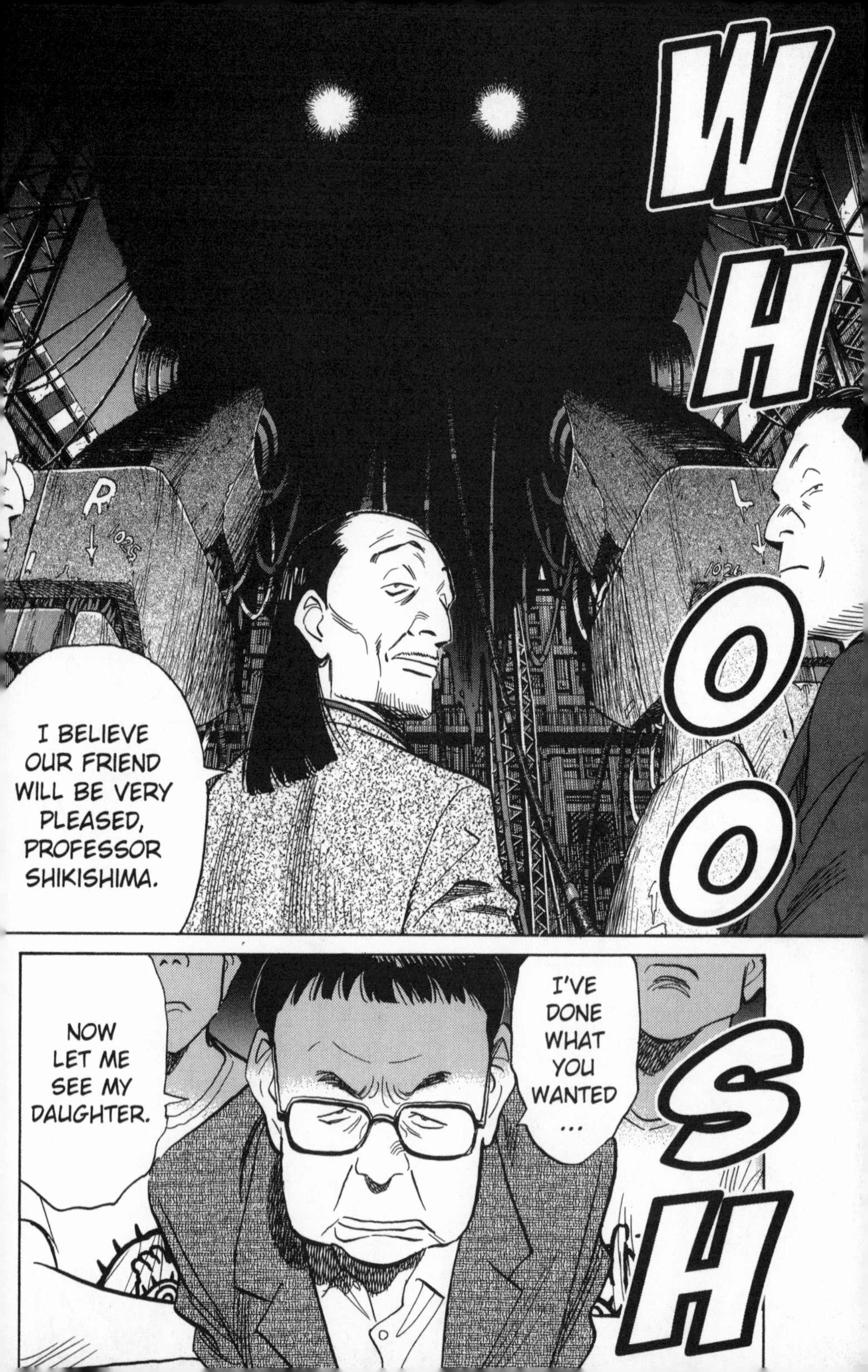
WHOOOSH
L
1026
R
1025
I BELIEVE OUR FRIEND WILL BE VERY PLEASED, PROFESSOR SHIKISHIMA.
I'VE DONE WHAT YOU WANTED ...
NOW LET ME SEE MY DAUGHTER.

Chapter 9 Robot Conference

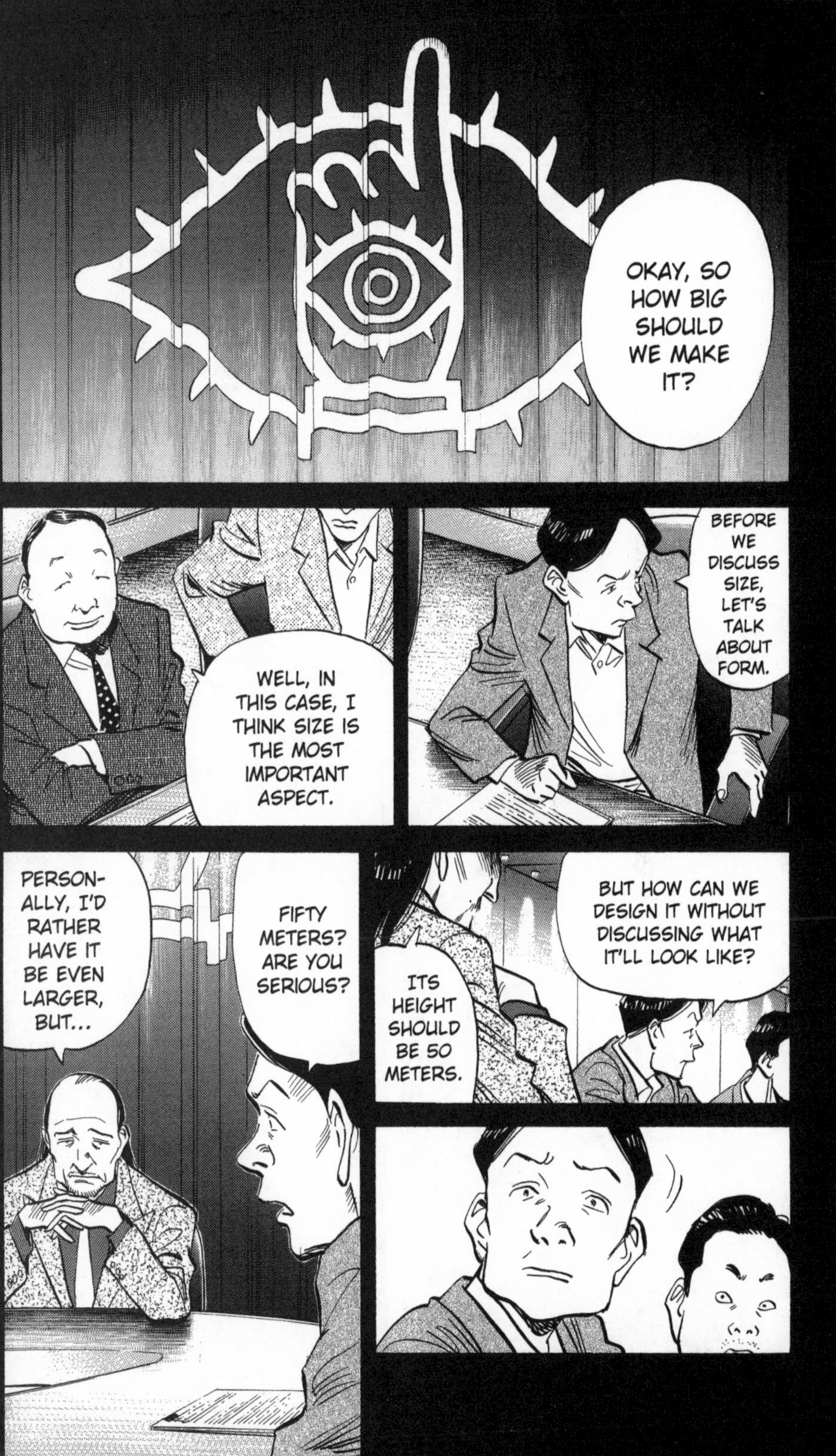
OKAY, SO HOW BIG SHOULD WE MAKE IT?
BEFORE WE DISCUSS SIZE, LET'S TALK ABOUT FORM.
WELL, IN THIS CASE, I THINK SIZE IS THE MOST IMPORTANT ASPECT.
BUT HOW CAN WE DESIGN IT WITHOUT DISCUSSING WHAT IT'LL LOOK LIKE?
ITS HEIGHT SHOULD BE 50 METERS.
FIFTY METERS? ARE YOU SERIOUS?
PERSONALLY, I'D RATHER HAVE IT BE EVEN LARGER, BUT...

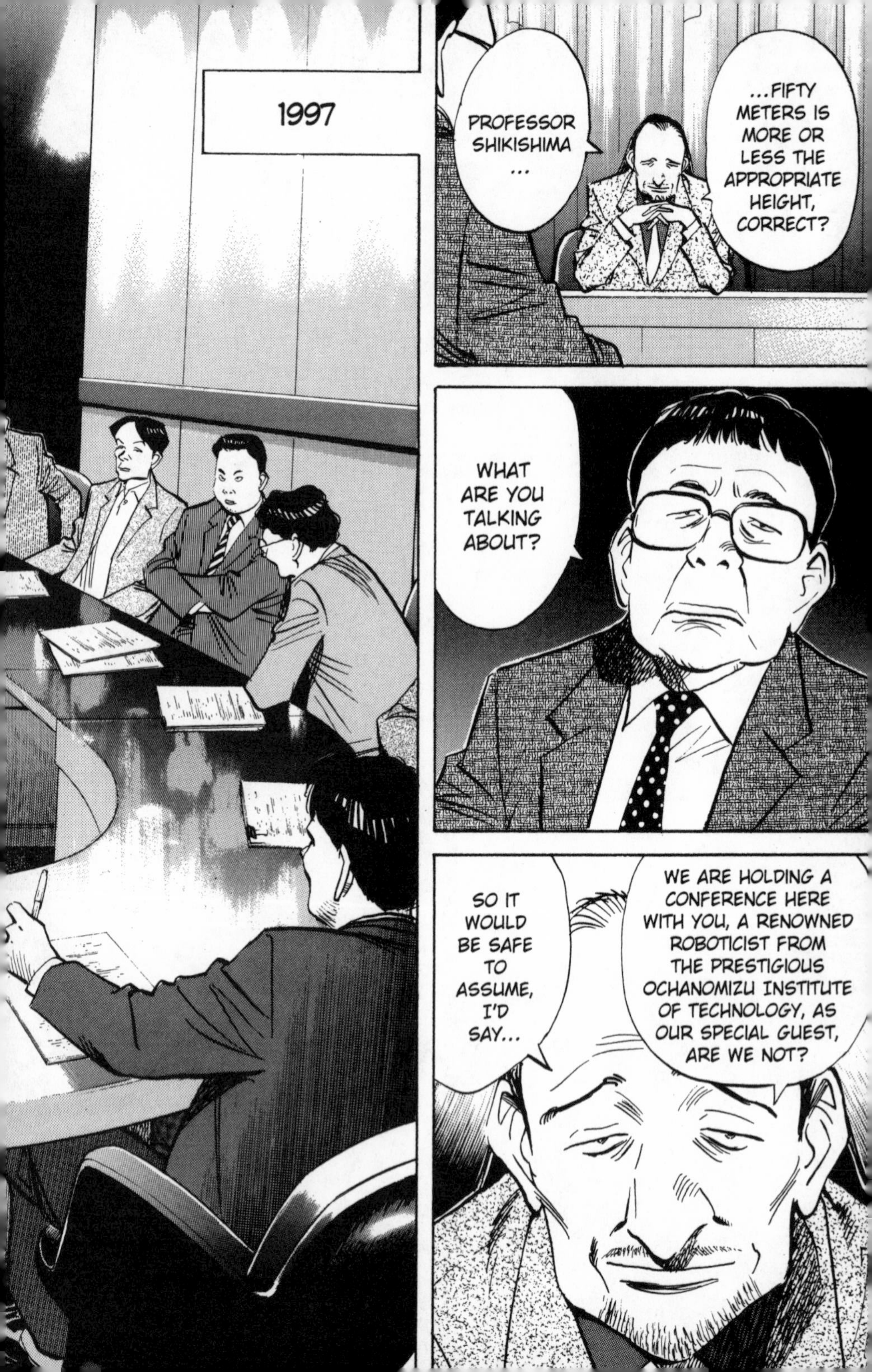
...FIFTY METERS IS MORE OR LESS THE APPROPRIATE HEIGHT, CORRECT?
PROFESSOR SHIKISHIMA ...
WHAT ARE YOU TALKING ABOUT?
WE ARE HOLDING A CONFERENCE HERE WITH YOU, A RENOWNED ROBOTICIST FROM THE PRESTIGIOUS OCHANOMIZU INSTITUTE OF TECHNOLOGY, AS OUR SPECIAL GUEST, ARE WE NOT?
SO IT WOULD BE SAFE TO ASSUME, I'D SAY...
1997

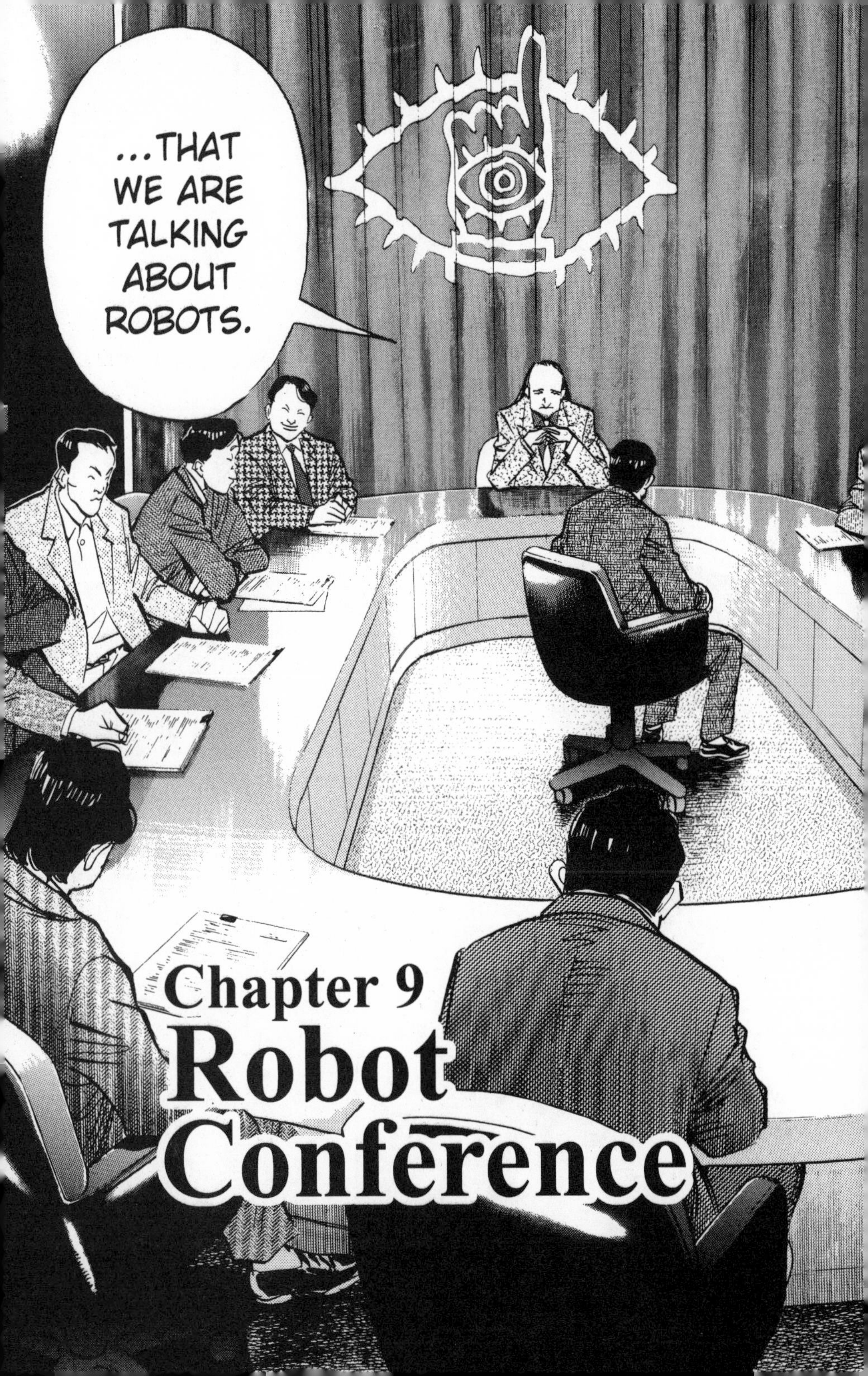
...THAT WE ARE TALKING ABOUT ROBOTS.
Chapter 9
Robot Conference

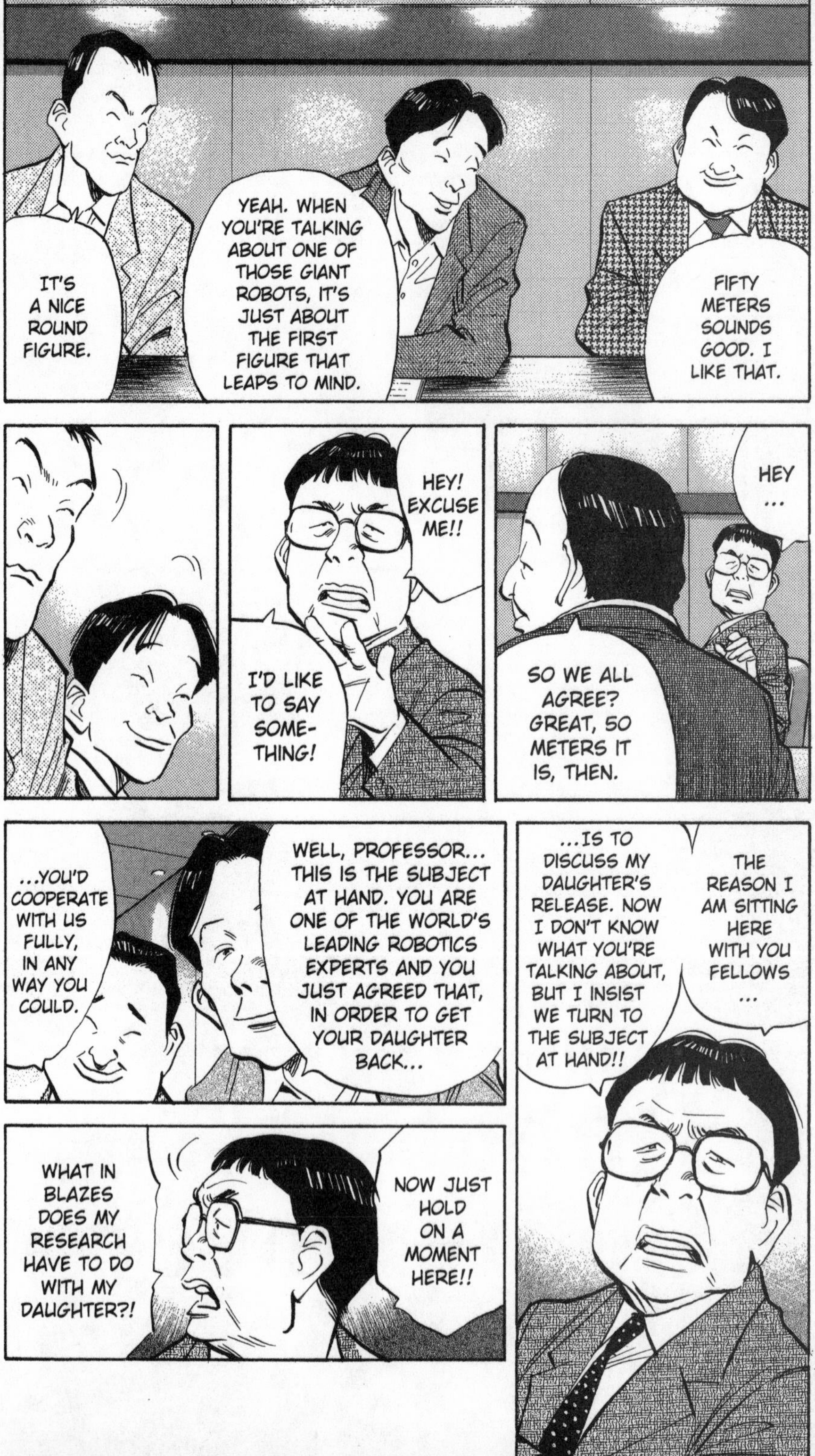
FIFTY METERS SOUNDS GOOD. I LIKE THAT.
YEAH. WHEN YOU'RE TALKING ABOUT ONE OF THOSE GIANT ROBOTS, IT'S JUST ABOUT THE FIRST FIGURE THAT LEAPS TO MIND.
IT'S A NICE ROUND FIGURE.
HEY ...
SO WE ALL AGREE? GREAT, 50 METERS IT IS, THEN.
HEY! EXCUSE ME!!
I'D LIKE TO SAY SOME-THING!
THE REASON I AM SITTING HERE WITH YOU FELLOWS ...
...IS TO DISCUSS MY DAUGHTER'S RELEASE. NOW I DON'T KNOW WHAT YOU'RE TALKING ABOUT, BUT I INSIST WE TURN TO THE SUBJECT AT HAND!!
WELL, PROFESSOR... THIS IS THE SUBJECT AT HAND. YOU ARE ONE OF THE WORLD'S LEADING ROBOTICS EXPERTS AND YOU JUST AGREED THAT, IN ORDER TO GET YOUR DAUGHTER BACK...
...YOU'D COOPERATE WITH US FULLY, IN ANY WAY YOU COULD.
NOW JUST HOLD ON A MOMENT HERE!!
WHAT IN BLAZES DOES MY RESEARCH HAVE TO DO WITH MY DAUGHTER?!

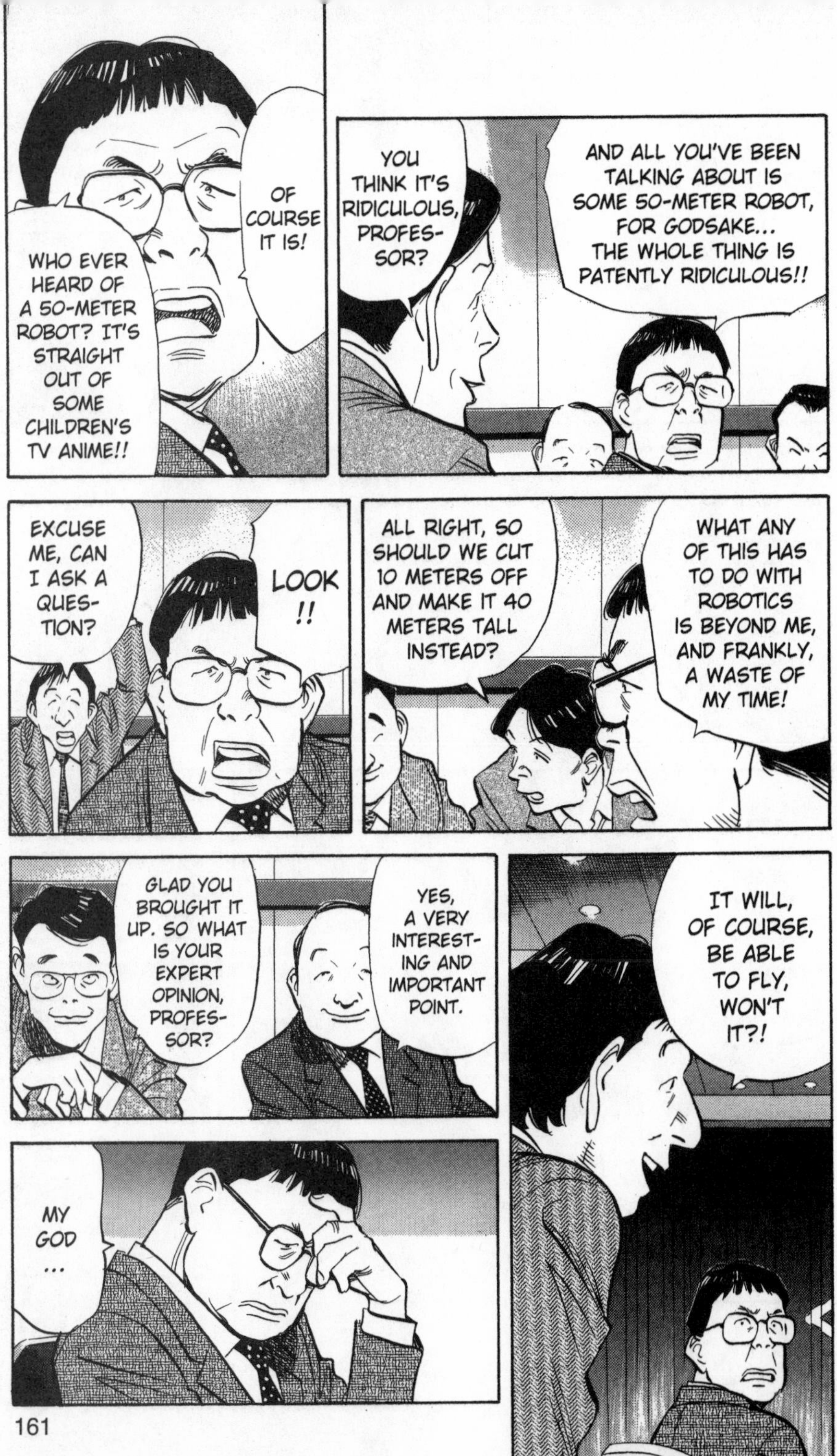
AND ALL YOU'VE BEEN TALKING ABOUT IS SOME 50-METER ROBOT, FOR GODSAKE... THE WHOLE THING IS PATENTLY RIDICULOUS!!
YOU THINK IT'S RIDICULOUS, PROFES-SOR?
OF COURSE IT IS!
WHO EVER HEARD OF A 50-METER ROBOT? IT'S STRAIGHT OUT OF SOME CHILDREN'S TV ANIME!!
WHAT ANY OF THIS HAS TO DO WITH ROBOTICS IS BEYOND ME, AND FRANKLY, A WASTE OF MY TIME!
ALL RIGHT, SO SHOULD WE CUT 10 METERS OFF AND MAKE IT 40 METERS TALL INSTEAD?
LOOK!!
EXCUSE ME, CAN I ASK A QUES-TION?
IT WILL, OF COURSE, BE ABLE TO FLY, WON'T IT?!
YES, A VERY INTEREST-ING AND IMPORTANT POINT.
GLAD YOU BROUGHT IT UP. SO WHAT IS YOUR EXPERT OPINION, PROFES-SOR?
MY GOD ...

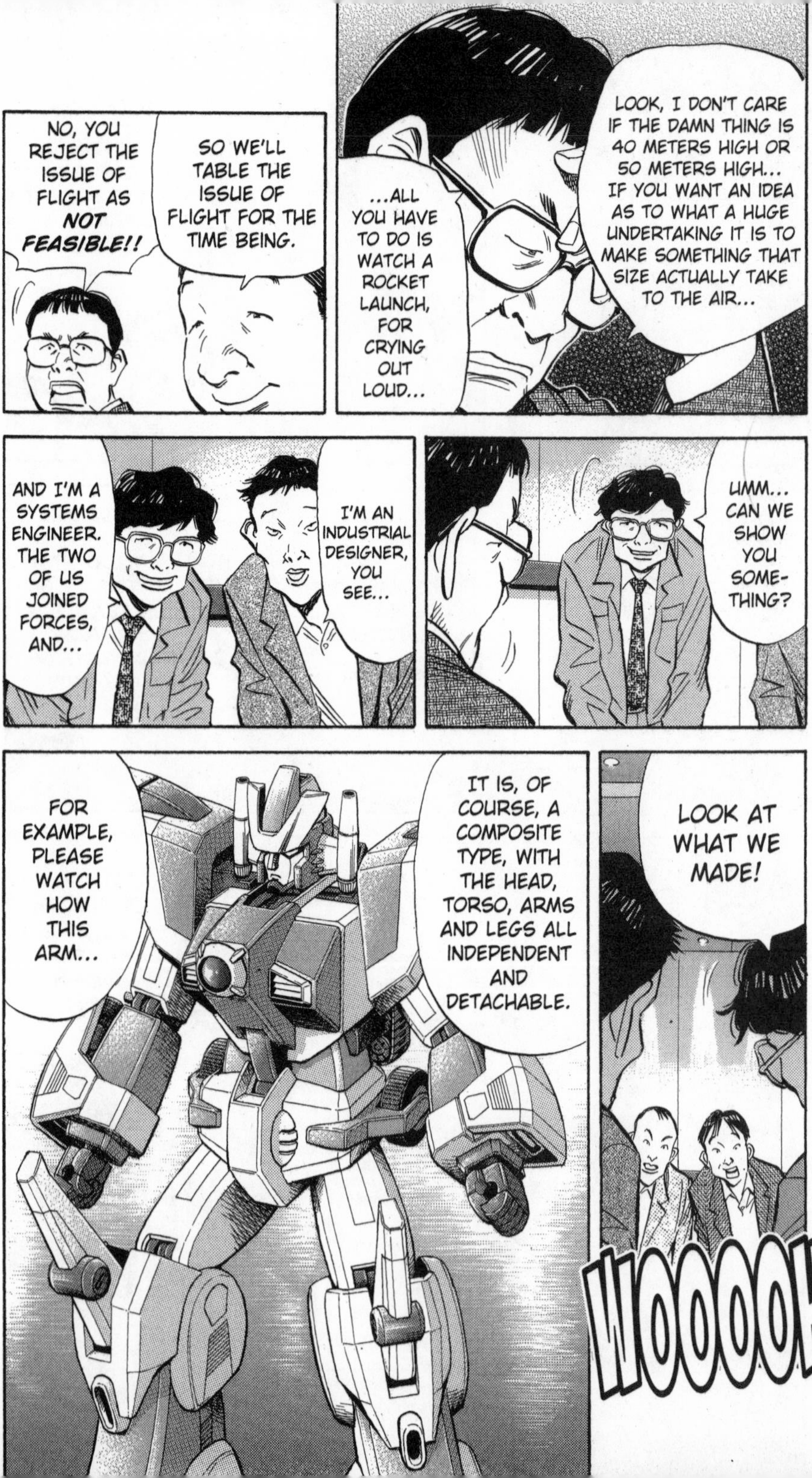
LOOK, I DON'T CARE IF THE DAMN THING IS 40 METERS HIGH OR 50 METERS HIGH... IF YOU WANT AN IDEA AS TO WHAT A HUGE UNDERTAKING IT IS TO MAKE SOMETHING THAT SIZE ACTUALLY TAKE TO THE AIR...
...ALL YOU HAVE TO DO IS WATCH A ROCKET LAUNCH, FOR CRYING OUT LOUD...
SO WE'LL TABLE THE ISSUE OF FLIGHT FOR THE TIME BEING.
NO, YOU REJECT THE ISSUE OF FLIGHT AS ***NOT FEASIBLE!!***
UMM... CAN WE SHOW YOU SOME-THING?
I'M AN INDUSTRIAL DESIGNER, YOU SEE...
AND I'M A SYSTEMS ENGINEER. THE TWO OF US JOINED FORCES, AND...
LOOK AT WHAT WE MADE!
WOOOOH
IT IS, OF COURSE, A COMPOSITE TYPE, WITH THE HEAD, TORSO, ARMS AND LEGS ALL INDEPENDENT AND DETACHABLE.
FOR EXAMPLE, PLEASE WATCH HOW THIS ARM...

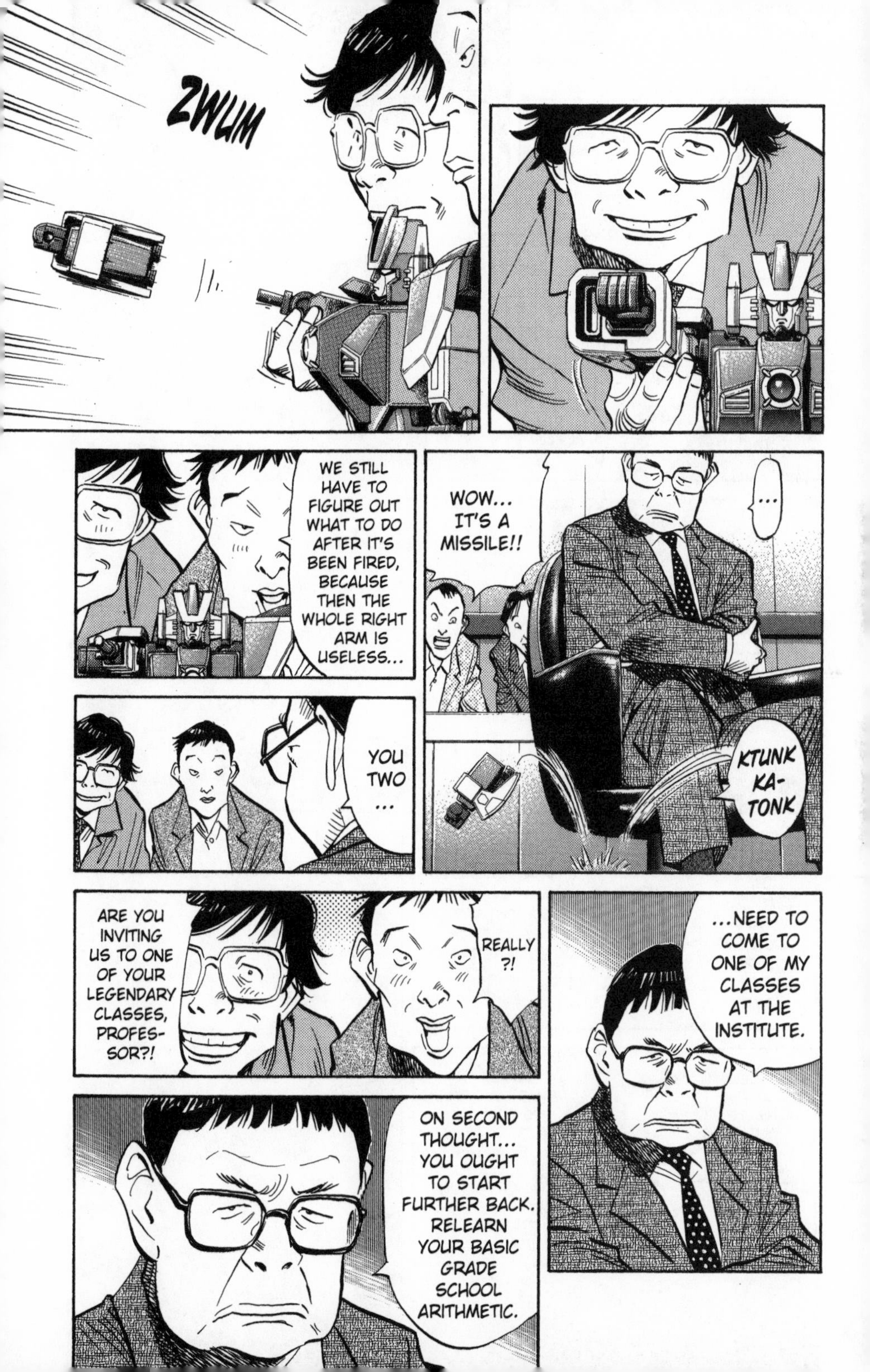
ZWUM
...
WOW... IT'S A MISSILE!!
KTUNK KA-TONK
WE STILL HAVE TO FIGURE OUT WHAT TO DO AFTER IT'S BEEN FIRED, BECAUSE THEN THE WHOLE RIGHT ARM IS USELESS...
YOU TWO ...
...NEED TO COME TO ONE OF MY CLASSES AT THE INSTITUTE.
REALLY ?!
ARE YOU INVITING US TO ONE OF YOUR LEGENDARY CLASSES, PROFES-SOR?!
ON SECOND THOUGHT... YOU OUGHT TO START FURTHER BACK. RELEARN YOUR BASIC GRADE SCHOOL ARITHMETIC.

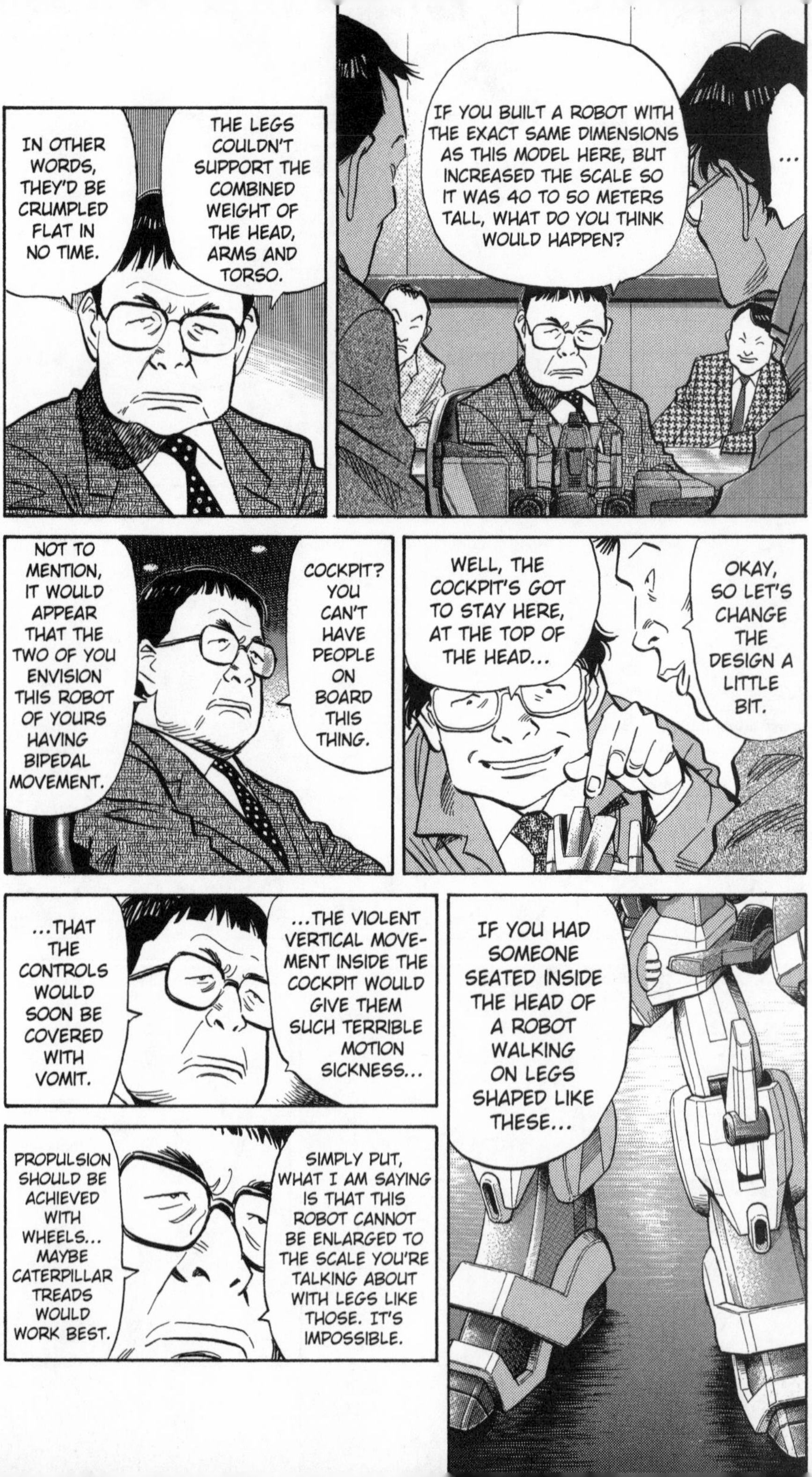
IF YOU BUILT A ROBOT WITH THE EXACT SAME DIMENSIONS AS THIS MODEL HERE, BUT INCREASED THE SCALE SO IT WAS 40 TO 50 METERS TALL, WHAT DO YOU THINK WOULD HAPPEN?
...
THE LEGS COULDN'T SUPPORT THE COMBINED WEIGHT OF THE HEAD, ARMS AND TORSO.
IN OTHER WORDS, THEY'D BE CRUMPLED FLAT IN NO TIME.
OKAY, SO LET'S CHANGE THE DESIGN A LITTLE BIT.
WELL, THE COCKPIT'S GOT TO STAY HERE, AT THE TOP OF THE HEAD...
COCKPIT? YOU CAN'T HAVE PEOPLE ON BOARD THIS THING.
NOT TO MENTION, IT WOULD APPEAR THAT THE TWO OF YOU ENVISION THIS ROBOT OF YOURS HAVING BIPEDAL MOVEMENT.
IF YOU HAD SOMEONE SEATED INSIDE THE HEAD OF A ROBOT WALKING ON LEGS SHAPED LIKE THESE...
...THE VIOLENT VERTICAL MOVEMENT INSIDE THE COCKPIT WOULD GIVE THEM SUCH TERRIBLE MOTION SICKNESS...
...THAT THE CONTROLS WOULD SOON BE COVERED WITH VOMIT.
SIMPLY PUT, WHAT I AM SAYING IS THAT THIS ROBOT CANNOT BE ENLARGED TO THE SCALE YOU'RE TALKING ABOUT WITH LEGS LIKE THOSE. IT'S IMPOSSIBLE.
PROPULSION SHOULD BE ACHIEVED WITH WHEELS... MAYBE CATERPILLAR TREADS WOULD WORK BEST.

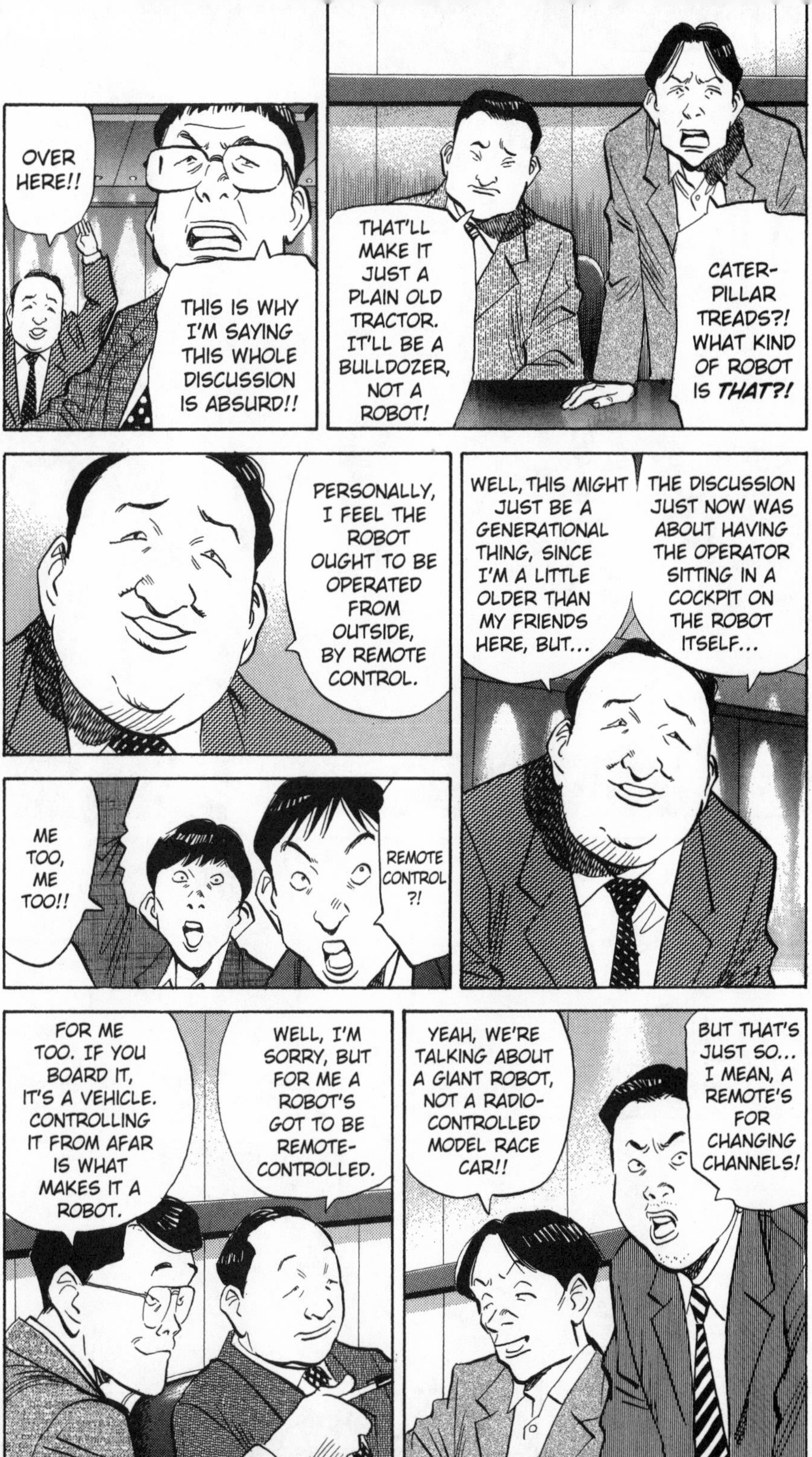
CATER-PILLAR TREADS?! WHAT KIND OF ROBOT IS *THAT?!*
THAT'LL MAKE IT JUST A PLAIN OLD TRACTOR. IT'LL BE A BULLDOZER, NOT A ROBOT!
THIS IS WHY I'M SAYING THIS WHOLE DISCUSSION IS ABSURD!!
OVER HERE!!
THE DISCUSSION JUST NOW WAS ABOUT HAVING THE OPERATOR SITTING IN A COCKPIT ON THE ROBOT ITSELF...
WELL, THIS MIGHT JUST BE A GENERATIONAL THING, SINCE I'M A LITTLE OLDER THAN MY FRIENDS HERE, BUT...
PERSONALLY, I FEEL THE ROBOT OUGHT TO BE OPERATED FROM OUTSIDE, BY REMOTE CONTROL.
REMOTE CONTROL ?!
ME TOO, ME TOO!!
BUT THAT'S JUST SO... I MEAN, A REMOTE'S FOR CHANGING CHANNELS!
YEAH, WE'RE TALKING ABOUT A GIANT ROBOT, NOT A RADIO-CONTROLLED MODEL RACE CAR!!
WELL, I'M SORRY, BUT FOR ME A ROBOT'S GOT TO BE REMOTE-CONTROLLED.
FOR ME TOO. IF YOU BOARD IT, IT'S A VEHICLE. CONTROLLING IT FROM AFAR IS WHAT MAKES IT A ROBOT.

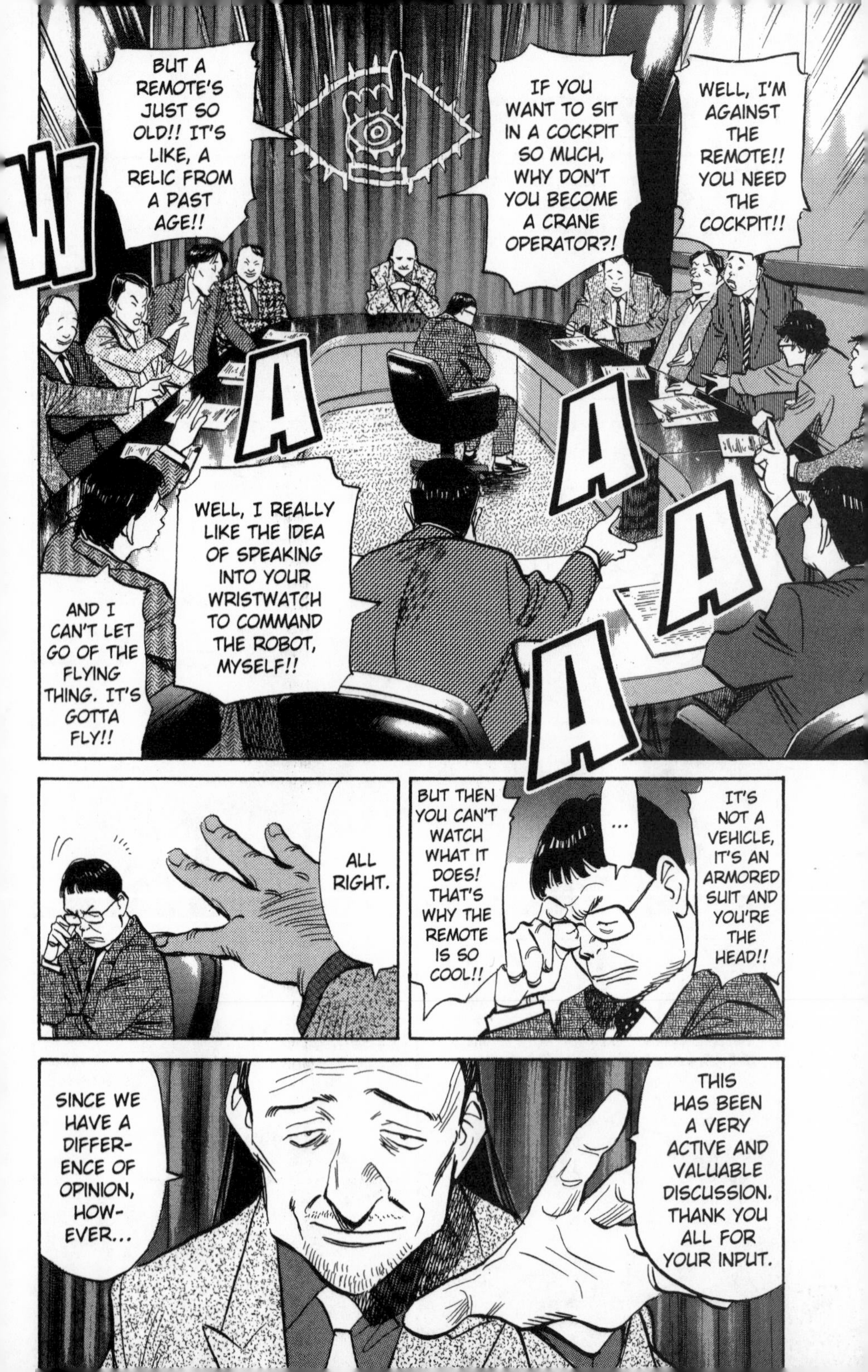
WELL, I'M AGAINST THE REMOTE!! YOU NEED THE COCKPIT!!
IF YOU WANT TO SIT IN A COCKPIT SO MUCH, WHY DON'T YOU BECOME A CRANE OPERATOR?!
BUT A REMOTE'S JUST SO OLD!! IT'S LIKE, A RELIC FROM A PAST AGE!!
WAAAAA
WELL, I REALLY LIKE THE IDEA OF SPEAKING INTO YOUR WRISTWATCH TO COMMAND THE ROBOT, MYSELF!!
AND I CAN'T LET GO OF THE FLYING THING. IT'S GOTTA FLY!!
IT'S NOT A VEHICLE, IT'S AN ARMORED SUIT AND YOU'RE THE HEAD!!
...
BUT THEN YOU CAN'T WATCH WHAT IT DOES! THAT'S WHY THE REMOTE IS SO COOL!!
ALL RIGHT.
THIS HAS BEEN A VERY ACTIVE AND VALUABLE DISCUSSION. THANK YOU ALL FOR YOUR INPUT.
SINCE WE HAVE A DIFFER-ENCE OF OPINION, HOW-EVER...

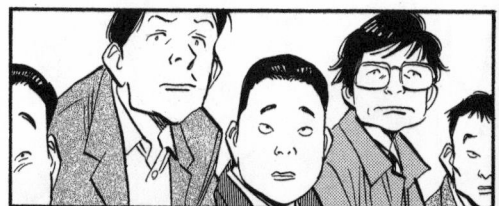

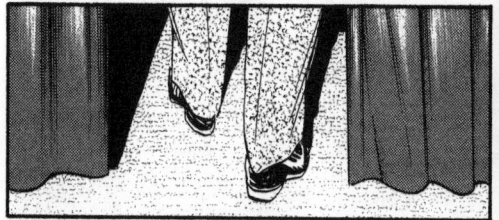

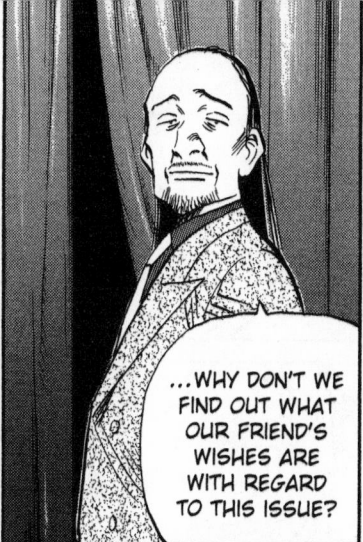

...WHY DON'T WE FIND OUT WHAT OUR FRIEND'S WISHES ARE WITH REGARD TO THIS ISSUE?
OUR FRIEND...
...LISTENED TO BOTH VIEWS WITH GREAT INTEREST.
LIKE SOME OF YOU, HE HAS A GREAT ATTACHMENT TO THE REMOTE CONTROL.
HOWEVER, HE BELIEVES THAT PLACING A COCKPIT AND CONTROLS INSIDE THE ROBOT IS ALSO A VERY GOOD IDEA.

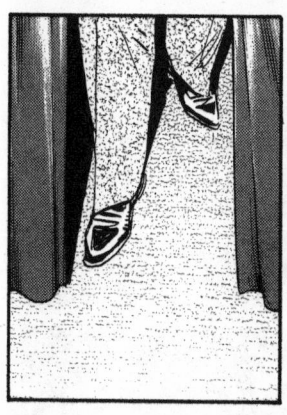

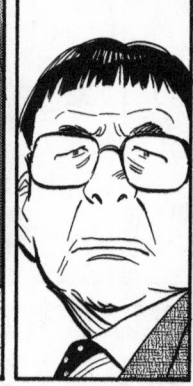

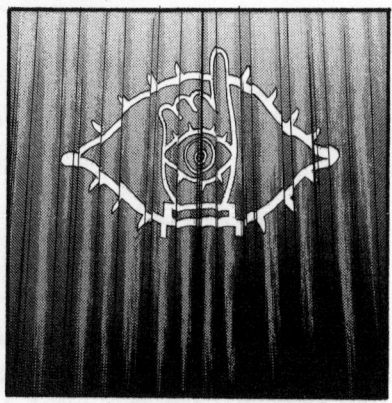

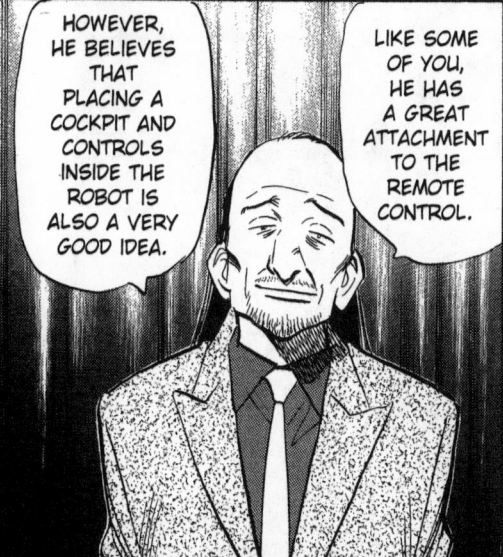

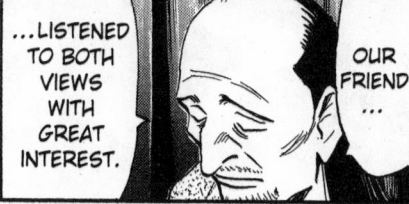

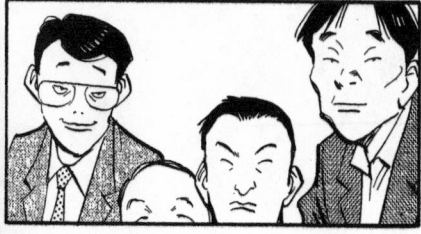

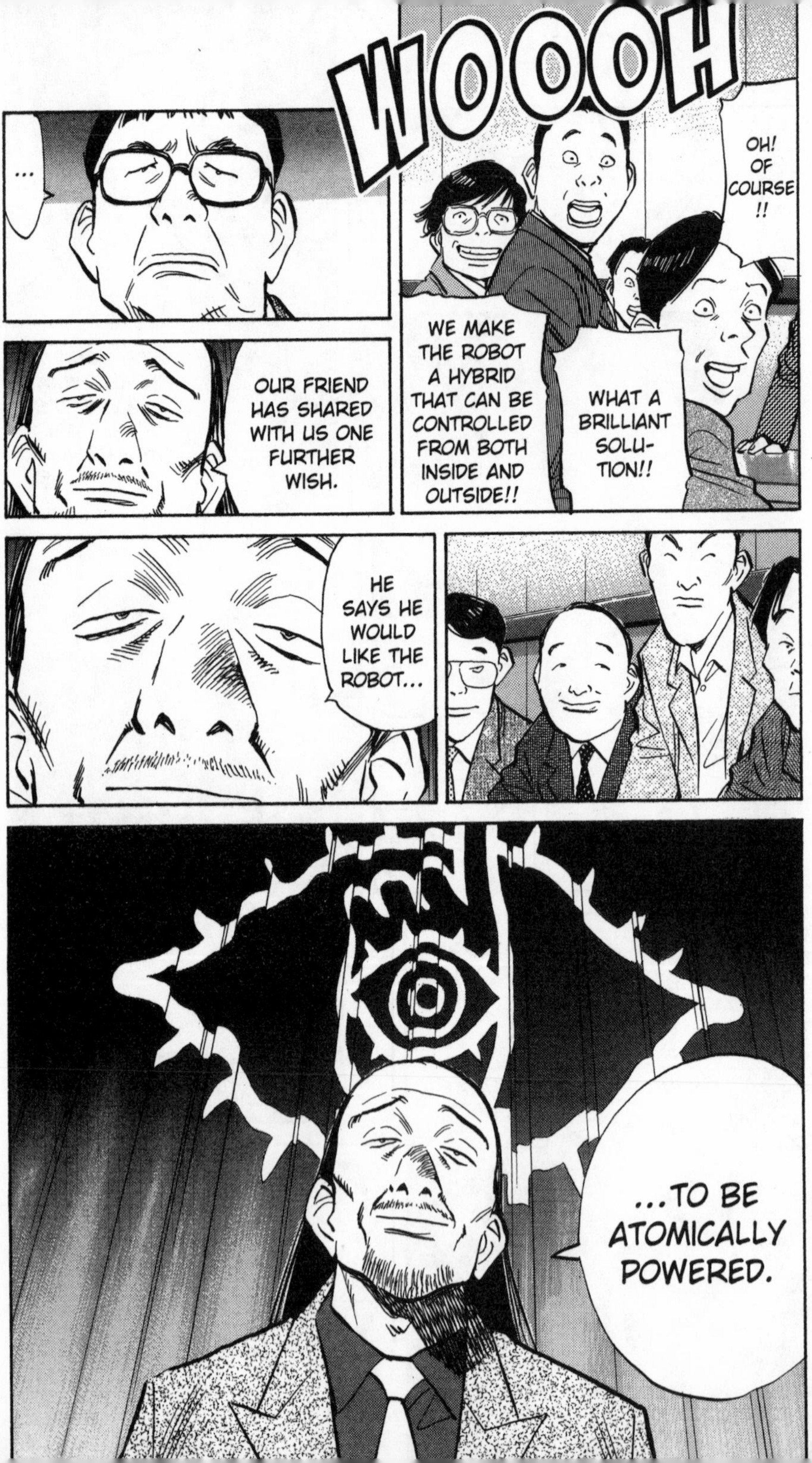
WOOOH
OH! OF COURSE!!
WE MAKE THE ROBOT A HYBRID THAT CAN BE CONTROLLED FROM BOTH INSIDE AND OUTSIDE!!
WHAT A BRILLIANT SOLU-TION!!
...
OUR FRIEND HAS SHARED WITH US ONE FURTHER WISH.
HE SAYS HE WOULD LIKE THE ROBOT...
...TO BE ATOMICALLY POWERED.

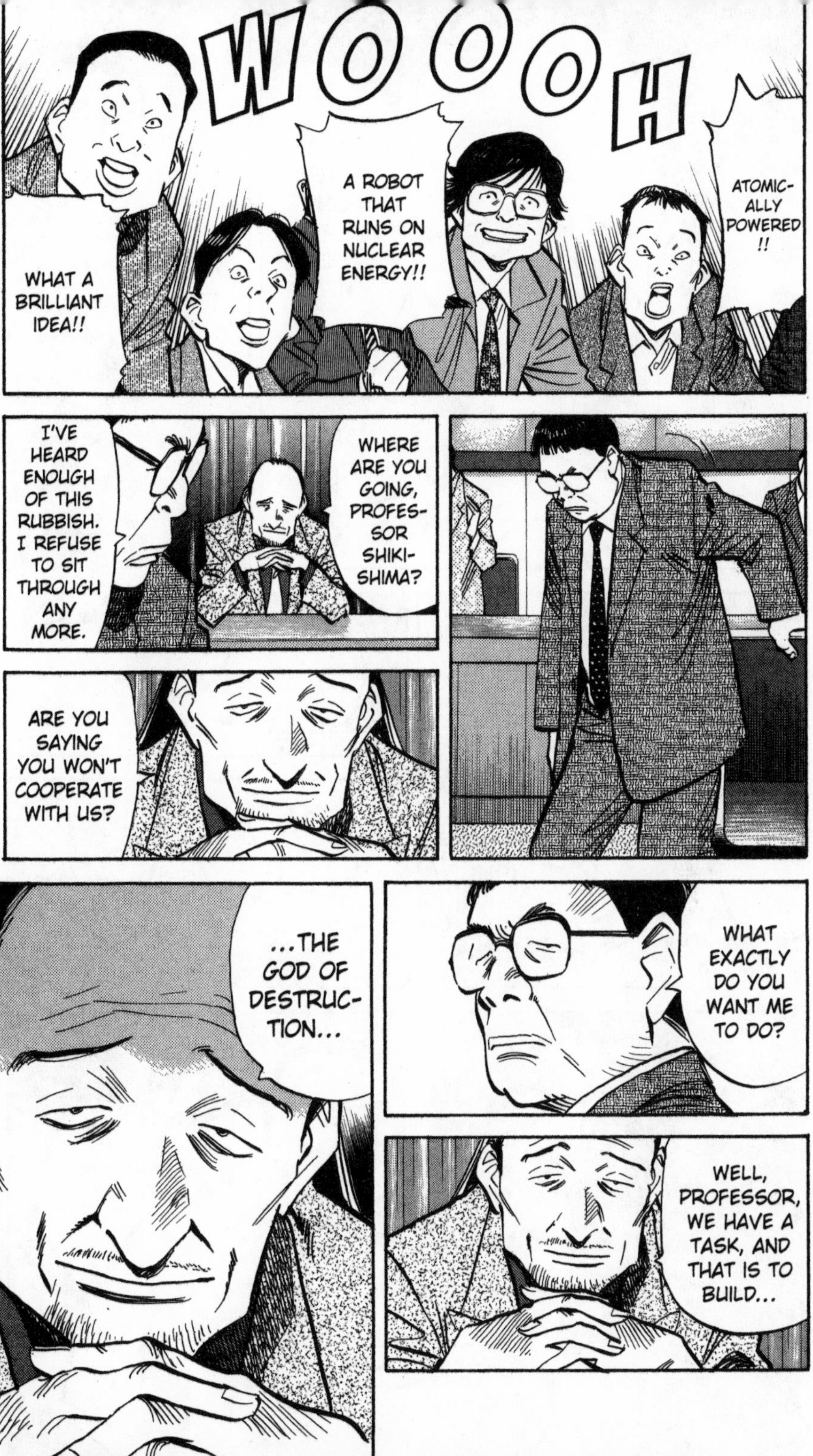
WOOOH
ATOMIC-ALLY POWERED!!
A ROBOT THAT RUNS ON NUCLEAR ENERGY!!
WHAT A BRILLIANT IDEA!!
WHERE ARE YOU GOING, PROFES-SOR SHIKI-SHIMA?
I'VE HEARD ENOUGH OF THIS RUBBISH. I REFUSE TO SIT THROUGH ANY MORE.
ARE YOU SAYING YOU WON'T COOPERATE WITH US?
WHAT EXACTLY DO YOU WANT ME TO DO?
WELL, PROFESSOR, WE HAVE A TASK, AND THAT IS TO BUILD...
...THE GOD OF DESTRUC-TION...

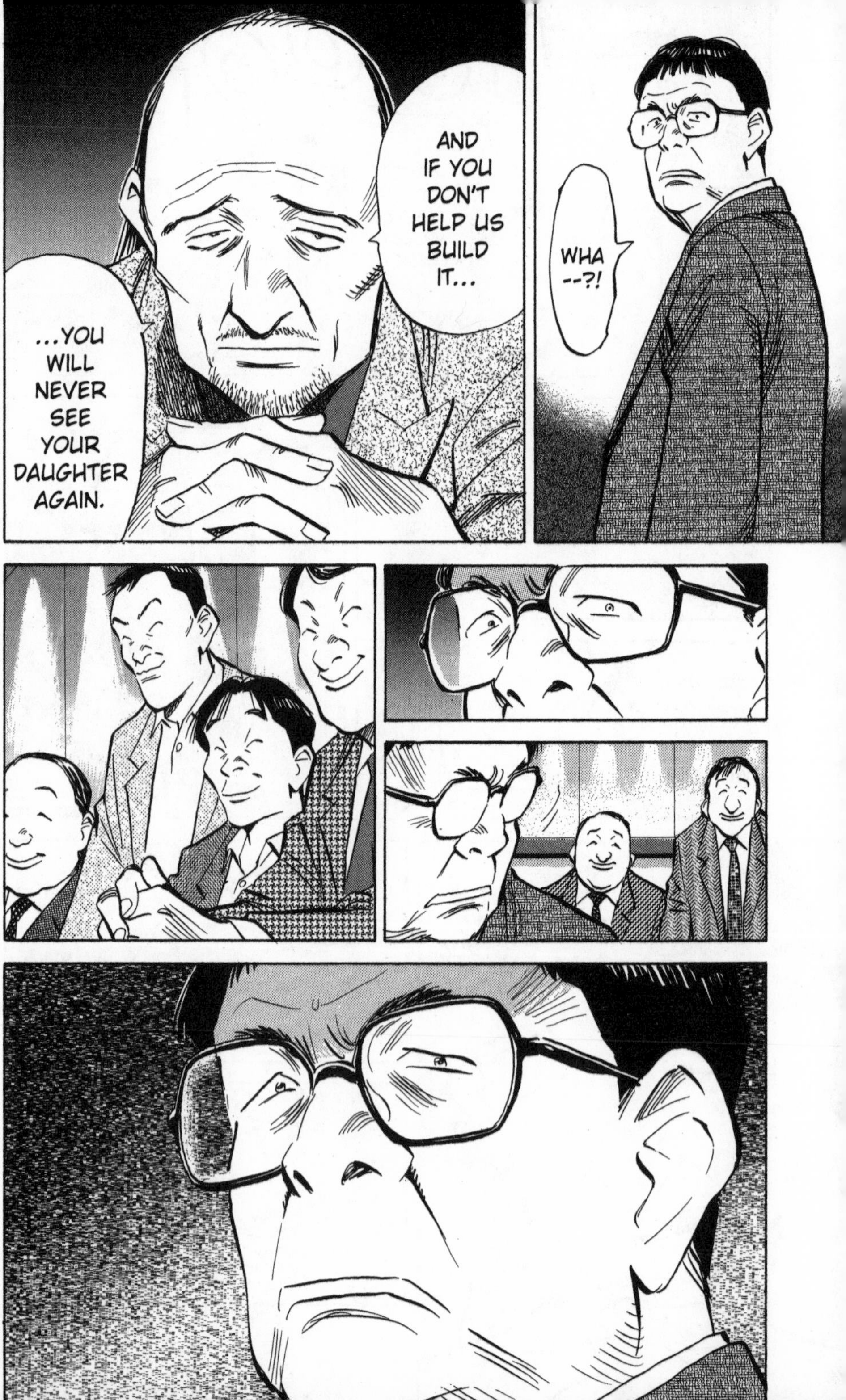
WHA --?!
AND IF YOU DON'T HELP US BUILD IT...
...YOU WILL NEVER SEE YOUR DAUGHTER AGAIN.

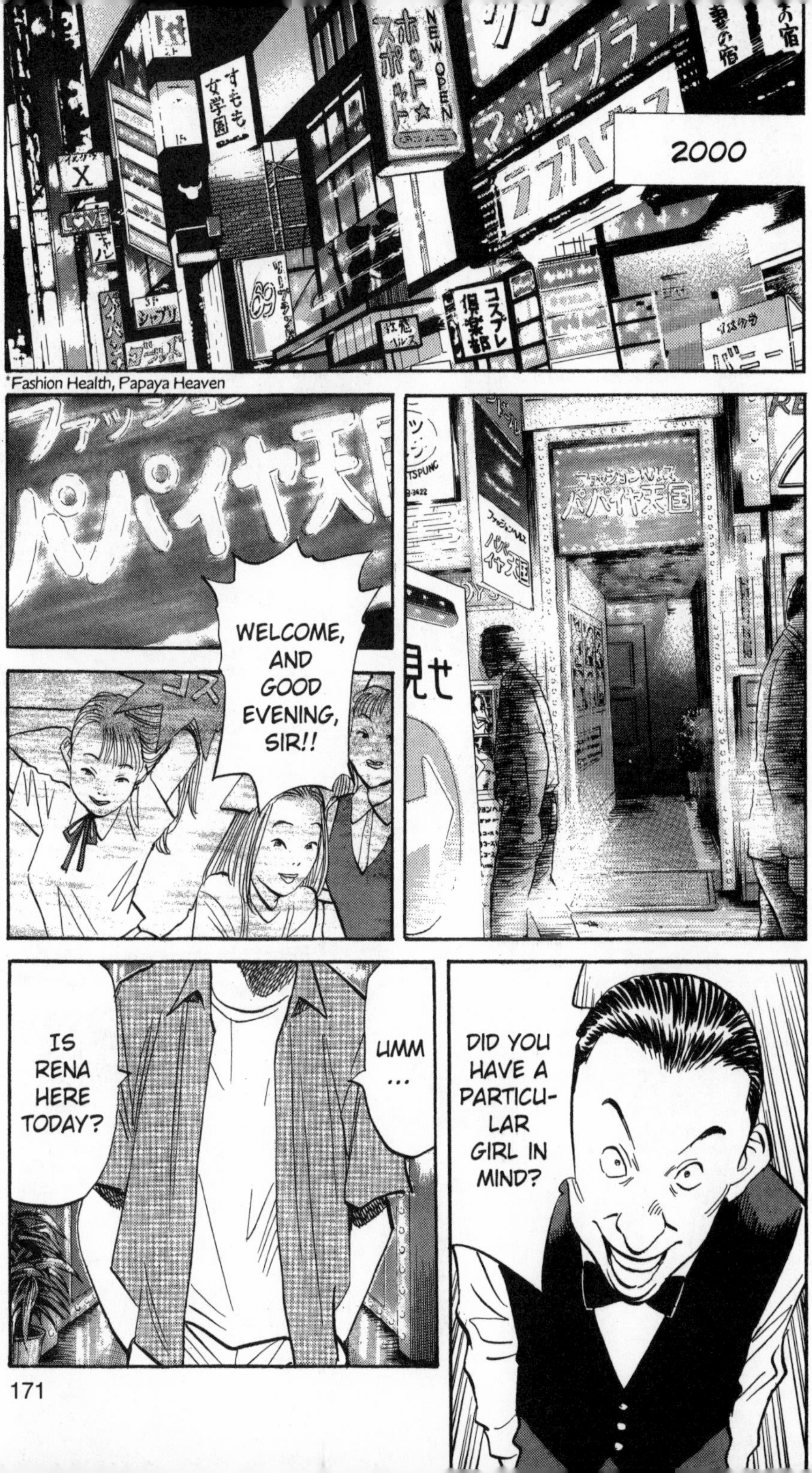
2000
*Fashion Health, Papaya Heaven
WELCOME, AND GOOD EVENING, SIR!!
DID YOU HAVE A PARTICU-LAR GIRL IN MIND?
UMM ...
IS RENA HERE TODAY?

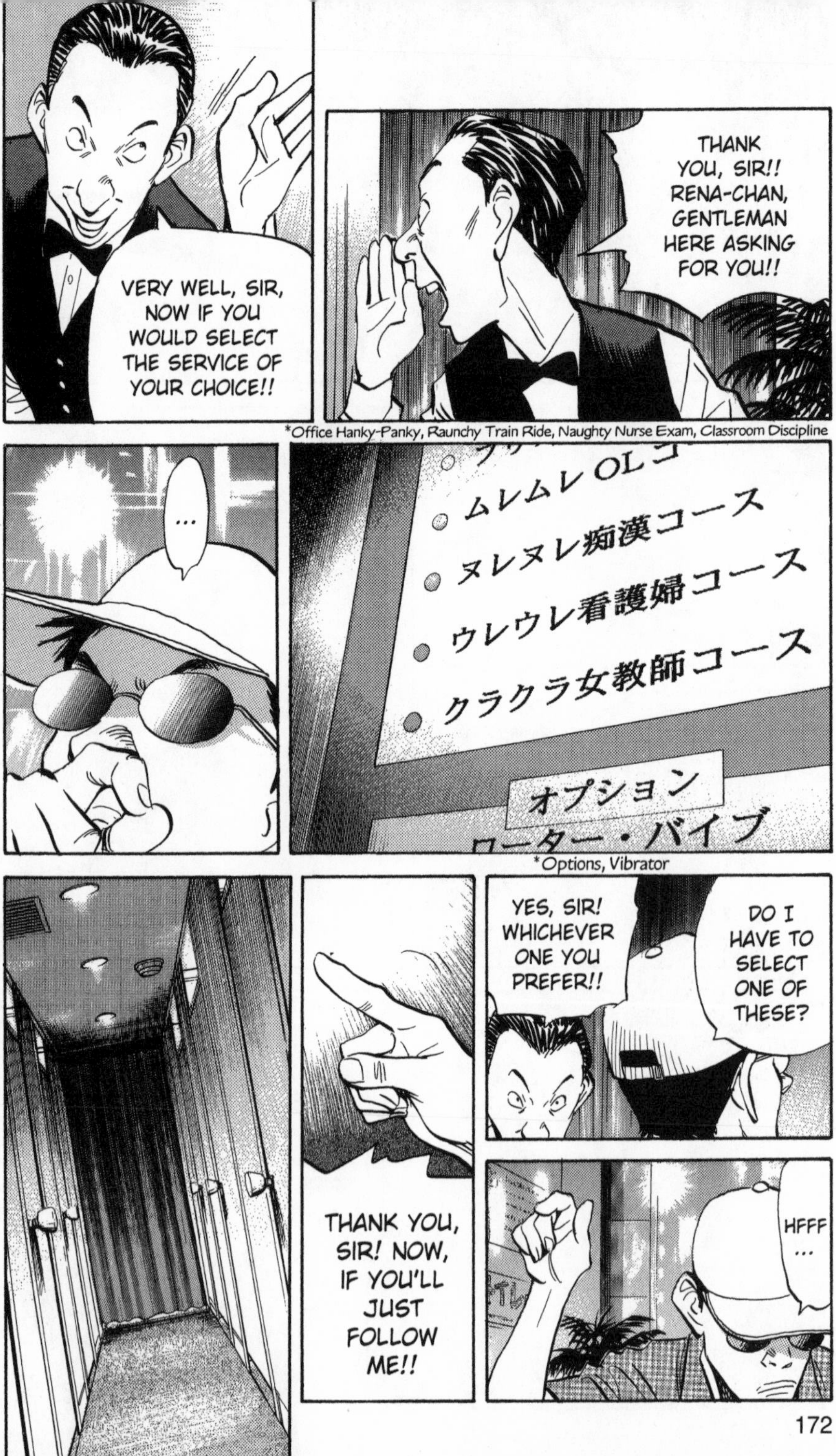
THANK YOU, SIR!! RENA-CHAN, GENTLEMAN HERE ASKING FOR YOU!!
VERY WELL, SIR, NOW IF YOU WOULD SELECT THE SERVICE OF YOUR CHOICE!!
ムレムレOLコ
ヌレヌレ痴漢コース
ウレウレ看護婦コース
クラクラ女教師コース
オプション
ローター・バイブ
...
DO I HAVE TO SELECT ONE OF THESE?
YES, SIR! WHICHEVER ONE YOU PREFER!!
HFFF ...
THANK YOU, SIR! NOW, IF YOU'LL JUST FOLLOW ME!!

*Office Hanky-Panky, Raunchy Train Ride, Naughty Nurse Exam, Classroom Discipline

*Options, Vibrator

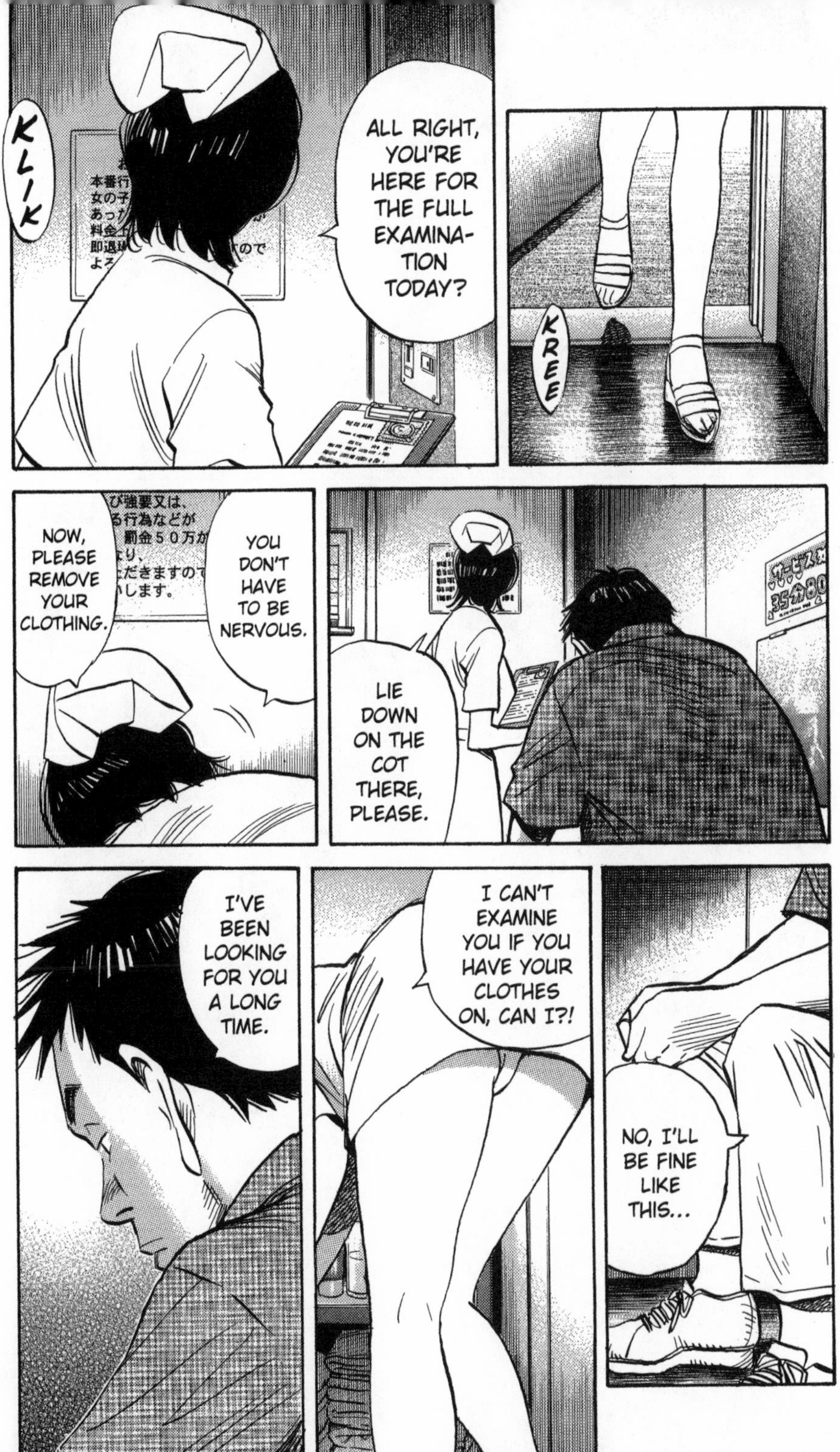
KREE
ALL RIGHT, YOU'RE HERE FOR THE FULL EXAMINA-TION TODAY?
KLIK
LIE DOWN ON THE COT THERE, PLEASE.
YOU DON'T HAVE TO BE NERVOUS.
NOW, PLEASE REMOVE YOUR CLOTHING.
NO, I'LL BE FINE LIKE THIS…
I CAN'T EXAMINE YOU IF YOU HAVE YOUR CLOTHES ON, CAN I?!
I'VE BEEN LOOKING FOR YOU A LONG TIME.

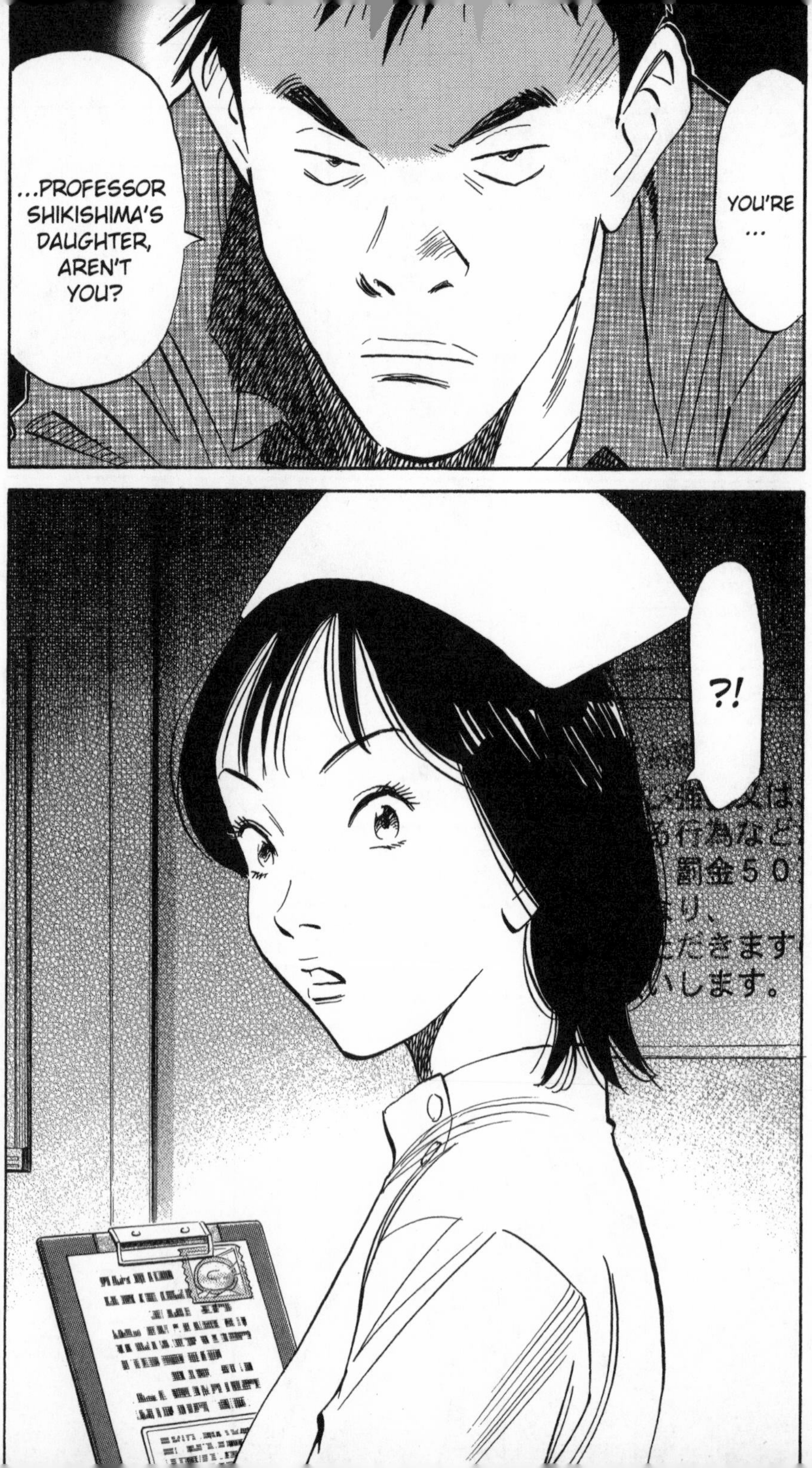
YOU'RE ...
...PROFESSOR SHIKISHIMA'S DAUGHTER, AREN'T YOU?
?!

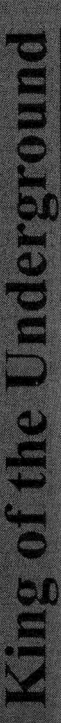

Chapter 10 King of the Underground

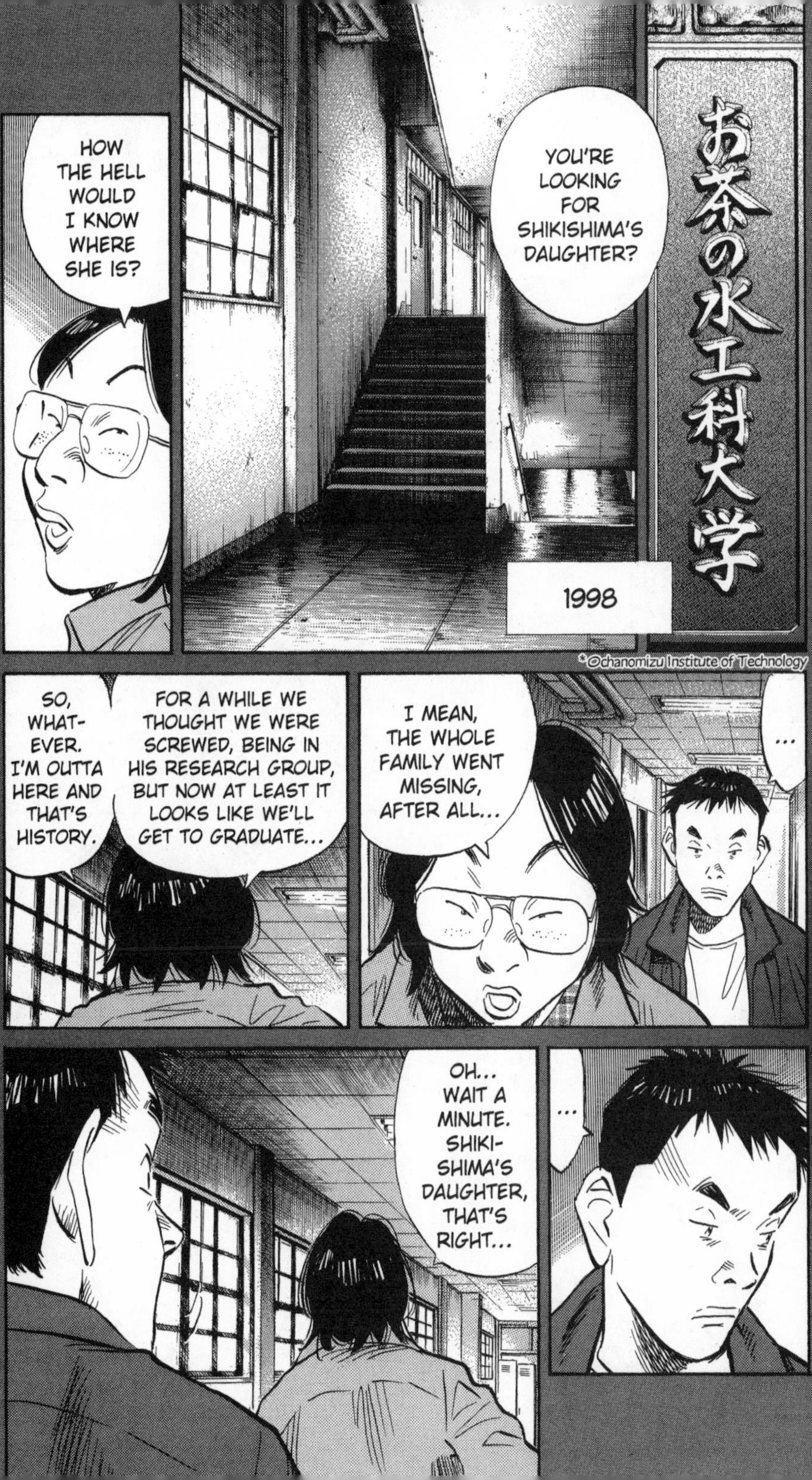
お茶の水工科大学
*Ochanomizu Institute of Technology
1998
YOU'RE LOOKING FOR SHIKISHIMA'S DAUGHTER?
HOW THE HELL WOULD I KNOW WHERE SHE IS?
...
I MEAN, THE WHOLE FAMILY WENT MISSING, AFTER ALL...
FOR A WHILE WE THOUGHT WE WERE SCREWED, BEING IN HIS RESEARCH GROUP, BUT NOW AT LEAST IT LOOKS LIKE WE'LL GET TO GRADUATE...
SO, WHAT-EVER. I'M OUTTA HERE AND THAT'S HISTORY.
...
OH... WAIT A MINUTE. SHIKI-SHIMA'S DAUGHTER, THAT'S RIGHT...

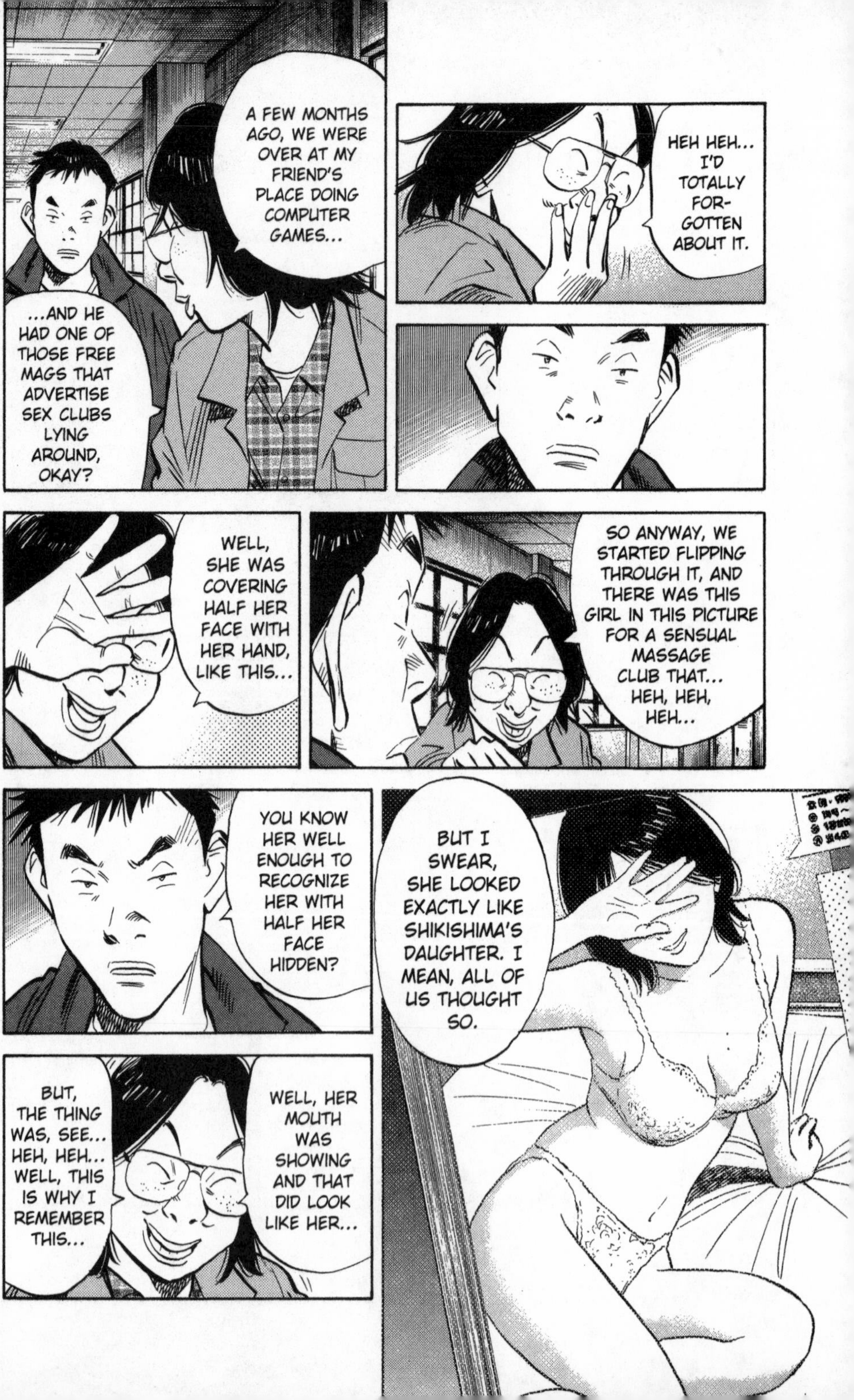
HEH HEH... I'D TOTALLY FOR-GOTTEN ABOUT IT.
A FEW MONTHS AGO, WE WERE OVER AT MY FRIEND'S PLACE DOING COMPUTER GAMES...
...AND HE HAD ONE OF THOSE FREE MAGS THAT ADVERTISE SEX CLUBS LYING AROUND, OKAY?
SO ANYWAY, WE STARTED FLIPPING THROUGH IT, AND THERE WAS THIS GIRL IN THIS PICTURE FOR A SENSUAL MASSAGE CLUB THAT... HEH, HEH, HEH...
WELL, SHE WAS COVERING HALF HER FACE WITH HER HAND, LIKE THIS...
BUT I SWEAR, SHE LOOKED EXACTLY LIKE SHIKISHIMA'S DAUGHTER. I MEAN, ALL OF US THOUGHT SO.
YOU KNOW HER WELL ENOUGH TO RECOGNIZE HER WITH HALF HER FACE HIDDEN?
WELL, HER MOUTH WAS SHOWING AND THAT DID LOOK LIKE HER...
BUT, THE THING WAS, SEE... HEH, HEH... WELL, THIS IS WHY I REMEMBER THIS...

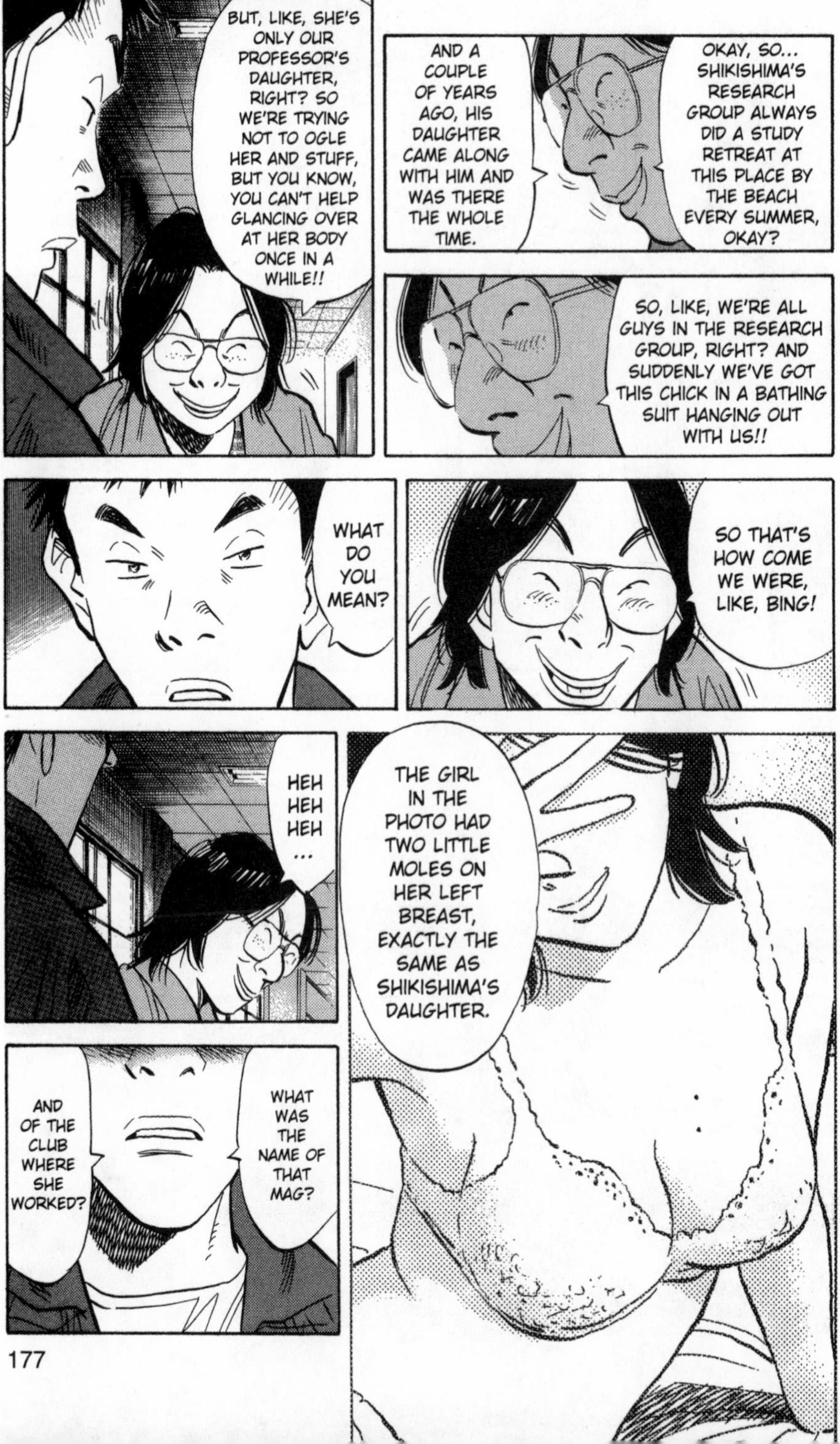
OKAY, SO... SHIKISHIMA'S RESEARCH GROUP ALWAYS DID A STUDY RETREAT AT THIS PLACE BY THE BEACH EVERY SUMMER, OKAY?
AND A COUPLE OF YEARS AGO, HIS DAUGHTER CAME ALONG WITH HIM AND WAS THERE THE WHOLE TIME.
SO, LIKE, WE'RE ALL GUYS IN THE RESEARCH GROUP, RIGHT? AND SUDDENLY WE'VE GOT THIS CHICK IN A BATHING SUIT HANGING OUT WITH US!!
BUT, LIKE, SHE'S ONLY OUR PROFESSOR'S DAUGHTER, RIGHT? SO WE'RE TRYING NOT TO OGLE HER AND STUFF, BUT YOU KNOW, YOU CAN'T HELP GLANCING OVER AT HER BODY ONCE IN A WHILE!!
SO THAT'S HOW COME WE WERE, LIKE, BING!
WHAT DO YOU MEAN?
THE GIRL IN THE PHOTO HAD TWO LITTLE MOLES ON HER LEFT BREAST, EXACTLY THE SAME AS SHIKISHIMA'S DAUGHTER.
HEH HEH HEH ...
WHAT WAS THE NAME OF THAT MAG?
AND OF THE CLUB WHERE SHE WORKED?

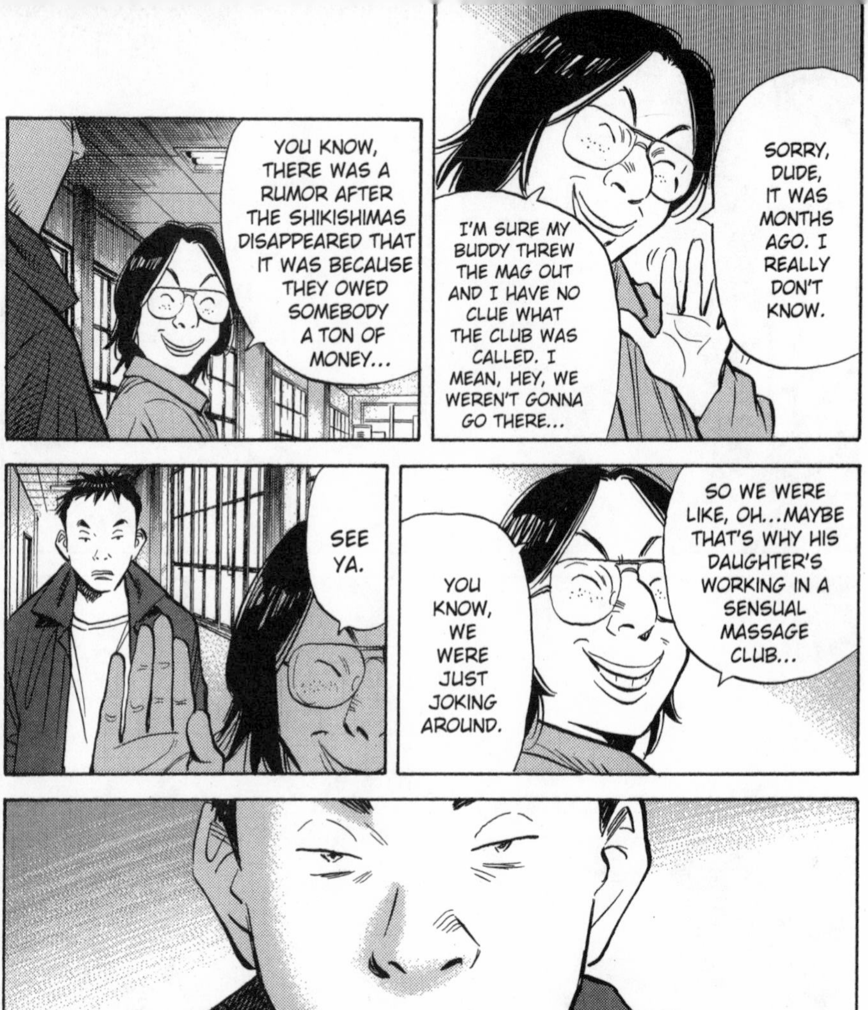
SORRY, DUDE, IT WAS MONTHS AGO. I REALLY DON'T KNOW.
I'M SURE MY BUDDY THREW THE MAG OUT AND I HAVE NO CLUE WHAT THE CLUB WAS CALLED. I MEAN, HEY, WE WEREN'T GONNA GO THERE...
YOU KNOW, THERE WAS A RUMOR AFTER THE SHIKISHIMAS DISAPPEARED THAT IT WAS BECAUSE THEY OWED SOMEBODY A TON OF MONEY...
SO WE WERE LIKE, OH...MAYBE THAT'S WHY HIS DAUGHTER'S WORKING IN A SENSUAL MASSAGE CLUB...
YOU KNOW, WE WERE JUST JOKING AROUND.
SEE YA.

*Fashion Health, Papaya Heaven

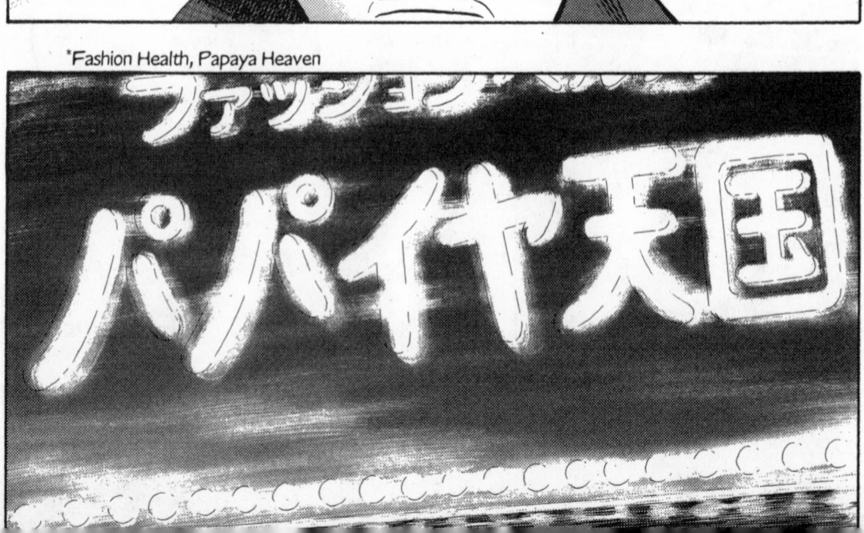
パパイヤ天国

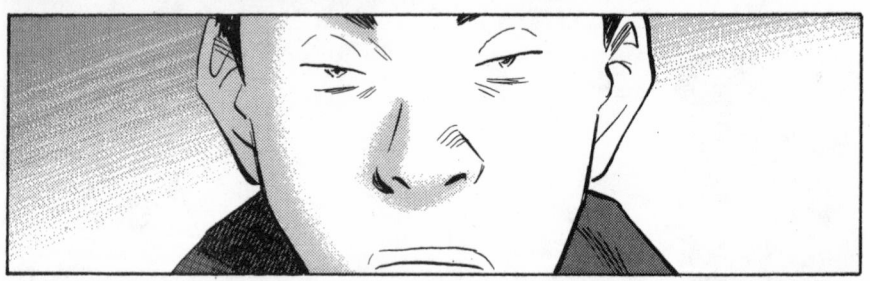

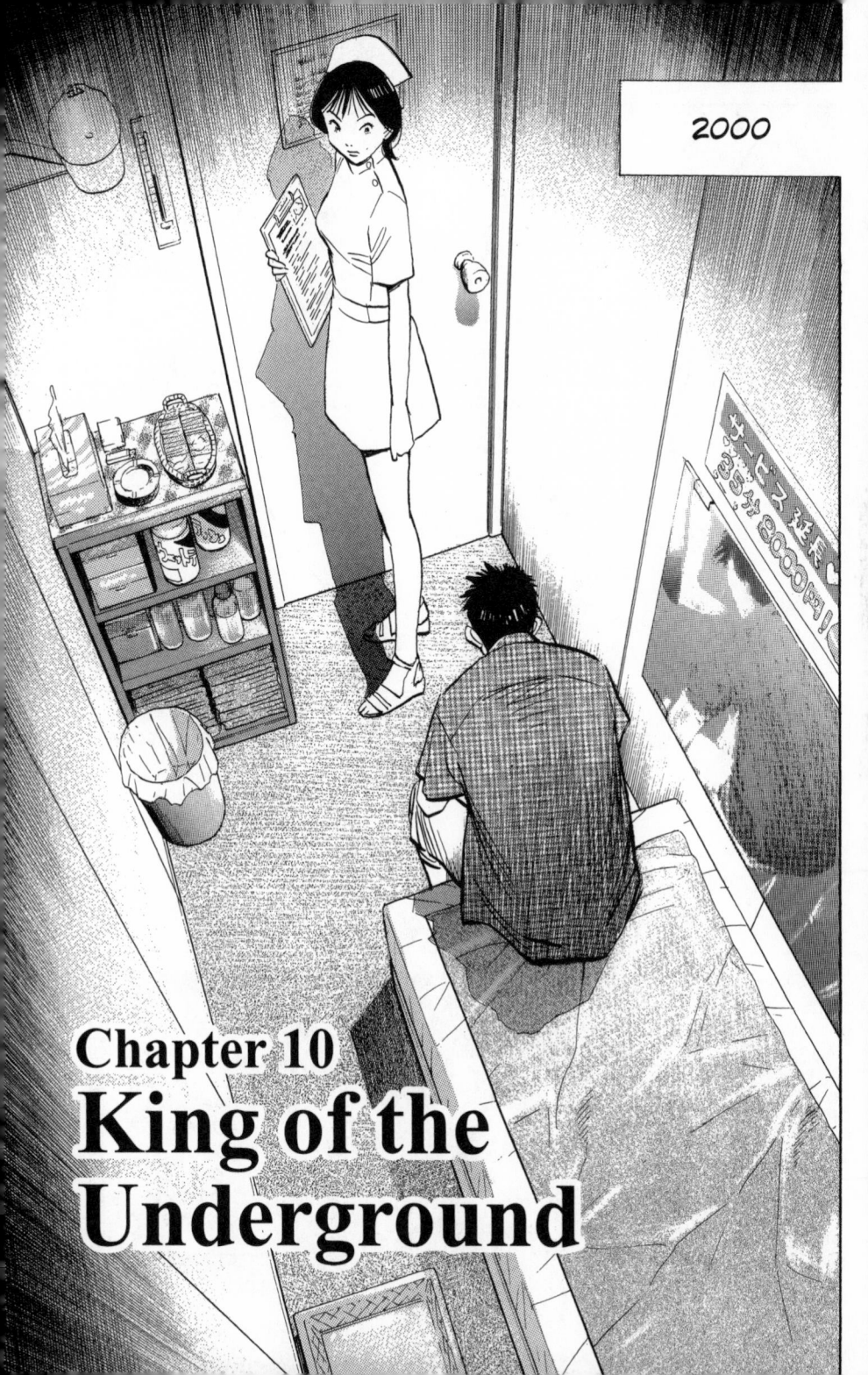

2000

Chapter 10
King of the Underground

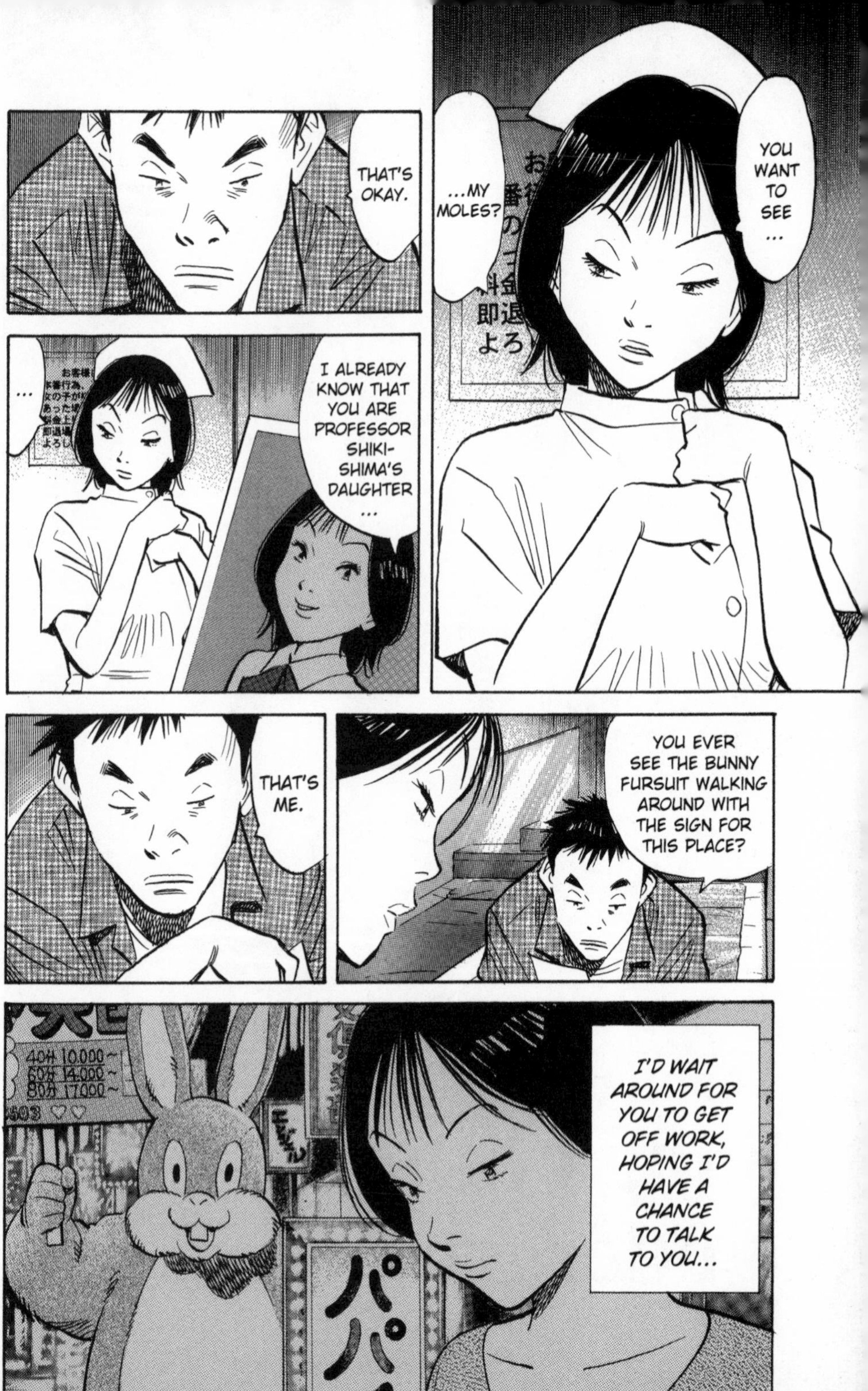
YOU WANT TO SEE…
…MY MOLES?
THAT'S OKAY.
I ALREADY KNOW THAT YOU ARE PROFESSOR SHIKI-SHIMA'S DAUGHTER…
…
YOU EVER SEE THE BUNNY FURSUIT WALKING AROUND WITH THE SIGN FOR THIS PLACE?
THAT'S ME.
I'D WAIT AROUND FOR YOU TO GET OFF WORK, HOPING I'D HAVE A CHANCE TO TALK TO YOU…
40分 10.000~
60分 14.000~
80分 17000~

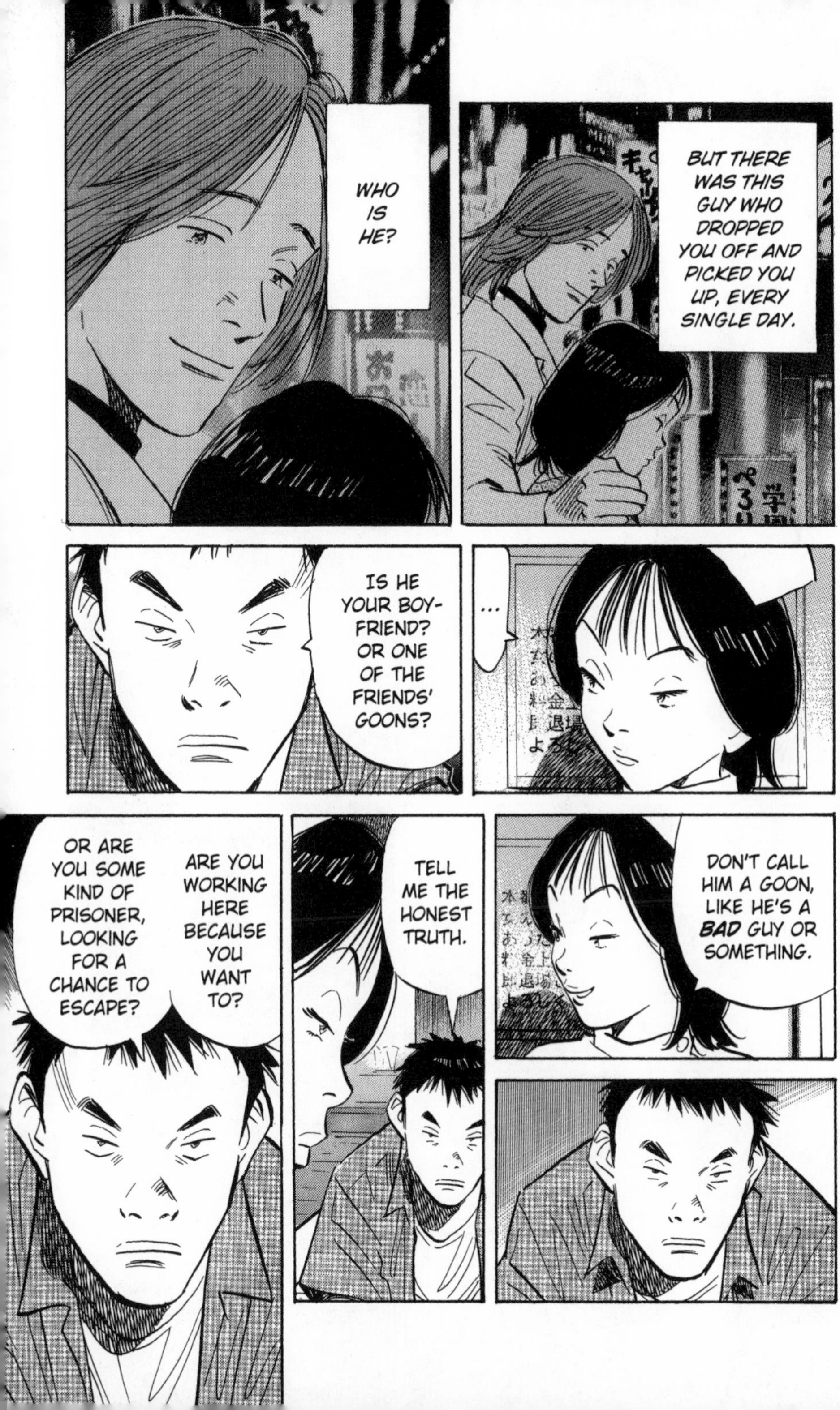
BUT THERE WAS THIS GUY WHO DROPPED YOU OFF AND PICKED YOU UP, EVERY SINGLE DAY.
WHO IS HE?
...
IS HE YOUR BOY-FRIEND? OR ONE OF THE FRIENDS' GOONS?
DON'T CALL HIM A GOON, LIKE HE'S A **BAD** GUY OR SOMETHING.
TELL ME THE HONEST TRUTH.
ARE YOU WORKING HERE BECAUSE YOU WANT TO?
OR ARE YOU SOME KIND OF PRISONER, LOOKING FOR A CHANCE TO ESCAPE?

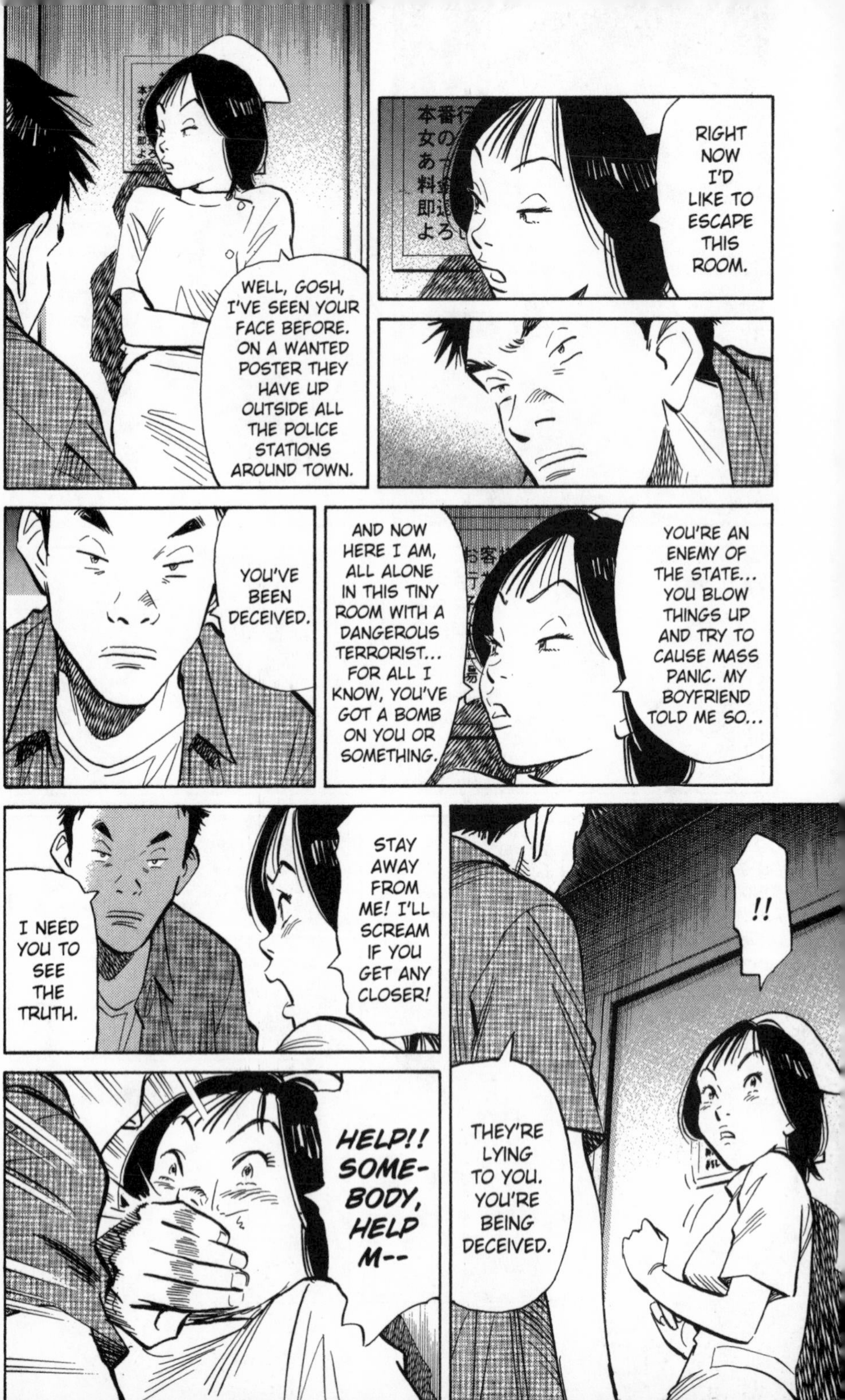
RIGHT NOW I'D LIKE TO ESCAPE THIS ROOM.
WELL, GOSH, I'VE SEEN YOUR FACE BEFORE. ON A WANTED POSTER THEY HAVE UP OUTSIDE ALL THE POLICE STATIONS AROUND TOWN.
YOU'RE AN ENEMY OF THE STATE... YOU BLOW THINGS UP AND TRY TO CAUSE MASS PANIC. MY BOYFRIEND TOLD ME SO...
AND NOW HERE I AM, ALL ALONE IN THIS TINY ROOM WITH A DANGEROUS TERRORIST... FOR ALL I KNOW, YOU'VE GOT A BOMB ON YOU OR SOMETHING.
YOU'VE BEEN DECEIVED.
!!
THEY'RE LYING TO YOU. YOU'RE BEING DECEIVED.
STAY AWAY FROM ME! I'LL SCREAM IF YOU GET ANY CLOSER!
I NEED YOU TO SEE THE TRUTH.
HELP!! SOME-BODY, HELP M--

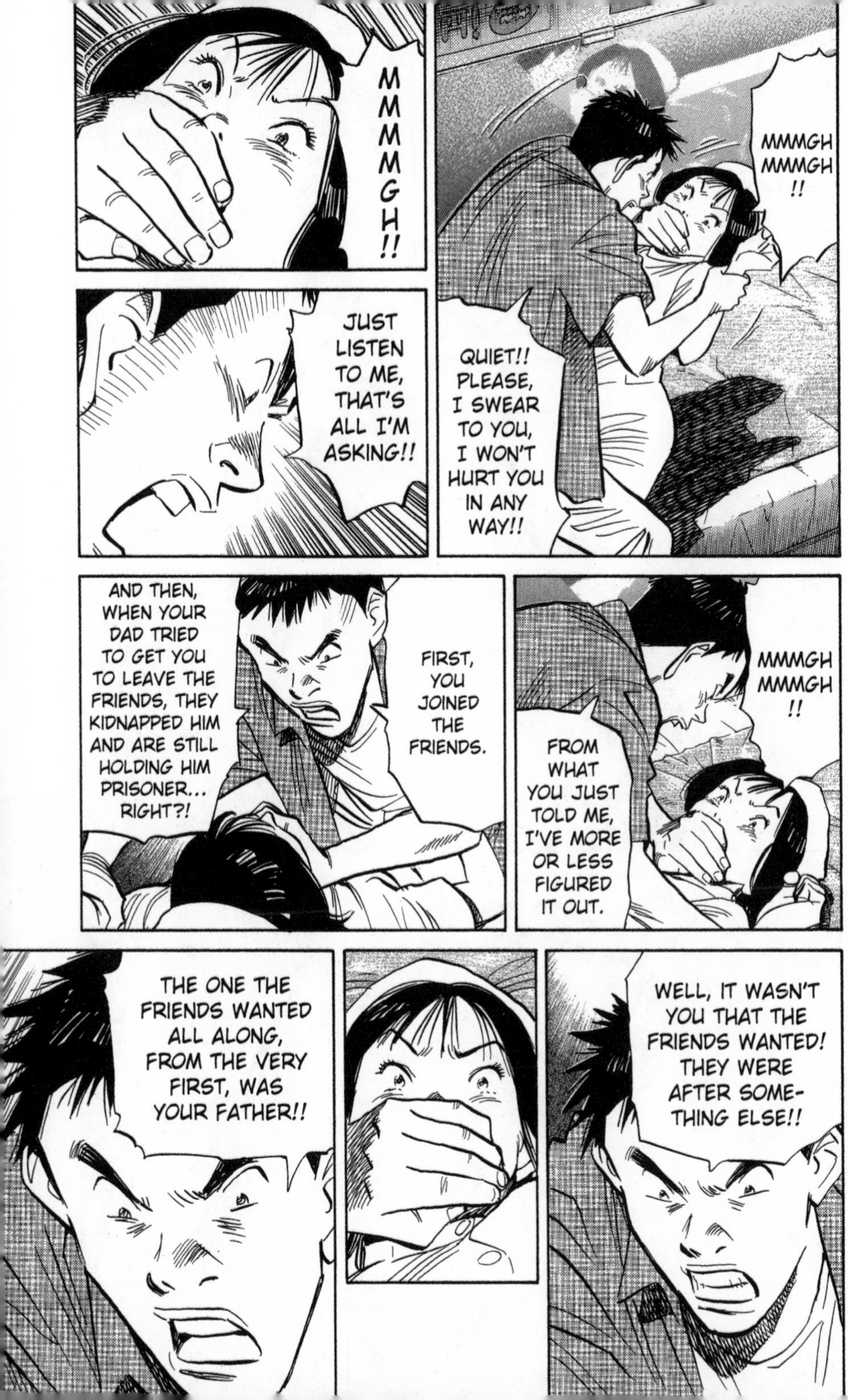
MMMGH MMMGH !!
QUIET!! PLEASE, I SWEAR TO YOU, I WON'T HURT YOU IN ANY WAY!!
MMMMGH!!
JUST LISTEN TO ME, THAT'S ALL I'M ASKING!!
MMMGH MMMGH !!
FROM WHAT YOU JUST TOLD ME, I'VE MORE OR LESS FIGURED IT OUT.
FIRST, YOU JOINED THE FRIENDS.
AND THEN, WHEN YOUR DAD TRIED TO GET YOU TO LEAVE THE FRIENDS, THEY KIDNAPPED HIM AND ARE STILL HOLDING HIM PRISONER... RIGHT?!
WELL, IT WASN'T YOU THAT THE FRIENDS WANTED! THEY WERE AFTER SOME-THING ELSE!!
THE ONE THE FRIENDS WANTED ALL ALONG, FROM THE VERY FIRST, WAS YOUR FATHER!!

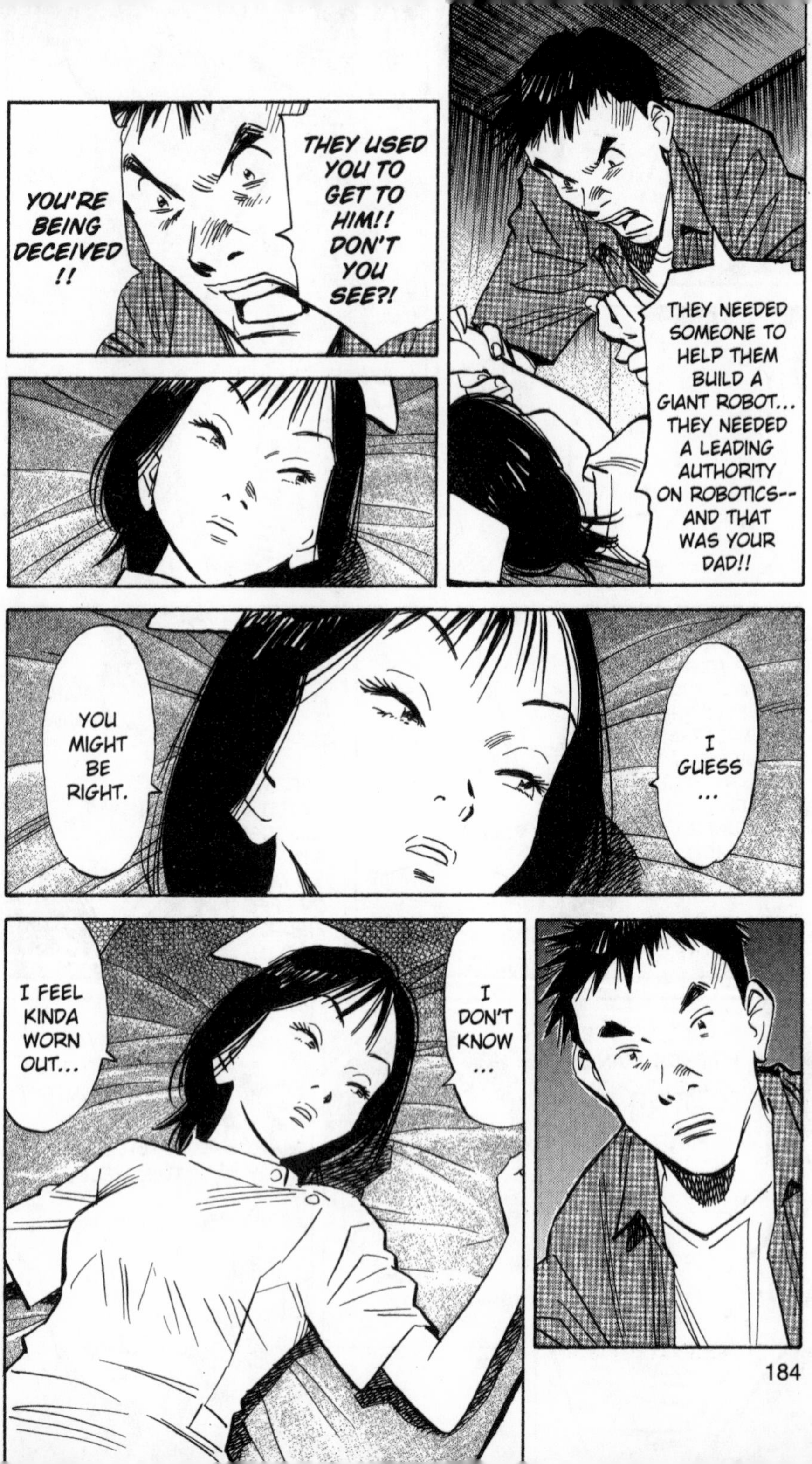
THEY NEEDED SOMEONE TO HELP THEM BUILD A GIANT ROBOT... THEY NEEDED A LEADING AUTHORITY ON ROBOTICS-- AND THAT WAS YOUR DAD!!
THEY USED YOU TO GET TO HIM!! DON'T YOU SEE?!
YOU'RE BEING DECEIVED !!
I GUESS ...
YOU MIGHT BE RIGHT.
I DON'T KNOW ...
I FEEL KINDA WORN OUT...

MY BOY-
FRIEND
TOLD ME
IT'S FOR
WORLD
PEACE...

THAT WE
NEED TO
RAISE
MONEY
TO SAVE
THE
WORLD
...

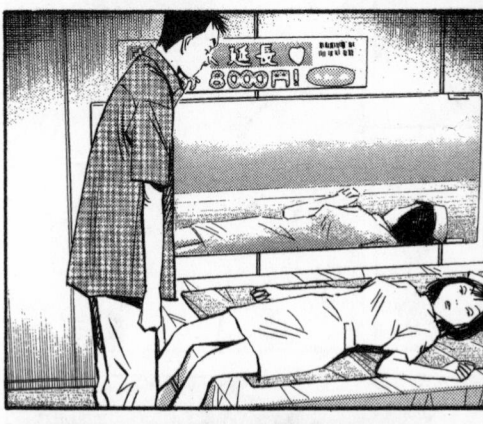

BUT,
GEE
...

I REALLY
DON'T SEE...
HOW
WORKING IN
THIS CLUB
IS GOING TO
HELP SAVE
THE WORLD.

SO
RUN
AWAY.
I'LL HELP
YOU...

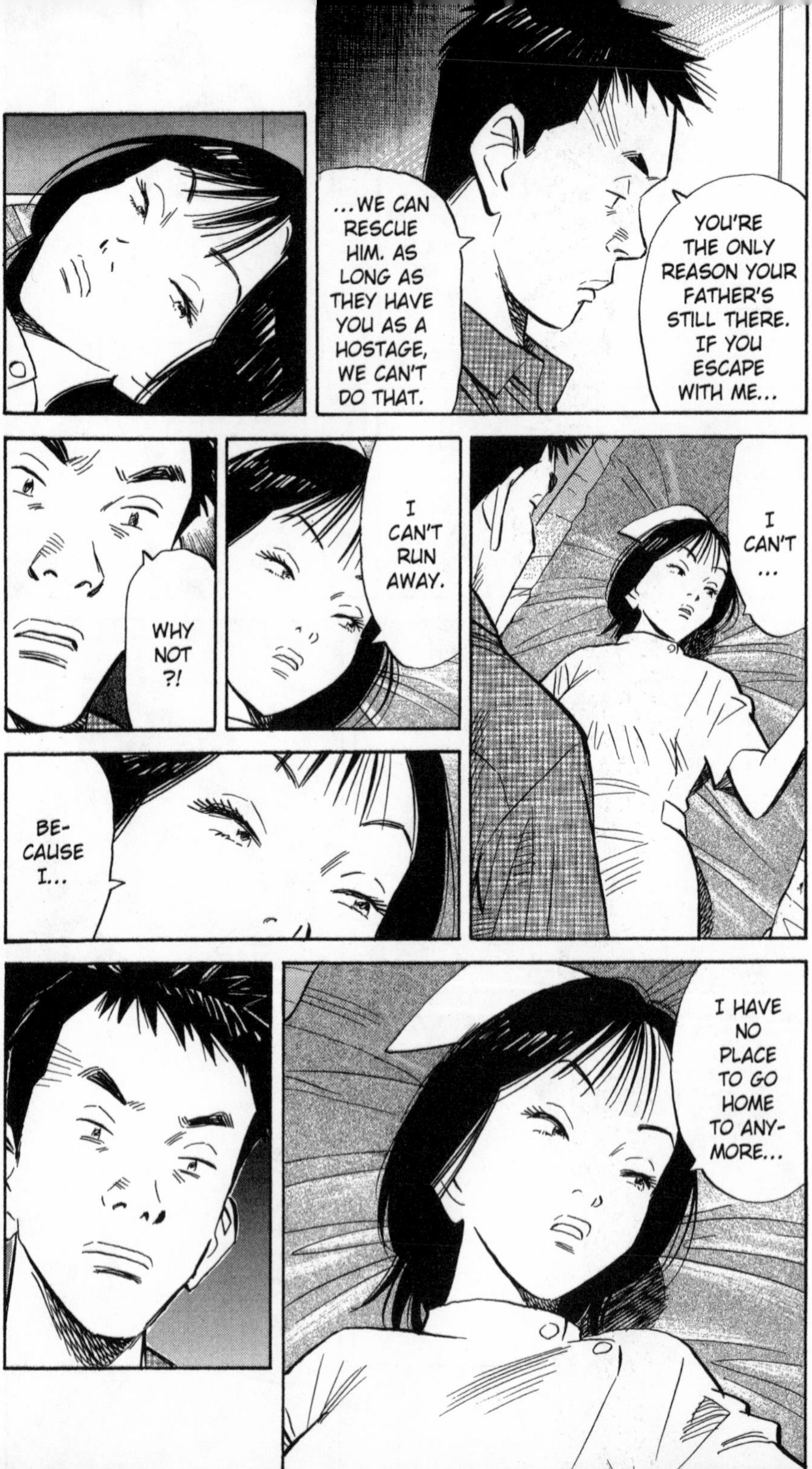
YOU'RE THE ONLY REASON YOUR FATHER'S STILL THERE. IF YOU ESCAPE WITH ME...
...WE CAN RESCUE HIM. AS LONG AS THEY HAVE YOU AS A HOSTAGE, WE CAN'T DO THAT.
I CAN'T ...
I CAN'T RUN AWAY.
WHY NOT ?!
BE-CAUSE I...
I HAVE NO PLACE TO GO HOME TO ANY-MORE...

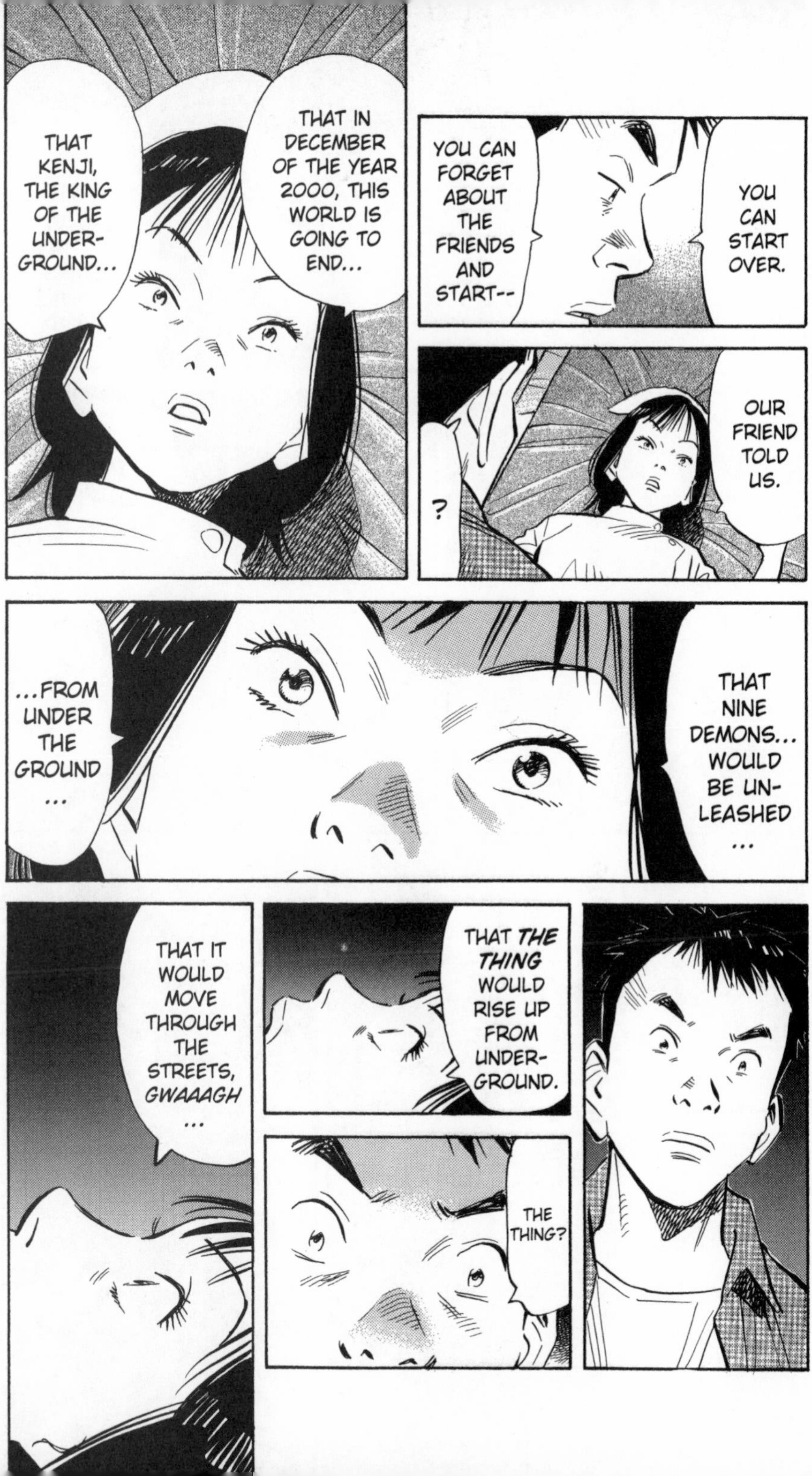
YOU CAN START OVER.
YOU CAN FORGET ABOUT THE FRIENDS AND START--
OUR FRIEND TOLD US.
?
THAT IN DECEMBER OF THE YEAR 2000, THIS WORLD IS GOING TO END...
THAT KENJI, THE KING OF THE UNDERGROUND...
THAT NINE DEMONS... WOULD BE UNLEASHED...
...FROM UNDER THE GROUND...
THAT *THE THING* WOULD RISE UP FROM UNDERGROUND.
THE THING?
THAT IT WOULD MOVE THROUGH THE STREETS, *GWAAAGH*...

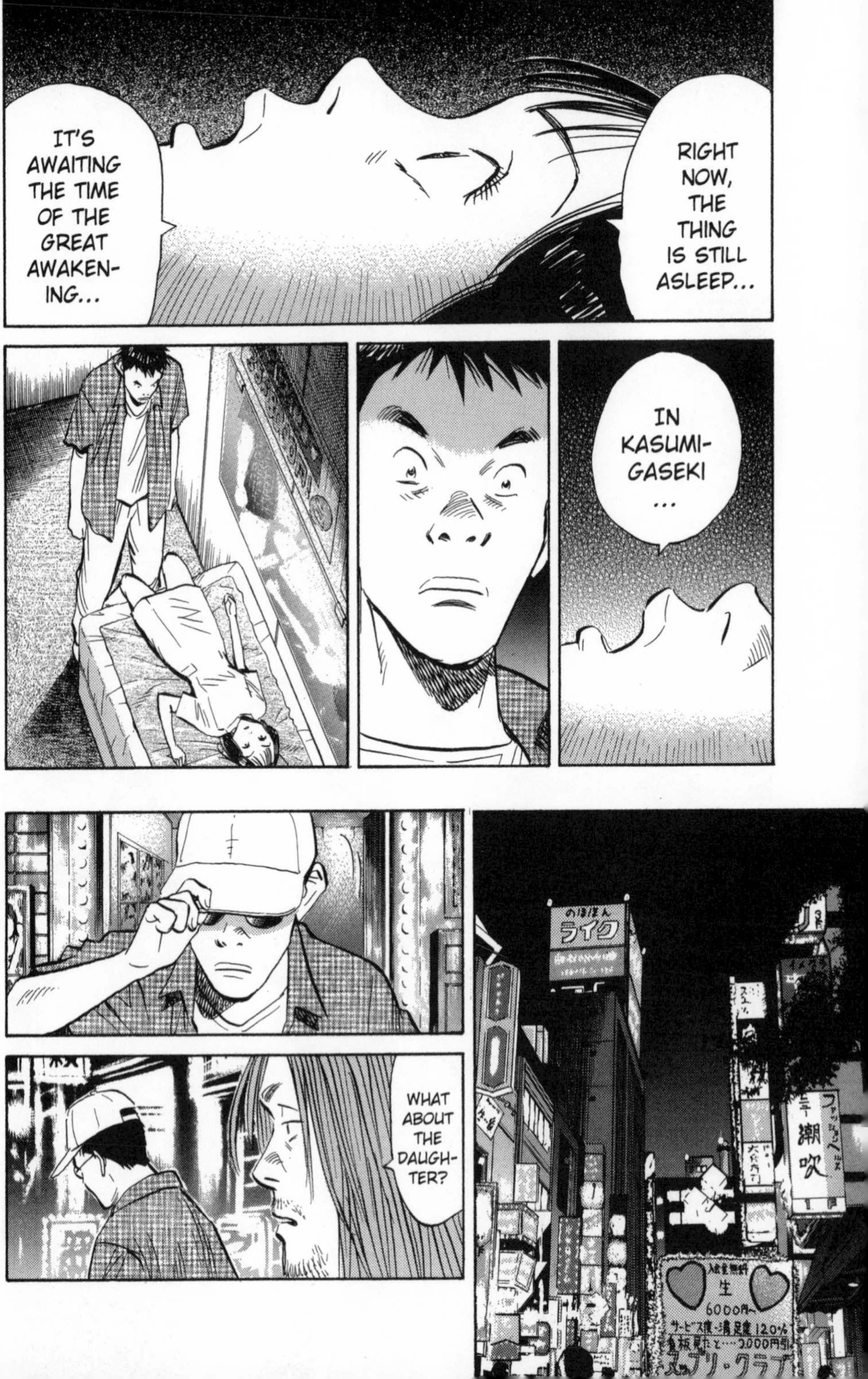
RIGHT NOW, THE THING IS STILL ASLEEP...
IT'S AWAITING THE TIME OF THE GREAT AWAKEN-ING...
IN KASUMI-GASEKI ...
ライク
WHAT ABOUT THE DAUGH-TER?

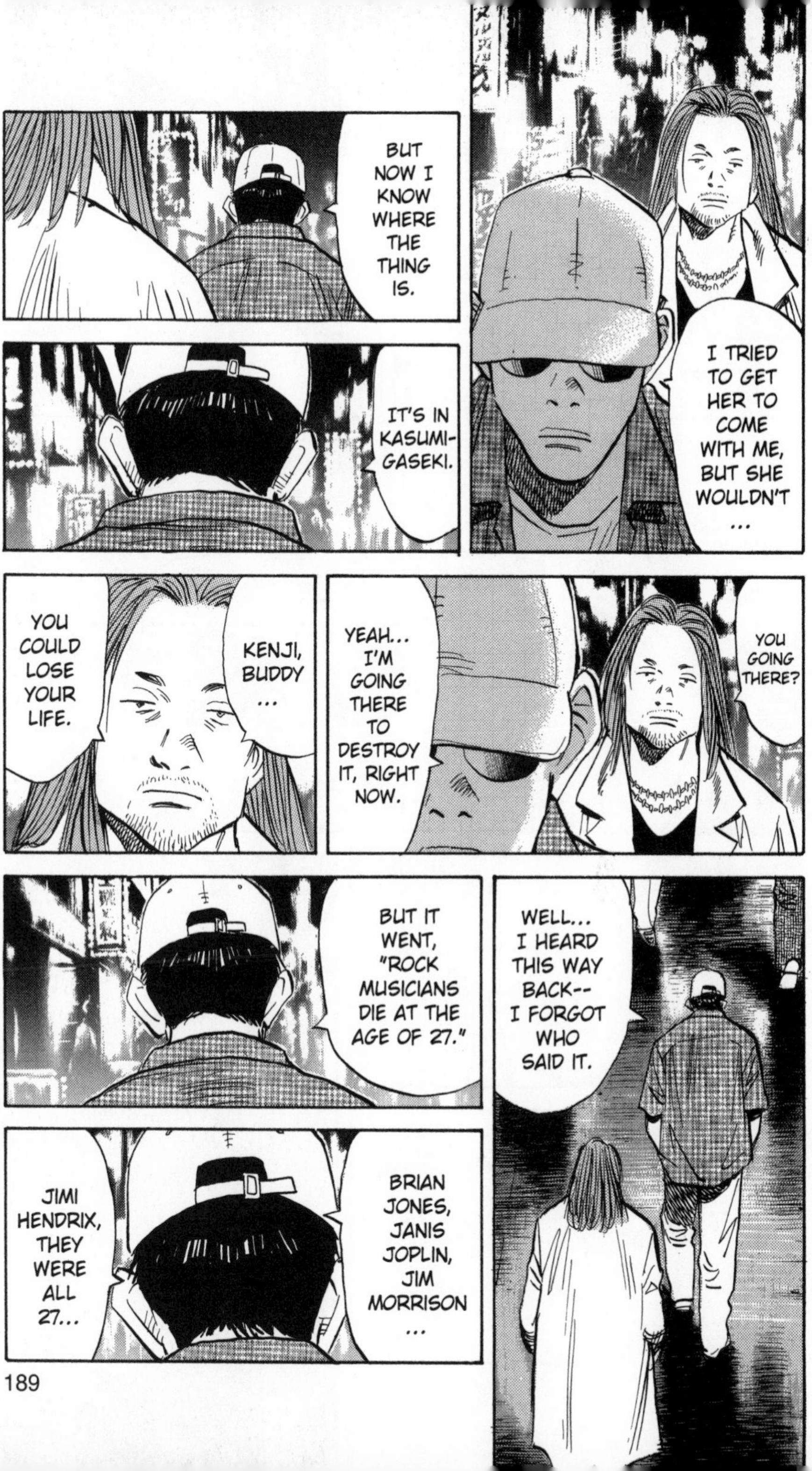
I TRIED TO GET HER TO COME WITH ME, BUT SHE WOULDN'T ...
BUT NOW I KNOW WHERE THE THING IS.
IT'S IN KASUMI-GASEKI.
YOU GOING THERE?
YEAH... I'M GOING THERE TO DESTROY IT, RIGHT NOW.
KENJI, BUDDY ...
YOU COULD LOSE YOUR LIFE.
WELL... I HEARD THIS WAY BACK-- I FORGOT WHO SAID IT.
BUT IT WENT, "ROCK MUSICIANS DIE AT THE AGE OF 27."
BRIAN JONES, JANIS JOPLIN, JIM MORRISON ...
JIMI HENDRIX, THEY WERE ALL 27...

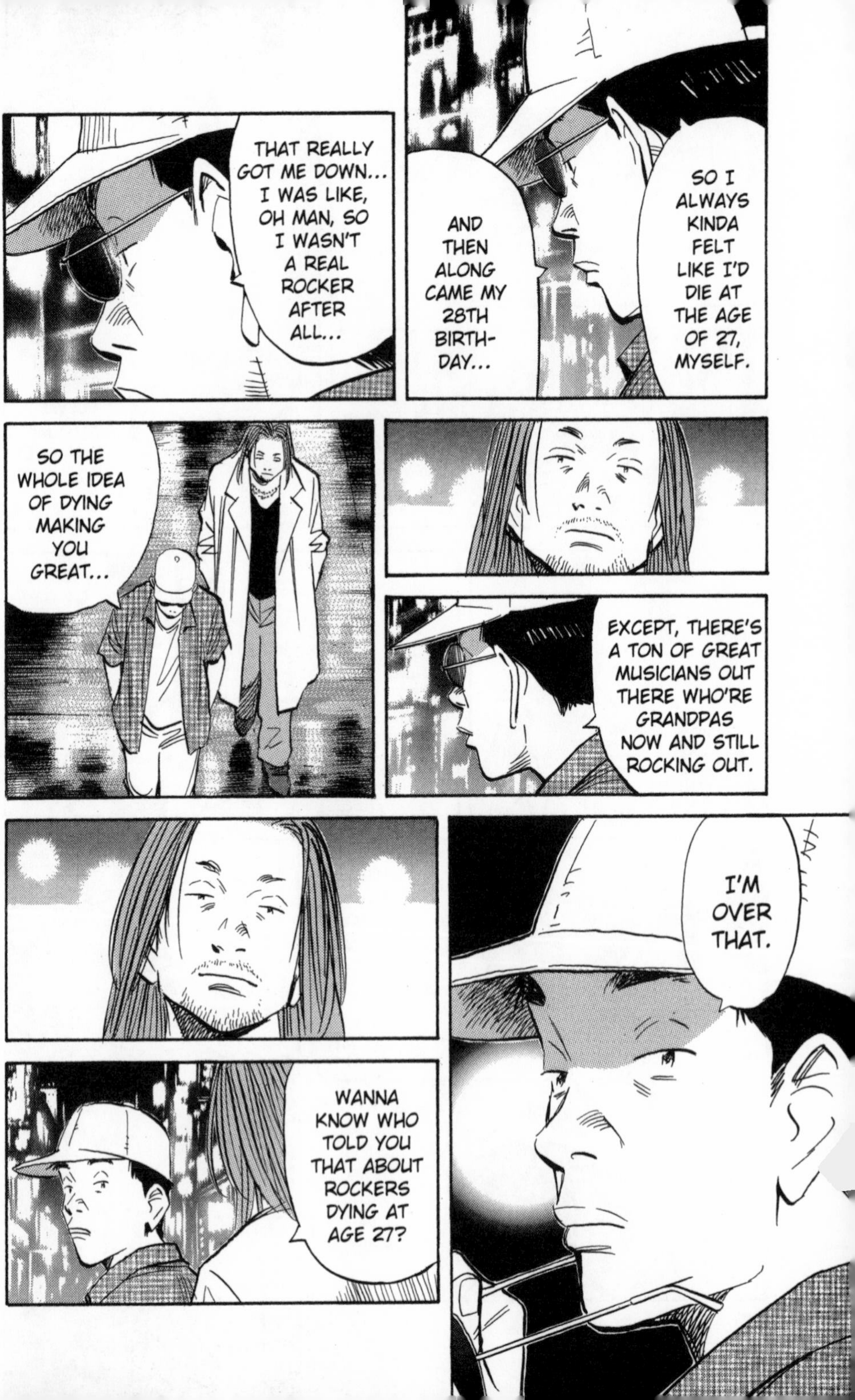
SO I ALWAYS KINDA FELT LIKE I'D DIE AT THE AGE OF 27, MYSELF.
AND THEN ALONG CAME MY 28TH BIRTH-DAY...
THAT REALLY GOT ME DOWN... I WAS LIKE, OH MAN, SO I WASN'T A REAL ROCKER AFTER ALL...
EXCEPT, THERE'S A TON OF GREAT MUSICIANS OUT THERE WHO'RE GRANDPAS NOW AND STILL ROCKING OUT.
SO THE WHOLE IDEA OF DYING MAKING YOU GREAT...
I'M OVER THAT.
WANNA KNOW WHO TOLD YOU THAT ABOUT ROCKERS DYING AT AGE 27?

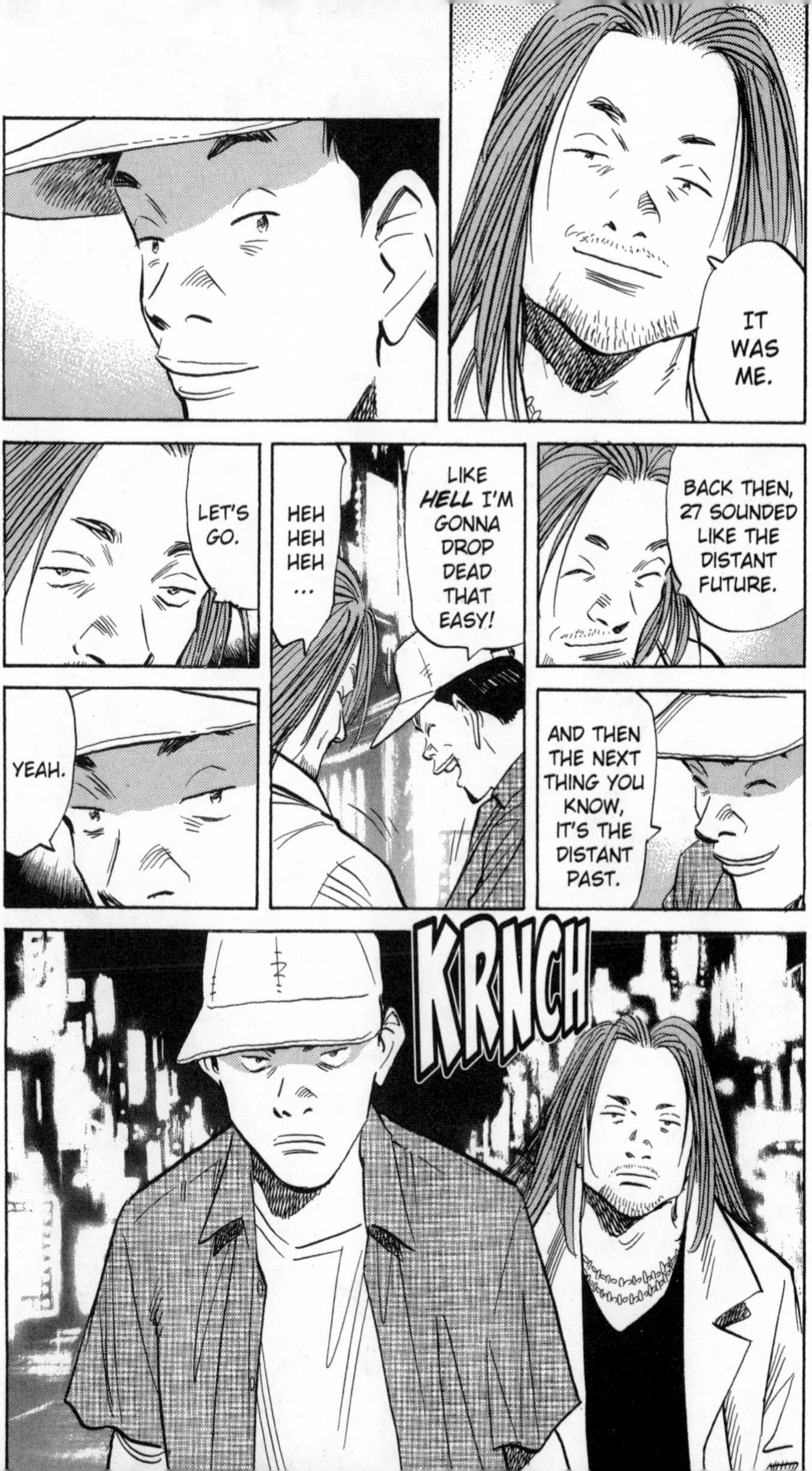
IT WAS ME.
BACK THEN, 27 SOUNDED LIKE THE DISTANT FUTURE.
AND THEN THE NEXT THING YOU KNOW, IT'S THE DISTANT PAST.
LIKE **HELL** I'M GONNA DROP DEAD THAT EASY!
HEH HEH HEH ...
LET'S GO.
YEAH.
KRNCH

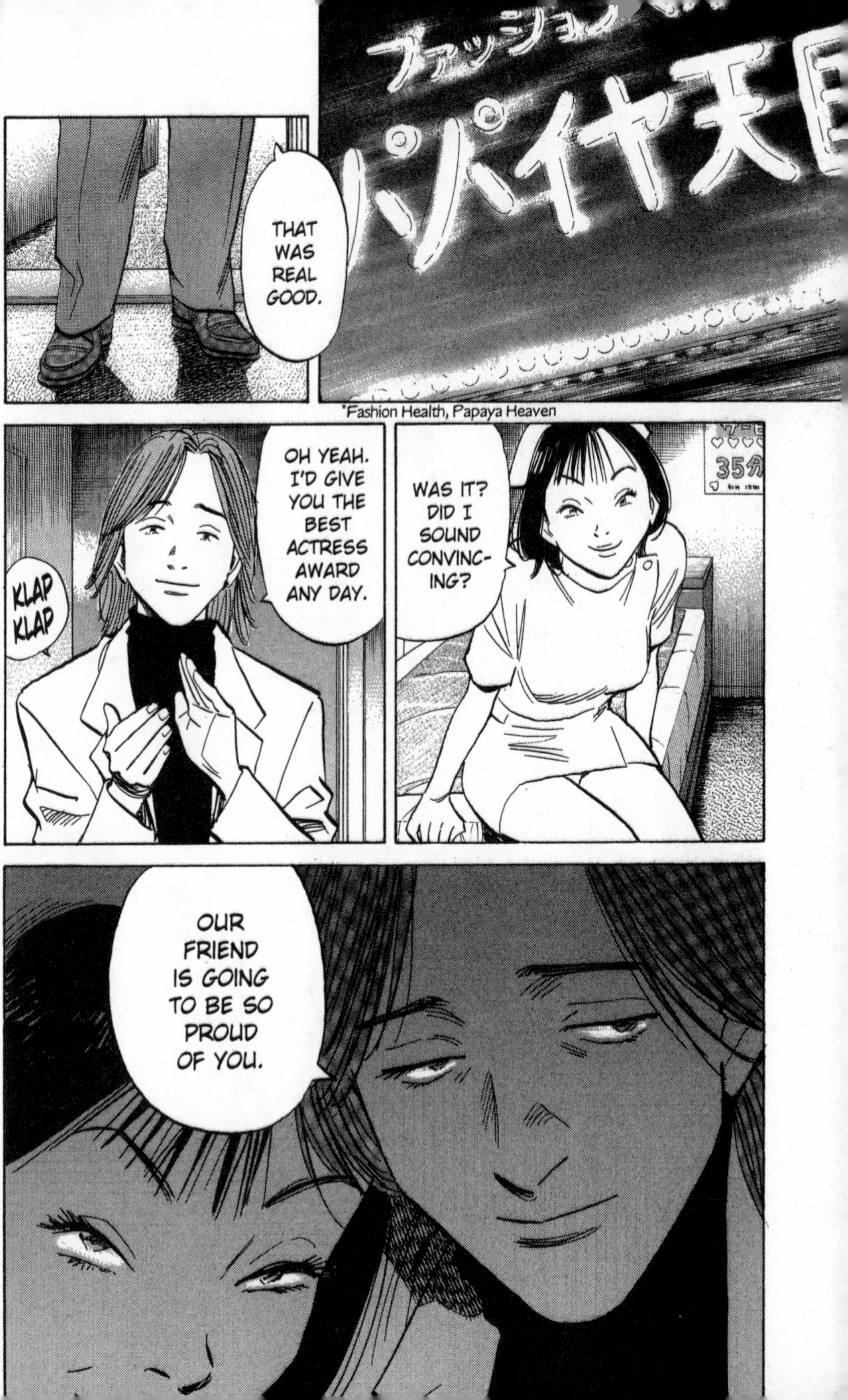
THAT WAS REAL GOOD.
WAS IT? DID I SOUND CONVINCING?
35分
OH YEAH. I'D GIVE YOU THE BEST ACTRESS AWARD ANY DAY.
KLAP KLAP
OUR FRIEND IS GOING TO BE SO PROUD OF YOU.

*Fashion Health, Papaya Heaven

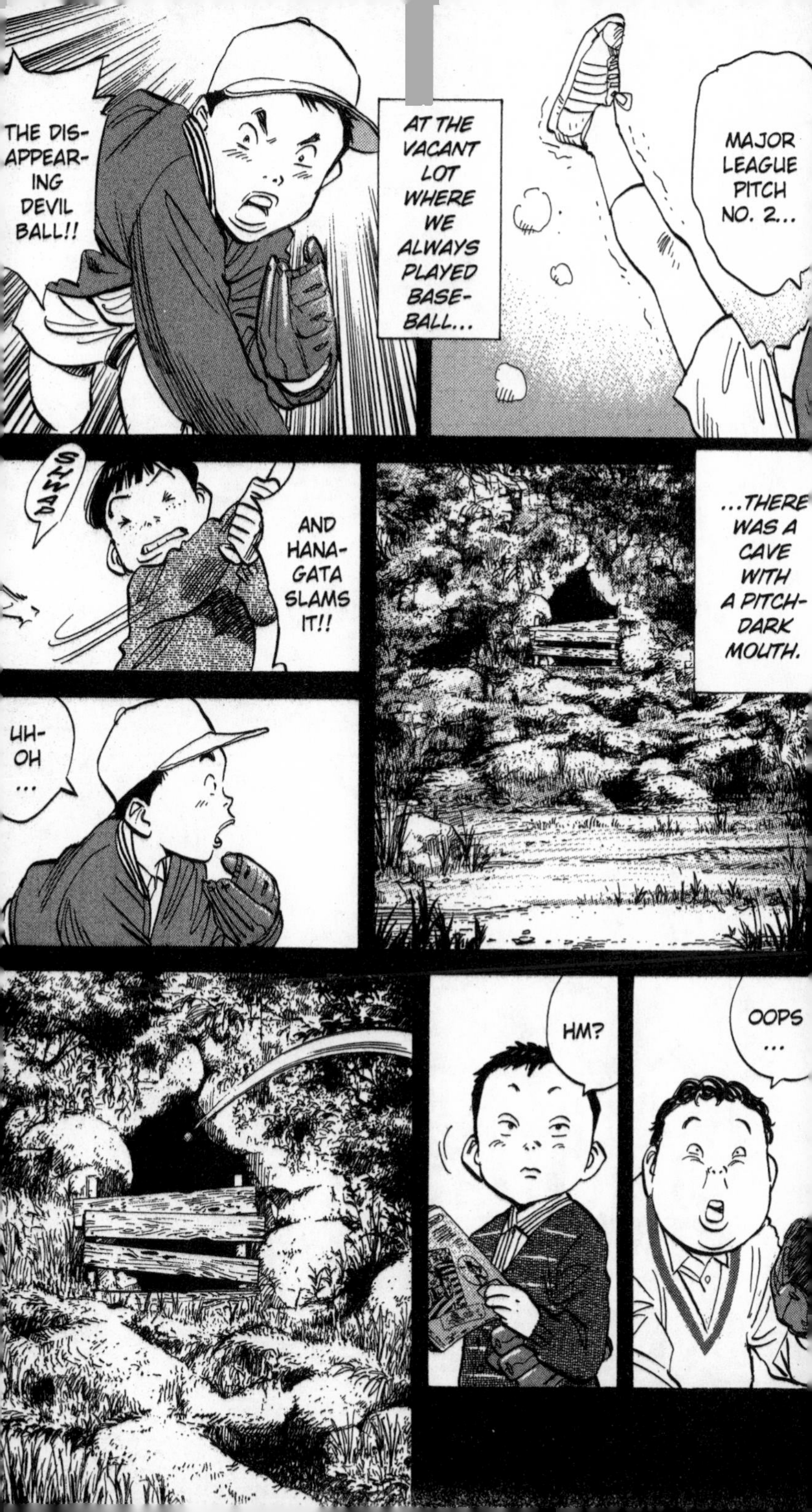
MAJOR LEAGUE PITCH NO. 2...
AT THE VACANT LOT WHERE WE ALWAYS PLAYED BASEBALL...
THE DIS-APPEARING DEVIL BALL!!
...THERE WAS A CAVE WITH A PITCH-DARK MOUTH.
SHWAP
AND HANA-GATA SLAMS IT!!
UH-OH...
OOPS...
HM?

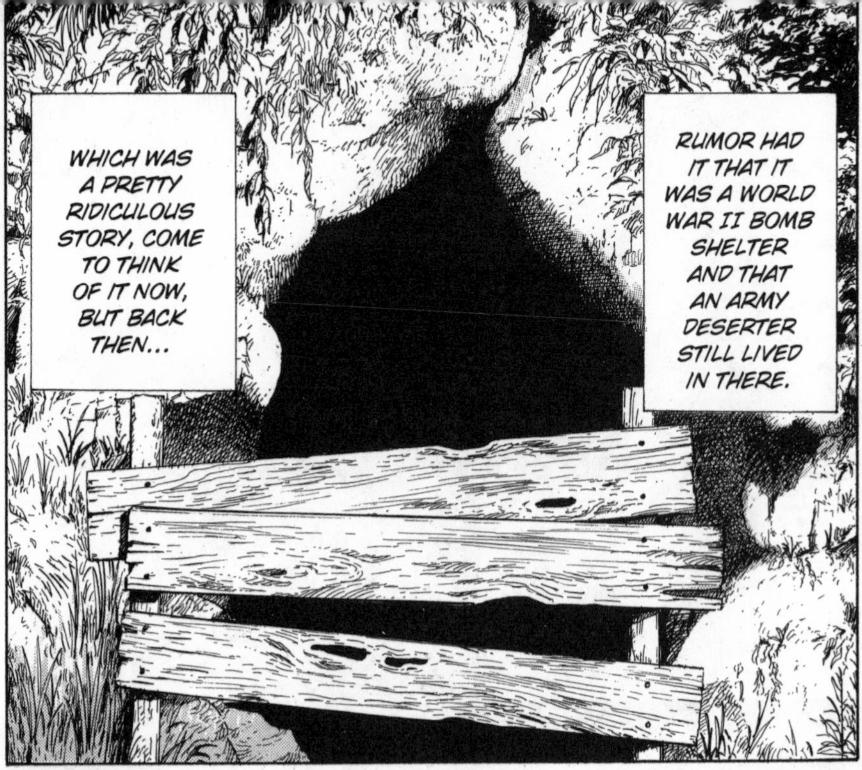
RUMOR HAD IT THAT IT WAS A WORLD WAR II BOMB SHELTER AND THAT AN ARMY DESERTER STILL LIVED IN THERE.
WHICH WAS A PRETTY RIDICULOUS STORY, COME TO THINK OF IT NOW, BUT BACK THEN...
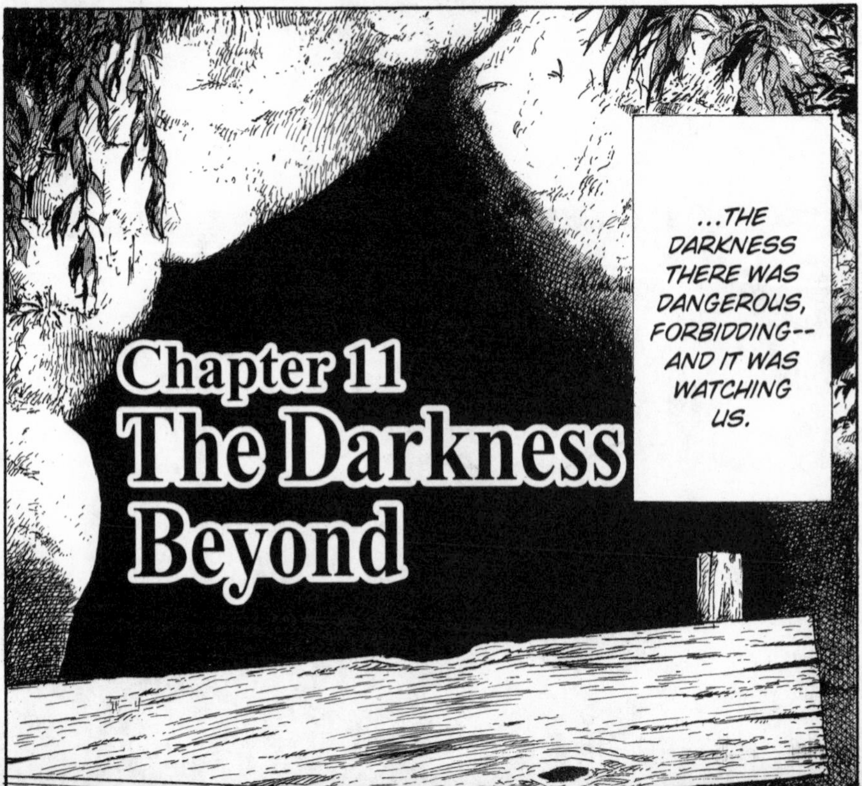
...THE DARKNESS THERE WAS DANGEROUS, FORBIDDING-- AND IT WAS WATCHING US.

Chapter 11
The Darkness Beyond

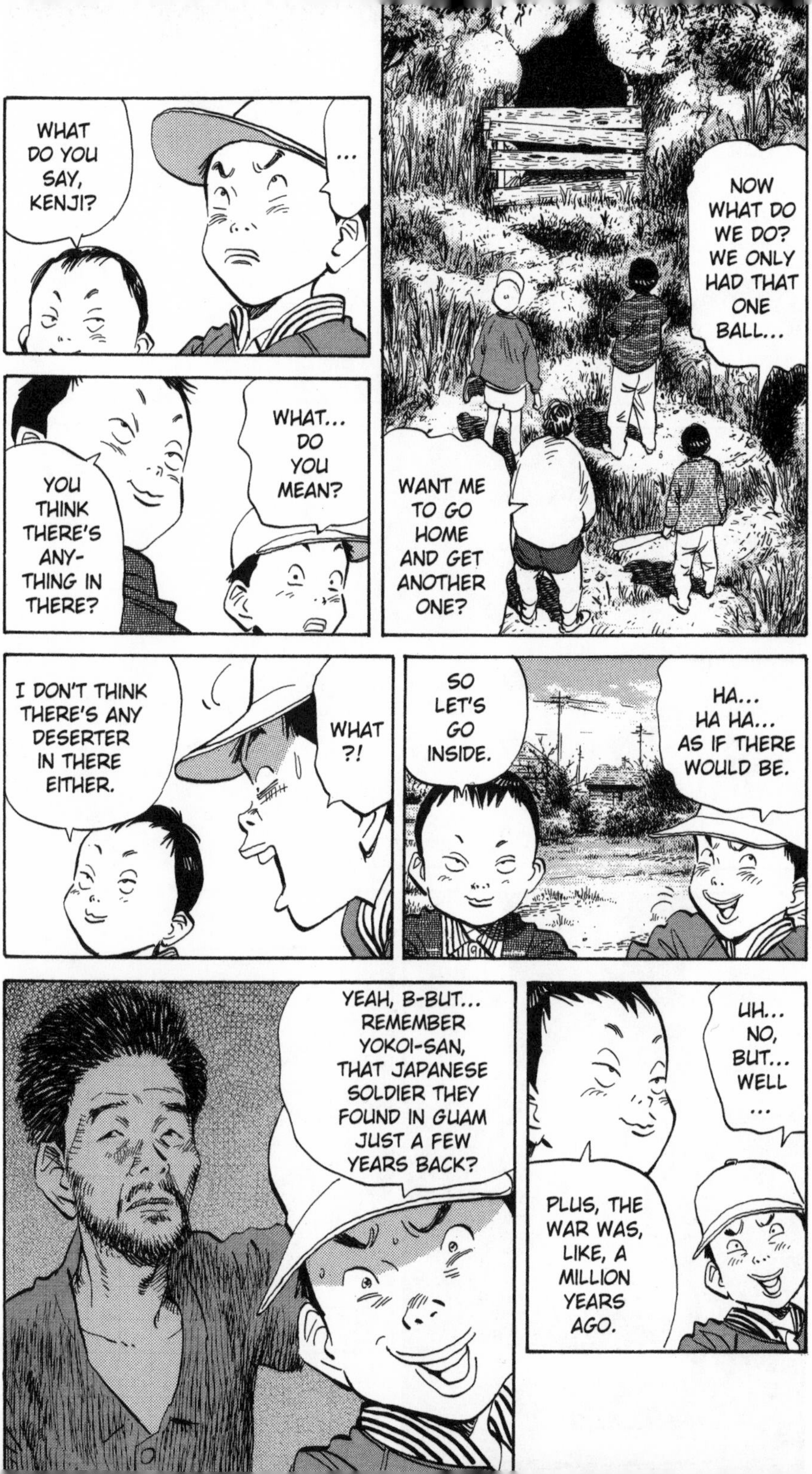
NOW WHAT DO WE DO? WE ONLY HAD THAT ONE BALL...
WANT ME TO GO HOME AND GET ANOTHER ONE?
...
WHAT DO YOU SAY, KENJI?
WHAT... DO YOU MEAN?
YOU THINK THERE'S ANY-THING IN THERE?
HA... HA HA... AS IF THERE WOULD BE.
SO LET'S GO INSIDE.
WHAT?!
I DON'T THINK THERE'S ANY DESERTER IN THERE EITHER.
UH... NO, BUT... WELL ...
PLUS, THE WAR WAS, LIKE, A MILLION YEARS AGO.
YEAH, B-BUT... REMEMBER YOKOI-SAN, THAT JAPANESE SOLDIER THEY FOUND IN GUAM JUST A FEW YEARS BACK?

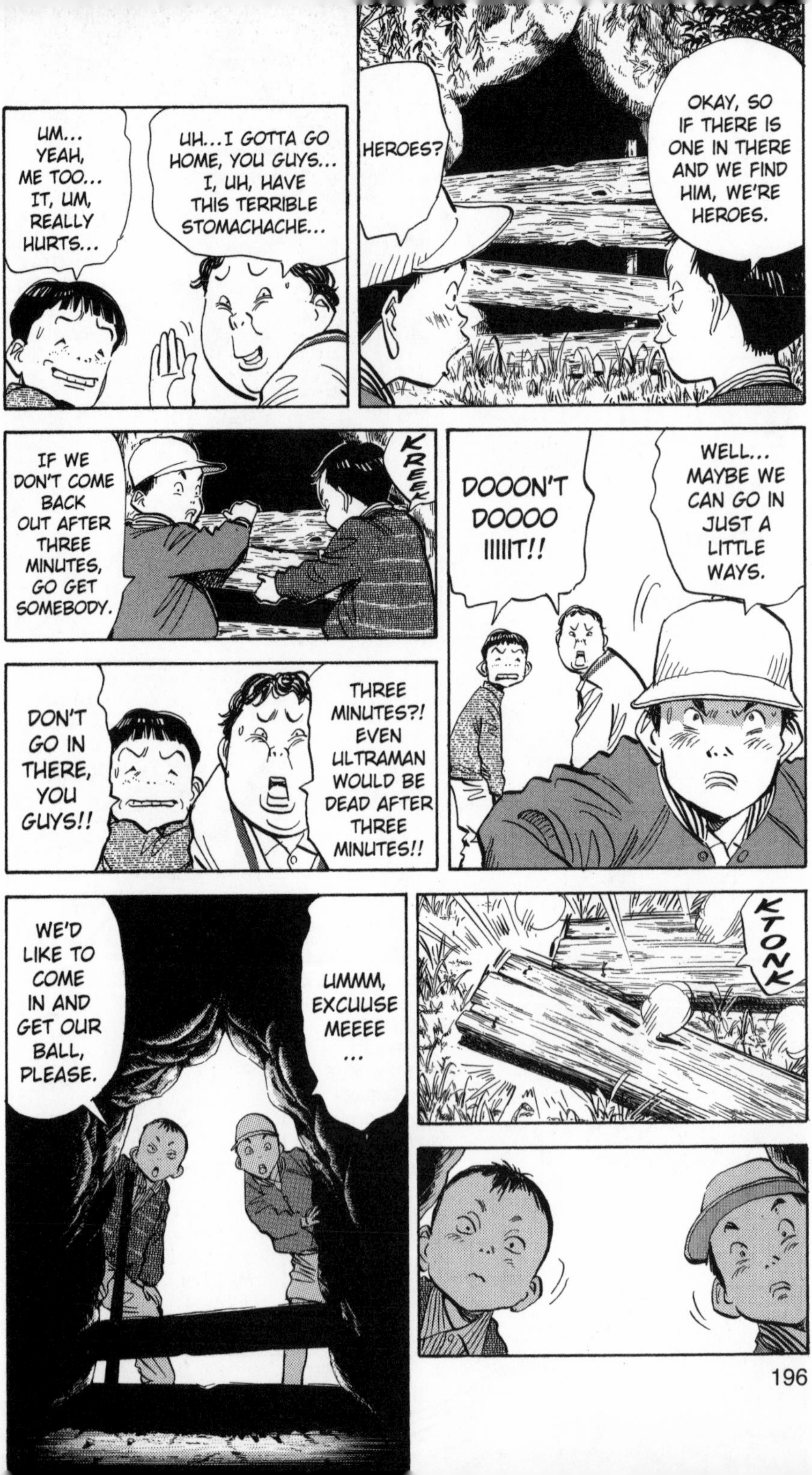

OKAY, SO IF THERE IS ONE IN THERE AND WE FIND HIM, WE'RE HEROES.
HEROES?
UH...I GOTTA GO HOME, YOU GUYS... I, UH, HAVE THIS TERRIBLE STOMACHACHE...
UM... YEAH, ME TOO... IT, UM, REALLY HURTS...
WELL... MAYBE WE CAN GO IN JUST A LITTLE WAYS.
DOOON'T DOOOO IIIIIIT!!
KREEK
IF WE DON'T COME BACK OUT AFTER THREE MINUTES, GO GET SOMEBODY.
THREE MINUTES?! EVEN ULTRAMAN WOULD BE DEAD AFTER THREE MINUTES!!
DON'T GO IN THERE, YOU GUYS!!
KTONK
UMMM, EXCUSE MEEEE ...
WE'D LIKE TO COME IN AND GET OUR BALL, PLEASE.

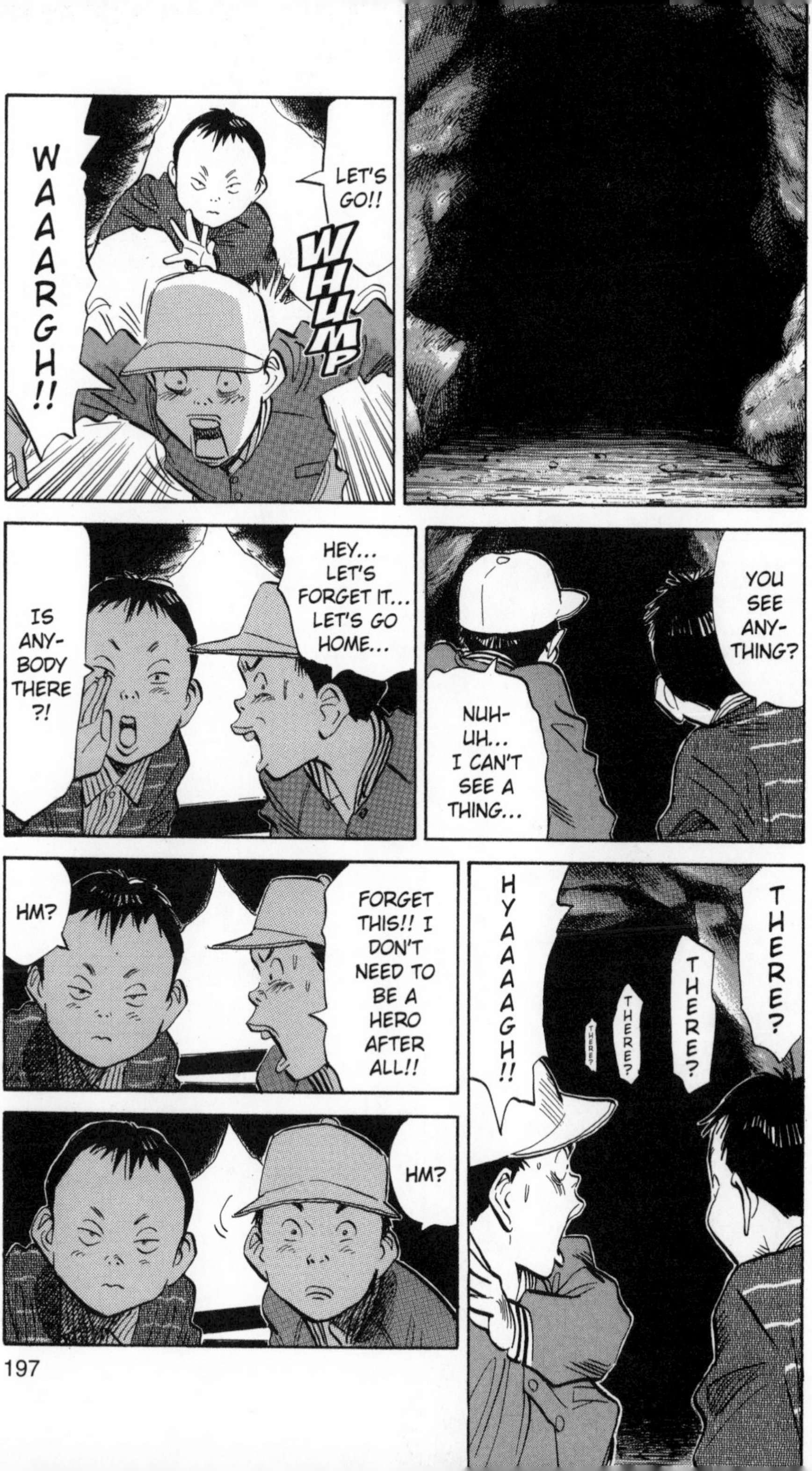
LET'S GO!!
WHUMP
WAAAARGH!!
YOU SEE ANYTHING?
NUH-UH... I CAN'T SEE A THING...
HEY... LET'S FORGET IT... LET'S GO HOME...
IS ANYBODY THERE?!
THERE?
THERE?
THERE?
THERE?
HYAAAAAGH!!
FORGET THIS!! I DON'T NEED TO BE A HERO AFTER ALL!!
HM?
HM?

TWOMP
TWOMP
SHWAK
HEY ...
HEY ...
GYAAAAAGH!!

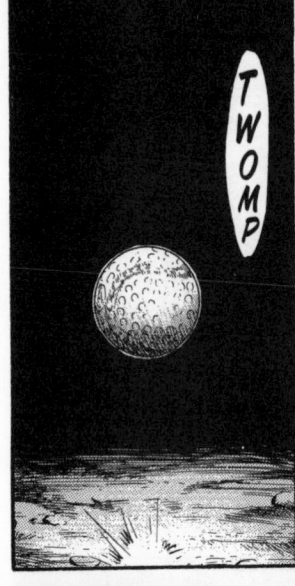

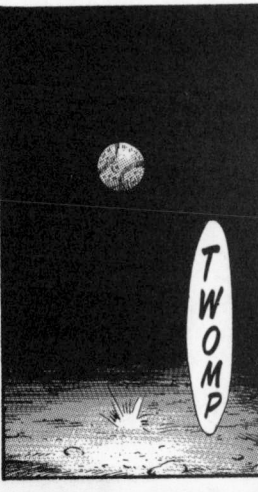

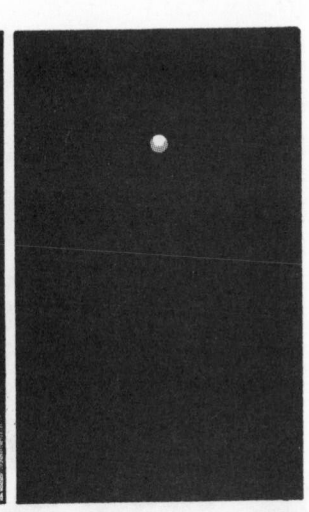

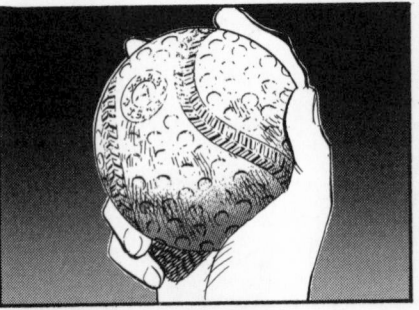

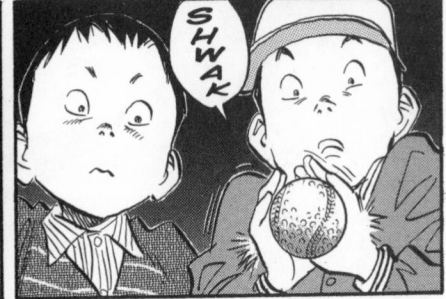

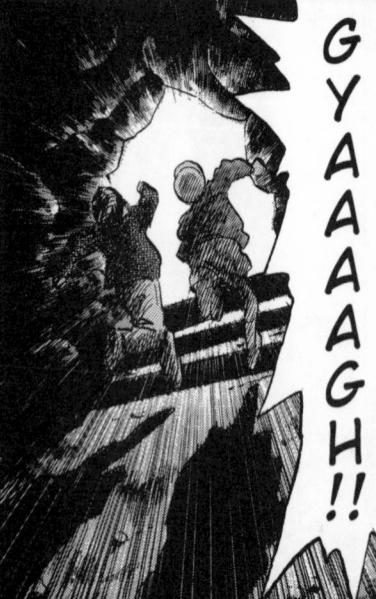

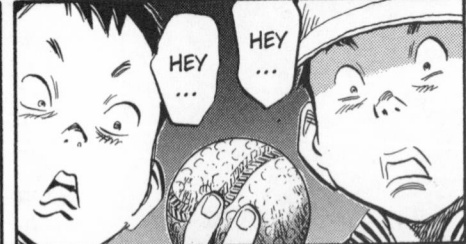

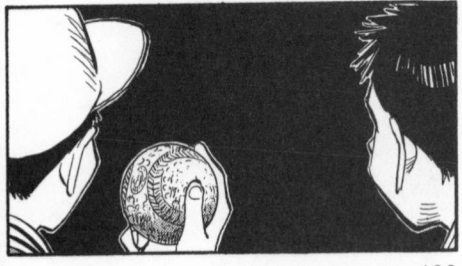

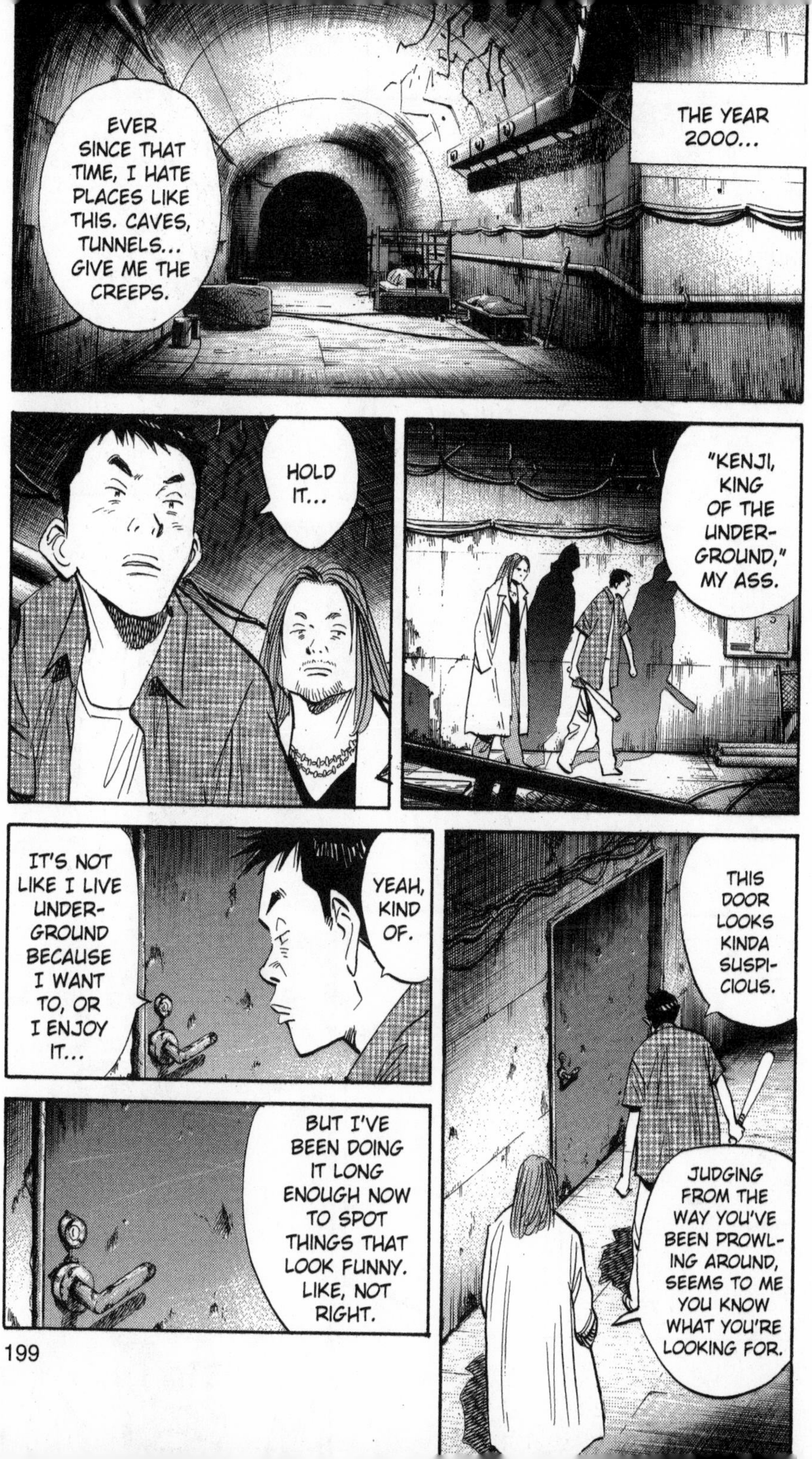
THE YEAR 2000...
EVER SINCE THAT TIME, I HATE PLACES LIKE THIS. CAVES, TUNNELS... GIVE ME THE CREEPS.
"KENJI, KING OF THE UNDER-GROUND," MY ASS.
HOLD IT...
THIS DOOR LOOKS KINDA SUSPI-CIOUS.
JUDGING FROM THE WAY YOU'VE BEEN PROWL-ING AROUND, SEEMS TO ME YOU KNOW WHAT YOU'RE LOOKING FOR.
YEAH, KIND OF.
IT'S NOT LIKE I LIVE UNDER-GROUND BECAUSE I WANT TO, OR I ENJOY IT...
BUT I'VE BEEN DOING IT LONG ENOUGH NOW TO SPOT THINGS THAT LOOK FUNNY. LIKE, NOT RIGHT.

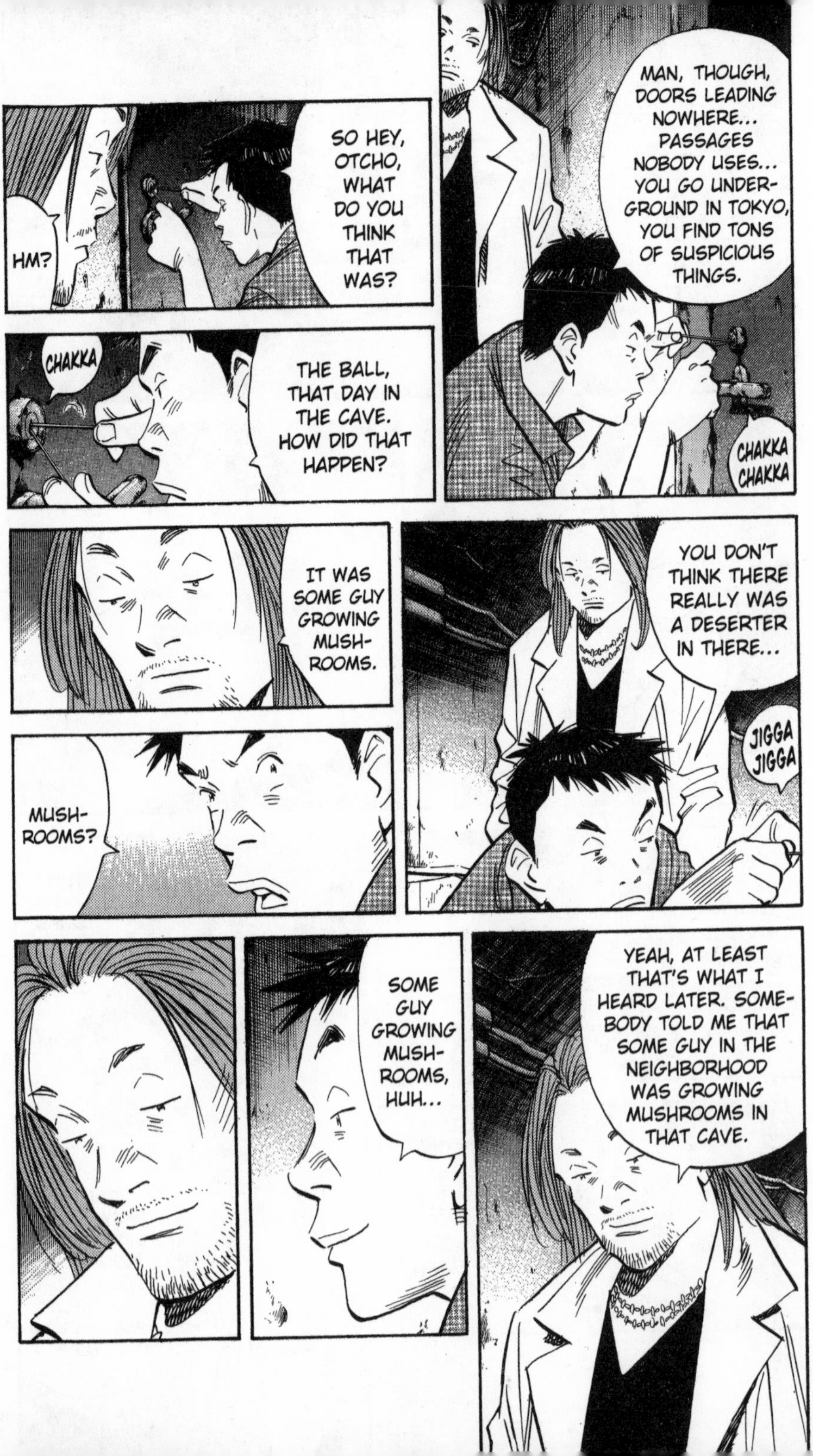
MAN, THOUGH, DOORS LEADING NOWHERE... PASSAGES NOBODY USES... YOU GO UNDER-GROUND IN TOKYO, YOU FIND TONS OF SUSPICIOUS THINGS.
CHAKKA CHAKKA
SO HEY, OTCHO, WHAT DO YOU THINK THAT WAS?
HM?
THE BALL, THAT DAY IN THE CAVE. HOW DID THAT HAPPEN?
CHAKKA
YOU DON'T THINK THERE REALLY WAS A DESERTER IN THERE...
JIGGA JIGGA
IT WAS SOME GUY GROWING MUSH-ROOMS.
MUSH-ROOMS?
YEAH, AT LEAST THAT'S WHAT I HEARD LATER. SOME-BODY TOLD ME THAT SOME GUY IN THE NEIGHBORHOOD WAS GROWING MUSHROOMS IN THAT CAVE.
SOME GUY GROWING MUSH-ROOMS, HUH...

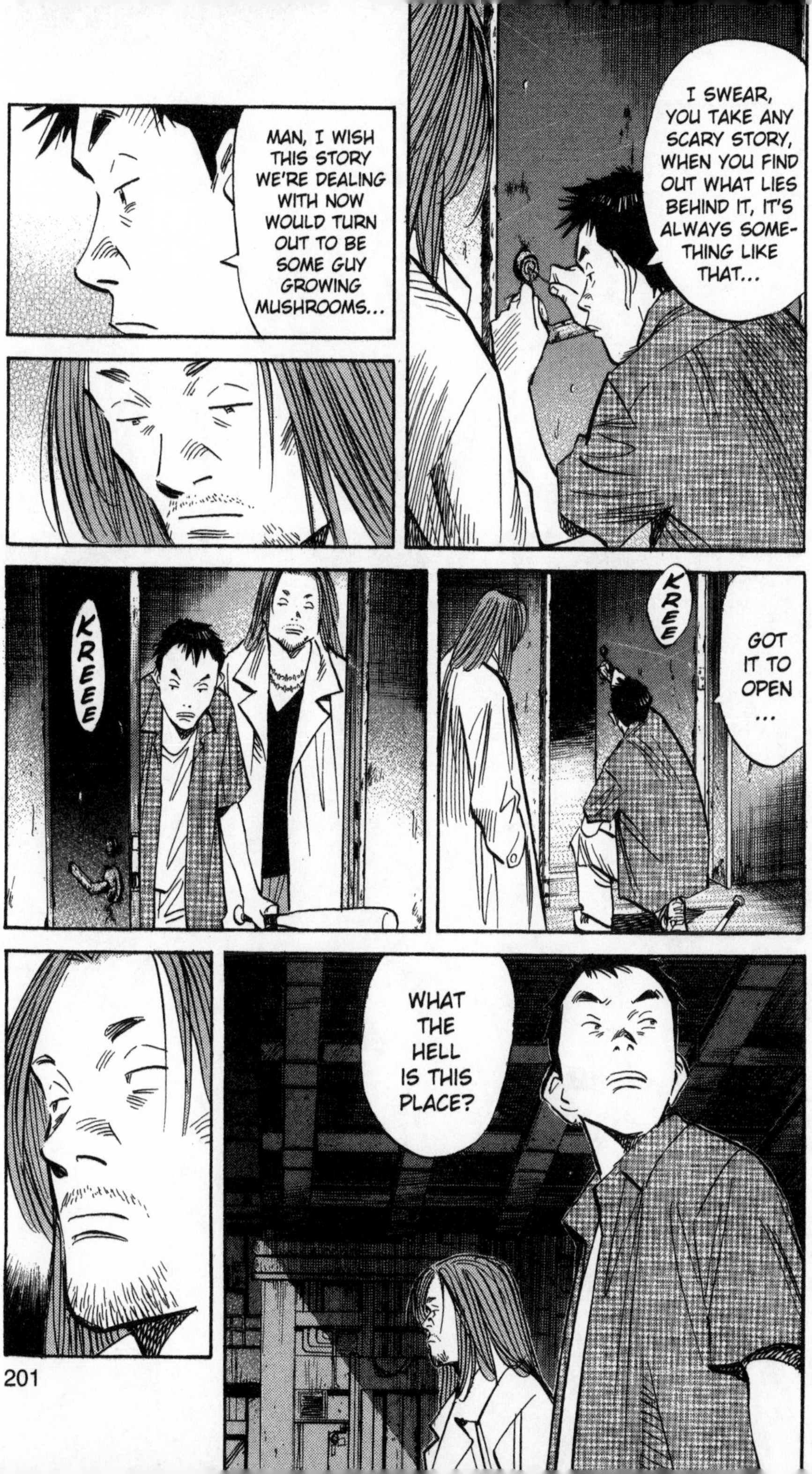
I SWEAR, YOU TAKE ANY SCARY STORY, WHEN YOU FIND OUT WHAT LIES BEHIND IT, IT'S ALWAYS SOME-THING LIKE THAT...
MAN, I WISH THIS STORY WE'RE DEALING WITH NOW WOULD TURN OUT TO BE SOME GUY GROWING MUSHROOMS...
KREE
GOT IT TO OPEN...
KREEE
WHAT THE HELL IS THIS PLACE?

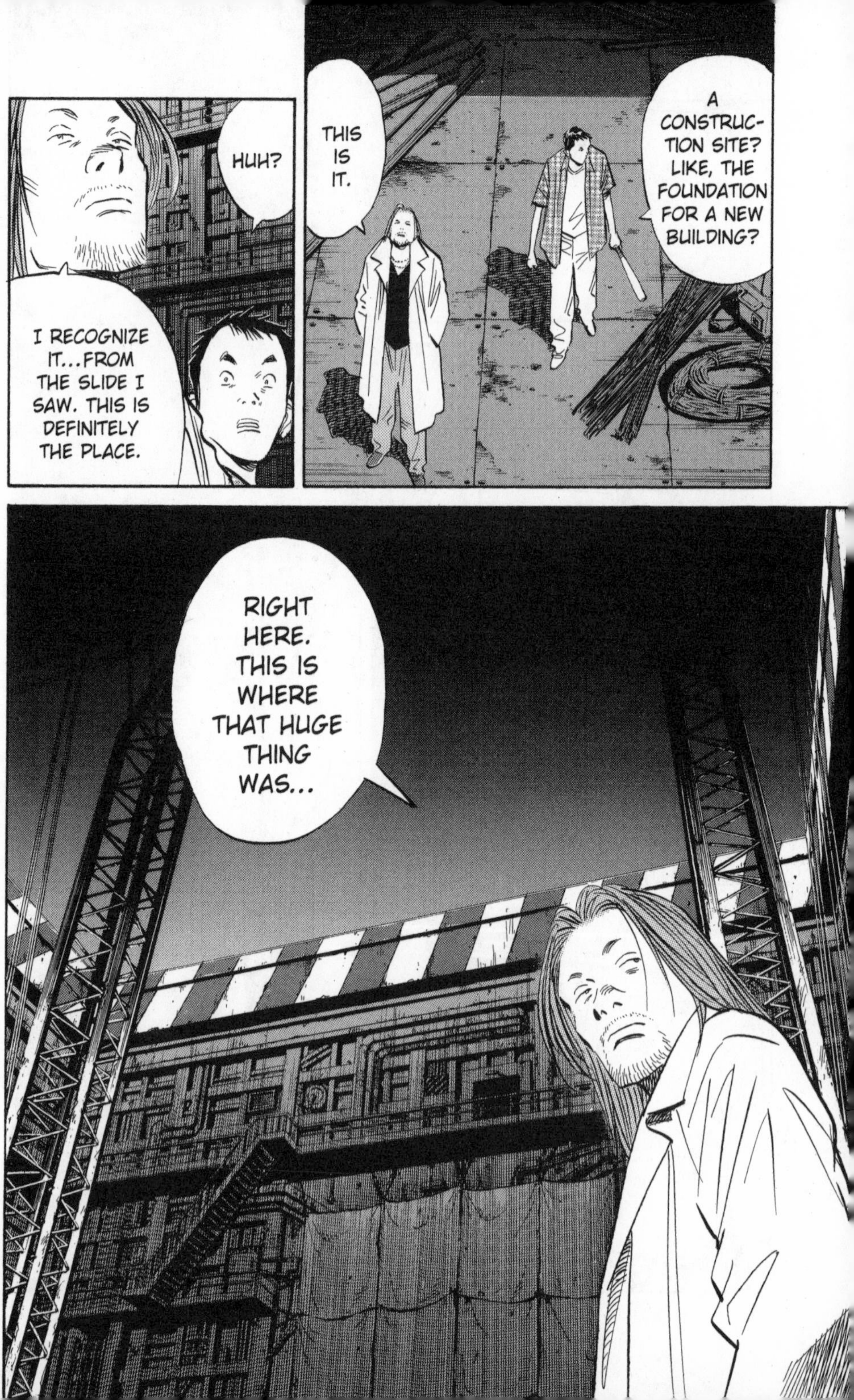
A CONSTRUCTION SITE? LIKE, THE FOUNDATION FOR A NEW BUILDING?
THIS IS IT.
HUH?
I RECOGNIZE IT...FROM THE SLIDE I SAW. THIS IS DEFINITELY THE PLACE.
RIGHT HERE. THIS IS WHERE THAT HUGE THING WAS...

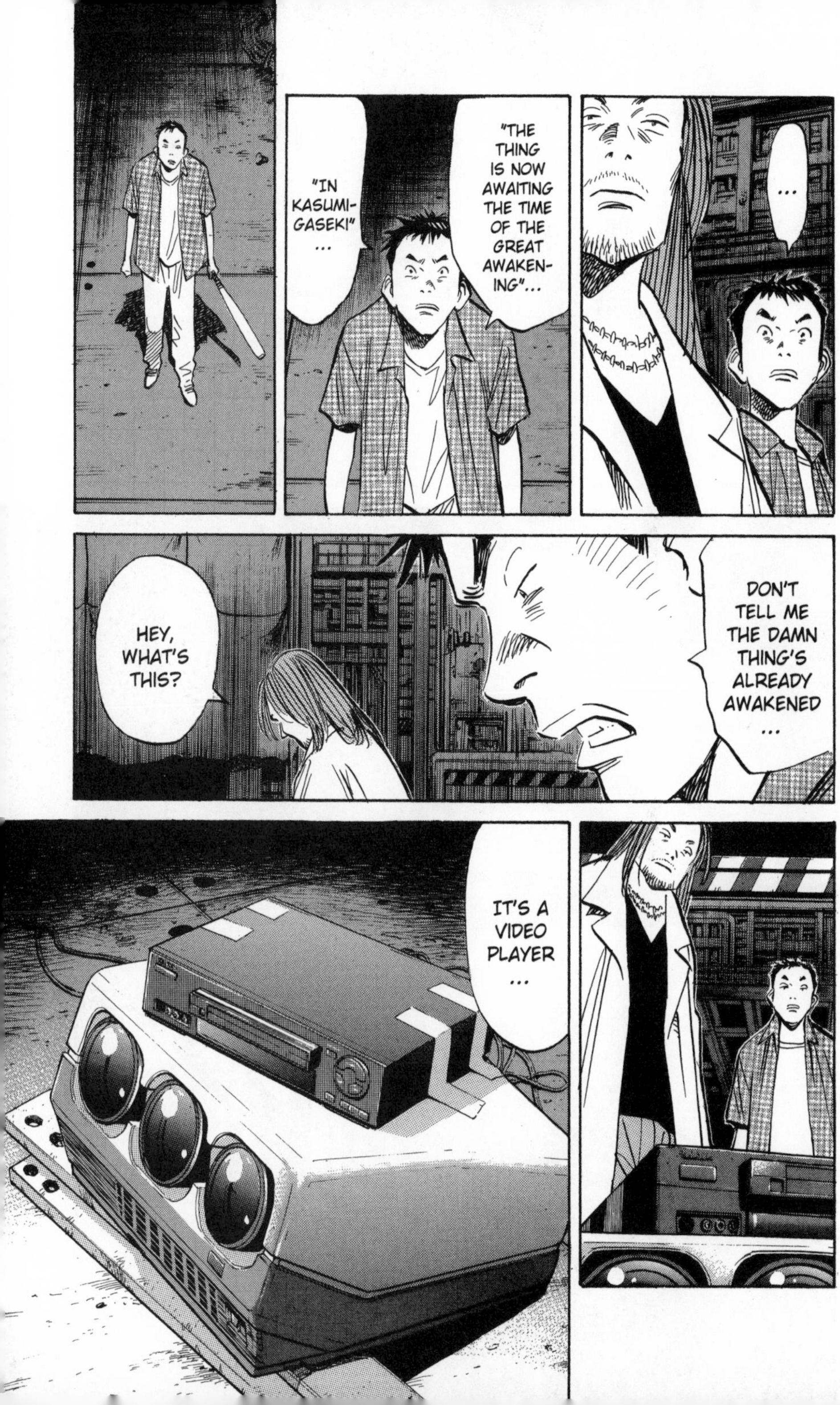
...
"THE THING IS NOW AWAITING THE TIME OF THE GREAT AWAKEN-ING"...
"IN KASUMI-GASEKI" ...
DON'T TELL ME THE DAMN THING'S ALREADY AWAKENED ...
HEY, WHAT'S THIS?
IT'S A VIDEO PLAYER ...

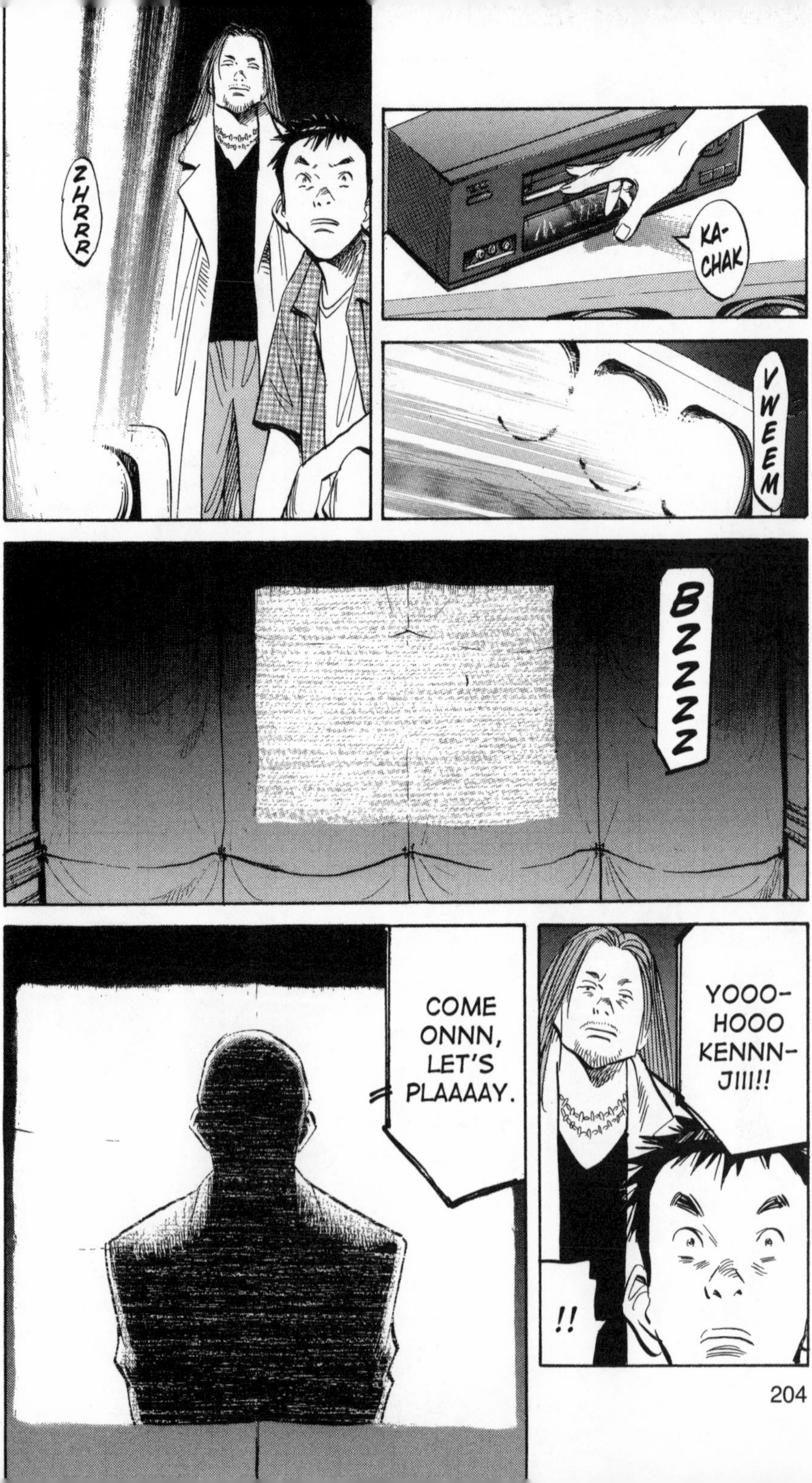
KA-CHAK
VWEEM
ZHRRR
BZZZZZ
YOOO-HOOO KENNN-JIII!!
!!
COME ONNN, LET'S PLAAAAY.

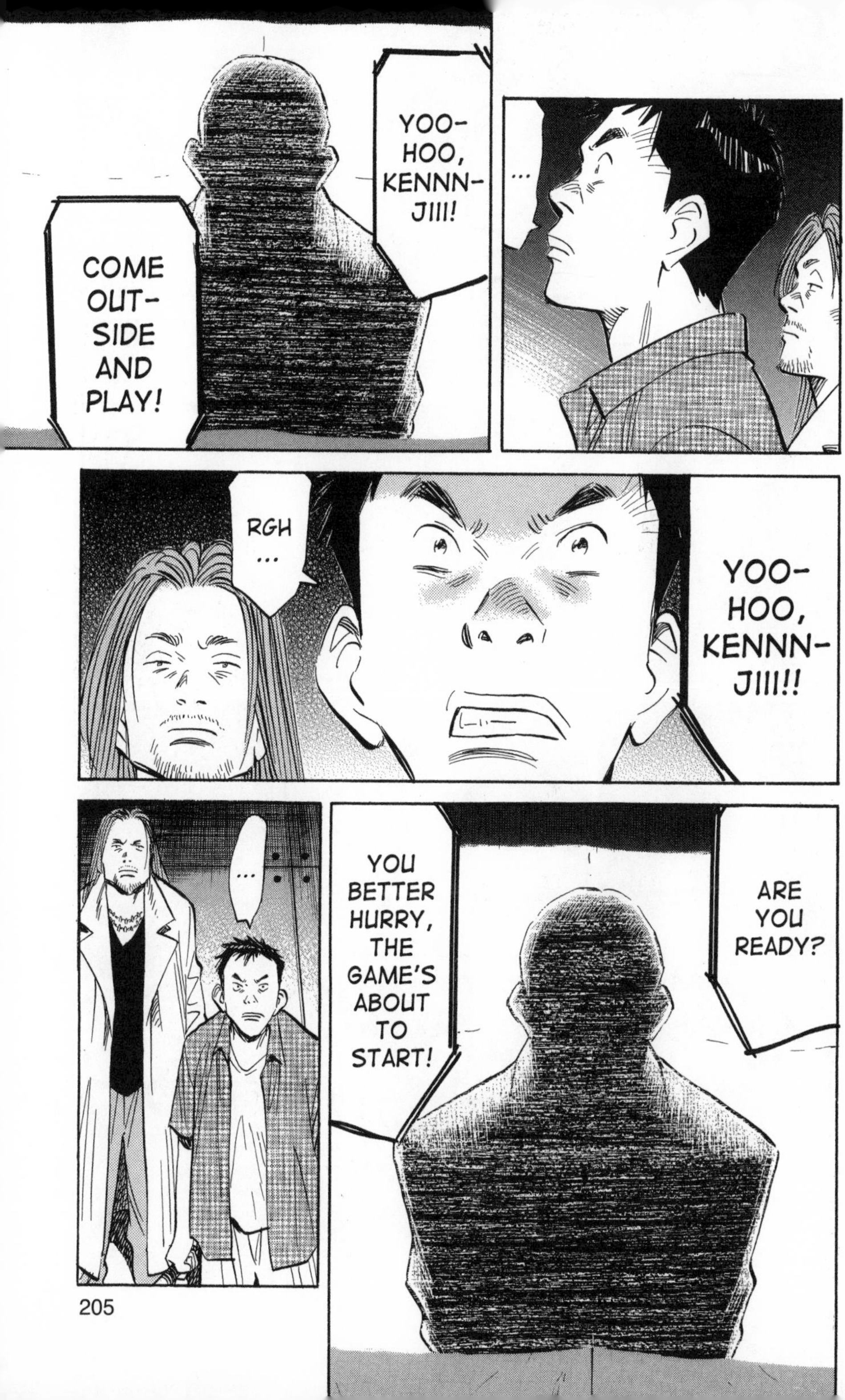
...
YOO-HOO, KENNN-JIII!
COME OUTSIDE AND PLAY!
YOO-HOO, KENNN-JIII!!
RGH ...
ARE YOU READY?
YOU BETTER HURRY, THE GAME'S ABOUT TO START!
...

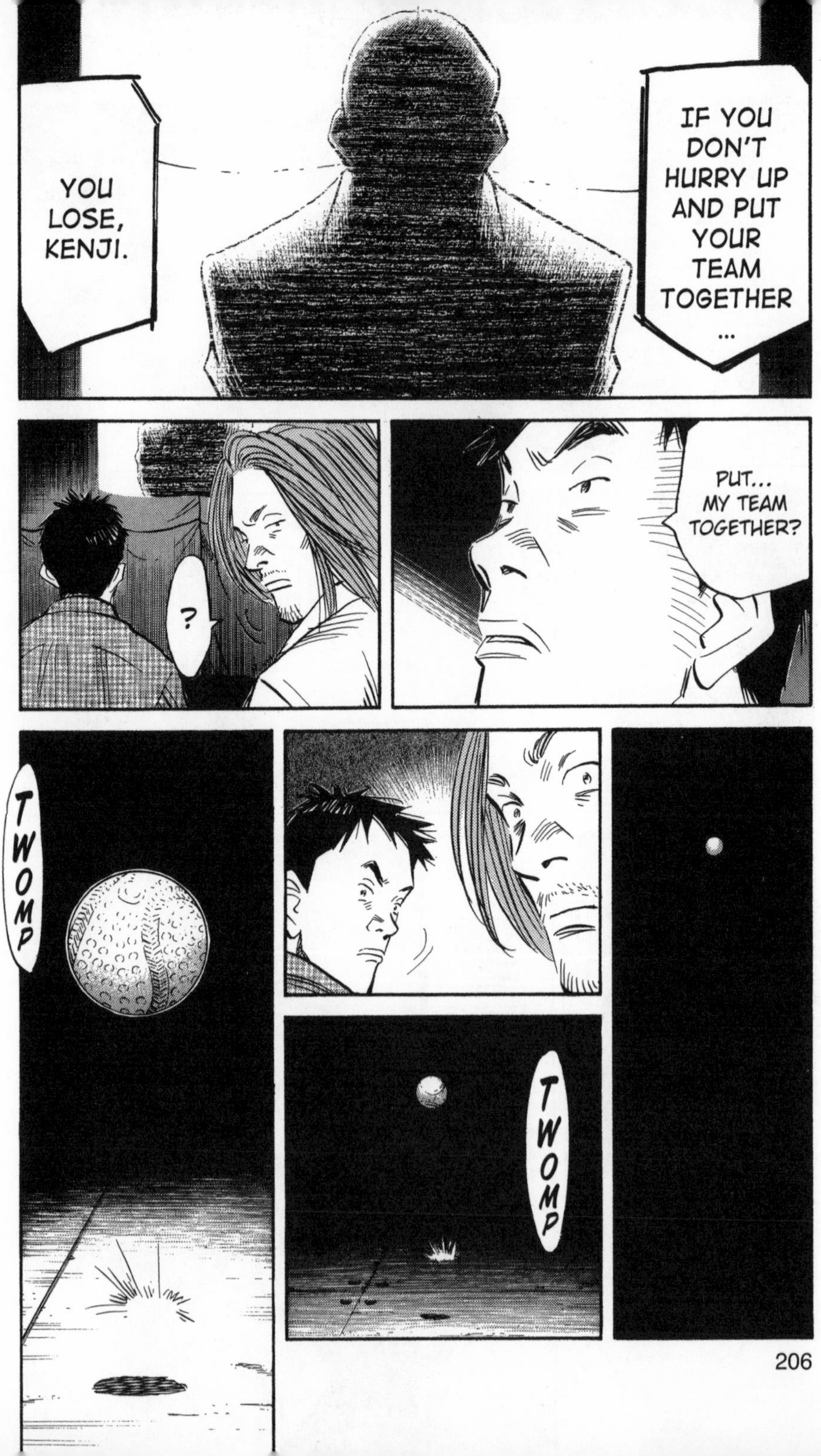
IF YOU DON'T HURRY UP AND PUT YOUR TEAM TOGETHER ...
YOU LOSE, KENJI.
PUT... MY TEAM TOGETHER?
?
TWOMP
TWOMP

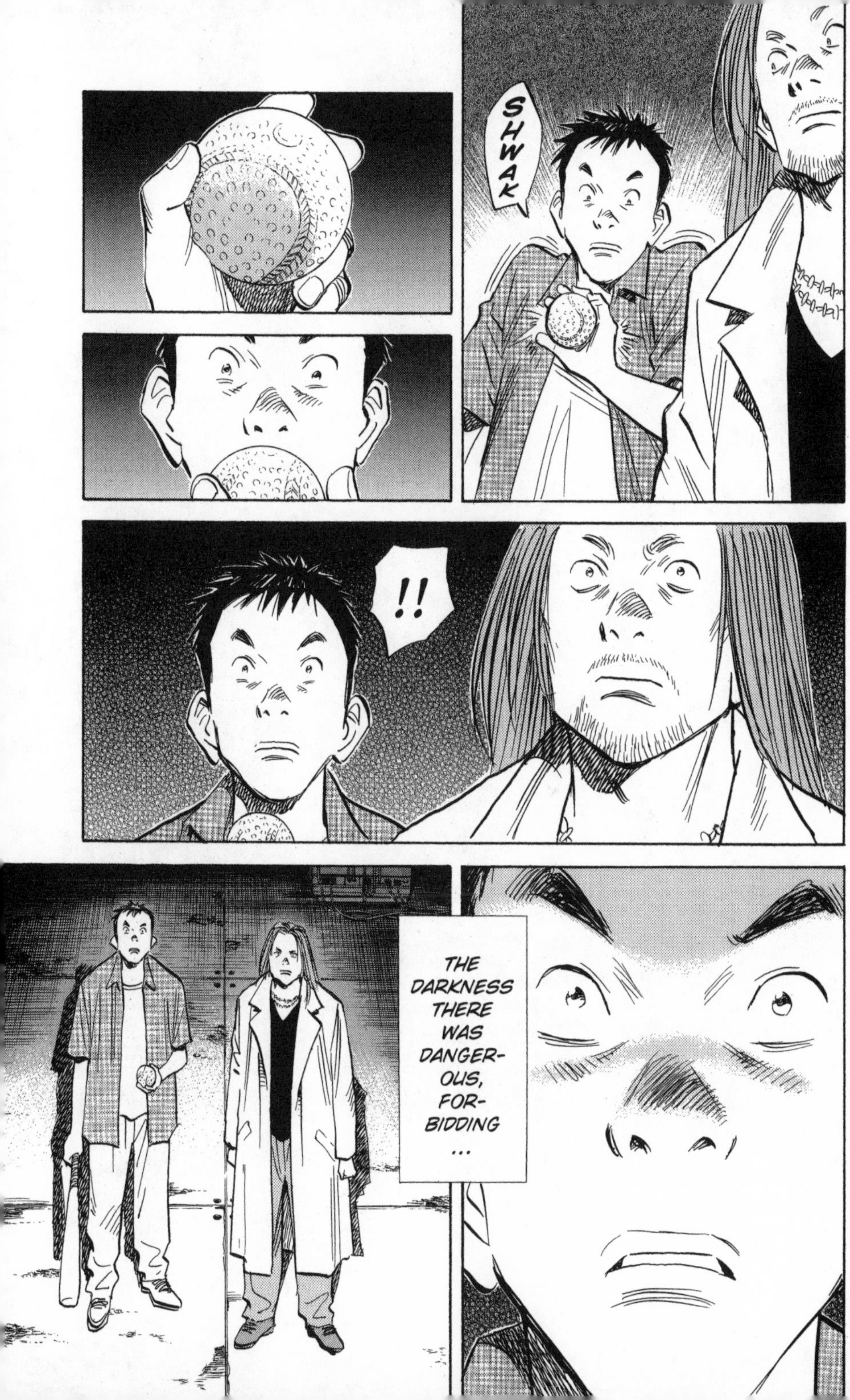
SHWAK
!!
THE DARKNESS THERE WAS DANGER-OUS, FOR-BIDDING ...

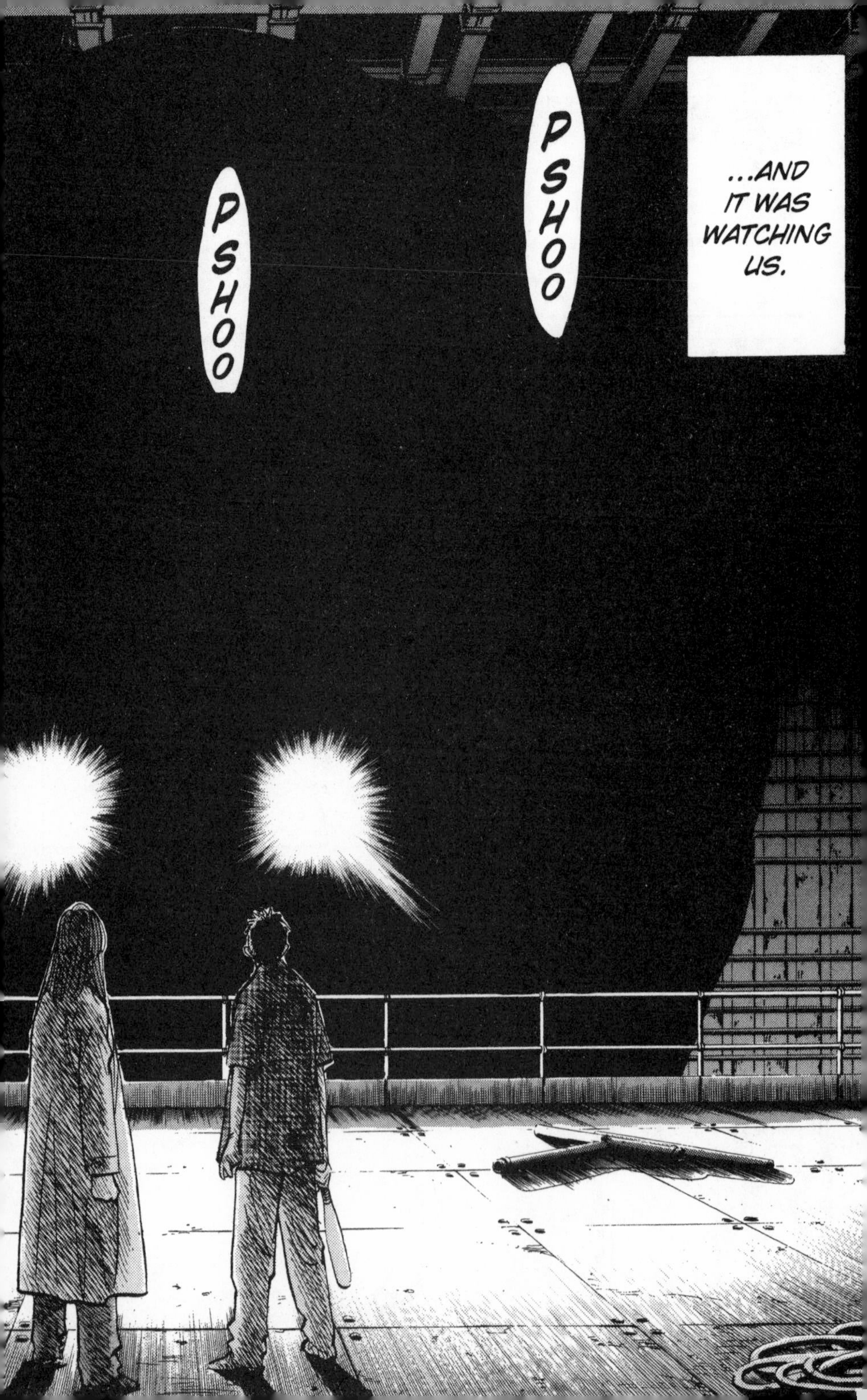
...AND IT WAS WATCHING US.
PSHOO
PSHOO

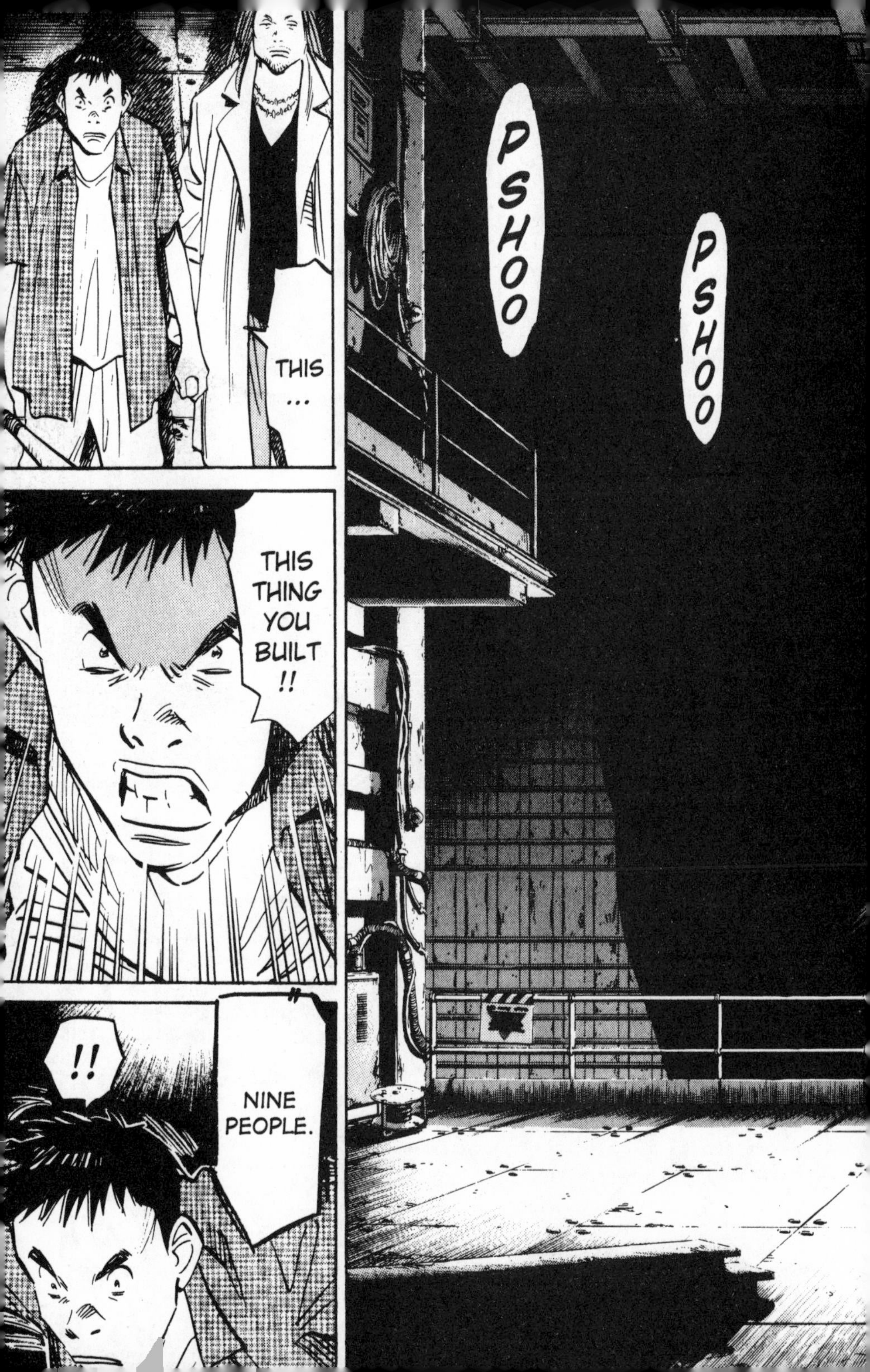
PSHOO
PSHOO
THIS ...
THIS THING YOU BUILT !!
NINE PEOPLE.
!!

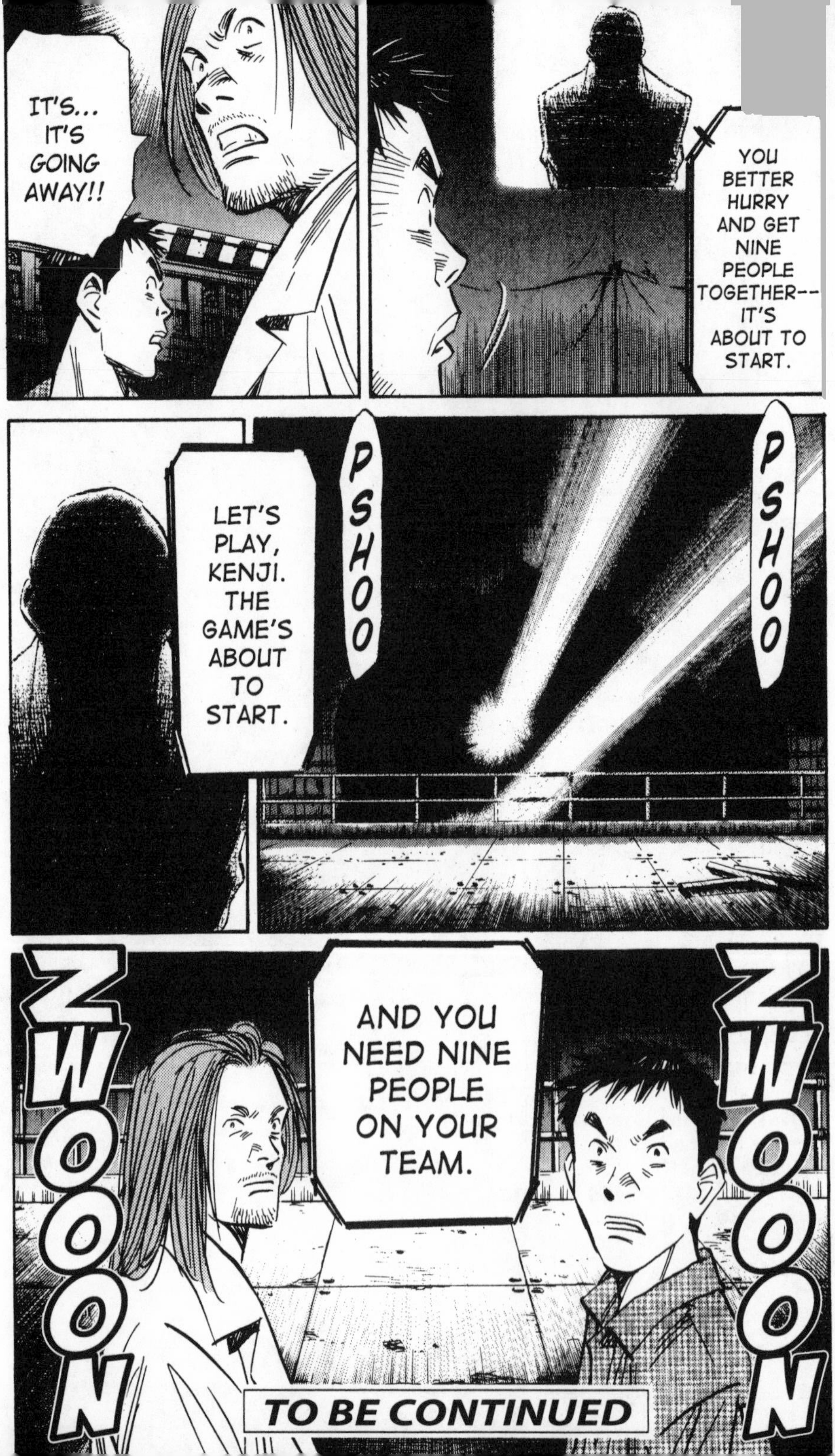
YOU BETTER HURRY AND GET NINE PEOPLE TOGETHER-- IT'S ABOUT TO START.
IT'S... IT'S GOING AWAY!!
PSHOO
PSHOO
LET'S PLAY, KENJI. THE GAME'S ABOUT TO START.
ZWOOOON
AND YOU NEED NINE PEOPLE ON YOUR TEAM.
ZWOOOON
TO BE CONTINUED

NOTES FROM THE TRANSLATOR

This series follows the Japanese naming convention, with a character's family name followed by their given name. Honorifics such as *-san* and *-kun* are also preserved.

Page 71: The protests in question refer to Japanese student protests against the war in Vietnam, the establishment, and above all, the Security Pact between the U.S. and Japan. Part of the worldwide student unrest of 1968–69, students at Tokyo University and Kyoto University, for example, took over university buildings, and riot police were eventually called in.

Page 142: The sign that Kenji is holding is an advertisement for a "sensuous massage" parlor. The sign itself reads:
>   Credit cards accepted
>   Advance payment required
>   Papaya Heaven
>   "Slippery" (balloon text)
>   40 min. ¥10,000
>   60 min. ¥14,000
>   80 min. ¥17,000

Page 162: In Japan, some mecha fall into a category known as *gattai-shiki*, translated here as "composite type"—meaning that the body, rather than being one piece, is an amalgam of detachable parts.

Page 188: Kasumigaseki is where most of the cabinet ministries are located.

Page 193: Kenji's lines in the first two panels are references to *Kyojin no Hoshi*, or "Star of the Giants," a popular baseball manga that first appeared in 1966. Also, the lead character Hyuma Hoshi's nemesis is Mitsuru Hanagata.

Page 196: Ultraman is only viable for three minutes and would die if he remained transformed for longer than that. As for Yoshitsune's line (which can be literally translated as "I got nothing to do with this"), this is another anachronism—a quote from *Kogarashi Monjiro*, a TV show that only aired from 1972 to 1973.

Orphaned on the mean streets of Treasure Town
From the creator of Blue Spring, No. 5 and Ping Pong
TEKKON KINKREET
BLACK & WHITE
by Taiyo Matsumoto
Manga on sale now—over 600 pages, complete with:
• Q&A foreword by TEKKONKINKREET film director Michael Arias and screenwriter Anthony Weintraub
• Exclusive, pull-out poster
• Special full-color manga pages
TEKKON KINKREET
BLACK & WHITE
All in One
TAIYO MATSUMOTO
EXPLICIT CONTENT
RATED M FOR MATURE
ratings.viz.com
VIZ Signature
Tekkon Kinkurito © Taiyo MATSUMOTO / Shogakukan Inc.
VIZ media
www.viz.com

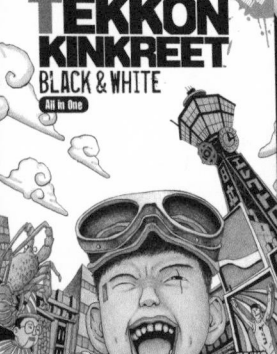

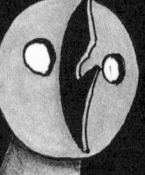

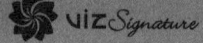

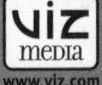

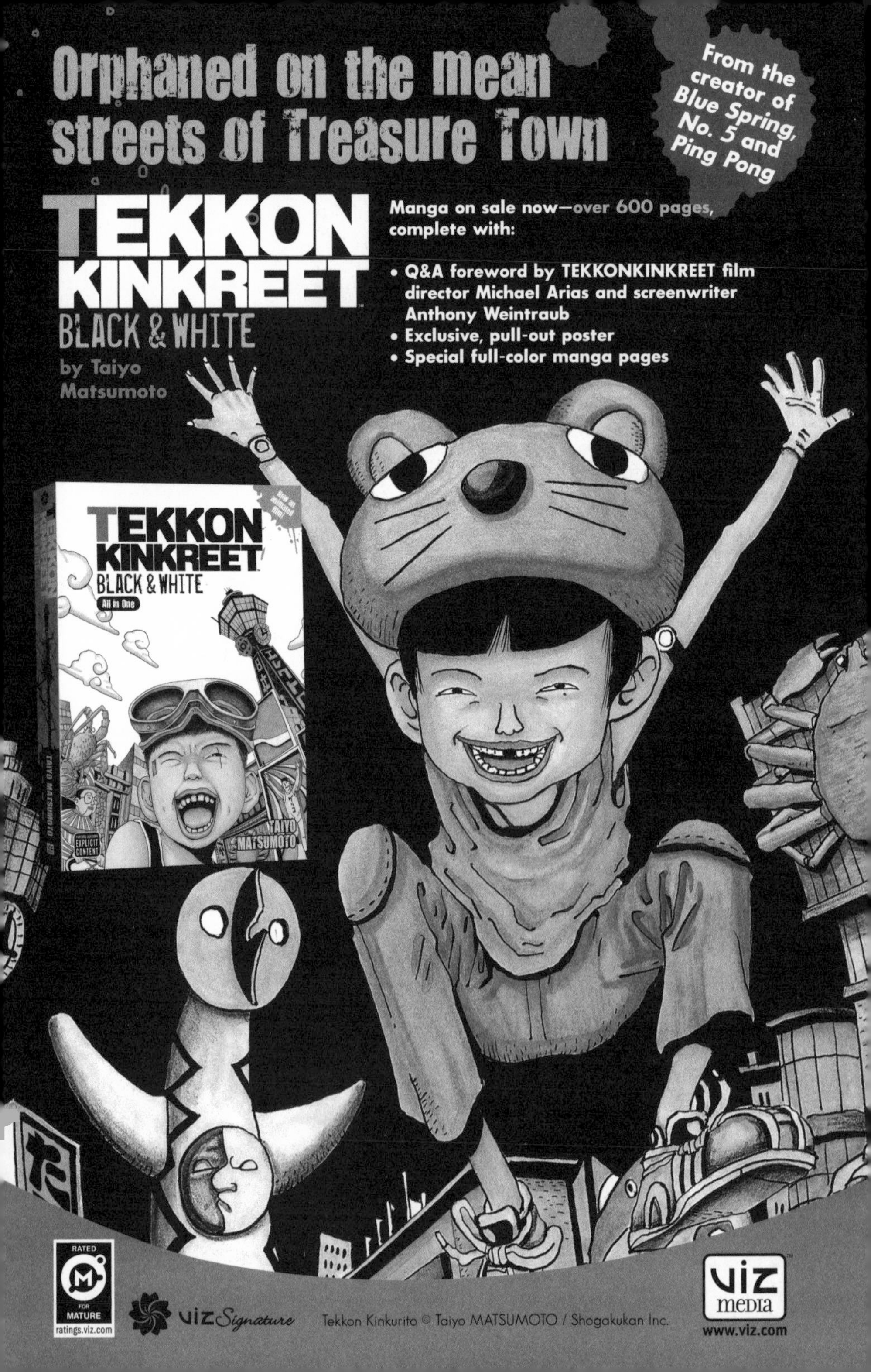

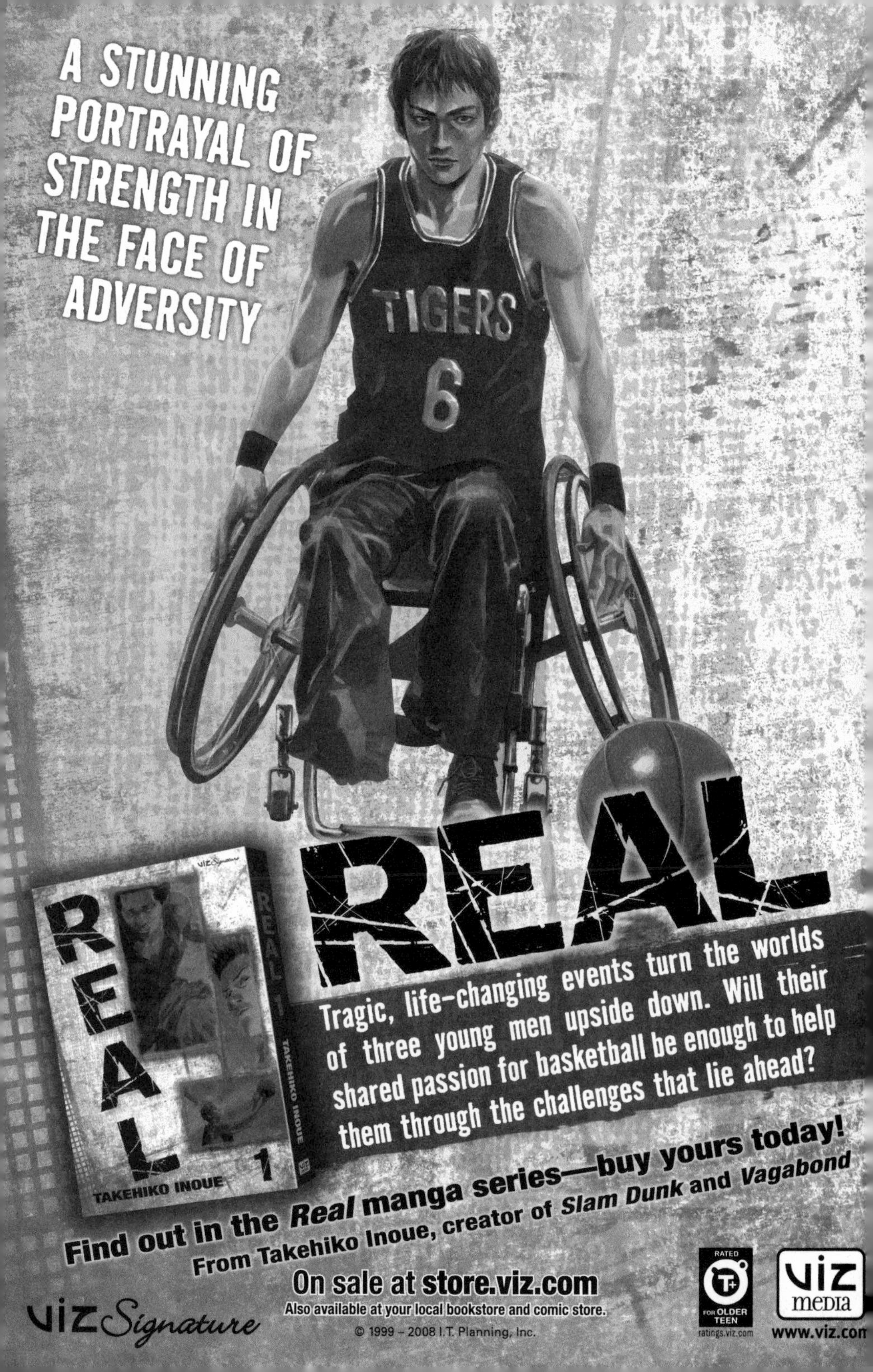
A STUNNING PORTRAYAL OF STRENGTH IN THE FACE OF ADVERSITY
TIGERS
6
REAL
TAKEHIKO INOUE
1
REAL
Tragic, life-changing events turn the worlds of three young men upside down. Will their shared passion for basketball be enough to help them through the challenges that lie ahead?
Find out in the Real manga series—buy yours today!
From Takehiko Inoue, creator of Slam Dunk and Vagabond
On sale at store.viz.com
Also available at your local bookstore and comic store.
© 1999 – 2008 I.T. Planning, Inc.
viz Signature
RATED T+ FOR OLDER TEEN
ratings.viz.com
viz media
www.viz.com

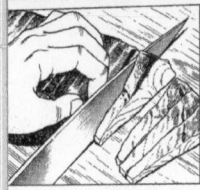

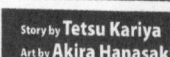
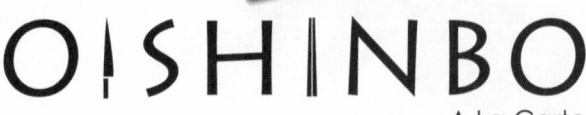